THIS BENEVOLENT EXPERIMENT

INDIGENOUS EDUCATION

Series Editors

Margaret Connell Szasz,
University of New Mexico

Brenda J. Child
University of Minnesota

Karen Gayton Swisher
Haskell Indian Nations University

John W. Tippeconnic III
The Pennsylvania State University

THIS BENEVOLENT EXPERIMENT

Indigenous Boarding Schools,

Genocide, and Redress in

Canada and the United States

ANDREW WOOLFORD

UNIVERSITY OF NEBRASKA PRESS | LINCOLN

© 2015 by the Board of Regents of the University of Nebraska

Published in the United States by the University of Nebraska Press
Published in Canada by the University of Manitoba Press
Manufactured in the United States of America

Library of Congress Cataloging-in-Publication Data
Woolford, Andrew John, 1971–
This benevolent experiment: Indigenous
boarding schools, genocide, and redress in Canada
and the United States / Andrew Woolford.
pages   cm.—(Indigenous education)
Includes bibliographical references and index.
ISBN 978-0-8032-7672-7 (hardback: alkaline paper)
ISBN 978-0-8032-8441-8 (ePub)
ISBN 978-0-8032-8442-5 (mobi)
ISBN 978-0-8032-8443-2 (pdf)
1. Indian children—Education—History. 2. Off-reservation
boarding schools—Manitoba—History. 3. Off-reservation
boarding schools—New Mexico—History. 4. Education—
Political aspects—United States—History. 5. Education—Political
aspects—Canada—History. 6. Indians of North America—Cultural
assimilation—History. 7. Genocide—North America—History.
8. Indians of North America—Reparations—History.
9. Reparations for historical injustices—Canada—History.
10. Reparations for historical injustices—United States—History.
I. Title.
E96.W66 2015
371.829'97073—dc23
2015013788

Set in Scala by M. Scheer.
Designed by N. Putens.

Dedicated to Ted Fontaine and his fellow survivors, who have inspired and challenged me. I am sure they will not agree with all of my interpretations of the boarding schools, but I hope I have done some justice to their experiences

Dedicated to my partner, Jess, who undertook her own journey of survival while I was working on this book

And dedicated to Ella, for being so brave during her mom's treatment and recovery

CONTENTS

ILLUSTRATIONS

PREFACE

Upon presenting this book, I am reticent to introduce myself into the text. I prefer to think that the scholarship can stand for itself and that criticism or praise will come as a result of my efforts. However, engaging in such a project, in which time and effort are invested in interrogating the Eurocentric presuppostions of government policy, educational practices, historical knowledge, and genocide studies, any trace of Eurocentricism that hides under a false notion of objectivity (and is partly a source of my reticence, though a working-class upbringing that stressed modesty and not talking too much about oneself is also in play) cannot be permitted. Self and research are intertwined. Although this story is not directly about me, I am implicated in it both as a scholar presenting it to my readers and as a non-Indigenous settler Canadian who is advantaged by the colonial world that emerged out of these and other historical processes; therefore, the reader should know a little about the position from which I approached this project.

I entered the field of genocide studies in 2000 with my sights set on the Holocaust and Rwanda. At the same time, I was conducting dissertation research on the British Columbia Treaty Process — a process of negotiation designed to address a historical wrong in my home province, whereby most Indigenous peoples had been dispossessed of their lands without treaties as existed elsewhere in Canada. In interviewing Indigenous leaders and elders about their understandings of land and territory as they related to treaty negotiations, my two research worlds bumped into one another. Before they could speak to me about treaties, many Indigenous respondents thought it necessary to tell me about genocide first, and they named it as such. Although at first I was unsure of their use of the term, and questioned whether or not it fit with what I thought I knew about genocide, my dissertation project was my first experience with multilogicity, and it gave me an initial awareness of settler epistemological violence. In particular, I was witness to this violence at the treaty table, which sought to erase Indigenous understandings of territory and history, but I was also a participant in this violence through my engagement with genocide discourses that ignored the destructiveness of Canadian settler colonialism or reduced it to a qualified form: cultural genocide. I eventually grappled with these issues in an article titled "Ontological Destruction: Genocide and Aboriginal Peoples in Canada" that appeared in the journal *Genocide Studies and Prevention*. This book represents an effort to build upon and intensify the ideas suggested in this earlier work through a more ambitious and empirically rich investigation of genocide in North America.

Although critical reflexivity and positionality are necessary scholarly practices when engaging with issues related to Indigenous peoples, they are ongoing efforts, and I cannot claim to have entirely "unsettled" myself, to use Paulette Regan's evocative term. However, I believe that such practices are necessary. As participants in settler societies, we live in a sociocultural space that made destructive Indigenous boarding schools, not to mention other colonial wrongs, possible. This places on the critical scholar an obligation to interrogate the social, institutional, and everyday contexts of settler colonialism. To do so, Indigenous voices must be presented. But these voices are not included here as reflections of a reified indigeneity or as a compendium of knowledge about Indigenous peoples. Instead, these voices are drawn on as counternarratives to jostle, disrupt, and unsettle taken-for-granted settler understandings of colonization, settlement, education, and assimilation. To this extent, the text that follows does not assume an authoritative voice on Indigenous experiences of boarding schools, nor does it seek to force these experiences into a European conceptual box (i.e., genocide); rather, it demands that the genocide concept be accountable to the variety of Indigenous experiences and knowledges. In short, I present a model for understanding and interpreting genocide that is attuned to the multiplicity and complexity of social life, including practices and experiences of attempted collective destruction. In this manner, I hope that this book will be perceived as an allied and decolonizing effort to the extent that my aim is not to present a final judgment on the past or prescription for the future but to open space for new engagements with history and the present in the United States and Canada.

I would like to thank the Truth and Reconciliation Commission of Canada and Fulbright Canada for the funding that made this project possible and for supporting the creation of the index. Many individuals assisted me in my research, including Konstantin Pethoukhov and Natalia Ilyniak, who provided excellent research support. I have benefited from conversations with Jeff Benvenuto, Theodore Fontaine, Jens Meierhenrich, Alexander Hinton, R. S. Ratner, Christopher Powell, Greg Bak, Tricia Logan, Robin Jarvis Brownlie, Adam Muller, Struan Sinclair, A. Dirk Moses, Paulette Regan, David MacDonald, Damien Short, Ted Jojola, Tifany Lee, Ben Madley, Joseph Gone, Ry Moran and Aimée Craft, Anthony Waterman, and many others who helped me, perhaps without knowing it, by asking tough questions or providing me with important insights. Special thanks is also due to Margaret Connell Szasz, who provided me wonderful advice and encouragement during my stay in Albuquerque. I greatly appreicate her support, as well as that from the other editors of the Indigenous Education Series, Brenda J. Child, Karen Gayton Swisher, and John W. Tippeconnic III.

I am deeply grateful to the many archivists who made it possible for a relative novice to find the information required: Tom Nesmith (University of Mantioba); Terry Reilly (Truth and Reconciliation Commission of Canada); Nancy Brown-Martinez, Ann Massmann, and Christopher Geherin (Center for Southwest Research, University of New Mexico); Sarah Hurford (Library and Archives Canada); Eric Bittner, Richard A. Martinez, Cody White, and David Miller (National Archives and Records Administration, Rocky Mountain Region). My thanks, as well, to the Santa Fe Indian School Board of Trustees, and Superintendent Roy Herera, for giving me permission to draw from the Santa Fe Indian School, The First 100 Years Oral History Interviews conducted by Sally Hyer. I also owe thanks to

Laurie Messer at the Truth and Reconciliation Commission for helping to facilitate my research. Finally, my experience working with the University of Nebraska and University of Manitoba Presses has been wonderful, and I thank Matthew Bokovoy, David Carr, Heather Stauffer, Glenn Bergen, Dallas Harrison, Trish Fobben, Martyn Beeny, Rachel Gould, and Erika Rippeteau, as well as my readers, Margaret D. Jacobs, Jacqueline Fear-Segal, and the anonymous Canadian reviewer, for making this a stronger book than it otherwise would have been.

THIS BENEVOLENT EXPERIMENT

1 | Introduction

In the 1940s, when Mary Courchene was only five, she and her brother were brought to Fort Alexander Indian Residential School by their mother.[1] It was not a far walk. Her family lived only a few minutes down the road from the school. Mary remembers her excitement at the prospect of learning a new language—a language that she had heard on the radio and seen in speech bubbles in comic books. Her parents had always refused to teach her this language, and they spoke only Ojibwe at home.

Despite Mary's excitement, her mother appeared to be withdrawn. When a nun came to the door of the school to let them in, Mary's brother began to cry. He was frightened by the figure in black and white with a red heart dangling from her neck. Mary, taking charge, kicked him in the shin. But during this moment of sibling confrontation, her mother disappeared without saying good-bye. "I learnt later," Mary recounts, "that that was the reason, because you see my mom was [a] first-generation residential school [survivor]. And she could not bear to talk to her children and prepare her children to go to residential school. It was just too, too much for her. So rather than tell us she, she just [left], because by then it was the law. I mean this was the 1940s, . . . and it was law for us to be in school, to be institutionalized."[2]

After that first day, the excitement about school quickly disappeared. Mary was subjected to personal humiliation and the degradation of her culture. And she learned to despise her Indigenous identity. She recalls that, when she was eleven years old, upon arriving home from school one summer,

> I just absolutely hated my own parents. Not because I thought they abandon[ed] me; I hated their brown faces. I hated them because they were Indians; they were Indian. And here I was, you know, coming from [the school]. So I, I looked at my dad, and I challenged him, and he, and I said, "From now on we speak only English in this house," I said to my dad. And you know when we, when, in a traditional home where I was raised, the first thing that we all were always taught was to respect your elders and never to, you know, to challenge them.[3]

Indigenous peoples were subjected to forced assimilation and other forms of violence through boarding schools in both the United States and Canada.[4] In each country, missionary societies established the first boarding schools in the seventeenth and eighteenth centuries, followed in the late nineteenth century by government-supported or government-run schools. During this latter period, conversations occurred across the border, as lessons and information traveled between the two nations, with both equally convinced of their need to contend with the so-called Indian Problem.[5] Yet, though both the American and Canadian governments committed to assimilative Indigenous education in the late 1800s, there has been little comparative analysis of how these two systems came into being, developed and instituted schooling policy, responded to challenges, adapted to changes in educational and colonial philosophies, and currently address the aftermath of these schools. In this book, broad-level similarities and differences between the two systems are identified and analyzed; however, specific attention is also given to local boarding school variations that are not simply the products of national differences but permutations of what I describe below as the *settler colonial mesh*. In brief, this approach is designed to avoid oversimplifying the boarding school experience in North America, which is always a risk when one reduces it to distinctly national (i.e., Canadian and American) patterns. Indeed, regional and temporal differences among Indigenous boarding schools are as significant and interesting as those that exist between the two countries. Therefore, the comparative approach that I use in this book will not be strictly national; instead, I will also seek to capture intranational and local discrepancies.

Although Indigenous boarding schools were often touted as a "benevolent experiment," such claims to benevolence are belied by the sheer destructiveness of these institutions.[6] In this book, benevolence and destruction are understood not as pure opposites but as potentially related terms, since perceived acts of benevolence, guided by an absolute moral certainty, can be experienced by the targets of such benevolence as painful and destructive. However, I also argue that benevolence was not the primary, motivation behind assimilative schooling, for discourses of benevolence were underwritten by a settler colonial desire for land, resources, and national consolidation.[7] For this reason, in titling this book *This Benevolent Experiment*, the emphasis is more on the word *experiment* than it is on the claims of benevolence made by settlers to rationalize their interventions in Indigenous lives. Indigenous boarding schools, as institutions imagined and guided by a diversity of individuals with motivations ranging widely in their benevolent or sinister intent, comprised a complicated experiment in the forcible transformation of multiple Indigenous peoples so that they would no longer exist as an obstacle (real or perceived) to settler colonial domination on the continent.[8] Like any complicated experiment, Indigenous boarding schools coordinated competing visions, organized multiple institutional auspices, enrolled a variety of actors, and enlisted sets of technologies, forces, and *things* (e.g., space, time, disease, food) within an overarching framework—in this case, a framework orchestrated around the theme of resolving the Indian Problem. The successes and failures of this experiment are many and must be examined empirically to gain as clear a picture as possible of the respective boarding school systems in the United States and Canada.

I chart the uneven development of Indigenous boarding schools in North America through a multilevel approach. In brief, I conceptualize settler colonial practices of assimilative education as a series of nets that operates at macro-, meso-, and microsocietal levels.[9] These nets tighten or slacken as they stretch across space and time, and when brought together, one on top of the other, they form a *settler colonial mesh*, which operates to entrap Indigenous peoples within the settler colonial assimilative project.[10] But it is also important to understand that this mesh is prone to snags and tears. That is, at specific points in the settler colonial mesh, relations among the actors and institutions engaged in processes of settlement and assimilation are such that they allow for a loosening of this mesh and for the emergence of resistance and subversion, even if the settler colonial power imbalance is such to prevent outright removal of the mesh.[11]

The various planes of colonial netting represent the different levels of analysis from which I approach the topic of Indigenous boarding schools. At the *macrosocietal level*, my emphasis is on the broader social terrain, comprised of fields such as economics, law, governance, culture, and science.[12] It is from here that a conceptualization of the Indian as a problem was formulated and policy interventions implemented by state institutions were derived. At the *upper meso- or institutional level* of the settler colonial mesh, various governmental and nongovernmental institutions contributed to a more precise formulation of and intervention in the Indian Problem. Here education as an institution had an obvious role to play, but its effects were complemented by other relevant governmental institutions, such as law (e.g., through laws that compelled Indigenous attendance at boarding schools), welfare (e.g., through the denial of social supports to parents who did not ensure their children's enrollment in boarding schools), health (e.g., through the provision of health services in boarding schools), and policing (e.g., through the use of officers to apprehend truants, nonattenders, and unenrolled students).[13]

The *lower mesolevel* consists of the various boarding schools as well as their competitor and feeder organizations. This network is where multiple schooling organizations—boarding schools (both reservation and non-reservation), mission schools, public schools, and day schools—worked in competition and cooperation to provide assimilative education to Indigenous children. Finally, at the *microlevel*, a specific boarding school can be conceived as a network of interactions and a site where school officials (e.g., principals, teachers, staff) innovated specific techniques to interact with students, their parents, and their communities and all parties formed relationships and alliances with other agents as well as nonhuman actors such as territory, food, and disease.[14] Inclusion of these nonhuman actors in our considerations is important for two reasons. First, it takes us beyond the human-centric limits of Eurocentric sociohistorical analysis, introducing a potentially decolonizing approach more in keeping with Indigenous epistemologies. Second, it allows for a more complex and multifocal analysis of social interactions and the mediated consequences of human intention.

I treat these multiple levels of analysis as a series of nets coordinated to forcibly transform Indigenous peoples and thereby destroy these groups. I suggest that this coordinated effort is consistent with sociological understandings of the concept of genocide. But these nets did not simply tighten and enact their destructive potential in an undifferentiated manner. Instead, resistance happened in different times and places, and at different levels, forcing openings in the mesh that allowed for the continued survival of Indigenous groups in North America. Therefore, I should stress up front that genocide is conceived in this book as a process and not as a total outcome. In most cases, Indigenous groups were not wholly destroyed, though many experienced destruction "in part," and all, to some extent, have experienced, and continue to experience, the settler colonial mesh.[15]

Comparing Boarding Schools in the United States and Canada

Despite the statement above about the need for attention to intranational differences, it is worthwhile to conduct a cross-national comparison of Indigenous boarding schools in the United States and Canada. This is because distinct patterns of Indigenous educational policy, its application, and experiences of assimilative schooling can be discerned, particularly at the macrolevel and upper mesolevel in each country.

To date, very little effort has been made to compare and contrast boarding schools in the United States and Canada. The literature that does exist tends to offer only brief comments, as in Reyhner and Eder's *American Indian Education*, which points out a few of the key differences between Canadian and American schools:

(a) Canadian residential schools lasted, on average, longer than American residential schools;

(b) Canadian policies were unrelentingly assimilationist, since no reformist period occurred in Canada as it did in the United States in the 1930s;

(c) Indigenous parents in Canada had less say regarding to which schools their children were sent; and

(d) some Canadian religious denominations lobbied vigorously to prevent diminishment of their control over or the closing of boarding schools.

The cumulative effect of these differences, Reyhner and Eder suggest, is that Indigenous children in Canada typically entered boarding schools at an earlier age than their U.S. counterparts, and the Canadian system affected more generations of Indigenous children, in a more brutal form, than was true for most parts of the United States.[16]

Reyhner and Eder's points are a useful starting point for a more intensive investigation of Indigenous boarding schools in the United States and Canada; however, few scholars have taken on this challenge. Moreover, the efforts at comparison that do exist are too often sweeping in their approaches to the schools, offering little attention to regional and temporal differences in the development, application, and experience of Indigenous boarding school policy in the United States and Canada. Such is the case with Ward Churchill's book *Kill the Indian, Save the Man*. Churchill brings useful critical insight to the topic of colonial genocide through his return to Raphael Lemkin's original understanding of the term that placed cultural genocide on par with physical and biological forms of destruction.[17] However, on an empirical level, Churchill fails to attend to the complexity of settler colonial genocidal processes. For example, he largely ignores the rise of John Collier to the role of commissioner of the Bureau of Indian Affairs (BIA) in 1933, which heralded a boarding school system much different from that in Canada during the same period. The Collier era certainly needs to be addressed more critically than it has been in some of the U.S. literature,[18] but the reforms of this period must also be thoroughly addressed in any serious comparison of Indigenous boarding schools in the two countries, since the Collier years have important consequences for how schools were experienced in the United States (see chapter 3) as well as for the urgency felt in terms of creating redress policy in each nation (see chapter 9).

Andrea Smith also offers a broader comparison of Indigenous schooling and forced assimilation in the United States, Canada, Australia, New Zealand, and several other countries. In her report for the United Nations Permanent Forum on Indigenous Issues, she outlines the common assimilative and genocidal purpose of schooling and child removals in each nation. Like Churchill, however, she focuses less on local and specific variations in attempts to assimilate Indigenous young people and more on a general pattern of destructive interventions in Indigenous communities.[19]

In contrast to these strongly critical comparative examinations, Charles Glenn's *American Indian/First Nations Schooling* offers a near-redemptive overview of Indigenous education in North America, treating European schooling as a good that was simply mismanaged for Indigenous pupils. Glenn discusses the hardships of the schools but is less interested in arguments of cultural genocide since he does not see clear intent in the actions of colonial agents. Nonetheless, he correctly observes a key difference between Canadian and American schools:

> There is a significant difference between the schools in the two countries. Residential schools in Canada were operated by various Christian denominations, with inadequate per-pupil funding from the federal government in Ottawa, until well after the Second World War. In the United States, while church-operated boarding schools have always played a role, by the 1890s public funds were being used almost exclusively to support government-operated schools; the big residential schools like Carlisle were created and operated by the Bureau of Indian Affairs, and seem in general to have been more adequately funded than their counterparts in Canada.[20]

This difference alone is not sufficient to account for the variances between American and Canadian schools (or among schools in the same country), and it overstates the "adequacy" of funding in U.S. schools. But it does touch on two key issues to which I give greater attention in this book: the roles of religion and funding in the schools on both sides of the Canada-U.S. border.

Although comparative discussion of Indigenous boarding schools in the United States and Canada is sparse and overly general, there is a wealth of historical work on Indigenous boarding schools in the two countries. Some of this work aspires to a comprehensive narrative overview of settler colonial schooling policy, with illustrative examples of how these policies were enacted, as well as of how students adapted to, resisted, and/or suffered from their time at the schools.[21] More recently, the historical trend has been to focus on specific schools. Such was always the case with Indigenous boarding school memoirs.[22] But current historians of Indigenous education more regularly seek to capture local characteristics of the schooling experience and to offer portraits of how specific Indigenous groups, rather than an assumed homogeneous Indigenous people, lived their boarding school days.[23] Some, such as Miller and Edmund Danziger Jr., argue that only through the study of local communities and schools is it possible to achieve a full and "balanced" understanding of the impact of residential schools.[24]

Most of these recent works are generally critical of schooling policy (some more than others), but they also seek to show the uneven application of this policy across time and space. It is within this unevenness that they locate examples of students who enjoyed aspects of their schooling experiences, connected with certain teachers or staff members, and went on to use their education for positive purposes unexpected by policy makers, such as by reinforcing rather than shedding their Indigenous identities or becoming leaders in the pursuit of Indigenous rights.[25] Others go further to emphasize how Indigenous students, parents, and communities came to claim and use boarding schools for their own purposes.[26]

By invoking the term "genocide," this book might seem to ignore the historical sophistication and debate engendered by these contemporary scholars.[27] However, the opposite is the case. My effort, in part, is to show how genocidal processes themselves are uneven and uncertain.[28] Like all grandiose modernist projects of state building, Indigenous boarding schools were prone to inconsistencies, variable applications, local resistances, and subversions. My concern is with the negotiation of genocide: that is, how groups intending to destroy other groups seek to mobilize their destructive powers, face obstacles and resistances, and either succeed (in whole or in part) or fail in their efforts. In particular, this book explores and analyzes the crucial role played by assimilative Indigenous boarding schools in the genocidal processes that unfolded in North American settler colonial nations.

For these reasons and others discussed below, I will argue that a nuanced understanding of the term "genocide" can offer a lens through which settler colonial impositions on Indigenous societies can be held to account, but also understood as imperfect projects carried out by imperfect actors, leaving space for the wide variety of actual experiences of Indigenous boarding school life, including those characterized by resistance to and subversion of the overarching purpose of the schools.[29]

Why Discuss Genocide?

In the introduction to his monumental history of Indigenous residential schools in Canada, *Shingwauk's Vision*, J. R. Miller describes the schools as "an instrument of attempted cultural genocide."[30] The phrase is striking in its caution. Given that the *United Nations Convention on the Prevention and Punishment of the Crime of Genocide* (1948, hereafter UNGC) refers to genocide as the *attempt* to destroy a group "in whole or in part," is not the word *attempted* here redundant? And why is it that we so often feel required to place the qualifier *cultural* before the word *genocide*? Although Lemkin, who coined the term "genocide" in 1943 and helped to frame the UNGC, distinguished among cultural, biological, physical, and other methods of genocide in his work, we seldom find it necessary to specify when we speak of physical or biological genocide.[31] So what particular work does the term "cultural" do for us? In this passage, I believe that Miller is responding to common misperceptions about genocide rather than its legal or social scientific definition. He tells us this was "attempted" because genocide tends to connote a sense of finality, of complete and utter annihilation. Such a view, when directed toward Indigenous peoples, would ignore their perseverance, resurgence, and adaptive resourcefulness in the face of potential colonial destruction. Likewise, we can assume that the term "cultural" is not intended to mark Indigenous boarding schools as a "lesser" genocide, since Miller is all too aware of the suffering and intergenerational effects of these schools. Instead, the word *cultural* reminds us that there are methods of collective destruction other than those that characterize the most known and iconic of genocides: the Holocaust. Unfortunately, when writing for a general audience, one often needs to provide the reminder that a group can be placed in precarious conditions that threaten its survival as a group without gas chambers or concentration camps.

Like Miller, Jacqueline Fear-Segal, at the beginning of her excellent *White*

Man's Club, which traces the contours of racialized thinking in American Indigenous education, offers the following distinction: "Reluctant to embark on an open policy of *genocide*, white Americans instead organized to incorporate the surviving remnants of Indian tribes into the nation through cultural reeducation. For contemporaries, the *ethnocidal* task of the schools was sanitized by being narrated within the ideological frame of national expansion or 'manifest destiny.'"[32] Fear-Segal then goes on to acknowledge that the consolidation of American nationality included the destruction of Indian nationalities, through geographical, legal, and political means. Here she deploys the term "ethnocide" to describe the destructiveness of boarding schools. For Lemkin, ethnocide was synonymous with cultural genocide and therefore an aspect of genocide proper.[33] Subsequent use of the term, however, tends to treat ethnocide as a different category of event than genocide, since physical annihilation is held by some scholars to be necessary to genocide.[34] Fear-Segal appears to embrace this latter move, though she certainly remains aware of and attuned to the destructive power of assimilative schooling.

The qualification of boarding schools as cultural genocide is starker in Reyhner and Eder's analysis of Indian education in the United States: "The era of government control sought to save the Indians from vanishing by substituting a policy of cultural genocide for the old policies of removal and actual genocide."[35] The meaning is unequivocal. Although the charge of *cultural* genocide is intended to have some critical bite, its juxtaposition with *actual* genocide informs the reader that this is a lesser form of genocide. Like many writing in the shadow of the Holocaust and its saturation of the concept of genocide, as well as those careful not to portray Indigenous peoples as passive victims of an absolute power, Reyhner and Eder wish to highlight the distinctiveness of forced assimilation as a destructive project. However, in so doing, they potentially minimize Indigenous boarding schools and their attempts to eliminate Indigenous groups, which, as we shall see, is what matters most when one views genocide as the attempted destruction of groups rather than simply a form of mass death.

Scott Trevithick expresses even greater concern over use of the term "genocide" when discussing Indigenous boarding schools, because he associates use of the term with the pollution of scholarly research by moral sentiment as well as with a tendency toward sweeping claims and oversim-plifications.[36] In criticizing the work of Agnes Grant, Trevithick charges that her use of the term is "inappropriate" and that she manipulates evidence to fit the UNGC.[37] Moreover, he claims, "by inferring that the Native residential experience was in the order of the Nazi Holocaust she perverts the concept of genocide and does a grave injustice to these highly distinct historical phenomena."[38] Here, again, the Holocaust overshadows the discussion and becomes conflated with the concept of genocide.

In the next chapter, I seek to correct some of these misconceptions about genocide and to offer it as a scholarly concept rather than strictly a touch-stone for activism. Genocide, I argue, is about the protection of groups, not individuals in the aggregate. Therefore, we cannot simply transpose our understandings of a crime such as homicide onto genocide, as when one assumes that, because homicide is the intended physical death of an individual, genocide is the intended physical, and only physical, death of a group. We must seek instead to understand what is specific to group life. What allows a group to persist, even if persistence occurs while the group itself undergoes change in reaction to variable circumstances, such as the introduction of new technologies or ecological shifts? What, as Lemkin would put it, are the "essential foundations of group life," and when can we consider them to be purposefully placed in jeopardy?[39]

While attempting to clarify genocide and its potential application to Indigenous boarding schools, I also offer a process-based and multilayered analysis that situates these schools within broader settler colonial processes. This approach is in keeping with recent developments in genocide studies, which aim to comprehend genocide not as a series of traits or characteristics intended to define genocide in all its times and spaces but as a dynamic process that ebbs, flows, and intensifies at specific historical moments and in specific places, while lessening its force in others. Such a process is seldom singular in how it unfolds, nor is it the product of the actions of a lone institution or actor; instead, genocide is typically comprised of the activities of multiple actors, who form networks of destructive forces that threaten the life of a group or the lives of multiple groups.[40] Following this approach, I treat Indigenous boarding schools as part of an uneven process comprised of numerous agents—government officials, military and police personnel, settlers, reformers, politicians, teachers, Indigenous leaders, parents and children, but also nonhuman actors such as disease, land, time, and food. Although it might seem strange at first to include nonhuman actors as participants in assimilative education, I make the case that a more complete understanding of genocidal processes can be obtained by inclusion of a wide variety of influencing forces that interact with and intervene in the social world.[41] Although human agents might seek at times to enlist pathogens and land in their efforts to bring order to the world around them, pathogens and land do not always respond in expected fashions. Therefore, treating such entities as actors allows one to better account for the unexpected consequences that often arise in processes of social engineering, such as in the "benevolent experiment" of assimilative education.

My objective in this book is to explain how settler colonial genocidal processes intensify and weaken across multiple social layers, spaces, and times and through the actions of a variety of actors. Genocide in this analysis is not merely an event perpetrated in a delimited region by a perpetrator against a victim; it is instead a networked process eclectic in its construction yet also an assemblage with a distinct and identifiable purpose: group destruction.[42] Moreover, in my discussion of redress efforts in the aftermath of residential schools, I argue that a sophisticated understanding of patterns of destruction wrought by settler colonialism offers a more promising path for redressing genocidal Indigenous-settler relations in a decolonizing manner, since we must understand the complexity of these patterns before we can transform them.

A Note on the Research

My approach in this project is a comparative, discourse-based analysis of historical documents and oral historical testimony. My objective is to avoid the tendency to use the term "genocide" to develop a single story or metahistory to apply to all Indigenous peoples in North America. It is not my intention to present a definitive narrative history of Indigenous educational policies in the United States and Canada, nor is it to provide comprehensive retellings of life experiences in the schools in New Mexico and Manitoba that I have selected to focus on at the microlevel: Albuquerque

Indian School (AIS), Santa Fe Indian School (SFIS), Fort Alexander Indian Residential School (FAIRS), and Portage la Prairie Indian Residential School (PLPIRS). This would require a more intensive and immersive knowledge of these schools and the Indigenous communities that they affected than I can claim to present in these pages. Instead, I extract from the secondary literature, archival documents, and oral histories that I reviewed common themes that emerged during my investigations and that serve as my basis for comparison. The multilevel and network-based theoretical model that I have developed for this project provided an initial map for identifying key points of comparison. In brief, this involved identifying key moments at the macro- (government policy), meso- (institutional and organizational), and micro- (everyday life within the schools) levels of the American and Canadian boarding school systems. This entailed (a) at the macrolevel, detailing the complex formulation of the Indian Problem in each country and the policy responses to this problematization; (b) at the mesolevel, examination of the multiple government and nongovernment institutions, as well as lower-level organizations (e.g., boarding schools, mission schools, and day schools), that sought to influence the formulation of government policy and were responsible for negotiating and implementing it on the ground; and (c) the everyday actors who drew on a variety of technologies (e.g., discipline, desire, knowledge, and violence, among others), and forged a variety of local alliances, to advance, adapt, resist, or subvert macro- and mesolevel conceptualizations of the Indian Problem. Through this model, I complicate and diversify understandings of settler colonial genocide in North America.

To cover all of these areas required a broad scan of primary and secondary literatures. Archival documents were useful for capturing policy-based ideas about and institutional applications of the Indian Problem, but they were generally less useful for obtaining glimpses of everyday life within the schools, though some hints about such life could be gleaned from inspector reports, superintendent and principal letters, letters from parents and students, diaries, and other such sources. Still, much of this information is overly formal and did not reveal much more than what those who controlled the schools wanted to show. For this reason, oral histories were important to my study.

For the U.S. cases, I reviewed over 500 oral historical interviews with Indigenous persons in the American Southwest through the Center for Southwest Research at the University of New Mexico. These U.S. interviews were conducted in the late 1960s and early 1970s as part of the Doris Duke American Indian Oral History Project, and they contain information related not only to education but also to Indigenous history, ceremony, art, and community issues. This broader context gave me access to information on other institutional and social pressures experienced by Indigenous peoples in the American Southwest that factored into their concerns about education. But it also meant that only a small portion of each interview focused on schooling, with current and former students discussing their experiences in boarding schools in a period that ranged from 1900 to 1970 in response to one or more questions from the interviewer. Add to this the fact that the University of New Mexico graduate students who often conducted the interviews were not always skilled methodologically, and it was clear that the interviews had to be reviewed with a careful eye. As well, the Indigenous respondents were often reticent to criticize the cultural community of their interviewers, and this reluctance required that the transcripts be read closely to find criticisms embedded within seemingly complimentary passages. Take the following example, in which the ambivalence of the speaker is prominent: "I think the white people were doing good for the Indians, but the Indians didn't realize what the white people were trying to do, the white people was trying to help us Indian. But still, at the same time, the white people was after our land."[43] In this statement, white motives of benevolence and land acquisition are placed side by side, without being assumed to be mutually exclusive. Although it is clear that the speaker is engaged in "giving face" to the interviewer by not criticizing too harshly the culture of that interviewer, one must also not discount entirely the sentiment that the speaker expresses—that (at least some) white people were trying to do good.[44]

More thorough and methodologically sound were the twenty-five transcripts of interviews conducted by Sally Hyer as part of the Santa Fe Indian School 100 years project. Transcripts of these interviews were also housed at the Center for Southwest Research, and they focused solely on students' experiences at SFIS. However, given that these interviews were conducted as part of a commemorative project for the school, and that some former students refused to be interviewed for the project, one must acknowledge that these interviews are not generalizable to the entire population of former students.[45]

In contrast to the U.S. materials, most of the oral history materials available with respect to Manitoba boarding schools have a different frame of reference. In 1990, Phil Fontaine, then grand chief of the Assembly of Manitoba Chiefs (the umbrella body representing First Nations across Manitoba), who later became grand chief of the Canada-wide Assembly of First Nations, revealed to the media his experiences of physical, sexual, and emotional abuse at Fort Alexander Indian Residential School, which he attended in the 1940s. This watershed moment appears to have opened the door for many survivors to come forward and tell their stories about the abuses and hardships of Indian residential schools, bolstering class action lawsuits that eventually led to the 2006 Indian Residential School Settlement Agreement (IRSSA), which was approved by the courts and came into effect in 2007.[46] Fontaine's revelation created an opening that made possible a new collective action frame through which survivors could process and better articulate their diverse experiences of the schools.[47]

For this reason, comparative oral history work must not be undertaken through a naive subjectivism. As much as one must respect and honor the words of the interviewees, one must also understand that the past is complicated and difficult to contain and articulate within a clear narrative. Survivors of trauma often look for what Jeffrey Alexander refers to as a "trauma drama" to introduce some structure into a difficult and complex past.[48] This is not to say that they misrepresent the past; instead, it is to acknowledge that they make choices in what they present from the past because they need to make their narratives comprehensible to their listeners, and a collective action frame gives coherence to the jumble of often confusing and traumatic experiences, making it communicable. In the United States, though criticism of boarding schools is certainly evident, such a collective action frame is less prevalent, especially in the late 1960s and early 1970s, when most of the interviews used in this book were conducted. In addition, Navajo (hereafter the preferred term "Diné" will be used when possible) and Pueblo interviewees appeared to be reluctant at the time to assert their criticisms of white Americans in interviews. Cultural values of politeness and humility restrained the speakers. These factors must be borne in mind so that the interviews can be located in their appropriate historical and cultural contexts.[49]

My oral history data from Canada are quite different. Although some of my oral sources were created in the 1980s, prior to Fontaine's disclosure, most come from the work of the Truth and Reconciliation Commission of Canada (TRC).[50] The TRC did its utmost to create an environment in which any story of Indigenous boarding schools could be told—good, bad, or both—but the TRC nonetheless existed in a new discursive landscape.[51] The wrongs of residential schooling had been acknowledged through Prime Minister Harper's public apology as well as the compensation programs that were components of the IRSSA. Moreover, since Fontaine's 1990 statement about his experiences at Fort Alexander, more and more survivors had come forward to add their own horrific experiences to the historical record. In such a context, even those who came to the TRC to tell of positive experiences at the schools felt the need to qualify their statements (e.g., "I know the schools did a lot of harm, but for me . . .").[52] Because of these differences in testimonial data in the two countries, I resist declaring Indigenous boarding schools to be worse in one country than the other. Such attempts at adjudicating suffering are in any respect unsavory. As well, I focus more on the mundane efforts to regulate and transform Indigenous populations through the order of the schools than on the more widely known sexual and physical violence of these schools. Although schools in both the United States and Canada could be brutally violent, and too often deadly, I am most interested in the more subtle techniques enlisted to destroy Indigenous peoples as groups.

It was also difficult to find a perfect balance between American and Canadian archival sources. Although Canadian residential school archives are known to be scanty and sanitized, a fact confirmed when I examined the government-prepared Fort Alexander Indian Residential School Individual Assessment Process Narrative, which, despite the widespread testimony detailing horrific violence at this school, lists only one instance of abuse in its entire history (a student who ran away from the school in 1963 and was reluctant to return for fear of punishment).[53] Thus, these official records in some respects were less detailed than those collected in the United States. However, the U.S. records also had their limitations, especially with respect to the Albuquerque Indian School, where records were destroyed at two different points in time, once by fire and once by vandals and squatters making use of the abandoned school building.[54] Enough archival material survived to offer a basic understanding of the school, but there are gaps in this information.

I should also note that comparative analysis often begins with an attempt to find somewhat analogous cases for comparison. Such an approach guided this project to the extent that I aimed to examine schools situated in regions with sizable and prominent Indigenous populations. However, the cases were also attractive as much for their differences as for their similarities. Based on an initial examination of the boarding school literature, it was clear that the regional differences among schools were significant, and I wanted to explore how a variety of factors might interrupt or adapt the assimilative intentions of federal planners. The primary communities that attended the schools that I examined—Pueblo, Diné, and Apache in the United States; Ojibway, Dakota Sioux, and to a lesser extent Cree in Canada—differ from one another in interesting ways in how they interacted with the schools, and their schools were distinct from one another. I thus selected these schools to help illustrate some of the many variations of the settler colonial mesh manifested through assimilative education rather than to serve as models of the American and Canadian systems.[55] That said, however, I make no claim in the pages that follow to offer a full and final interpretation of the experiences of these Indigenous groups in North American boarding schools. I draw on oral histories so that their voices might counter the dominant narratives of the schools obtained from the archives, but my focus is still on the schools themselves as settler colonial institutions and more broadly on the destructive character of the settler colonial mesh. As a non-Indigenous member of a settler colonial society, I find myself still working to unsettle all that I have taken for granted from a lifetime within my formative context, and I find it necessary to use the tools of critical sociology to interrogate the institutions and practices of settler colonialism that have placed, and continue to place, limits on how we, as settlers, live and experience our relations with Indigenous peoples.

The Chapters that Follow

Chapter 2 demonstrates the applicability of the term "genocide" to Indigenous boarding schools by tracing the origin, legal application, and sociological purpose—protection of the life of a group—of the term. This chapter destabilizes assumptions built into much thinking about genocide that privilege European understandings of group life, and it stresses the importance of conceptualizing settler colonial genocide in terms of process, rather than in an oversimplified and overgeneralized fashion that ignores its uneven spread, as well as the multiple points where resistance occurs within genocidal contexts.

Chapter 3 provides a comparative analysis of Indigenous boarding school policy and its application in the United States and Canada, focusing on the macrolevel and upper mesolevel of the settler colonial mesh. At the macrolevel, the chapter shows that a common collective action frame—a lens for understanding and acting on the Indian—formed in both the United States and Canada under the auspices of the Indian Problem. These commonalities of vision in each country begin to diverge, however, as solutions to the Indian Problem are institutionalized. In Canada, the decision is made to rely on existing networks of Christian missions to implement assimilative schooling, whereas in the United States the system is largely directed and operated through the federal Bureau of Indian Affairs (and its earlier manifestations). Under these circumstances, Canadian Christian denominations lobbied to prevent changes to the institutional structure of Canadian residential schools, and the Canadian bureaucracy tended to be more stagnant and disengaged in its approach to the schools. In contrast, the United States showed greater variation in its policies with respect to Indigenous boarding schools, and the government intervened more directly into the operation of these schools.

In Chapter 4, four schools are introduced as the foci for microlevel analysis. These schools are placed at the lower meso-, or organizational, level of the settler colonial mesh, and they are examined both as stand-alone schools and in their interactions with other schools—not only other boarding schools but also day schools, public schools, and other related bodies. In addition, at the microlevel, the principal actors at the schools—staff, parents and communities, and students—are considered with respect to the various ways in which they engaged with forced assimilation. Some found opportunities to resist enrolment and to lessen the genocidal violence of the settler colonial mesh, whereas others committed fully to the settler colonial project. This largely descriptive chapter sets the stage for the next three chapters, which provide a closer look at how these four schools enlisted various techniques and nonhuman actors in the project of assimilation and did so in ways that either contributed to or lessened the genocidal impacts of these specific schools.

Chapters 5 and 6 examine some of the techniques employed by school staff to forcibly transform Indigenous children and to destroy Indigenous communities. The goal of each chapter is not to provide a comprehensive catalog of settler colonial assimilative strategies but to illustrate some of the ways in which the settler colonial mesh sought to tighten around Indigenous young people at the microlevel. In most cases, these techniques provoked resistances that prevented the total assimilation of students to European ways. But at certain times and in certain spaces, the combined force of violence, discipline, desire, managerialism, and aggressive resocialization (i.e., disconnecting children from their families and inserting them into new family-like relations), not to mention other factors, tightened the settler colonial mesh and made it nearly impossible for children to maintain connections to family and community, leaving them either isolated or in search of new forms of collective affiliation.

In Chapter 7, the analysis moves beyond human-centric examinations of genocidal destruction by delving into the roles played by nonhuman actors in producing the intended and unintended consequences of the American and Canadian boarding school systems. Here territory, space, time, disease, health, hell, food, and poverty receive discussion as actors enlisted either in facilitating or in resisting assimilative education. Other actors could have been added, but those assessed in chapter 7 provide a sense of the complicated local context of Indigenous boarding schools and the changes that occurred over time in terms of how these actors were enrolled in resolution of the Indian Problem and formation of the settler colonial mesh.

In Chapter 8, I argue that both Canadian and American Indigenous peoples continue to suffer from the aftermath of Indigenous boarding schools as well as other ongoing mutations in the settler colonial mesh. Moreover, I briefly discuss the legal channels available in each nation for the pursuit of reparations. I note that, based on similar experiences and legal resources, the different pathways to redress taken in the United States and Canada require explanation. I offer three reasons why Canada arrived at the IRSSA, whereas efforts to achieve redress in the United States remain minimal. These reasons are (1) *discursive*: based on differences in how the respective boarding school systems have been interpreted and represented; (2) *political*: based on the different nature of pan-Indigenous politics and governmental Indigenous policy in each country; and (3) *structural*: based on the different characteristics of neoliberalism in the United States and Canada. In light of these three reasons, the chapter concludes with a critique of the Canadian IRSSA as a model for redress as well as the argument that too often such redress policies represent further mutations of rather than clear breaks with the settler colonial mesh. I suggest that American Indigenous groups approach their efforts to achieve redress with this caution in mind.

Chapter 9, the concluding chapter, braids together the strands of assimilation, education, genocide, and redress that run throughout the book. The chapter ends by presenting a politics of decolonizing redress in North America that holds genocide as a key stake within such redress.

2 | Settler Colonial Genocide in North America

Other scholars have explored the legal case for a charge of genocide against the United States and Canada based on the historical and contemporary treatment of Indigenous peoples, including in boarding schools.[1] This chapter, in contrast, offers a primarily sociological and historical conceptualization of the term. It is not that legal and sociological conceptions are completely unrelated, for both are founded on the work of Polish Jewish jurist Raphael Lemkin, whose work crossed multiple disciplines. However, contrary to much genocide law, my emphasis is on collective and structured forms of social patterning and action as well as on the ways in which individuals negotiate and make meaning within group life. Thus, my concern is less with prosecuting specific individuals for their participation in genocide and more with understanding how destructive social relations emerged and were sustained, intensified, dampened, or countered within a broader social network.

In short, my focus is on the collective nature of genocide perpetration and victimization. This leads, for example, to concerns with the victim group as a collectivity targeted for destruction and how such collectivities come to be placed under threat.[2] Genocide can be directed either at a group of actors who co-produce the boundaries of their group through ongoing interactions or at a group that exists largely, or even solely, in the imagination of the perpetrator, though both internal and external forms of collective identity formation are typically involved.[3] My interest lies in groups of the former rather than the latter kind. Moreover, my concern with collectivities extends to an examination of the perpetrator as a collective actor that seeks the destruction of a targeted group.[4] It is a concern with how actors enact and experience potentially genocidal relations in concert rather than as individuals. In contrast, in the realm of international criminal law, the focus of genocide trials to date has been predominantly on the specific intent of the individual accused of having deliberately sought the full or partial destruction of the target group.[5]

Raphael Lemkin, Genocide, and the Americas

As Leo Kuper notes with regard to genocide, "the word is new, the concept is ancient."[6] Indeed, the slaughter of opponents has a long history, from the Roman siege and eventual razing of Carthage at the close of the Third Punic War (149–146 BCE), which historian Ben Kiernan has labeled "the first genocide,"[7] to the Athenian destruction of Melos during the Peloponnesian War (fifth century BCE).[8] Reflecting on the history of group destruction, and most immediately the crimes committed by the Ottoman Turks against Armenian and other minorities living in their shrinking empire (1915–18), Raphael Lemkin made it his life's mission to give a name to, and create a legal mechanism to prosecute and prevent, the destruction of such groups. Lemkin began in 1933 with a paper that he prepared for a conference in Madrid in which he proposed the crimes of barbarity and vandalism. Barbarity was "the premeditated destruction of national, racial, religious and social collectivities," and vandalism was the "destruction of works of art and culture, being the expression of the particular genius of these collectivities."[9] One can see in this early definition his interest in the life of a group. For him, law already existed to defend the life of an individual, but the group, as well as the cultural means for its persistence, was unprotected.

Lemkin's initial attempt at legal definition failed to gain traction in the international community. But Lemkin endured nonetheless. However, after the Nazi invasion of Poland, he had to avoid becoming a victim of genocide himself. He escaped capture and eventually settled in the United States in 1941.[10] It was there that he witnessed the power of commercial branding and sought a new term for what he had previously referred to as barbarity and vandalism—a term that would be as memorable as "Kodak" or "Xerox."[11] Thus, in 1943, he coined the term "genocide," combining the Greek *genos* (for "type" or "group") and the Latin *cide* (from *cidere*, "to kill"), to describe the crime of group destruction.[12]

For Lemkin, genocide was not limited to the physical annihilation of peoples:

> Generally speaking, genocide does not necessarily mean the immediate destruction of a nation, except when accomplished by mass killings of all members of a nation. It is intended rather to signify a coordinated plan of different actions aiming at the destruction of essential foundations of the life of national groups, with the aim of annihilating the groups themselves. The objectives of such a plan would be disintegration of the political and social institutions, of culture, language, national feelings, religion, and the economic existence of national groups, and the destruction of the personal security, liberty, health, dignity, and even the lives of the individuals belonging to such groups. Genocide is directed against the national group as an entity, and the actions involved are directed against individuals, not in their individual capacity, but as members of the national group.[13]

Clear here is that Lemkin thought that the group was worthy of protection in and of itself, not just in terms of the physical lives of its members.[14] This is further evident in the fact that he saw the Nazi march across Europe not solely as an assault on European Jews but also as leading to the potential destruction of Poles, Slavs, Roma, and many others, through diverse methods that extended beyond mass murder.

Moreover, for Lemkin, practices of colonization were intimately related to those of genocide: "Genocide has two phases: one, destruction of the national pattern of the oppressed group: the other, the imposition of the national pattern of the oppressor. This imposition, in turn, may be made upon the oppressed population which is allowed to remain, or upon the territory alone, after removal of the population and the colonization of the area by the oppressor's own nationals."[15] Imposition on an oppressed population, in his analysis, is more than simply a demand that the oppressed group take on some of the cultural qualities of the oppressor. Instead, the national pattern of the oppressor is imposed in such a way that little to nothing will remain of the national pattern of the oppressed. The genocidaire seeks to eliminate the oppressed group as a physical and biological entity bound together by the strands of culture.

Lemkin was a tireless advocate of his concept, and his first great success came when his new word was included in the Nuremberg indictment, though it was not among the charges laid by the International Military Tribunal against Nazi war criminals (1945–46). After Nuremberg, Lemkin worked with the United Nations to devise a law against genocide. Indeed, he played an instrumental role as a consultant in preparation of the 1947 secretariat's draft convention on the crime of genocide. In this draft, his tripartite division of the concept of genocide—into physical, biological, and cultural patterns—is clearly expressed. Damien Short, however, remarks that these three aspects of genocidal destruction are not to be understood as mutually exclusive forms of genocide. Instead, Lemkin viewed them as interrelated components of a destructive process directed toward the elimination of a group.[16]

Assimilation, the primary focus of this book, was considered by Lemkin to fall under the pattern of cultural genocide; however, he was careful to point out that only specific strategies of forced assimilation should be considered genocide. He argued that assimilation, in and of itself, does not necessitate a charge of genocide if the methods are moderate, such as when attempts are made to gradually acculturate an immigrant minority group to the dominant culture.[17] In contrast, drastic policies aimed at the "rapid and complete disappearance of the cultural, moral and religious life of a group of human beings" did, in his view, amount to genocide.[18] But such rapid and forced assimilation was not solely cultural in practice or outcome. Lemkin understood it to combine with physical and biological patterns of destruction and thereby contribute to the elimination of the group as a physical, biological, and cultural entity.

The final version of the 1948 *United Nations Convention on the Prevention and Punishment of the Crime of Genocide* (UNGC) dispensed with Lemkin's emphasis on cultural genocide, which had been present in early drafts of the convention, including Article III of the Ad Hoc Committee on Genocide's 1948 draft. The article read thus: "In this Convention genocide also means any deliberate act committed with the intent to destroy the language, religion or culture of a national, racial or religious group on grounds of national or racial origin or religious belief such as: 1. Prohibiting the use of the language of the group in daily intercourse or in schools, or the printing and circulation of publications in the language of the group; 2. Destroying, or preventing the use of, libraries, museums, schools, historical monuments, places of worship or other cultural institutions and objects of groups."[19] Although the majority of delegates to the UN General Assembly voted to remove Article III, settler colonial nations such as the United States and Canada were the most strongly opposed to inclusion of the language of cultural genocide in the UNGC. But this occurred in contradiction to Lemkin's intentions; a fragment from his autobiography reveals that Lemkin opposed the removal of Article III from the UNGC.[20]

Article II of the UNGC, the most frequently cited portion of the convention, reads as follows:

> In the present Convention, genocide means any of the following acts committed with intent to destroy, in whole or in part, a national, ethnical, racial or religious group as such:
> a. Killing members of the group;
> b. Causing serious bodily or mental harm to members of the group;
> c. Deliberately inflicting on the group conditions of life calculated to bring about its physical destruction in whole or in part;
> d. Imposing measures intended to prevent births within the group;
> e. Forcibly transferring children of the group to another group.[21]

Some read inclusion of the clause on the forcible transfer of children as an acknowledgment of one specific type of cultural genocide.[22] However, scholars examining the *travaux preparatoires* of the UNGC suggest that the clause was intended to speak only to physical destruction,[23] or to biological destruction,[24] since it was assumed that the removal of children would threaten the viability of targeted groups.

After helping to draft the UNGC, Lemkin continued to gather information on genocides in world history. In his effort to produce a major volume on the topic, he prepared, or had his research assistant prepare, notes on a wide range of cases. Among these cases were the harms experienced by

Indigenous peoples in the Americas at the hands of colonizers.[25] In these notes, as well as examining instances of physical and biological annihilation, Lemkin turned his attention to cultural patterns of destruction. Indeed, A. Dirk Moses suggests that he was "more concerned with the loss of culture than the loss of life."[26] Lemkin was influenced by the anthropology of Sir James George Frazer and Malinowski and saw culture as essential to the functioning of collectivities, since it assisted groups in meeting their survival needs and allowed them to form a "family of mind."[27] In his view, the destruction of culture undermined the very ability of a group to persist. Moreover, Lemkin believed that the destruction of a group's culture depleted the richness and diversity of global life.[28]

With particular reference to Lemkin's study of North America, John Docker notes that

> we can see Lemkin focusing on aspects of genocide perpetrated by the English, French, and postindependence Americans that constitute a comprehensive historical process over a number of centuries, including deep into the nineteenth century: dispossessing indigenous peoples of their land (with or without permission of central authorities), kidnapping, enslavement, removal, and deportation often involving forced marches, taking of children, disease through overcrowding on reservations with inadequate food and medicine, self-destruction brought on by introduction of the sale of liquor, curtailing and deprivation of legal rights, cultural genocide (as in re-education of children in boarding schools, cutting off of braids, forbidding native languages, prohibitions on Indian culture and banning of religious ceremonies, forcing children to become Christians), and mass death.[29]

One can see in this list the diverse actions that comprise settler colonial genocidal processes in North America, of which residential schools are but one significant moment. Thus, though the focus of this book is on settler colonial genocide and Indigenous boarding schools, such schools are not to be taken alone as instances of genocide—following Lemkin's lead, they should be considered components of genocidal processes that involve a range of complex interventions in Indigenous life.[30]

Within the diversity of actions that Lemkin identifies as constitutive of genocide, there are a variety of intents and motives at work. It is in this context that one can better understand what Tony Barta, in his important essay that helped shape the field of colonial genocide studies, refers to as "relations of genocide." He posits that genocide was endemic to colonization. For Barta, even those among settler colonial populations who worked against the destruction of Indigenous peoples, or who expressed a desire to let Indigenous peoples simply die out, were nonetheless complicit in a broader ideological vision that prescribed the destruction of Indigenous worlds, albeit by different means.[31] My approach is certainly indebted to Barta's work, though my goal is to give more attention to local applications of settler colonial "relations of genocide" and to gauge some of the ways in which they actually play out in practice.

Cultural Destruction and Genocide Definition

Despite Lemkin's interest in and affirmation of the genocidal nature of many aspects of North American settler colonialism, the tendency in scholarship has been to use notions of "cultural genocide" or "ethnocide" when discussing transgressions against Indigenous peoples, including assimilative boarding schools.[32] Unfortunately, such terms too often come across as presenting forced assimilation as a "lesser" form of genocide. "Cultural," in such instances, signifies that one is speaking of a qualified genocide not to be confused with "real" genocide.

"Indigenocide" is another term used to refer to the particular experiences of Indigenous peoples under colonialism. In explaining the rationale behind the term, Raymond Evans refers to the "lack of fit" between the UNGC and the "disastrous process of indigenous dispossession occasioned by settler colonialism."[33] With Bill Thorpe, he coined the term "indigenocide" to communicate "an interdependent, three-way onslaught upon lives, land, and culture."[34] Evans and Thorpe provide an important acknowledgment of the overlap between the lives of group members and their territory, since territory is too often treated in genocide studies as merely a resource needed to preserve the life of the group rather than as an element integral to its collective identity. However, Evans and Thorpe's variation on the term "genocide" also has the unfortunate effect of removing Indigenous peoples from the more general category of protection suggested by the UNGC—as persistent and valued groups that, like all other such groups, have a right to protection and survival. The term "indigenocide" tends to particularize indigeneity to the point that it remains exotic and otherworldly and therefore potentially perceived as part of a different universe of obligations than that which typically animates discussion of genocide. In other words, it has the potential to conceive Indigenous peoples as "absolute others" protected because they are essentially different from rather than in crucial respects similar to us.[35] Understood in Lemkinian terms, the UNGC should protect various forms of group life, since each is a valued part of our plural humanity, and we should not need a separate term for certain types of groups.

However, though the UNGC can speak to a wide diversity of group forms, it is not without its limitations in terms of how it imagines group life. In particular, many early genocide scholars expressed concern about the narrow band of groups targetable under the UNGC—that is, racial, ethnic, religious, and national groups. For example, the omission of political groups from the UNGC definition has been criticized, for this omission fails to reflect the fact that political identifications can persist across time and are central to collective identity.[36] Because of such perceived problems with the UNGC, genocide scholars have proposed numerous variations on this definition.

One of the most widely cited definitions is offered by the sociologist Helen Fein, who writes that "genocide is sustained purposeful action by a perpetrator to physically destroy a collectivity directly or indirectly, through interdiction of the biological and social reproduction of group members, sustained regardless of the surrender or lack of threat offered by the victim."[37] In this definition, the groups targeted by genocide are left open, so that any cohesive group that reproduces itself across time could be considered a victim of genocide. Others, such as Frank Chalk and Kurt Jonassohn, shift emphasis to the role of the perpetrator in imagining the target group as a unified and dangerous entity: "Genocide is a form of one-sided mass killing in which a state or other authority intends to destroy a group, as that group and membership in it are defined by the perpetrator."[38] Unfortunately, Chalk and Jonassohn's approach, unlike that proposed by Fein, dispenses with the group as the object of concern, for it simply protects individuals, who might be perceived as members of a group by a perpetrator, rather than members of actually existing groups.[39]

Some contemporary genocide scholars have tried to answer Christopher Powell's provocative question "what do genocides kill?" by turning toward more relational or negotiated understandings of group life rather than treating the group simply as a static or fully coherent entity.[40] Feierstein, for example, defines genocidal social practices as "a technology of power that is intended to destroy social relations based on autonomy and cooperation by killing a significant portion of society (significant in numbers of influence) and that then attempts to create new social relations and identity models through terror."[41] And, though Powell's own definition of genocide, "an identity-difference relation of violent obliteration,"[42] does not explicitly mention group relations, for Powell "groups do not exist only in the minds of individuals; they also exist in practical relations among people, relations that can be observed empirically."[43]

As one moves from definitions like those provided by Fein and Chalk and Jonassohn, which seek to determine the key traits that characterize genocide, to more relational understandings of genocide, the emphasis also shifts from strictly physical to other forms of destruction. For many years, genocide scholars largely abided by Chalk and Jonassohn's argument that there is an "analytical" difference between physical and cultural destruction.[44] One basis of this analytical difference is argued to be that, whereas collectivities can regroup and revive after experiences of cultural destruction, physical destruction leaves no such option.[45] But several contemporary scholars have found this sharp divide between the cultural and physical life of the group difficult to sustain.[46] What makes a group a group, and what allows a group to survive? Although defining group survival in terms of the physical lives of a certain portion of group members might seem to be the simplest way to answer this question, it brings us no closer to understanding the "essential foundations" of group life that Lemkin thought it important to protect. Discovering these foundations of group life requires familiarity with actual groups and in particular with group cultures.

Culture is a central and necessary component of the continued existence of a collectivity, since culture is part of what helps us to preserve the relations of group life. In contemporary terms, culture is understood as both a product of and a constitutive component of group relations. But such a conceptualization of culture has not always been reflected in notions of cultural genocide. Indeed, early definitions of cultural genocide and ethnocide tended to treat culture as a fixed entity rather than a collectively negotiated aspect of group life. For example, Monroe Beardsley defines ethnocide as the "intent to extinguish, utterly or in substantial part, a culture. Among such ethnocidal acts are the deprivations of opportunity to use a language, practice a religion, create art in customary ways, maintain basic social institutions, preserve memories and traditions, and work in cooperation toward social goals."[47] Culture here appears to be little more than a static set of practices and ways of being that need to be preserved as part of the store of the particular group's traditions. But culture is something other than this. As James Clifford suggests, it is a "deeply compromised" notion that has too often been used to place firm boundaries around what is in truth a complex set of relationships.[48] Culture is a loose grouping of values, practices, and behaviors never wholly legible but always in interaction with historical processes of "appropriation, compromise, subversion, masking, invention, and revival."[49] Culture, in brief, is the stuff in between us; it shifts and moves as our relationships unfold. In this sense, it cannot be frozen into some permanent quality, but it is also that crucial glue that helps to hold together group relations.[50] Therefore, what is at stake in discussions of cultural genocide is not some never-changing quantity or quality; instead, it is a set of relations that allows groups to form and reform as they develop and adapt to changing circumstances.[51] This raises a vexing question for genocide scholars. How does one protect something that is fluid and changing? As well, such an understanding of culture reminds us that it is a site of contest and debate, and therefore collectivities are not monoliths. Thus, a further question arises. How does one protect something that itself is beset by internal divisions?

I will address these issues below, but before I do it is important to acknowledge that, though they are by and large my focus in this book, cultural techniques of group destruction are not the only ones evident in North American settler colonialism. Massacres and even group annihilation were not foreign to Canadian and American settler colonial societies.[52] Indeed, even when we look at residential schools as a form of genocide, many deaths could be addressed through a genocide studies lens.[53] But I wish to focus primarily on so-called cultural forms of attempted destruction because they are often perceived to be softer or less catastrophic than outright physical assault, which can give one the erroneous impression that forced assimilation through boarding schools represents a more enlightened and gentler form of attempted destruction, no matter how strange that sounds.

Many scholars deploy genocide terminology in discussing Indigenous boarding schools,[54] and therefore use of the term within this book is hardly original—it is more with respect to how the term is used that this book makes its contribution. Some of the literature that seeks to demonstrate the genocidal nature of Indigenous boarding schools does so by using the UNGC as a grid or framework for assessment and prosecution. Some, such as Agnes Grant and Kevin Annett, direct their attention to the five types of genocide listed in Article II of the UNGC (see above), and they seek to demonstrate how Canadian Indian residential schools fit these criteria.[55] By forcibly fitting the experience of residential schooling into this set of criteria, much historical nuance is lost, and all that is distinct about the destructive or genocidal quality of the schools is diluted as residential schools are asked to become like concentration camps or some other space that better fits popular notions of genocide.

More useful have been attempts to grapple with Indigenous boarding schools in relation to the *travaux preparatoires* of the UNGC and to show how these framing documents, as well as subsequent case law, create space for consideration of the destructiveness of these schools.[56] However, my own approach has been to try to distill the Lemkinian conceptual essence of the UNGC and to deconstruct its most basic terms so that it is no longer simply a Eurocentric grid for evaluating group rights to existence. In this manner, my focus is on the statement of general principles, or *chapeau*, of Article II, which comes before the five types of genocide: "Genocide means any of the following acts committed with intent to destroy, in whole or in part, a national, ethnical, racial or religious group." In short, genocide refers to acts committed with the *intent* to *destroy* a *group*. It is worthwhile to take a moment to interrogate each of these highlighted terms.

TARGETED GROUPS

As mentioned above, there has been much consternation over the limited set of targetable groups acknowledged in the UNGC. The move to more relational understandings of genocide has sought to push this debate forward by understanding groups as sets of relations rather than essentialized identities that do not change over time. The group, therefore, is to be preserved not as a museum piece set behind glass and observed with passing curiosity but as an ongoing set of interactions and negotiations through which group members make and remake their group. In other words, following this understanding of the group, a set of group relations is observed to exist and possess value in that the group offers its members a space for attachment and identity formation. Based on this insight, genocide is important not so much because it targets the bodies of group members but because it targets the relations that hold the group together as a persistent yet changing entity.[57]

Group identity formation, of course, takes place not solely through internal negotiation but also through external perceptions of the group. The gaze of others imputes to the group characteristics that in certain conditions might be integrated into the group's self-conception.[58] However, external identifications can also serve to disrupt or destroy internal identifications. For example, when confronted with the challenge of governing multiple and distinct Indigenous groups in North America, the settler response was to homogenize these differences into a single, governable category: the Indian.[59] With this invention in place, additional law was created, and a diverse population was targeted for government intervention. Such acts of definition, Dan Paul reminds us, have severe consequences for Indigenous peoples. He writes that "centralization caused many hardships among the Mi'kmaq. It was a terrible and unwarranted assault upon the village structure of a great civilization . . . It's probably very difficult for most non-Indians to conceive of having a plan for the life of their race mapped out and implemented by government against their wishes."[60]

In genocide, it is often the perpetrator who attempts to impose a permanent categorization on the group. Under the perpetrator's gaze, targeted group members often become an undifferentiated danger to the perpetrator's own group. I say "often" here because it is not always the case that target groups are treated as threatening. Such dehumanization is a frequent component of genocide and other forms of mass violence,[61] but as Henry Theriault notes genocide can also occur when perpetrators imagine themselves possessed of an exceptionalism that makes their actions beyond reproach, regardless of any threatening qualities possessed by the targeted group.[62] Notions such as manifest destiny or civilization therefore can guide genocidal destruction even in cases in which an absolute debasement of Indigenous peoples is not clearly evident, such as when they are treated simply as backward races to be civilized through schooling. This is not to suggest that Indigenous peoples were not demeaned and diminished by colonial powers—such debasement certainly occurred within schools and through other settler institutions. However, this debasement did not need to approach the level of utter dehumanization, since settler colonialism also sought to *rehumanize* Indigenous individuals to make them fit a European image.

The UNGC restricts genocide's targets to racial, national, ethnic, and religious groups but gives us little guidance on how such groups are constituted and persist across time. Moreover, by specifying the types of groups targetable by genocide, the UNGC veers dangerously close to practices of forced identification mobilized by settler colonial regimes within genocidal contexts (e.g., the Canadian Indian Act). Too often, in reading the UNGC, the tendency has been to treat the potentially targeted groups in an essentialist manner: that is, as possessing ascribed identities that largely shape the lives of their members. Even Lemkin was prone to such essentialism.[63] But this approach does not help us to protect actually existing groups in all of their dynamism and fluidity, and a more supple understanding of genocide, and of a group's risk of destruction, needs to make space for understandings among group members of how they reproduce their group's life on a day-to-day basis. Genocide definition cannot prescribe the nature of group life, since to do so would be to engage in a further act of violence against the group.

DESTRUCTION

Unless there is space available for the group in question to assert how it constitutes itself as a group, and to assert the dynamics and resources that make its group life possible, it is difficult to assess the ways in which such a group might be destroyed. For this reason, testimony from survivors of attempted destruction is crucial, since they are best positioned to identify what they believe was lost or almost lost. This is not to suggest that genocide scholars must naively accept all survivor claims and descriptions as unadulterated truths; the methods of sound critical scholarship must still be in place. But these methods must be combined with an ethical sensibility that strives to better understand the experiences of the other, even if we can never put ourselves fully into his or her shoes.[64]

To date, much genocide scholarship has focused on physical and biological destruction.[65] This approach is not only inconsistent with Lemkin's early framing of the definition of genocide but also evinces a liberal and Eurocentric focus on the lives of individuals as the ultimate object of moral concern.[66] But groups are not simply associations of individuals; they are entities comprised of, but that exist beyond, their individual members. The term "genocide," if it is to be used to protect groups from destruction (as Lemkin intended), needs to be sensitive to the relations and processes that sustain the group and make it a valued source of identity and meaning for individual members. Under such a conceptualization, acts usually considered under the rubric of cultural genocide are no longer relegated to a place of being "lesser" forms of genocide, since they can destroy the group as a group, even if the blood of group members is not spilled in the process.[67] Certainly, the murder of a large number of group members places a group's persistence in jeopardy, but this persistence can also be threatened by multiple acts intended to fray the bonds of group association, such as through the prohibition of practices such as language use, spiritual worship, self-governance, and transmission of cultural knowledge. These are merely examples, since the social relations that hold the group together will be specific to the group in question. For example, in the case of many Indigenous peoples, land or territory is viewed as an important participant in the formation of collective identity, an identity not simply based on a specific geographical location but also infused by this location. Here land is not only a thing that makes possible group subsistence but is also entwined with and part of the group, and therefore its removal, development, or devastation constitutes a potentially destructive assault on the group.[68]

The suggestion is sometimes made that American and Canadian governments did not actively seek destruction of Indigenous groups as groups.[69] The harm done, according to this view, derived not from a racist animus (and therefore clear genocidal intent) but as a consequence of the settler colonial desire for Indigenous land and a less fractured nation-state. Likewise, it is argued that settler governments and missionaries framed (or even believed) their interventions to be benevolent, providing assistance to peoples struggling with group-threatening situations, such as loss of the bison as a source of subsistence on the prairies and plains. Is it possible that misguided acts of human welfare can be perceived as genocidal? Even if one accepts such redemptive narratives of settler colonial benevolent intent, there still exists deep disrespect for Indigenous groups in such attempts at "help." In this vein, van Krieken argues that what is genocidal in, for example, policies of Indigenous child removal lies "less in an unambiguous 'intent to destroy' a human group . . . than in the presumption that there was not much *to* destroy."[70] But can such a willful denial of the value of the culture of a targeted group, and a sincere belief in the "white man's burden," amount to the same thing as genocidal intent?

In genocide trials, based on the UNGC or subsequent reinterpretations in international law, emphasis thus far has been placed on "specific" or "special" intent, which means that the perpetrator exhibited a distinct purpose to destroy a group "in whole or in part." This intent has been determined in three ways: (1) through the destructive magnitude of the actions of individual perpetrators; (2) through evidence of participation in a comprehensive plan of destruction; and (3) through evidence of a consistent pattern of action. With "specific intent," the emphasis is squarely on individual perpetrators. This makes legal sense, for it can be more difficult to determine the intention of collective action under the standards of international law.[71] But it does not always help us to better comprehend the collective sociohistorical processes through which intentions take shape.

Historically speaking, discussion of intent in Canadian Indigenous boarding schools has typically followed one of two pathways. Trevithick differentiates between "traditional" and "revisionist" interpretations of the intention behind boarding schools. The traditional view emphasizes the assimilationist intentions of residential school planners. These intentions are viewed as based either on misguided benevolence or cynical desire to open land to settlement or resource extraction and remove federal obligations to Indigenous peoples. The revisionist understanding offers a slight variation on these themes but tends to view assimilationist discourse as a rhetorical guise for pursuing self-interested motives.[72] In his introduction to the Truth and Reconciliation Commission of Canada's Interim Report, Chief Commissioner Justice Murray Sinclair offers a version of the traditional view: "Residential schools disrupted families and communities. They prevented elders from teaching children long-valued cultural and spiritual traditions and practices. They helped kill languages. These were not side effects of a well-intentioned system: the purpose of the residential school system was to separate children from the influences of their parents and their community, so as to destroy their culture."[73] However, Justice Sinclair also suggests that the "revisionist" story is not without merit: "To gain control of Aboriginal land, the Canadian government signed treaties it did not respect, took over land without making treaties, and unilaterally passed laws that controlled nearly every aspect of Aboriginal life."[74] Ultimately, Justice Sinclair suggests, this was a "complicated" story. But how does one locate intent within such a complicated story?

To begin, moving away from individualist notions of intent allows one to incorporate both traditional and revisionist perspectives. Within collective projects of group destruction, multiple individual intents and motives can be in play under a broader, more generalized, intent, and the meaning and purpose of destructive interventions are negotiated among several actors, each potentially mobilizing different objectives and idealized outcomes.[75] What matters for the enactment of group destruction is that these diverse perspectives can cohere or congeal around a common collective action frame that enables coordinated interventions rather than completely haphazard interactions.[76] In the next chapter, I will argue that this is the work done by the language of "assimilation" and "civilization"—these terms allowed people with different views and interests to act together in pursuit of their goals within a shared universe of meaning.[77] Whether their goal was the dispossession of Indigenous lands, the cultivation of souls, or both, they could fit their efforts within the collective action frames of assimilation and civilization, which united multiple motives within a North American context—it opened up lands for exploitation, souls for conversion, and a nation for consolidation. In pursuit of these motives, the notions of assimilation and civilization thus represent an attempt to deliberately direct social change: namely, the destruction of Indigenous peoples as groups.[78]

Such an understanding takes us away from a strict juridical understanding of intent. In criminal law, motive, that which impels a person to action, is separate from intent, the *mens rea* (the state of mind) that gives purpose to the offender's actions. Courts typically are interested in intent rather than motive, though in certain cases, such as hate crimes, motive is used as a basis for establishing that the crime was committed because of the defendant's prejudice or hatred toward a specific group of people. For reasons similar to those marshaled with respect to hate crimes, motive should not be ignored in legal questions about genocide. But do motives such as those discussed above suggest that actions intended to destroy Indigenous peoples were genocidal?

If the UNGC is to serve as a basic guide for our analysis, then we must pay careful attention to the "as such" that precedes the five types of genocide listed in Article II, since the UNGC specifies that there be "intent to destroy, in whole or in part, a national, ethnical, racial or religious group, as such." This suggests that the intent of the perpetrator is to destroy the target group as a group and not for some other objective, the pursuit of which leads to the incidental destruction of the group.[79] Elsewhere I have criticized the Eurocentric assumptions that often guide our reading of such terms, but this does not diminish the fact that the UNGC requires that perpetrators seek to destroy groups "as such" or for who they are.[80] Drawing on a Holocaust frame of reference, our expectation is often that genocide is motivated by a racist animus that dehumanizes the target group to the point that their survival can no longer be permitted. But this is not the only manner in which such intent might be expressed. Indeed, I argue that, through formulation of the Indian Problem in terms of assimilation and civilization, Indigenous peoples were constructed as backward, savage, barriers to progress, and they needed to be forcibly transformed in order to meet the designs and appease the motives of the settler colonial society. That multiple motives were behind this forcible transformation matters less than the fact that there was widespread agreement on the need to eliminate Indigenous groups, *as such*, from settler society. Indigeneity was a *problem* to be *solved*.

But what about those teachers, principals, and other staff who showed kindness in their interactions with Indigenous students or who even assisted Indigenous peoples in their resistance to assimilation?[81] Stories of such individuals arise with relative frequency in boarding school memoirs, though such people appear to have been a minority in the schools. But the outpouring of horrific tales from Canadian residential schools has provoked a defense from those who believe that there is "another story" to tell, such as Eric Bays, former bishop of the Diocese of Qu'Appelle in southern Saskatchewan: "I think all those who have written historical accounts of the schools would admit that there were, in some schools and in some eras, good staff people who were doing their best for the students under their care. Unfortunately, the story reported in recent years has often lumped all residential schools together, putting all the schools, at all times, under suspicion of wrongdoing."[82] Questions of good and bad individuals can certainly be problematic when investigating cases of attempted genocide, since genocides are collective projects involving individuals with different levels of motivation and involvement as well as different dispositional engagements with the processes of destruction. Christopher Browning, for example, compares the men of Police Battalion 101, who participated in some of the most horrific killings in Poland in the early stages of the Nazi "Final Solution," with the guards of Philip Zimbardo's Stanford prison experiment, described as falling into one of three groups: kind guards who sought to ease the suffering of inmates to the extent possible in the existing structural conditions, guards who followed orders but were not excessive in their cruelty toward prisoners, and guards who were devious and creative in the cruelties that they imposed on prisoners. This division of guards, of course, is a simplification of the diverse ways in which people participate in the suffering of others, but it captures how those who provide human labor in genocidal spaces are not necessarily full embodiments of these spaces. They are actors within a larger collective project who seek lines of action that reflect and are consistent with their personal dispositions and orientations.[83]

George Tinker responds to claims of benevolence among missionaries and religious groups with the argument that "the motivation and the theoretical basis for the missionary endeavor, apparent both from the actual practice of the missionaries and from their writings, will demonstrate that they not only preached a new gospel of salvation, but also just as energetically imposed a new cultural model for existence on Indian people." In so doing, he suggests, missionaries became "partners in genocide."[84] Tinker refers specifically to the notion of cultural genocide, which reflects for him a more subtle but equally catastrophic mode of destruction to physical genocide, as well as one that operates with or without intention, since it is also embedded in systems as much as in individuals. His conceptualization elides as much as it resolves the problem of intention, however, since it basically emphasizes the motives behind and destructiveness of individual actions or the unmitigated destructiveness of social systems. But these two levels are conjoined and not separate. Thus, as we grapple with this notion of intent central to legal thinking on the concept of genocide, we must pay critical attention to the fact that the notion of intent remains lodged in a series of unstable modernist dyads: for example, those between structure and agency or conscious and unconscious activity. From a more relational perspective, however, one could argue that agency operates in and contributes to the production of social structure, and that the conscious and unconscious are more interlinked and overlapping, as the thought and unthought combine to form our tactical and habituated actions.[85] Under these terms, intention serves as a juridical fiction, a means of tidying up a complex world, that isolates one side of these hybrid equations. Its emphasis is on the individual, the agentic, and the conscious. We need to find a means to comprehend intention in its hybrid complexity as a negotiation of structural conditions as well as the actions of other agents. It is formed by both the habituated dispositions and the tactical machinations of the actor, who might often act with only a partial or incomplete understanding of the purpose of his or her actions.

Such a discussion is not intended to serve as an apologia for those who participate in attempts at group destruction ("they could not help themselves; they were locked into structural conditions that determined their actions"). Instead, my goal is to offer a sociologically enriched understanding of what intent might mean in genocidal contexts, since the legal concept does not adequately account for human action. In this sense, intent is not reducible to the thoughts or practices of a single actor. Instead, it is negotiated under structural and discursive conditions. These conditions give shape to a collective action frame that is both the product of social interactions and a force conditioning social interactions. Under the guidance of such a collective action frame, institutional and personal interventions in the lives of others are made possible but not without degrees of freedom that allow for individual negotiation of the collective action frame: that is, for specific adaptations and motivations to arise in particular settings. Sociologically speaking, then, intention in genocide is often more "generalized" (rather than simply "general" or unspecified) than "specific," since collective action bent on the destruction of another group is made possible through a combination of broad social pressures and widely circulating discourses, as well as immediate situational factors, such as the institutional organization of destruction, patterns of fear of the other, desire for the land or resources possessed by the other, and multiple other interests or concerns.[86] In short, the generalized intent identifiable in the collective action frames that set the course for destruction makes possible instances of specific intent among individuals, but it is not necessary that specific intent be observable in all participating actors, since this generalized intent can have a momentum of its own and carry along with it actors not fully conscious of (or willfully blind to) their roles in genocide or even those who find novel and unexpected ways to adapt themselves to this collective action frame in order to subvert it or lessen its impact.

Colonial Genocidal Processes

To address some of the challenges faced when examining questions of intent in group destruction, more recent literature has moved toward a processual approach to understanding colonial genocide.[87] Such an approach better captures historical nuances, such as regional and temporal differences, as well as individual and local adaptations, in the ways that Indigenous peoples experienced (and continue to experience) and settlers implemented (and continue to implement) colonialism. This allows one to avoid the reductive character of legal analysis or of earlier definitions of genocide based on identification of a set of common criteria held to be true for all genocides. In contrast, there is a building consensus in genocide studies that genocide is a process, not an outcome or a set of clearly definable traits.[88] This means that our attention is increasingly turned not toward the results, which can lead to unsavory comparisons of death tolls or a teleology of intent that traces genocide linearly and simplistically from utterance to action, but toward the dynamics of genocide. How do various ideologies (promoting different levels of destructiveness) meld into a genocidal outlook? How are the actions of numerous actors and institutions coordinated over time and in a range of territorial settings? Which obstacles to genocide arise, and, if they are overcome, how is this done? Such questions demand that our approach to the topic of genocide not be focused solely on narrowly delimited periods of time but offer a diachronic lens sensitive to moments of foundation, interruption, expansion, contraction, and so forth, within genocidal processes.

The analysis that follows is in keeping with this more contemporary approach to genocide studies. My framework for the study of settler colonial genocide, described in chapter 1, traces its movement across three levels—macro, meso, and micro—conceived of as series of nets that tighten and loosen across time and space. This framework is designed to attend to the unevenness of genocidal processes. Moreover, it follows the advice of Ernesto Verdeja: "We [i.e., genocide scholars] should explain, in other words, variability in violent outcomes. With a few exceptions, our comparative theories have yet to develop systematic theoretical accounts for the interactions of these various levels of violence (micro, meso, macro) and consequently the onset and diffusion of genocidal violence; nor do they investigate cases where genocide did not occur."[89] Verdeja adds that, "outside of anthropological and historical studies, there is relatively little work that systematically explains internal differences across space and time. Genocide is understood as an aggregate outcome of country-level factors, while variation within states and regions is ignored."[90] In this book, I show some of the local variation mentioned by Verdeja by examining at the microlevel specific schools in New Mexico and Manitoba, and the particular networks that formed at these schools, which took distinct shapes in response to both broad and local conditions.

However, prior to beginning this analysis, I should take a moment to consider the relationship between colonialism and genocide. When referring to colonial genocide as a process, we assume that there exists a level of connection between the terms "colonialism" and "genocide." So, one might ask, what makes genocide colonial? Drawing from the work of Jurgen Osterhammel, Moses defines colonialism as "the occupation of societies on terms that robs them of their 'historical line of development' and that transforms them 'according to the needs and interests of the colonial rulers.'"[91] This is an ongoing project. Thus, like capitalism, colonialism is totalizing rather than a totality.[92] It is always expansive and therefore always incomplete in its aspirations. It is a process. It spreads across regions and times in an often uneven and variegated manner, adapting to the local networks that give shape to colonialism on the ground.

Following in the footsteps of Hannah Arendt,[93] as well as drawing on diverse traditions that range from world systems theory to poststructuralism, several contemporary historians have drawn links between colonialism and genocide.[94] In considering similarities between colonialism and the Holocaust, Jurgen Zimmerer writes that "historical scholarship has largely ignored structural similarities and avoided direct references between the two. Instead, the investigation of the colonial enthusiasm of National Socialists has been restricted prematurely to the reacquisition of the German empire in Africa."[95] Although such approaches do generate some controversy,[96] they are nonetheless instructive on the importance of avoiding reductive national approaches to the study of genocide. They give us reason, at the outset of this book, to be skeptical of its initial premise—a comparison between Canadian and American settler colonial processes—since one cannot help but note the many intersections and overlaps between these processes.

Of course, one must also be aware that there are analytically distinct forms of colonial rule. In particular, for my purposes here, the difference between colonialism, in which the colonizer establishes only a base in the colonized land and rules from outside while exploiting the labor of the "native," and settler colonialism, in which the colonizer establishes a dominant settler population in the colonized territory and that population rules that territory from within while seeking the removal or disposal of the "native," is of central importance.[97] Patrick Wolfe more than anyone has set the standard for examination of processes of "settler colonialism," which he argues are defined by a "logic of elimination." Although such a logic might be genocidal, he prefers his term because he believes that it better captures the specificity of settler colonialism as a social formation bent on dispossession and erasure, and he doubts that this term would be very useful for understanding other genocides, such as Rwanda and the Holocaust.[98] He is thus less interested in tracing the links between events like the Holocaust and colonialism than other genocide scholars, but he shares with them an emphasis on process. In particular, Wolfe suggests that, when examining colonial genocide, one is not assessing a single event but a structure or wide range of actions. The primary factor animating this structure is the settler desire for Indigenous lands, not for Indigenous labor, which thus marks Indigenous peoples as dispensable and replaceable.[99] In contrast to Wolfe, I prefer genocide as a rubric for examining specific forms of settler colonial elimination, since, in my understanding, the logic of elimination is a component of the collective action framework that makes settler colonial genocidal processes possible. Although I note the distinctiveness of settler colonial versus colonial or noncolonial genocidal contexts, there is purpose in a common definition of harm, as is encapsulated in the term "genocide," since it provides a means to specify what is common within these different contexts: the rights of collectivities to protection against destruction.

In this respect, the work of Moses has been significant in guiding my approach to the study of genocide in a settler colonial context. Moses offers a nuanced view of settler colonial processes and their potential for destruction. Speaking of Australia, he writes that,

> instead of arguing statically that the colonization of Australia was genocidal tout court, or insisting truculently that it was essentially benevolent and progressive, albeit with unfortunate ramifications, it is analytically more productive to view it as a dynamic process with genocidal potential that could be released in certain circumstances. The place to look for genocidal intentions, then, is not in explicit, prior statements of settlers or governments, but in the gradual evolution of European attitudes and

policies as they were pushed in an exterminatory direction by the confluence of their underlying assumptions, the demands of the colonial and international economy, their plans for the land, and the resistance to these plans by the indigenous Australians.[100]

In this manner, Moses identifies the confluence of factors that must be examined for an assessment of genocidal intent, potential, and outcome.

These factors include acknowledging the resistance presented by those targeted for destruction, the omission of which has made Indigenous scholars in the past hesitant to draw on genocide terminology, since they believed that it connoted passivity.[101] Lomawaima summarizes how an understanding of resistance is crucial in the study of Indigenous boarding schools:

> Indian people at boarding schools were not passive consumers of an ideology or lifestyle imparted from above by federal administrators. They actively created an ongoing educational and social process. They marshaled personal and shared skills and resources to create a world within the confines of boarding-school life, and they occasionally stretched and penetrated school boundaries. In the process, an institution founded and controlled by the federal government was inhabited and possessed by those whose identities the institution was committed to erase.[102]

As Ellis similarly states, "that Indian people used the schools to suit their needs and purposes is an important consideration, for it raises the often-overlooked notion of agency."[103]

Although recognition of such agency is crucial to the study of Indigenous boarding schools, both Lomawaima and Ellis risk reversing the terms of the debate, committing to a sociology of the subject that overemphasizes agency in their eagerness to move past an objectivist sociohistoriography that denies agency. Without a doubt, students acted and reacted to the confines of boarding schools and renegotiated the terms of these schools. But just as the schools were not able to impose their ideology in a straightforward and unproblematic manner on pupils, so too the pupils did not see their resistance realized in an even and direct way. Instead, their negotiations of self, community, and resistance in the face of assimilative pressures took place amid a complex of actors, networks, and negotiations, and social outcomes were produced through a difficult social alchemy.

In this chapter, I have sought to clarify my use of "genocide" as a term in this book. Beginning with the origins of the term in the work of Raphael Lemkin, and through its legal definition at the United Nations, I have sought to specify what I believe to be most important about the term: its capacity to protect the collective efforts of groups to constitute and reproduce themselves as groups. In this respect, I have drawn the discussion away from essentialized notions of group identity and treated the nature of the group and its potential for destruction as empirical questions rather than legally codified facts. Moreover, I have argued for a broadening of the notion of intention to better capture the complexity of social action, so that perpetrator actions and intentions can be considered diverse, albeit under a forceful and dominant collective action frame that pushes toward the destruction of a targeted group or set of groups. Finally, I have presented settler colonial genocide as a process, rather than as an outcome, so as to better capture the uneven and complex nature of colonial interventions in the collective lives of Indigenous peoples. In short, if the term "genocide" is to have any scholarly utility in the sociohistorical study of intra- and intergroup relations, we must avoid using it as a reductive shorthand that deprives historical events of their complexity and specificity. Instead, genocide, as a conceptual rubric, must open itself to allow for the examination of multiple and often conflicting motives, intents, and actions, as well as structural and discursive pressures on actors (e.g. the collective action frame, which Wolfe would describe as a logic of elimination), that shape often uneven genocidal processes. The settler colonial mesh, as a conceptual framework for examining macrolevel formulations of destructive intentions, mesolevel institutional manifestations of these intentions, and microlevel interactions that both realize and thwart such intentions, provides a means for examining the multiplicity and variability of settler colonial assimilative education in North America.

3 | Framing the Indian as a Problem

This chapter focuses on two levels of the settler colonial mesh. The first, the macrolevel, is discussed in terms of the broad frameworks and interests that guided settler colonial thinking on the so-called Indian Problem, which informed government policy and offered a collective action frame for assimilative Indigenous schooling. The second, the upper mesolevel, consists of those institutions, governmental and nongovernmental, that took on the task of implementing these policies. Education, as a social institution, is my primary topic of concern, but it is important to remember that education did not operate alone in efforts to resolve the Indian Problem. For example, the testimony of Lords Dufferin, Lorne, and Lansdowne about their experiences in the Canadian Northwest soon after the 1885 uprising illustrates the multinodal nature of Canada's approach to the Indian Problem. In their report, they discuss the positive influence of farm instructors and Christian missionaries and suggest that their efforts need to be combined with education, health promotion, and policing. They also note how the reserve system, recently established Canadian Pacific Railway, and Canadian military together provided ultimate recourse for the Canadian government if Indigenous peoples did dare to rebel again:

> Under the treaty, the Indians are obliged to stay upon their reserves—a
> refusal to comply entailing forfeiture of the Government annuity.—So

that they are thus kept from commingling and plotting treason. This precaution is one of the wisest adopted by the Canadian Government. Then again, the fact should not be lost sight of, that with the excellent railway facilities now afforded, since the completion of the Canadian Pacific Railway, four thousand troops from Eastern Canada could, if necessary, be transported to quell any disturbance that might arise, in a time not exceeding three or four days from the receipt of intelligence of such troubles.[1]

Not only were educational institutions supported by other institutions, such as law, health, and policing, but also these other institutions often carried out independent efforts to encourage assimilation. Canadian colonial law not only provided a basis for compelling children to attend boarding schools in the early twentieth century but also partnered with religious institutions to try to prohibit Indigenous cultural practices, such as through prohibition of the potlatch.[2] As well, colonial law legitimated settler land appropriation and prevented Indigenous demands for return of their territories through mechanisms such as the Canadian ban against Indigenous communities hiring lawyers.[3]

Although this chapter concentrates on broader developments both within and between the United States and Canada, it remains attentive to the fact that the policy and institutional developments discussed below took distinct shapes when applied in specific regions. As Margaret Szasz writes, "the uniqueness of each boarding school seems to defy comparison. Yet beneath the surface surprising commonalities connected the experiences of students at these diverse Indian boarding schools, whether they were located in the East or the West, in the colonial era or the late nineteenth century."[4] Among the commonalities that she identifies is the fact that all Indigenous children sent to boarding schools experienced removal from their families and communities and insertion into a foreign, disciplinary environment. How is it that this came to pass?

The focus of this book is on the settler colonial era, in particular those periods after the American Indian Wars abated and assimilation became the basis of Indian policy.[5] However, before turning to the conceptualization of the Indian Problem and the move toward mass assimilative schooling, I will briefly explore education prior to the development of the Indigenous boarding school systems in the United States and Canada.

Indigenous Education

It can be very difficult to convince Westerners to look on education, even in its most assimilationist form, as a potential source of harm much less genocide. So often, when faced with contemporary social problems, our automatic response to the question of "what is to be done?" is to suggest that "more education is needed!" Education, in our world, is what gives us opportunities in life. As well, education is idealized as a means for overcoming ignorance and intolerance. Add to this the fact that boarding school education was traditionally practiced among Western elites,[6] and it becomes very challenging to convince others that not only the abuses that occurred in boarding schools, but also the ethnocentric design of the schools, should be considered an intentionally destructive form of harm.

In contrast to more sanguine views of education, Pierre Bourdieu asserts that "one of the major powers of the state is to produce and impose (especially through the school system) categories of thought that we spontaneously apply to all things of the social world—including the state itself."[7] Thus, it is through education that various forms of state messaging, and the social construction of the state itself, occur. This includes transmission of the qualities of the ideal citizen to children. But when it is imposed on the children of a subjugated group, the transformative power of citizenship education can be harnessed to objectives of cultural destruction, especially when combined with disciplinary techniques that sometimes employ brutal force toward this end. This can occur to include the subjugated group in the dominant society or to foster obedience among the marginalized, destabilizing their identity so that they no longer pose a threat to the dominant order.[8] In this sense, education is not simply a means by which we learn about our world; it is also a means whereby we produce or reproduce this world in the minds of the young. Even without the added violence that characterized Indigenous boarding schools, education that ignores the culture from which the student is drawn threatens to disrupt that student's ability to understand himself or herself as part of, and find meaning within, his or her cultural group.

To the extent that education has an important societal role to play, it is a component of most organized societies. It is thus a mistake of ethnocentrism to assume that education in the Americas began with the arrival of Europeans. Indigenous communities have always had their own forms of education. It is beyond the scope of this book to describe the many and varied methods of precontact education in North America; however, common practices included learning through observation and experience, subtle forms of parental guidance, freedom to explore one's surroundings, ceremony and ritual, as well as didactic storytelling.[9] For the Ojibway (Anishinaabe), education began at a young age through play that mimicked adult tasks. For high-status Ojibway, education could continue through involvement in the Midewiwin, an institution designed for fostering "cultural unity, preserving traditions, healing sickness and educating its members."[10] Among the Navajo (Diné), House describes the following educational practices:

> There were songs, prayers, and other lessons that accompanied sheep-herding and gardening, weaving and basket making, bearing and tending children, greeting and interacting with others. One learned by doing and observing. In addition, many important and sacred teachings took place during ceremonies and other events that centered on the creation of the Navajo people and all that exists in the world and on the Navajo emergence into the present White or Glittering World through a succession of previous worlds. The telling of winter stories late at night around the fire in the center of the Hogan, like the playing of the shoe game, a reenactment of the gambling contest in which the animals decided the duration of night and day, was an occasion for transmitting this cultural knowledge. Yet another source of instruction about how Navajos were to behave and live in their world was the Coyote stories.[11]

None of this is to suggest that some Indigenous people were not interested in the forms of education that the Europeans promised. Indeed, many envisioned European schooling for their children as a means by which they would learn to better adapt to a changing world while still holding on to their cultures.[12] Unfortunately, the education that they received from the earliest days after contact was predominantly assimilative in its approach; rather than sharing knowledge, it imposed a way of life.

Early Forms of Assimilative Schooling

Industrial- or vocational-style boarding schools in the United States and Canada are the products of an institutional legacy that stretches well back in European history. The antecedents of these assimilative institutions were not just the European schools that long existed but also workhouses, missionary schools, and other European spaces designed for disciplining the bodies of those perceived to be unproductive, shiftless, or sinful.[13] Indeed, the reigning sentiment in both Europe and North America, especially in the aftermath of Enlightenment reforms to education that saw it as a tool for shaping more than just the upper classes, was that institutions could be rationally designed to rehabilitate the criminal, cure the insane, or transform the backward and make them productive members of society.[14]

Mission schools directed toward educating Indigenous youth appeared in North America even prior to such reform. For example, Reyhner and Eder note that the first permanent mission was established in what is now the state of New Mexico in 1598.[15] Similar missions were also present in what is now California. However, these early mission schools did not initially assume the form of Indigenous schooling with which we are now most familiar. Although Indigenous peoples were gathered to live within mission compounds under the direction of missionaries, little formal education took place in these settings.[16] In contrast, Jesuits in the northeast of what is now the United States did establish a seminary for Indigenous students in about 1637. The six young students enrolled in this seminary abided by a schedule that included mass, prayers, catechism, reading, and writing. Two of the six died of sickness, and another left prior to graduation.[17] Slightly more successful were the efforts of Protestant missionaries, such as John Eliot, Thomas Mayhew Jr., and Eleazor Wheelock, who sought to convert and enlighten Indigenous young people in the United States through Christian teaching. Eliot, for example, set up fourteen "praying towns" between 1651 and 1674, and some of the Indigenous inhabitants of these towns were instructed in how to read and write in their native languages, as well as English, so that they could teach others. The inhabitants were also encouraged to change their appearance and disposition to adhere to European norms.[18]

In what is now Canada, in 1620, the Récollets, an order of Franciscans, established the first known boarding school for Indigenous children. The goal of their short-lived seminary was to convert Indigenous children, who might then return to and proselytize within their communities.[19] As the Récollets faded in their educational efforts, the Jesuits, who began in 1633 their own movement toward seminary-style schooling for Indigenous children, replaced them. Under their model, Indigenous children were removed from the influence of their families, provided with a Christian education, and sent back to their communities to convert others.

Up to this point in time, from the perspective of colonial governments, Indigenous education for the most part was simply tolerated rather than encouraged. Although some saw advantages to integrating Indigenous peoples into colonial society, and to spreading among them Christian beliefs and norms, others thought that these were futile endeavors and countered that the best measure was to keep Indians isolated and segregated from white society.[20] Still others saw some strategic advantage to holding Indigenous children in schools; indeed, some in the French government believed that these children could be used as leverage to ensure fur-trade and military cooperation as well as peaceable behavior within the communities from which the children were drawn. Nonetheless, government support for these educational efforts, at least in terms of resource allocation, was minimal at best.

Without the support of colonial governments, this early attempt at assimilative schooling was a failure, and it was largely abandoned by the 1680s. It was beset by familiar challenges: parents were reluctant to hand over their children, children resisted the restraints of European schooling, and Indigenous peoples refused to relinquish their cultures for an allegedly superior one derived from the cultures of Europe. J. R. Miller adds that "a major reason that the experiment in residential schooling failed in New France was that an assimilative educational program made no sense in an extractive commercial economy or in a martial world where northeast woodlands people were excellent warriors and allies just as they were."[21] To this extent, the political-economic conditions of colonialism had not shifted to a point where Indigenous education became a viable or even desirable option for the colonial societies beginning to take shape on the continent.

More concerted colonial involvement in Indigenous schooling would begin earlier in the United States than Canada, albeit in a tentative fashion. A 1774 treaty with the Oneida, Tuscarora, and Stockbridge Indians included provisions for the employment of one to two instructors to educate members in the skills of miller and sawyer. This promise was followed up on July 12, 1775, when the Continental Congress set aside $500 for Indigenous education at Dartmouth College, New Hampshire. As well, the U.S. government encouraged religious missions to educate Indians. In 1810, under such encouragement, the American Board of Commissioners for Foreign Missions, a joint project of the Presbyterians and Congregationalists, launched an "aggressive and well organized" attempt to civilize and assimilate Indigenous peoples.[22]

A wider policy with respect to Indigenous education began to emerge in 1818 when, on January 22, the House Committee on Indian Affairs presented a report in which it argued that

we are induced to believe that nothing which it is in the power of Government to do would have a more direct tendency to produce this desirable goal [civilization] than the establishment of schools at convenient and safe places amongst those tribes friendly to us. . . . Put into the hands of their children the primer and the hoe, and they will naturally, in time, take hold of the plow, and as their minds become enlightened and expand the Bible will be their book, and they will grow up in habits of morality and industry, leave the chase to those whose minds are less cultivated, and become useful members of society.[23]

This report influenced the first government policy on Indigenous education, when an act passed on March 3, 1819, set aside $10,000 in the Indian Civilization Fund for the employment of people of "good moral character" to instruct those Indigenous peoples who had shown potential for improvement "in the mode of agriculture suited to their situation."[24] This act was described to be "for the purpose of providing against the further decline and final extinction of the Indian tribes adjoining the frontier settlements of the United States."[25] With this latter sentiment, we witness a classic tension that permeates discussions on cultural forms of genocide—a foundational policy that initiates the movement toward Indigenous assimilation is presented as a measure intended to protect Indigenous peoples from seemingly more ominous colonial threats.[26] In Lemkinian terms, this tension amounts to one between different patterns of group destruction. But in the universe of European liberal individualism, such a tension is parsed to suggest that settler colonizers chose to avert rather than facilitate such destruction.

It is also worth highlighting the fact that the pathway to assimilation was contested by those involved. There was no singular intent that guided a fully defined project of Indigenous destruction. The lines of debate included questions such as should the Indians be transformed first into white men or Christians? Should emphasis be placed on the skills and habits required by white society? Or should it be on the rigors of Christian discipline and scripture?[27] As we immerse ourselves in the actual unfolding of genocidal processes, attention to such lines of debate gives us richer insights into genocide as a collective project. Seldom do such collective projects emerge uncontested or without multiple potential paths of action.

By the mid-1800s, there were sixteen manual labor schools, eighty-seven boarding and other schools, and several more schools under contract in the United States. These schools were funded by money held in trust for Indigenous groups as well as by an increased budget for Indian schooling, which rose in 1849 from $10,000 to $50,000 and then to $100,000 in 1855.[28] Most of the schooling was operated by missionary societies, which ran the schools under contract with the U.S. government, and hence they are often referred to as "contract schools." By 1873, the government began to state its preference that these schools be operated as boarding schools in order to better disrupt the influence of the "wigwam" and to shift the children toward speaking English rather than their "native tongue[s]."[29] In subsequent years, the government would begin its experiment in federally run boarding schools, discussed in the section below. With this occurrence, and particularly between 1885 and 1888, under the leadership of Commissioner John Atkins, Indian Affairs would decrease funding to mission-based contract schools and instead concentrate its resources on the federal boarding schools.[30]

Turning now to the emergence of the residential school system in Canada, we can see a similar pattern, albeit with a slight lag behind the U.S. system. In the early 1800s, Canadian grammar and day schools for non-Indigenous children were of limited number and often understaffed, poorly equipped, and prone to abuses against students.[31] Thus, most non-Indigenous children in this period did not attend school. Moreover, very few Indigenous students ever willingly enrolled in such schools. Part of the challenge faced by these schools in attracting Indigenous students was the fact that the western treaties had not yet been signed, and Indigenous peoples were not strongly tethered to their reserves, which made any prospect of mass Indigenous schooling unlikely given the dispersed and mobile nature of many Indigenous communities. Moreover, many Indigenous peoples during this period were still part of a frontier economy that involved hunting and trapping. During the nineteenth century, the devastating collapse of the bison, and the push to intensify settlement on the prairies, would bring schooling to the fore as a means for adapting Indigenous peoples to changing economic realities.[32]

In Rupert's Land and the North-Western Territory, the Hudson's Bay Company (HBC) was the dominant player in the early 1800s. As settlers came to the Red River area, in what is now Manitoba, the HBC started to see promise in allowing "civilizing agents" to freely enter the territory. This began with an 1818 invitation to the Catholic bishop of Quebec to provide missionaries. That summer Joseph Provencher led three Roman Catholic priests from Quebec to Red River, where after six months they established a Métis day school as well as another at Pembina. But the Métis were invested in hunting and trapping and therefore less interested in the agricultural instruction offered at these schools. Wesleyan missionaries entered the picture in the early 1840s as they sought to establish missions and offer education beyond Red River. However, the man leading the Wesleyan efforts, James Evans, ran afoul of both the Hudson's Bay Company and Indigenous groups since he was accused of meddling in HBC affairs and fondling children. He left the region and returned to England in 1846.[33]

Much like the experience in the United States, early boarding schools in Canada were based in and operated by religious missions, though during this era Canada showed more commitment to acculturation than military confrontation (still common in the United States).[34] But by the mid-1800s, Catholic mission schools began to take firmer root in western Canada as the Sisters of Charity of Montreal and the Oblates of Mary Immaculate became involved in educational work. By 1861, the Oblates had spread as far west as the Rockies and north to the Mackenzie River.[35] When residential schools eventually opened in the west, many were managed by the Oblates.

Protestant experiments with boarding schools also occurred prior to establishment of the Indian residential school system in Canada. The Protestant missionary organization the New England Company attempted to establish schools in New Brunswick, but they were closed in the 1820s because of complaints about the ineffectiveness of the schooling on offer, among other concerns. As well, the company established the Mohawk Institute in 1828 and began to train Six Nations children in the skills of manual labor as the fur trade began to provide less economic opportunity.[36] By the 1840s, this school was full, with several potential students on a waiting list for enrollment.[37]

In short, early efforts at Indigenous schooling were sporadic and disorganized. Although there was some interest among religious bodies in converting Indigenous communities through the education of their children, colonial governments had little interest in offering anything more than verbal and minor economic support for such institutions, since the colonial economy did not yet rest entirely on the acquisition of Indigenous lands and the complete pacification of Indigenous peoples, who still had utility as allied warriors or hunters. However, a shift in the political economy of the colonies was beginning to take place. By the mid-nineteenth century, European influence had grown significantly. Settlements were well established, particularly on the east coast, and population movements had begun, while Indigenous populations suffered great declines.[38] As well, the networks formed through fur-trade and military alliances started to unravel, diminishing the bargaining power of Indigenous groups.[39] But as the fur trade dwindled and the English asserted their dominance over and settlement of the continent, Indigenous groups found themselves faced with a massive land grab that threatened not only their territories but also their very existence as Indigenous peoples.

The Indian Problem: Defining and Governing the Indian

At a basic level, assimilative education is an example of what James C. Scott describes as "thinking like a state" to the extent that it represents an ambitious modernist attempt at social engineering spawned by a specific governmental problematization of an issue perceived to be solvable through a strictly managed or scientifically guided intervention in the social world.[40] However, the networks of institutions and agents that governed Indigenous peoples in colonial North America were complex,[41] and the state is better conceptualized here as a field of activity rather than a unified or wholly consistent entity.[42] Thus, rather than assume a monolithic state formed around a single ideological platform, I will examine the negotiation and coalescence of a collective action frame. A frame is a "schemata of interpretation" that provides the means through which people construct and understand the social world.[43] It is not an ideational straightjacket; frames shape rather than determine our thoughts and actions; to this extent, they open up to multiple adaptations and lines of action.

For boarding schools, the Indian Problem provided the basic formulation of the problem to be solved as well as guidelines for state intervention. Problematization of the Indian was noticeable as soon as settlement became the priority, after British control over most of North America was secured. But in the late nineteenth century, this problematization took specific form and was organized around principles of assimilation and aggressive civilization.[44] Of course, the term "Indian Problem" or "Indian Question" was not newly coined for the purpose of establishing Indigenous boarding schools; assimilation and civilization through such schools represented merely one solution to ongoing perceptions of the Indian Problem. Moreover, the North American Indian Problem was not the only Indian Problem that the British Empire thought it faced, since the expression was also often applied to British efforts in India.[45]

As a rubric of problematization, the Indian Problem allowed for complex deployment of techniques of governance, framed around notions of protection, moral uplift, assimilation, and civilization, that served the common purpose of removing the Indian as an obstacle to nation building, settlement, and government.[46] But before the Indian Problem could be fully articulated and enlisted into governance, it was necessary that there be an "Indian" to govern. Certainly, from the time of contact forward, the diverse Indigenous peoples of Turtle Island were mischaracterized as "Indians" based on the initial mistake of Columbus about where he had landed.

Through periods of trade, warfare, and then settlement, this homogenizing attribution was the basis for efforts to create laws and policies with respect to Indigenous persons.

The Canadian example helps to illustrate how this naming took shape as a basis for Indigenous governance. Prior to settlement, decrees of the British crown for the territories that would become Canada, such as the Royal Proclamation of 1763, issued after the British gained control over French territories in North America, operated to constitute an Indian subject at the same time that they sought to define the legal rights of Indians to their territories. Later, once settlement was under way in the mid-nineteenth century, specific legislation would be enacted in Lower Canada to define more strictly who was and who was not an Indian in the eyes of the law, without any consultation on the matter with those designated Indians.[47] Such early efforts to legally codify an Indian subject would receive broader application throughout the Canadian dominion through the 1869 Gradual Enfranchisement Act and 1876 Indian Act, both of which drew the distinction between status and nonstatus Indians.[48] In these and other cases, such legislation manufactured a governable Indian who could be made the target of programmatic interventions or be denied an Indian identity through legislative fiat.[49]

Thus, Canada's Indian Act did more than simply define who was and who was not an Indian. It introduced a raft of laws intended to manage and assimilate "Indians." For example, each Indian reserve was to be surveyed so that a band member could be issued "location tickets" that would allow him to gain ownership of this land if he successfully demonstrated his ability to make proper use of it during a three-year probationary period. In addition, the Indian Act, both in its original form and through later amendments, challenged the governance, marriage, religious, sexual, economic, spiritual, justice, and cultural norms of Indigenous societies.[50]

In the United States, efforts to create a classificatory algorithm of Indianness did not emerge until territorial expansion was largely complete: that is, after the Indian Wars and removals secured American domination from coast to coast. It was at the time of the Dawes Act (discussed below), which sought to distribute collectively owned Indigenous lands through individual allocations, that the blood quantum model for determining

Indigenous identity was instituted. Part of the logic of this model was that a certain amount of mixed blood in the individual would dilute his or her indigeneity, making it less necessary to impose policies of assimilation and segregation.[51] Blood quantum, or the percentage of Indian parentage, also factored into determinations of Indigenous identity in Canada.

Law and definition of the Indian were not the only techniques drawn on to make Indigenous peoples legible and to contend with their claims to their territories. In the United States and Canada, the settler population continued to grow, reaching hungrily for Indigenous lands and resources by any means necessary. As the colonial economy shifted more concertedly toward agricultural production and resource extraction, the perception of Indigenous peoples as a unitary, homogeneous obstacle to progress grew, and colonial grasping for Indigenous lands increased. Indeed, particularly in the United States, violence was a common method of removing and eliminating Indigenous peoples to make way for settlers.

Competing Solutions to the Indian Problem

There existed no single solution to the perceived Indian Problem. Many different strategies were attempted, though none offered a lasting solution. Some American policies, such as removals and reservations, simply displaced the problem.[52] Likewise, settler violence failed to provide a solution to the Indian Problem on the frontier. Indeed, the American Indian Wars of the eighteenth and nineteenth centuries were an object lesson for governments in both the United States and Canada, for efforts to defeat Indigenous nations militarily proved to be an extremely costly approach to national consolidation and economic development.[53]

The costs of these wars generated much discussion among military and spiritual leaders, economists, and legislators, among others. For example, Francis Amasa Walker, the commissioner of Indian Affairs from 1871 to 1872, considered such lessons in his monograph *The Indian Question:* "The Indian question naturally divides itself into two: What shall be done with the Indian as an obstacle to the national progress? What shall be done with him when, and so far as, he ceases to oppose or obstruct the extension of railways and settlements?"[54] Walker disagreed with the notion that treaties should be made with Indigenous nations as though they had rights to sovereignty, and he felt little sympathy for Indigenous peoples, representing them as backward, savage, and insolent. However, all-out war with the Indian was too expensive a proposition for Walker, and he recommended instead that Indians be segregated on even fewer reserves than those that were, in his time, recognized by the U.S. government. When isolated on reserves, Walker argued, Indians could "pursue their customs and habits of life, and indulge themselves in savagery,"[55] and not be intruded on by settlers. Moreover, he believed that it was only when they were isolated as such, and prevented from leaving reserves to pursue the hunt or trade, that Indians could be educated in the arts of industry and self-improvement. In the end, he claimed, the nation's goal was to "assimilate much and rid itself of more, until in the course of a few human generations, the native Indians, as a pure race or distinct peoples, shall have disappeared from the continent."[56] For Walker, this approach was the most humane; he thought it too cruel to simply allow Indians to die of hunger, disease, and pauperism, in contrast to which he thought that even a war of extermination would be more benevolent.

Likewise, Lieutenant Colonel Elwell S. Otis, in an 1878 monograph also titled *The Indian Question*, worried about the costs of war, while simultaneously dismissing Indian claims to sovereignty and the need for treaties. He was skeptical of the possibility of quickly civilizing the Indian, since he believed European civilization to be the perfect result of a long historical development. Therefore, like Walker, he also thought it necessary that the Indian be isolated on reserves and subject to the threat of external force to compel good behavior. He wrote that "henceforth the United States must labor to improve the Indian as well as to localize him, and abridge his territory. Under present circumstances it is of vital importance that his disposition and nature be so transformed, that he may be induced to quietly live in the neighborhood and peaceably follow the pursuits of whites."[57] In such circumstances, Otis held, schools for Indians were of some value, as long as Indian children were compelled to attend them.[58]

One can see between these two men multiple plans of action to potentially resolve the Indian Problem. Should there be war or education? Indigenous immersion or isolation? Or perhaps some combination of these approaches? Carl Schurz, U.S. secretary of the interior from 1876 to 1881, himself a reformer who only slowly came to embrace assimilationist policies, mapped out nicely his government's multipronged response to the Indian Problem, which incorporated a few of these, as well as other, strategies:

> To set the Indians to work as agriculturalists or herders, thus to break up their habits of savage life and make them self-supporting.
>
> To educate their youth of both sexes, so as to introduce to the growing generation civilized ideas, wants, and aspirations.
>
> To allot parcels of land to Indians in severalty and to give them individual title to their farms in fee, inalienable for a certain period, thus to foster the pride of individual ownership of property instead of their former dependence upon the tribe, with its territory held in common.
>
> When the settlement in severalty with individual title is accomplished, to dispose, with their consent, of those lands on their reservations which are not settled and used by them, the proceeds to form a fund for their benefit, which will gradually relieve the government of the expenses at present provided for by annual appropriations.
>
> When this is accomplished, to treat the Indians like other inhabitants of the United States, under the laws of the land.[59]

Education, under this formulation, was part of a broader approach to the Indian Problem that also targeted patterns of property ownership, land use, and perceived dependency, in addition to extending U.S. law across the continent.

Likewise, in Canada, one also sees the early emergence of a multipronged approach to the Indian Problem. For example, the Bagot Commission, which operated between 1842 and 1844, was tasked with reviewing the Canadian Indian Department and producing recommendations to better integrate Indians into Canadian society, reduce the costs of Indian administration, and improve the Indian Affairs record-keeping system. With respect to Indigenous education, the report proposed the establishment of industrial boarding schools some distance from the influence of parents and communities. The removal of children from parents, combined with subtle compulsion by which Indian children would "imperceptibly acquire the manners, habits and customs of civilized life," was viewed in Canadian government circles as a promising means to resolve the Indian

Problem well before the onset of the residential schooling system.[60] This view was also evident in Egerton Ryerson's 1847 evaluation of prospects for the industrial education of Indigenous children. At the time, Ryerson was the chief superintendent of education in Upper Canada, and like Bagot he recommended boarding schools as a solution, adding that they should be placed under religious authority. In his view, only Christianity could bring civilization to the Indians.[61] But Canada was slow to react to Bagot's and Ryerson's proposals, and some thought that the boarding schools in existence at the time of these reports were already a failure.[62] Rather than invest in systemic schooling, Canada sought to accomplish Indigenous transformation *en masse* through its Gradual Civilization Act of 1857, which attempted to wipe away Indigenous affiliations by asking Indians to withdraw from their tribes and accept individual parcels of land carved from their reserves. Indigenous peoples widely refused this option, seeing it for what it was: an attempt to destroy their societies.

The costs of military engagement were of issue not only in the American formulation of the Indian Problem, though in Canada the concern was more with avoiding such costs than with extricating the nation from their burden. In Canada, Indigenous groups had allied with the British during the War of 1812, and still played a role in the fur trade, which remained an important part of the Canadian economy in the early nineteenth century. This context, as well as external pressure from UK-based advocacy societies to protect Indians, and from the British government to keep costs in check, resulted in Canadian policy being directed more toward strategies of acculturation different from the warfare and removal policies prominent in nineteenth-century United States.[63]

Assimilative Education as a Solution to the Indian Problem

So if war, physical extermination, and forced removal were largely off the table, then what was to be done with the Indian? A distinction is typically drawn between those settlers who perceived Indigenous peoples to be part of a dying race that should be left or encouraged to fade away and those who saw hope in the possibility that they might be civilized.[64] But these ostensibly competing points of view are essentially conjoined within a colonial dyad, the fulcrum of which rests on the assumption that Indigenous peoples were passive agents incapable or unworthy of weighing in on their own futures. These perspectives were thus two sides of the same destructive reasoning.[65] Although they differed in their solutions to the Indian Problem, both sought to impose a solution that, in one way or another, resolved the Indian Problem by doing away with Indians (whether physically or culturally). In so doing, these twinned perspectives offered to address a number of settler concerns, including access to land for industry and agriculture, nation building, and citizenship formation.

A shift occurred at the end of the nineteenth century across multiple social fields and a confluence of material interests and facilitative discourses that created the conditions for the formulation of a new solution to the Indian Problem. Agricultural, industrial, and resource interests asserted an increased demand for Indigenous lands. Religious and rights-based organizations advanced forms of Christian and liberal universalism that proposed to save Indigenous peoples by changing them. Scientific theories of social evolution suggested a more gradual, yet also progressive, model for Indian transformation. And government institutions sought a more economically rational and administratively efficient means to overcome costs of Indian Wars, reservations, treaties, and other perceived challenges of Indigenous governance.[66]

By 1879, boarding schools began to win out on both sides of the border as the solution to the Indian Problem—schools were perceived to be the best strategy to meet the needs of those with economic, religious, governance, and educational stakes in the lives of Indigenous peoples and their lands. Of course, other institutional interventions into Indigenous lives continued alongside and in combination with the schools. But driving the establishment of the schools was the belief that Indigenous adults were too stubborn in their traditions for effective assimilation, making children the best targets for a more rapid transformation of Indigenous communities away from their cultural past and toward a more Europeanized future.[67] Debates persisted about the level of civilization possible for Indigenous peoples, with evolutionary and scientific racism-based arguments that suggested only a limited or gradual uplift becoming especially prominent in the early twentieth century. To some degree, these arguments supplanted Christian or liberal universalism, according to which all Indigenous children were blank slates on which civilization and Christianity could be written. Yet, despite such tensions, general agreement was achieved on the necessity of schooling, and the language of civilization and (full or partial) assimilation served as a shorthand to draw together what might otherwise have been disparate views about, and to coordinate a broad variety of, policy interventions in Indigenous lives.[68]

A key difference in the U.S. context for such debates, however, was the presence of influential reform groups that advocated effectively on behalf of certain directions in Indian policy.[69] The exception to this rule was the Canadian Indian Research and Aid Society, but it survived for only two years after its formation in 1890,[70] and it did not have the same impact as groups such as the Indian Rights Association, a well-organized and powerful U.S. group whose members believed that Indians could be fully assimilated into American society and that the primary barrier to this assimilation was a lack of political will.[71] To cultivate this will, the association launched several endeavors, including its well-known meetings at Lake Mohonk between 1883 and 1913, at which policy recommendations were developed and reform was strategized.[72] The Indian Rights Association, and like-minded groups, provided important support for assimilative boarding school innovations in the late 1800s. Key among these innovations was the Dawes Act, or General Allotment Act, which the U.S. Congress passed in 1887. This act was the product of lobbying by Indian rights reformers, who thought that Indian peoples needed to be encouraged to gradually change their ways and embrace assimilation and that redistributing land in severalty was key to this process.[73] Under the Dawes Act, reservations were surveyed and divided accordingly: 160 acres to the head of a family, eighty acres to single persons and orphans over eighteen years of age, and forty acres to those below the age of eighteen. The deed for this property remained in the hands of the government for twenty-five years to prevent greedy whites from buying up Indigenous lands on unfair terms. Citizenship was also bestowed on Indigenous persons, expanding the empire of U.S. law to cover all first peoples. And finally, under the act, all remaining unallotted property could be sold to white settlers.[74] These changes set the stage for the consolidation and expansion of the Indian education system. They also disrupted Indigenous relationships with territory and finessed

American law so that it could apply more effectively to Indigenous peoples. Indian schools, moreover, in the vision of reformers, would reinforce policies on land and law, since young Indians would be habituated to individual forms of labor and trained to see themselves as citizens and subjects of the United States.[75] The Dawes Act was an attempt to coordinate multiple upper mesoinstitutions in resolving the Indian Problem.

It is worth mentioning, however, that the conversations held by such reform groups were not restricted to national landscapes, and lessons from other colonial contexts were often taken into consideration. For example, Theodore Roosevelt, when he participated in the 1886 Mohonk Conference in his capacity as U.S. civil service commissioner, noted the following about Canada's Indian Problem:

> We have paid ten and fifteen times as much in proportion to the Indian as to the foreign whites. While I would never say one word in extenuation of the outrages really committed, we must bear in mind, too, that as a people, we have striven, haltingly and blunderingly, to do the best that we could with the Indians. We are often taunted with the fact that we have not done as well as Canada. Well, Canada had two rebellions of half-breeds in her territory. We have not had any in ours. It would be foolish to say, therefore, that we know how to deal with half-breeds better than Canada. We have a difficult Indian problem; they have not. And there have been no such outrages by government with us as have been attributed to the French in Algiers, and, but the other day, to the Germans in New Guinea. The Indian can largely stand by himself after he has been shown the way. I have seen this on my own ranch.[76]

Canada is referred to elsewhere in the conference proceedings as a model for the "reasonable" treatment of Indians and the benefits of absorption.[77] Thus, in many ways, the settler colonial mesh stretched across borders, seeking to strengthen its force over Indigenous peoples through knowledge of analogous situations, as well as key differences, in the neighboring nation.

Although the focus of this chapter is on the development and institutionalization of Indigenous boarding school policy in the United States and Canada, and on the non-Indigenous actors often at the forefront of policy discussions, one should not have the mistaken impression that Indigenous peoples were entirely absent from such discussions. As will be more evident when our attention turns to the lower meso- and microlevels of Indigenous boarding schools in chapters 4, 5, and 6, Indigenous people worked vigorously to influence this policy and its implementation. But my purpose here is not to relate the efforts of these actors to influence the policy imposed upon them but to give a sense of the complex manner in which the settler colonial mesh established and implemented its general intent.

Institutionalizing Education to Solve the Indian Problem

The institutionalization of assimilative education as a solution to the Indian Problem began even as macrolevel discussions on this supposed problem continued. Thus, the institutionalization of assimilative education should not be viewed as directly or unproblematically derived from macrolevel policy discussions. Instead, the two levels interact and intersect, for knowledge drawn from and material practices used in experiments with Indigenous schooling reinforced the power of the vision of assimilation and aggressive assimilation put forward by reformers, government officials, religious leaders, and others. Likewise, the vision possessed by supporters of assimilation created openings for such practitioners to continue their innovations.

As earlier sections of this chapter attest, mission-based schools preceded the grander "benevolent experiment" of mass assimilative schooling. But innovations in assimilative education did not emerge entirely, or even primarily, out of the mission schools that had long experimented with dormitory-based education for Indigenous children. These mission schools were sparsely sited, proselytizing institutions limited in their power to compel attendance.[78] Although efforts were made to establish industrial-style boarding schools under their auspices, the birth of the modern industrial Indigenous boarding school is often credited not to the missions but to Lieutenant Richard H. Pratt, who began his experiment in Indigenous education in the late 1870s, working on seventy-two captured Indian warriors (thirty-four Cheyenne, two Arapaho, twenty-seven Kiowa, nine Comanche, and one Caddo) at the Fort Marion prison in Florida.[79] Pratt was given some license with respect to how he dealt with the prisoners, and, rather than simply let them sit in their cells and perish, he opted to launch a school of civilization, using his prison as a space in which to educate Indians. This education presented a welcome contrast to the brutal conditions of the prison, and many prisoners succumbed to Pratt, accepting his lessons and the improvements to prison life that came with them over the isolation of their cells. Pratt knew, though, that his experiment would gain recognition only if it were visible, and thus he made sure to place his prisoners, and their emergent civilized habits, on regular public display. As public acclaim for his methods grew, Pratt pressed his superiors to allow him to release some of the younger prisoners to an institution where they could continue their education. After some searching, Pratt received word in 1878 from Samuel Chapman Armstrong, founder and principal of the Hampton Normal and Industrial Institute, a school that taught African American freedmen, that he would accept seventeen of Pratt's pupils.[80] Following on this success, in 1879 Pratt opened his own school in an abandoned army barracks in Carlisle, Pennsylvania. His vision of the nonreservation boarding school, which he enacted at Carlisle, became the model for the early U.S. federal boarding school system: Indigenous children were to be removed from their communities and habituated to the ways of European life in close proximity to white civilization. As Pratt stated, "we make our greatest mistake in feeding our civilization to the Indians instead of feeding the Indians to our civilization."[81]

The assimilative work of Pratt at Carlisle and Armstrong at Hampton was foundational for the emerging U.S. federal boarding school system.[82] Within twenty years of the opening of Carlisle, twenty-three nonreservation boarding schools, and numerous reservation schools that subscribed to similar principles, were established. For Pratt, his model represented a radical break with all forms of Indigenous education that had come before Carlisle. This break was reflected in the training for work provided through the school, the intensive efforts to remove attachments to Indigenous cultures, and the level of integration into the white population experienced by Carlisle students.[83] Subsequent U.S. Indian boarding schools did not slavishly follow Pratt's formula, but the general model was observable across the growing number of federal schools. It included military marching, which Pratt thought necessary to increase student discipline, and the outing system, which placed students in work, typically as farm laborers or domestic help, on weekends or during their short summer vacations. Pratt saw the outing system as the "right arm" of his school in that it required students to adapt to and fit in settler communities, learning to emulate the conduct of a Euro-American existence through immersion.[84]

Near the time that Pratt was opening Carlisle, Nicholas Flood Davin was sent by John A. Macdonald's Conservative government in Canada to investigate Indian education in the United States.[85] Davin completed a short tour that included stops in Washington to meet Secretary of the Interior Carl Schurz, Commissioner of Indian Affairs E. A. Hayt, as well as chiefs from the Five Civilized Tribes.[86] He also traveled to Minnesota, where he observed a mission-run contract boarding school. In his report, Davin cites favorably U.S. efforts to have Indigenous peoples concentrated on a few reservations, possessing lands in severalty rather than in common, and prepared for citizenship through industrial education. Like others at the time, Davin was unconvinced that day schools, in which children returned to their homes after a day's education, would work for Indigenous children and force them to overcome the "influence of the wigwam."[87] The industrial boarding school, in his view, was therefore the best option for Indians and "half-bloods" "to be merged and lost" within the idea of the nation.[88] But Davin also thought that the migratory nature of Indigenous groups in the northwest made the establishment of government-run industrial boarding schools potentially expensive and inefficient, and therefore he argued that it was best to use the already existing network of denominational missions as the foundation for Canada's residential schooling system. Soon after Davin's report, industrial-style boarding schools were opened. The Oblates initiated schools in Qu'Appelle, Saskatchewan (Qu'Appelle Industrial School), and Dunbow, Alberta (St. Joseph's School). As well, they continued to run their preexisting schools in St. Boniface, Île-à-la-Crosse, Lac la Biche, Lake Athabasca, and Fort Providence. Likewise, the Anglicans opened the Battleford Industrial School in Saskatchewan.[89]

Macdonald initially sent Davin to the United States out of concern over unrest among the Métis.[90] Although his worries about the Métis initially subsided prior to the opening of the first schools, the Northwest Rebellion of 1885 would awaken further concerns. In the aftermath of the Red River Resistance, through which Métis leader Louis Riel helped to shape the province of Manitoba and the rights of citizens in the province, Métis and settler populations in Saskatchewan also hoped that he could assist them in their complaints about neglect from the federal government. Riel, now possessed by a prophetic zeal, assembled a small military force that engaged in combat with government troops. At the same time, Indian groups were staging resistance in response to their grievances over land and hardship caused by loss of the bison.[91] In the face of such disruptions, J. A. Macrae, the department inspector of schools for the Northwest, noted that "it is unlikely that any Tribe or tribes would give trouble of a serious nature to the Government whose members had children completely under Government control."[92] Indeed, after this point, Canadian policies on Indigenous peoples became more extensive and controlling, stepping up the project of assimilation.[93] These battles also served as a warning to Indigenous groups about the ever-present potential for their physical annihilation, and future policy on the Indian Problem would be imposed on Indigenous peoples in the shadow of settler colonial physical violence.

Subsequent reports from the Department of Indian Affairs show that boarding schools soon became the primary strategy enlisted by the department to attend to the Indian Problem. In 1878, Macdonald returned to power as prime minister and made himself minister of the interior, thereby giving him responsibility for Indian affairs.[94] In an 1880 report, he declared that Indian day schools were a failure and remarked that "the Indian youth, to enable him to cope successfully with his brother of white origin, must be dissociated from the prejudicial influences by which he is surrounded on the reserve of his band. And the necessity for the establishment more generally of institutions, whereat Indian children, besides being instructed in the usual branches of education, will be lodged, fed, clothed, kept separate from home influences, taught trades and instructed in agriculture, is becoming every year more apparent."[95] By the middle of the decade, Macdonald argued that boarding schools be expanded to include Indigenous girls.[96] Indeed, the schools continued to grow as a matter of government concern, and by the late 1880s Indigenous education was a significant component of the newly formed Department of Indian Affairs, and its annual reports featured detailed updates on all schools and regions. At this time, Edgar Dewdney, now in the role of superintendent general of Indian Affairs, acknowledged that Indigenous assimilation through schooling would be gradual, but he expressed great hope about its prospects:

> As, however, the improved methods now employed for the amelioration of the condition and the mental enlightenment of many are applied to all of the bands, the progress of the Indian towards complete civilization will be more rapid, and his eventual emancipation from the present state of ignorance, superstition and helplessness, in which too many of them still remain, will be more assured; and it is submitted and earnestly pressed that the most essential lever for the elevation of the race would be the adoption of a vigorous policy of imparting to the young a thorough practical knowledge of mechanical arts and of agriculture, as well as of other employments, including a systematic method of ordering and managing their domestic affairs—in short, a complete training in industries and in domestic economy.[97]

Thus, in several ways, notions of Indigenous education began to merge in the United States and Canada as each nation sought a rapid, fully immersive, and industry-based solution to its Indian Problem. But Canada would remain steadfast that its system needed to be run through the Christian denominations. Whereas the United States began its experiment in Indigenous education with widespread involvement of the Catholic and Protestant churches, the Protestants were more willing to end their relationship with contract schools than the Catholics, who sought to keep their schools running. Protestant reformers, especially those who were involved at Lake Mohonk, pushed their changes in part out of concern about the role of Catholicism in Indigenous schooling. In this sense, though American Indigenous boarding schools were divorced from direct religious influence at a much earlier stage than was the case for Canadian schools, competition between Catholics and Protestants did have a definite impact on the shape taken by the U.S. system.[98]

As noted previously, the settler colonial mesh is not, in its entirety, a national project, since the mesh stretches across borders through intergovernmental negotiations and communications. Curiosity about Indian policy in the neighboring nation continued to be evident after Davin's initial journey to learn about the U.S. system. In 1889, Canadian Indian Commissioner

Hayter Reed reported on a visit to the Mohawk and Muncey schools in Canada as well as to Carlisle in the United States. His trip to Carlisle left him with the impression that the U.S. system for educating Indians was more advanced than that in Canada, and he brought home some key lessons. For one, prohibition of the use of Indigenous languages at Carlisle reinforced his sense that Indian dialects should be banned entirely from the Canadian schools; Reed thought that they should not even be used to translate the teachings of European civilization to Indigenous pupils. He also reported his beliefs that the practice of allowing boys to return home during vacations be discontinued and that a program similar to Pratt's outing system be introduced to prevent them from reimmersion in the habits of their Indigenous communities. Finally, though Reed saw economic advantages in the Canadian pattern of having religious denominations operate schools on the government's behalf, he did express curiosity about the possibilty of whether a nonsectarian school could one day be experimented with in Canada.[99] However, the economic motive would prevent Canada from ever seriously pursuing this final point.

Later several senior members of Canada's Department of Indian Affairs would visit Carlisle to observe Pratt's system in operation. However, as impressed as they were with the school, they held to Davin's perspective that it was more ambitious than was practical in the Canadian context.[100] Therefore, though Canada did establish several industrial-style boarding schools located near urban centers, where great emphasis was placed on manual, agricultural, and domestic forms of labor, systemic and institutional differences began to arise between schools in each country, despite their common roots in a similar conception of the Indian Problem.

Compelling Indigenous Education

Both the Canadian and the American systems, for the most part, attempted to maximize the number of students exposed to assimilative schooling. Although neither was particularly successful in forcing assimilative education on Indigenous children because of a number of intervening factors, at the level of policy and institutional setup, the goal was to have as many children as possible brought under the force of aggressive civilization.

At the close of the nineteenth century, efforts were made to persuade

Indigenous groups in the United States to offer up their children to schools. In 1891, the commissioner of Indian affairs was empowered "to make and enforce by proper means such rules and regulations as will secure the attendance of Indian children of suitable age and health at schools established and maintained for their benefit."[101] Then, in 1893, the Indian Office was permitted to deny rations, clothing, or other desired objects to Indigenous parents or guardians who did not enroll their children. But, in the same year, nonreservation schools were also restricted from drawing children to them without parents' permission.[102] Thus, parental consent was perceived to be desirable, but it was also the case that Indian agents and superintendents were permitted to use inducements such as resource denial and moral suasion to influence this consent.[103]

In her 1900 annual report, Estelle Reel, superintendent of Indian schools in the United States, made a passionate defense of compulsory Indian education: "Civilization only comes to a people by the slow process of education, and unless we educate and civilize the majority of the children the down pull of the ignorant will be greater than the uplift of the educated."[104] She added that, "if the Indian will not accept the opportunities for elevation and civilization so generously offered him, the strong hand of the law should be evoked and the pupil forced to receive an education whether his parents will it or not."[105] Assimilative education was thus believed to be so imperative that it had to be imposed on those not yet civilized enough to see its value. The notions of "uplift" and elevation in Reel's statements communicate that Indigenous cultures were understood as debased, lesser cultures; under such a conception, Indigenous cultures were devalued to the point that children's attachment to them could be destroyed as a matter of perceived benevolence. This is a frequent cognitive strategy of settler colonialism; overconfident in its own superiority, it operates on a plane of rationality that does not permit it to see (or allows it to willfully ignore) the value of Indigenous cultures to those who participate in the co-creation of these worlds.

To accomplish the task of making children and their parents accept this reputed benevolence, the force of law was enlisted. For example, in the early 1900s, according to New Mexican territorial law, Indigenous children could be compelled to attend public schools. When New Mexico officially became a state in 1912, the AIS superintendent, Rueben Perry, recommended to the state's chairman of the Committee on Education that this law be revised so that Indigenous children from ages seven to sixteen (instead of fourteen) be compelled to attend school and that it be expressly noted that federal day and boarding schools were public schools within the terms of the law.[106]

In the early 1920s, U.S. legislators sought to refine earlier compulsory education legislation. During this period, Indigenous children who were wards of the state were required to abide by state education laws, including requirements that nearby public or private schools be attended. Where distance to such schools made enrollment impractical, children were instructed to attend boarding schools. Refusal by parents to send children to schools resulted in fines.[107] Such laws were part of the arsenal available to legislators who hoped to compel Indigenous assimilative education; nonetheless, they were not able to fully overcome the challenges presented by Indigenous resistance and poor accessibility to schools.

In Canada, the push to compulsory Indigenous education occurred about the same time as in the United States. Amendments to the Indian Act in 1894 and 1895 advanced the objective of compulsory schooling. These amendments gave the government authority, among other things, to require school attendance for Indigenous youth until they reached the age of eighteen. Another amendment allowed for involuntary schooling under specific circumstances.[108] By 1920, compulsory pressures were increased. An amendment to the Indian Act allowed government to compel attendance for children between the ages of seven and fifteen and authorized a truant officer to enter "any place where he has reason to believe there are Indian children between the ages of seven and fifteen years."[109] The amendment also set penalties for Indigenous parents who resisted sending their children to school. Finally, the amendment stated "that no Protestant child shall be assigned to a Roman Catholic school or a school conducted under Roman Catholic auspices, and no Roman Catholic child shall be assigned to a Protestant school or a school conducted under Protestant auspices"[110] Of course, the law showed no compunction about removing children from the influence of Indigenous spiritualities and imposing Christian teachings on them.

The moves to make assimilative education compulsory, and to intensify efforts to compel schooling, occurred at similar points in time in both the

United States and Canada. Many children managed to evade school, despite these stringent policies. However, such acts of resistance do not diminish the fact that there existed an intention to impose European education on as many Indigenous children as possible, with the goal of severely transforming their Indigenous identities.

Implementing Assimilative Education: Tightening and Loosening the Settler Colonial Mesh

In both counties, the Indian Problem provided a collective frame for settler colonial intervention through assimilative education, and compulsory education laws sought to impose this education on all Indigenous children. However, there are distinct national differences that arise at the upper mesolevel, where the Indian Problem was institutionalized.

In Canada, the residential school system unfolded in a somewhat haphazard manner. This is not to say that the assimilative practices and destructive negligence witnessed at these schools were accidental. Rather, because the government sought to achieve the forcible transformation of Indigenous peoples with only a modest investment of time and money, an institutional opening was created that various Christian denominations sought to fill. These denominations were motivated by a variety of interests, as were the various actors performing missionary work under their auspices. These included earnest desires to help Indigenous groups perceived to be in difficult circumstances and accumulative desires to gather more Indigenous souls than their rivals. As well, denominational communities themselves were spaces of debate and disagreement about how Indigenous education should be conducted, with some in specific denominations even critical of the entire boarding school system. In this respect, none of the Christian denominations that lobbied the government of Canada for grant support to open schools can be treated as a monolith.[111] Nonetheless, despite these variations of belief and purpose in the Christian denominations, a collective project of Indigenous transformation was attempted under their watch.

But before examining the role of the Canadian churches in more detail, I must consider the issue of cost. The economics of the Indian Problem was a source of worry in both countries. But in Canada the division of labor between government policy makers and denominational educators created a peculiar boarding school market. For example, in 1892, concerns about the cost of residential schools led the Canadian government to seek changes to its funding method.[112] In 1893, it introduced a per capita financing arrangement to encourage the churches to run the schools with the greatest economic efficiency.[113] This funding method placed considerable budget pressures on the schools, resulting in increased emphasis on student labor (such as farming) and poor nutrition for the students, as the schools sought ways to cut corners on expenses and generate revenue. Still, even these measures were insufficient to make Canadian boarding schools economically viable under the per capita funding arrangement. Indeed, only one year after the transition to per capita funding, institutions in the North-West Territories began to report deficits.[114]

Funding also resulted in a preference for smaller residential schools rather than large-scale industrial schools in Canada.[115] At the onset of the Canadian system of Indigenous boarding schools, the Conservative government, which oversaw the systematic introduction of these schools, favored Carlisle-like industrial schools that would remove children far from their homes in order to implement rapid assimilation. In contrast, when the Liberal Party of Canada came to power in 1896, it considered the industrial school system to be too expensive to run. Furthermore, it argued that it had failed to encourage the rapid transformation of Indigenous children.[116] The Liberal government prior to its election had also expressed doubts about rationality of the denominational system of Indigenous schooling, but it did not challenge the arrangement with the churches once elected to form the government.[117] Instead, it closed some industrial schools and transformed others into more basic boarding schools. At the same time, it promoted the use of day and reservation-based boarding schools, which served the added purpose of maintaining past governmental practices of Indigenous isolation by keeping Indigenous children within their communities.[118]

In general, then, Canadian industrial schools were located near "civilized" urban centers, whereas residential schools were placed closer to Indigenous communities. At the former, male children were instructed in agriculture and trades, whereas female children learned domestic skills. At the latter, children were instructed in the subsistence skills that the government and churches deemed necessary for them to survive as adults on their reserves, such as agriculture and domestic labor, and training in the trades was less on offer. But concerns about funding resulted in an underinvestment in school structures. Missionaries tended to set up small residential schools near their missions as well as in existing but deteriorating or poorly built new buildings. The poor quality of these initial school buildings was later reflected on by the deputy superintendent of Indian affairs, Duncan Campbell Scott: "It was clear that one of the chief causes of criticism was the condition of the buildings in which the schools had been established, these buildings were nearly all owned by the missionary societies, and the character of their construction had been influenced prejudicially by limited resources. The result was that the buildings in many respects were inadequate; they were unsanitary and they were undoubtedly chargeable with a very high death rate among the pupils."[119] Such schools came to be the norm in the Canadian context in the early nineteenth century in a system that, as we will see, was less centralized than that in the United States. Funding shortfalls also contributed to the redirection of labor in schools since it served more to sustain the school and supplement school coffers than to train children.

That these Canadian schools were run by Christian denominations introduces a distinct quality. The Catholic, Anglican, and United Churches in Canada were the primary players in operating the boarding schools, with the United Church divided into Presbyterian, Methodist, and Congregationalist denominations prior to its unification in 1925. Of the denominations in control of Canadian residential schools, the Catholic Church was the most prominent. Close to 60 percent of the schools established in the nineteenth century were Catholic run.[120] The Anglican Church was the next most prevalent, with 30 percent of schools operated by this denomination. Troubles arose, and children suffered at schools run by all of the denominations; however, institutional differences are evident among the various denominations, making broad coverage of the schools difficult. In general, though, the churches jealously guarded those Indigenous people whom they considered to be "theirs," complaining vociferously to the federal government if another denomination recruited a student who at birth had been assigned to their denomination. As well, they raced to established residential schools near their assigned communities to ensure control over education of the Indigenous children. Yet the missions of specific denominations at specific schools did not always match exactly the Indian Problem as envisioned by the federal government. Depending on the church involved, as well as the local relations between church and community, such as whether the church's agents sought assimilation or cultural exchange, strictly enforced church doctrine, or allowed a degree of syncretism, a tightening or loosening of the settler colonial mesh could occur.[121]

In general, the Canadian residential school system took shape from negotiations between the state and the church denominations that operated the schools. Milloy writes that "the system grew and was shaped, in the main, by federal reactions to the force of missionary efforts and in response to persistent lobbying by church hierarchies for school subsidies. Party politics and patronage played a role, as well."[122] Because of this dual structure, the system operated with very few changes in terms of funding increases or policy, for both parties to the residential school system, church and state, worked hard to preserve their respective domains of control, rarely giving an inch to the other.[123] Moreover, there was little turnover in the Department of Indian Affairs bureaucracy, which contributed to greater stagnancy in terms of policy on and institutionalization of the Indian Problem. Nichols notes of Canada that "between 1862 and 1900 only three men directed the policies of the Department of Indian Affairs. . . . At the same time in the United States, sixteen men held the office of commissioner of Indian affairs."[124] Moreover, the Canadian system changed little into the 1950s. Federal Indian policy remained in the hands of very few men over this period. For example, Duncan Campbell Scott, who began work in Indian Affairs in 1880, before joining the accounting branch of the department in 1891, held the role of deputy superintendent of Indian Affairs from 1913 to 1932.[125]

Yet, though Canadian residential school policy, in many respects, was remarkably consistent and showed fewer variations than evident in the United States, residential schools did not go without criticism from representatives of both church and state. In 1905, S. H. Blake from the Mission Society of the Church in Canada (a body of the Anglican Church) wrote to the deputy superintendent of Indian Affairs that, based on conferences among Anglican, Presbyterian, and Methodist denominations, the objectives of Indian education had not been fully achieved. To remedy the situation, he recommended that day schools be dispensed with and that more resources be directed toward boarding and industrial schools. Blake also recommended that Indian youth be provided with a portion of land to be tended, as well as support in getting started in farming, after their education was completed, so that they would not simply return to the reserve or "hunting lodge."[126] The deputy superintendent general responded positively to several of these suggestions, which in many respects echoed the efforts of U.S.-based Indian reformers, and agreed that day schools were undersubscribed and that more needed to be done to assist students after the completion of their education. However, he also thought that starting to educate children at as young as six years of age could place great hardship on them and their families.[127] Such critical reflection on child removal, however, did not stem the practice; for years to come, Indigenous children continued to be removed from their parents at very young ages and sent to Canadian residential schools.

In contrast to Canada, in the United States, after the federal boarding school system began, state funding for church-run charter schools was reduced and then largely eliminated by the 1890s.[128] This resulted in an institutional structure more defined by trending practices of governance within the American Indian service and in many ways less static than the Canadian system. In addition to the aforementioned differing roles played by religion in each boarding school system, major discrepancies between the two systems in the early stages include (1) a clearer *division of labor* between nonreservation boarding, reservation boarding, and day schools in the United States; (2) *older students,* typically, in U.S. federal boarding schools; and (3) *greater turnover* of bureaucrats in the American Indian service, which resulted in more *dramatic policy breaks.*[129]

First, under the leadership of Thomas J. Morgan, commissioner of Indian Affairs from 1888 to 1893, three levels of schooling—day schools, reservation boarding schools, and nonreservation boarding schools—were organized so that the first two would serve as feeder institutions for the nonreservation schools.[130] Second, this division of labor meant that children generally arrived at boarding schools at a later age than they did in Canada.

In typical circumstances, American Indigenous children first attended local day schools, which allowed them a more gradual immersion into the world of European schools and spared them the extreme disruption of removal from their parents at an early age. Of course, their cultural and linguistic attachments were nonetheless challenged via the education that they received in the day schools. The division of labor among school types is noted in the 1900 annual report of Estelle Reel, the superintendent for Indian schools: "Nonreservation schools are not intended to give instruction in the kindergarten and lower grades. Children in such grades should be kept in the day schools, or at least in reservation schools, until they are of an age to partake of the advantages of a nonreservation school. In this way much of the educating power of the nonreservation schools is used in doing the work which properly belongs to and should be done by the schools of lower grade."[131]

Some Indigenous children, however, were placed in boarding schools at as young as four or five years of age, especially if they were perceived or presented as having been "orphaned" or their parents were deemed in some way unfit for child rearing.[132] For example, Wolf Rob Hunt (Hopi) was removed from his parents in his early years. He says of his time at Albuquerque Indian School that, "it was a boarding school that I went to, and I was picked up on the reservation when I was six years old, taken away, and you have to spend nine months at school, a six-year-old kid gets mighty lonesome for mother and daddy if you have to spend nine months, but you get used to it over the years, you know, and you are sent back during summer vacation."[133]

Third, policy changes were far more frequent in the United States. At the turn of the century, emphasis was placed on vocational education for Indigenous children. Although education for industrial/agricultural or domestic purposes had long been part of the U.S. government vision for Indian education, increased pessimism about the possibility of rapidly assimilating Indians led BIA bureaucrats to stress the need for fitting education to what were believed to be realistic vocational ambitions for Indigenous youth. Like workhouses, or other institutions of social control, the schools then sought to slot pupils into specific vocational categories suited to their racial status and discipline them to the behaviors appropriate to this level.[134] This change was particularly evident in the early twentieth century under the more racializing leadership of Commissioner Francis Leupp, who considered Indigenous peoples limited in their ability to take advantage of schooling. Like his Canadian counterparts, Leupp worried that the boarding school system was not effectively fostering Indigenous transformation, despite the inordinate expense associated with running the schools. He also feared that the schools were setting Indians up for economic failure. Under Leupp, the BIA began to explore the closure of boarding schools and the expansion of day schools, considered better value. As well, it was widely accepted at the time that there were evolutionary limits on what could be achieved by Indians, and less emphasis was thus placed on training Indian youth for jobs inappropriate to what their everyday lives were imagined to be like on reserves.[135]

Policy Variability in the United States: The Meriam Report and the Collier Years

It is worth spending some time on the period from 1928 to 1945, when changes took place in U.S. Indian policy that had no analogue in the Canadian context. In contrast to the Canadian system, in which Duncan Campbell Scott in particular held control over Indian Affairs for many years, the American system was marked by multiple reforms and redirections in policy. None of these policy changes was more dramatic than the reforms that occurred under Commissioner of Indian Affairs John Collier from 1933 to 1945.

Collier's initial reforms occurred in the aftermath of the Meriam Report, also known as *The Problem of Indian Administration* (1928), which had received input on questions of Indigenous education from W. Carson Ryan, an experienced educator. Ryan was a proponent of progressive education, and conditions in the boarding schools were in direct contradiction to the principles of this approach. Inadequate nutrition, crowded dorms and classrooms, poor health treatment, student labor, poorly trained teachers, and excessive discipline all came under criticism for failing to provide an adequate learning environment. The Meriam Report also took the government to task for trying to run education on the cheap: "Cheapness in education is expensive. Boarding schools that are operated on a per capita cost for all purposes of something over two hundred dollars a year and feed their children from eleven to eighteen cents worth of food a day may fairly be said to be operated below any reasonable standard of health and decency. From the point of view of education the Indian Service is almost literally a 'starved' service."[136] The Meriam Report further argued that Indigenous traditions, beliefs, and knowledge should be integrated into the Indigenous child's learning experience, and it reiterated that boarding schools should be reserved for older children, presumably more ready to be separated from their families and communities.

The Meriam Report was remarkable for offering drastic criticism of Indigenous education at a time when retrogressive views of Indigenous peoples persisted and were dominant in many regions. Yet, despite its critical vigor, the Meriam Report was not a complete refutation of the notion of the Indian Problem, and it should not be read as a complete break with the idea that settler colonial intervention in the lives and governance of Indigenous peoples was both necessary and obligatory. Indeed, it is accepted in the report that education is important because it is the key to Indian integration. The report's criticism of aspects of schooling, such as its routine and repetitive nature, or the trauma of separating children from their families, are framed less as concerns about the oppressiveness of such practices or their violation of principles of Indigenous self-determination and more as concerns about how the Indian was being ill prepared for "independent citizenship."[137] The Indian Problem thus shifts from being a problem to be tackled by force or faith to being a problem to be addressed through modern techniques of administration. The Meriam Report marks the move from social control through disciplinary education to new liberal welfarist models of intervention in the lives of those viewed to exist at the outskirts of society. This report signals the arrival of a new cadre of professionals who would insert themselves more deeply into American Indigenous communities to enroll parents and children in what was still a transformative project. On this score, the report argues that

> merely using police methods may perhaps be defended as a necessary step at one stage, but long experience in city and rural school administration, with children situated very much as Indian children are, has

shown that attendance officers of the school social worker type rather than of the police officer kind are needed for this work. It is, indeed, much more than a matter of mere school attendance. What has to be worked out is a home and school relation whereby the parents will be enlisted in having their children go to school regularly and the home in return will be directly affected by the school.[138]

Moreover, new methods of measurement and assessment are advised in the Meriam Report, not to confirm the prejudices of scientific racism, but to "study the individual child" so that education can be better directed toward his or her particular needs. Knowledge of the Indian therefore shifts with the report from the racial to the personal. The report reflects what was, at the time, cutting-edge pedagogy but not one that is separate from or inimical to colonial ordering. It also represents an extension of the web of governance into Indigenous communities and lives, moving administration and control from the centers of government to local sites. Such a shift to what can be referred to as a welfarist-administrative model of Indigenous control eventually took place in Canada too, but not until the 1950s.[139]

A few of the reforms recommended in the Meriam Report were initially implemented under Charles J. Rhoads, commissioner of Indian Affairs from 1929 to 1933. The fact that Rhoads placed W. Carson Ryan as his education director in 1930 certainly facilitated these early changes. Indeed, upon appointment, Ryan immediately directed his energy toward educational reform.[140] Under his guidance, for example, federal Indigenous education programming was fashioned with greater recognition of differences among Indigenous groups. No longer was it assumed that a standardized educational scheme could be developed for all Indigenous children as putative Indians; instead, specific knowledge of the Indigenous group in question was sought for inclusion in the design of localized educational programs.[141] However, these changes advanced only so far under Rhoads, since he was a reformer in the late-eighteenth-century sense of the term. He favored assimilation and allotment as the solutions to the Indian Problem, and, for this reason, he found himself under heavy criticism from a new class of reformers, including John Collier, an Indian rights activist, drawn more deeply into Indian advocacy after a two-year visit (1919–21) with his friend

Mabel Dodge in Taos Pueblo.[142] The experience led to Collier's involvement in the American Indian Defense Association during the 1920s, a group that helped to pressure the government to undertake the Meriam study and remained active in the aftermath of the Meriam Report recommendations.

Based on his time at Taos Pueblo, Collier feared that Indigenous cultures were in danger from encroaching European settlements. In many respects, he shared with Raphael Lemkin a pluralist belief in the value of group diversity, since for him each group's distinct culture contributed to the wealth of collective existence. On this issue, Collier wrote that,

> on the purely cultural side, only sheer fanaticism would decide the further destruction of Indian languages, crafts, poetry, music, ritual, philosophy, and religion. These possessions have a significance and a beauty which grew patiently through endless generations of people immersed in the life of nature, filled with imaginative and ethical insight into the core of being. To destroy them would be comparable to destroying the rich cultural heritage of the Aryan races — its music and poetry, its religion and philosophy, its temples and monuments. Yet through generations the Government did deliberately seek to destroy the Indian cultural heritage; and only because the roots of it lay so deep in the Indian soul, and only because age old, instinctive modes of thought and expression were so much less destructible than individual life itself, has the Indian culture stubbornly persisted.[143]

Although Collier located Indigenous culture as a deeply embedded, unchanging component of the Indian's constitutional makeup, as did Lemkin,[144] his recognition of assimilation as a destructive force coincided with, or perhaps even preceded, Lemkin's thoughts on these matters.[145]

Collier would give Meriam-era reforms their strongest push when he assumed the position of commissioner of Indian Affairs in 1933. Prior to becoming commissioner, he was a vocal supporter of the Bill of Indian Rights, also referred to as the Howard-Wheeler Bill, which under his tenure as commissioner would be signed into law as the Indian Reorganization Act.[146] This act undid the Dawes Act allotment system and paved the way for greater powers of Indigenous self-government. Collier defended the act, when it was still in the form of the Howard-Wheeler Bill, using the following terms: "The allotment system has been disastrous for the Indians because it has taken away from them the only means of self-support which most of them are equipped to use, namely, the land. The Allotment Act of 1887 is largely responsible for the existence of one hundred thousand landless Indians, most of whom are paupers."[147] But as Collier worked to shape the bill into law, he faced complaints from religious groups and others invested in the project of assimilation. For example, some missionaries opposed the bill, fearing that it would return Indians to "paganism." In one instance, a resolution from the conference of (Protestant) missionaries argued that "this Bill glorifies segregation of the Indians and makes it permanent. We believe, however, that the Indian must be saved by a process of Christian assimilation into American life, not by carefully guarded and subsidized segregation."[148] Other interest groups, such as those representing mining, forestry, and cattle ranching, worried about the loss of access to Indian lands. Collier dismissed these voices as "selfish interests" and held fast to defending what he viewed as the Indian "Constitution."[149]

The politics of New Deal America provided the space for a reformer such as Collier to rise to the fore and the resources to initiate policy changes. The cross-national experience of economic depression, and the historic compromise with working people to deflate the influence of communism, made room for new Indian policies by redirecting funds toward matters of social welfare such as employment and education. Changes were wrought across U.S. society in order to reinvigorate economic activities, opening political opportunities and providing funds for new approaches to Indigenous economic conditions. Moving away from the exploitative and assimilative policies of the Dawes Act, the Indian Reorganization Act ended the practice of allotment, established a credit fund, facilitated the preservation of Indigenous resources, opened the door to Indian employment in the civil service, and created new pathways to tribal organization and incorporation.[150] But for Collier, such measures were not in contradiction to the goal of better integrating Indigenous peoples into American society: "Assimilation and preservation and intensification of heritage are not hostile choices, excluding one another, but are interdependent through and through."[151] Yet, with respect to Indigenous schooling, Collier overrode the views of those most committed to aggressive assimilation, the missionaries, and he could do so because he was not institutionally dependent on them for the operation of Indigenous schools, as was the case in Canada.

More specifically, Collier sought to reduce reliance on federal boarding schools by directing more funds toward day schools that were to become community-based and community-serving institutions. In his view, and according to research provided to the BIA at the time, the federal boarding schools had been a colossal failure. Attended by 20,000 children, the boarding schools ate up approximately 80 percent of the educational resources of the BIA. The yearly per child cost for boarding schools was estimated at $550, in contrast to $125 for day schools—a figure that included schooling, transportation, lunch, and clothing at each location. Moreover, these studies showed that boarding schools were inferior "both educationally and in social effect."[152] Ryan, who remained director of Indian education until the summer of 1935, continued the push that he had begun under Commissioner Rhoads for more reliance on a decentralized community school system that would be oriented to local needs rather than government standards, including emphasis on connecting the Indian child to his or her community and on vocational training so that Indian students would be prepared to find jobs and earn livelihoods. Collier's leadership provided a more welcoming environment for such reforms, and the reforms continued when Willard Walcott Beatty replaced Ryan as the director of Indian education. Based on the efforts of Collier, Ryan, and Beatty, between 1933 and 1941, day schools increased in number from 132 to 226, whereas boarding school enrollments decreased by one-third.[153]

However, it is still the case that, under Collier, Indigenous schools were largely directed by non-Indigenous ideas about how Indigenous children should be educated. Therefore, his approach was not entirely inconsistent with the pattern of paternalism that guided much previous U.S. educational policy.[154] Moreover, Margaret Connell Szasz notes that the more culturally inclusive curriculum of the 1930s was often delivered in piecemeal form, rather than in an integrated whole, so that it did not necessarily open up sustainable spaces for Indigenous identity formation and social engagement.[155] As well, the Collier period did not represent a permanent transformation of American Indian policy. Rather, many of these initiatives were halted by the onset of the Second World War, and a concomitant shift in the distribution of government resources, before they were reversed when Indigenous education returned to its assimilative focus in the late 1940s under the federal policy of termination. During this latter period, Hildegard Thompson assumed command of Indian education at the BIA (1952–65), and, despite her time working under Ryan and Beatty, her leadership saw the reinvigoration of more destructive educational policies.[156]

One should also not overstate the progressive nature of Collier's leadership. The danger with the welfare-era softening of Indigenous educational policy is that under it a superficial form of cultural preservation could serve as a wedge into Indigenous communities, allowing a more subtle extension of the assimilative project. Although it is difficult to doubt the sincerity of Collier as a pluralist and Indigenous romantic, his reforms were facilitated by new developments in knowledge/power and the shape of social control. Specifically, his interest in Indigenous cultures and societies led him to place higher value on learning about these cultures and societies, and this knowledge was rearticulated in new means for extending the reach of paternalistic governance over more Indigenous children. The more that was known about the children, the more effectively they could be readied for inclusion in a non-Indigenous world, preserving aspects of their traditional identities but nonetheless making them better suited to American citizenship and resolution of the Indian Problem. As well, these policies furthered the involvement of settler professionals in Indigenous communities as they were deployed to offer community-level services through various reforms.[157]

Collier's progressive reforms also occurred at the level of the Bureau of Indian Affairs and did not always reach down to the ground, where teachers and principals, at times, resisted these changes.[158] Thus, the dream shared by Collier, Ryan, and Beatty—of an educational experience that would not seek to remove and belittle Indigenous traditions but be rooted in the needs and practices of Indigenous communities (and organized through day rather than boarding schools)—was occasionally obstructed by those positioned closest to Indigenous communities. Examining the day schools opened in 1935 in Diné territory, Jenson notes how teachers sent to this region faced challenges of geographical isolation, language and cultural barriers to communication and cooperation, lack of a coherent curriculum, as well as sufficient and suitable textbooks. Moreover, the lack of training among teachers made it difficult to fulfill the progressive vision in Diné territory.[159]

In sum, despite the microlevel limits of the reforms attempted in American Indigenous education, we can see more variance in policy and its attempted institutionalization than was the case in Canada. Indeed, the dual structure of Canadian residential schooling discouraged the policy changes that occurred in the United States. As Dyck writes, "the joint operation of residential schools by churches and government fueled ongoing squabbling concerning the relative responsibilities of each side. The funding of residential schools through per capita government grants inclined each partner to seek to keep its own expenditures and obligations to the minimum and to blame the other side when the shortcomings, inevitably generated by this strategy, eventually came to the surface."[160] This "squabbling" produced standstill rather than policy change. For example, the end of the nineteenth century and the beginning of the twentieth century brought frustrations with the lack of success and deplorable conditions in Canadian residential schools. Although some would have preferred to see the schools disappear as a failed experiment, by 1911 the government committed more funds to the schools, distributing these funds unevenly so that the needs and accomplishments of specific schools were better reflected in the funding formula. As well, increased commitments to inspections and medical care of infected students were made.[161] Moreover, industrial schools were phased out by 1923, and the term "residential school" became widely used, replacing the no longer relevant distinction between industrial and boarding (reservation-based) schools. This change was motivated by concerns about their cost and the same evolutionary pessimism that also marked the Leupp years in the United States.[162] But more radical changes to the practices of residential schools were rare. Here we gain a sense of the more problematic institutional structure that supported the Canadian Indigenous boarding school experiment, which discouraged all but the most minor policy adaptations.

However, policy changes in the United States should not be taken as signaling that boarding schools were ever operated as a humanitarian venture in that country. As argued in the chapters that follow, U.S. boarding schools still sought the destruction of Indigenous peoples as peoples, only through sometimes different means and with brief pauses in the policy (though not necessarily the practice) of destruction. In Canada, such regulatory and administrative reforms were hampered by the partnership formed between Christian denominations and the state whereby the latter sought to keep costs unreasonably and dangerously low and the former sought to maintain autonomy of oversight of the schools. Under such conditions, reformist voices in the Canadian system—whether they came from the state, specific churches, the general public, or Indigenous communities—had greater difficulty gaining traction for proposed changes. Moreover, the shift toward civil service involvement in residential schools took place far more gradually, since religious allegiance remained a primary basis for employment in the IRS system.[163]

The Demise (and Mutation) of Indigenous Boarding School Systems in North America

Discussion of the end of genocidal processes is always risky terrain. The reverberations of such processes tend to stretch well beyond supposed end dates, and there is the danger of forcing closure on what is an ongoing and still developing set of harms. This is particularly true when the techniques of cultural destruction are multiple and not reducible to a single intervention or act. Such is the case in North America, where Indigenous communities were not solely under assault at the hands of assimilative schooling but also faced further appropriations of their territories, forced reworkings of their governments, laws against their spiritual practices, and other efforts to weaken them as self-constituting peoples.

With this in mind, we must look carefully at the demise of assimilative education in both the United States and Canada. It would be naive to suggest that assimilative strategies have not mutated and taken on new forms in both educational and other persistent colonial institutions, such as prisons or child welfare services. With respect to the latter, both Canada and the United States would see a shocking increase in child removals from Indigenous homes just as boarding schools were declining in use.[164] But we can nonetheless chart distinct changes in the systems of assimilative education that occurred starting in the mid-twentieth century.

This was a period during which shifts in Indigenous politics became evident in Canada and the United States. In the aftermath of the Second World War, race-based exclusions seemed to be less acceptable, civil rights championed notions of color blindness, and European liberalism in North America shifted toward practices of enforced citizenship that translated past practices of Indigenous erasure into a new language of equal rights. This moment took shape with the ascendance of neoliberalism under which governments prioritized the shrinking of the welfare state and the devolution of responsibilities to decentralized actors. With these political and economic transformations, policies directed toward Indigenous peoples adapted, sponsoring new techniques, albeit techniques still directed toward resolution of the Indian Problem. Instances of settler colonial erasure took on the form of a homogenizing liberal equality. In the United States, this was evident in the era of termination, during which the government sought to end its special relationship with Indian peoples, bestow on them the rights and responsibilities of U.S. citizenship, and encourage their integration into the American economy.[165] Likewise, in Canada, the 1969 white paper attempted to replace Indigenous rights, including protections of Indigenous territories and reserves, with Canadian citizenship rights before it was defeated by Indigenous opponents.

With respect to boarding schools, Indigenous peoples became even more vocal in their complaints about a Canadian residential school system that sought to alienate them from their communities and traditions while offering them few useful skills and opportunities in return. They sought, instead, nondenominational schools as well as inclusion in the public school system.[166] Expectations grew that the 1951 reforms to the Indian Act would end, or at least change, residential schooling, but such change did not transpire. In general, Indigenous leaders were dissatisfied with the limited reforms offered by the government at this time. For example, some minor advances were achieved: the half-day system of work was officially ended, though many schools still depended heavily on student labor. But the per capita system, with its incentive for overcrowding, remained in place until 1957.[167]

Also during the 1950s, the schools in southern Canada increasingly came to be used as child welfare facilities. In 1953, almost 40 percent of the students in the schools had been placed there because the government had judged them to be neglected by their parents.[168] Of this period, the Royal Commission on Aboriginal Peoples notes that,

> in 1948, 60 per cent of the Indian school population was enrolled in federal schools. In 1969, 60 per cent were in provincial schools, and the number of residential schools and hostels was reduced from the 72 schools operating in 1948, with 9,368 students, to 52 schools with 7,704. That the number of schools and students did not fall proportionately was attributable not only to local circumstances but to two further difficulties—opposition to closures and the emergence of a new role for the schools as social welfare institutions.[169]

Similar patterns can be found in the United States, where boarding schools fell out of favor during the termination era as the government sought to devolve Indigenous education to the state level. Indigenous children were still too often removed from their families, but fostering and adoption were viewed as the preferred means of removal. In some instances, boarding schools remained as necessary holding spaces for those children removed through child welfare for whom homes could not be found. However, schools were viewed as less cost effective than adoption or fostering, which more effectively privatized the Indian Problem by placing responsibility for education on non-Indigenous adoptive parents and public schools.[170]

Criticisms of Indigenous boarding schools, though well founded, also played into the state's preference for lightening its financial and administrative burdens with respect to Indigenous schooling. In Canada, the 1960s report by Richard King on *The School at Mopass* portrayed the poor conditions and outcomes of residential schools, while the 1966–67 Hawthorn Report, otherwise referred to as *A Survey of the Contemporary Indians of Canada: Economic, Political, Educational Needs and Policies*, advised a gradual move toward integrated schooling for Indigenous students.[171] Such indictments of Indigenous boarding schools made it increasingly difficult for churches to justify their so-called benevolence at the schools, and cracks began to appear in the religious institutional matrix that had long buttressed the Canadian residential school system. Space opened for the Canadian state to adjust its Indigenous educational strategy.[172]

In the late 1960s and into the 1970s, residential schools began to be phased out in Canada, but some schools survived under Indigenous control, a move based on recommendations in a report of a committee sent to Arizona to study Indigenous-led schools there. The government also intensified its negotiations with local school boards to have the latter educate Indigenous students.[173] Finally, denominational involvement in residential schools was significantly curtailed in 1969, when the federal government assumed control of most residential schools in the south. At the same time, northern schools were brought under the auspices of the Yukon and Northwest Territories governments. Most boarding schools were closed over the next decade; however, following the government's usual formula, this was done without input from Indigenous families and communities.[174] Gradually, some schools were placed under Indigenous control, but such policy was enacted somewhat sporadically and usually continued under some level of government oversight. By the 1990s, residential schools, whether government or Indigenous controlled, disappeared from the Canadian landscape, though other approaches to boarding Indigenous students attending schools away from home persisted.[175]

As already noted, twentieth-century shifts in U.S. boarding school policy were more frequent. Likewise, the pathway to the demise of assimilative schooling south of the border was also somewhat more circuitous. Although the Collier years appeared to mark the beginning of the end for nonreservation boarding schools, public schools had already surpassed federal schools in the number of Indigenous children enrolled by 1928, five years before Collier took office.[176] But this number began to rise more dramatically with the onset of Collier's reforms. Between 1930 and 1970 occurred the largest increase in Indigenous enrollment in public education in U.S. history.[177] This increase was facilitated by the 1934 Johnson-O'Malley Act, which made legal the signing of contracts between federal and state governments to provide education, health care, social welfare, and agricultural assistance to Indigenous persons.[178]

Of course, one cannot assume that increased enrollments in public schools are synonymous with the end of assimilative education. Public schools also serve as assimilative institutions, and, as noted earlier, state-sponsored schooling serves as a means for citizenship formation.[179] Likewise, instances of superficial cultural recognition in public schools can exacerbate resentment rather than facilitate Indigenous integration by reinforcing stereotypes about Indigenous students (through presentations of Indigenous art or dance without sufficient cultural context) or sponsoring backlashes against Indigenous territorial or sovereignty claims.[180] Such moments were notable in both American and Canadian efforts to integrate Indigenous students into public schools, alongside occasions when a lack of kindness and cultural sensitivity was exhibited by public school teachers toward Indigenous students. Too often Indigenous students experienced hostility from the communities in which they were to be schooled as well as insufficient provisions for clothing, food, and transportation.[181]

After the Second World War and the end of the Collier years, the "termination era" of Indian policy also brought forward a new era of assimilation. At this time, growing numbers of available jobs in urban centers inspired Indian Affairs leaders to focus on preparing Indigenous students for employment.[182] Also during this era, there was a desperate push to enroll greater numbers of Diné students in public and boarding schools, since this group possessed the largest proportion of Indigenous children in the United States who had, by choice or circumstance, evaded assimilative schooling.[183] Finally, it became more common in this period for boarding schools to operate as child welfare institutions and for the federal government to promote fostering and adoption of Indigenous children as alternatives to institutionalization.[184]

By the late 1960s and early 1970s, Indigenous leaders in the United States began a vigorous public push for self-determination in Indigenous education. The 1969 Kennedy Report, or *Indian Education: A National Tragedy—a National Challenge*, which shared with the 1928 Meriam Report a strong critique of American Indigenous education, supported their efforts. The report called for greater involvement of Indigenous parents in school, cultural respect, and recognition of the importance of Indigenous communities.[185]

Support from the Kennedy Report opened new opportunities for devolved responsibility in Indigenous education, but the move toward Indigenous-controlled schools began before the report was released. Schools such as the Rough Rock Demonstration School opened in Diné territory as early as 1966. The Diné also established Navajo Community College in 1969 for more advanced students. Other such schools followed, including transformation of the Santa Fe Indian School into a Pueblo-controlled and -operated institution, and the first Indian contract school, in 1975. In addition, Indigenous leaders pressed for greater inclusion of Indigenous cultures in the public school system and fought against the misrepresentation of Indigenous peoples and colonial history in school textbooks.

Boarding schools remained present in the United States, though a number gradually came under Indigenous control.[186] But in both the United States and Canada, Indigenous peoples continued to struggle for more powers of self-determination with respect to education. A 1998 information pamphlet produced by the government of Canada described Indigenous education in the two countries as follows:

> In *Canada*, First Nations are increasingly taking control of the federal government's budget for their children's elementary and secondary education. In 1998–99, about 88 percent of the $929-million budget was under First Nations' management. In addition, 98 percent of the schools on reserves are administered by First Nations themselves. In the *U.S.*, the BIA funds several educational programs to supplement those of public and private schools. The BIA also funds 185 schools, most of which tribes administer themselves. Over 90 percent of Native American students, however, attend private, public or religious schools.[187]

However, despite the positive gloss that this pamphlet gives to the Canadian situation, many Indigenous peoples continued to press the Canadian government for educational reform that not simply devolved responsibility to Indigenous school boards but also enhanced the powers of Indigenous groups to make all decisions about the very nature of education in their communities. These discussions are ongoing; at the time of writing, Prime Minister Stephen Harper's First Nations Education Act faced grassroots resistance even as it gained assent from the Assembly of First Nations. For many in Indigenous communities, this act, which promised increased funding for Indigenous schools, also continued the practice of placing control over schools ultimately in the government's hands.[188]

The emergence of aggressively assimilative schooling institutions in the United States and Canada suggests a general intent by both governments to destroy Indigenous groups as groups. Beginning with the formulation of an Indian Problem, and bolstered by institutional networks that permitted the combined forces of law, religion, military, policing, medicine, and other institutions to compel Indigenous children to attend boarding schools, efforts were made to systematize enrollment and ensure that children would be separated from their Indigenous cultural traditions and adopt European ways. However, these projects unfolded differently in each country, especially in terms of how religious institutions maintained significant power over assimilative schooling in Canada, whereas the U.S. system was more subject to trends in the strategies of governance embraced by the U.S. civil service. Also, in the United States, Indigenous education was defined by more radical shifts, especially during the Collier years, when attempts, though imperfect, were made to fashion an education that would not entirely eliminate the vestiges of Indigenous cultures from the lives of Indigenous students. In this sense, assimilative education was not a constant across all eras and in all regions, as far as policy formation is concerned (I will turn to the actual policies in subsequent chapters). The settler colonial mesh tightened and loosened at various points in time; in some instances, Indigenous communities could take advantage of the loosening of this mesh to push schooling in directions that were at least, on the surface, affirmative of their traditions and values, though these moments are more apparent in the U.S. case studies investigated in subsequent chapters.

In this chapter, I have purposely sought not to rest my discussion of settler colonial genocide through residential schooling on a single statement intended to encapsulate genocidal intent, such as Duncan Campbell Scott's now infamous statement of Canada's desire "to get rid of the Indian problem. . . . Our object is to continue until there is not a single Indian in Canada that has not been absorbed into the body politic, and there is no Indian question, and no Indian Department."[189] Or Richard Pratt's claim: "Kill the Indian in him, and save the man."[190] Although these statements do capture the ethos that guided the aggressive assimilation attempted through Indigenous boarding schools, especially in their early years, ascribing authoritative credence to such statements paints the picture of collective settler action forming in an overly unified and singular manner around the Indian Problem. Such quotations do not capture the extent to which multiple actors, approaching the issue from different vantage points and with varied interests, negotiated U.S. and Canadian Indian policy and the very notion of an Indian Problem. This is not to suggest that there were no actors intent on the destruction of Indigenous peoples as Indigenous peoples; the quotations above from Scott and Pratt demonstrate that such purposeful visions of destruction, or specific intent, did exist. However, they existed in a universe of multiple intentions, in which an ethos of Indigenous destruction formed amid competing theories of the Indian and his or her ability to be civilized, against various forms of contestation and opposition, and alongside ideological, institutional, and governmental shifts. This complexity prevents us from drawing a simplistic straight line from intention, to action, to outcome, though it does not prevent us from identifying a generalized intent within the collective action frame of the Indian Problem.

4 | Schools, Staff, Parents, Communities, and Students

As one moves closer to the actual boarding schools, national-level comparisons become less salient. Although American and Canadian policies and institutional frameworks both differed from each other in important ways and shared equally significant similarities, the schools themselves were spaces of invention and adaptation. The staff at the schools did not simply implement federal policy in a straightforward manner; instead, they shaped it to local circumstances and developed novel managerial approaches in contributing to (or in rare cases subverting) resolution of the Indian Problem. As well, they enlisted an assemblage of nearby actors in their efforts, including parents, neighbors, and community members, as well as nonhuman actors, such as space, time, and poverty. But these actors could also band together to challenge the Indian Problem's assimilative ethos. The techniques for managing local school populations, and the nonhuman actors enlisted in specific schools, comprise my topics for chapters 5, 6, and 7. This chapter provides a brief overview of the four schools on which this study is focused and then introduces the human actors engaged in negotiating the conditions at each school. Distinct national policy and institutional frameworks offer important contexts for consideration of experiences at each school, since they give us a glimpse of the circulating frames and logics that structured thought and action on the ground at Indigenous boarding schools. But these frames were not simply applied in the schools in automatic fashion. They were interpreted, negotiated, and adapted based on microlevel factors that interacted with meso- and macrolevel constraints. Degrees of freedom were found for novel mutations in the settler colonial mesh, and it is to these instances that we now turn our attention.

The schools that I selected for this study were not chosen because they resembled one another in key ways. I did not seek out American analogues of Canadian schools or vice versa. I was concerned with illustrating local variations in boarding school experiences rather than offering a definitive description of boarding schools in each country. The schools discussed below were not selected because they were deemed by some criteria to be representative of Canadian and American experiences. Based on my reading of both the American literature and the Canadian literature on boarding schools, there were no typical schools on which such a comparison could be made. This limits any claims to generalizability that one might be tempted to make about the information presented below; however, my goal is not to generalize but to develop a framework attentive to both broader genocidal processes and differences and irregularities within such processes.

Although these schools are imperfect cross-border matches, they do reflect some general tendencies in the American and Canadian systems. For example, a Canadian memorandum of February 22, 1934, offers a comparison of Indigenous education in the United States and Canada. At this time, there were 197 schools (reservation, nonreservation, and day) in the United States and 349 in Canada. But U.S. schools handled 29,062 students (68,123 if we include those for whom tuition was paid at public schools), whereas Canadian schools handled only 17,425 students. As the author of the memo indicated, "you will note, from the above, that we have considerably more schools on reserves." As well, in the United States, when one includes all forms of schooling, even public, these schools received $133 per student, whereas the Canadian average was $98.[1] Based on the national tendencies identified by the author of this memo, the fact that I examine smaller reserve-based schools in Canada, and larger nonreserve institutions in the United States, follows the general pattern in the latter country of larger federal boarding schools than those in Canada.

My focus is on schools located near the reserves or territories from which the majority of their students were drawn. Although Albuquerque Indian School (AIS) and Santa Fe Indian School (SFIS) in New Mexico are often considered nonreservation boarding schools, they were near enough to various Pueblo communities to allow parental and community access to children. Portage la Prairie Indian Residential School (PLPIRS) and Fort Alexander Indian Residential School (FAIRS), both in Manitoba, were smaller mission-run boarding schools located very close to the Long Plain and Sagkeeng communities, from which they drew most of their students. The proximity of each of these schools to a primary Indigenous community allows for comparisons of the ways in which territory was allied with or used to resist assimilative practices, an area of concern in chapter 7. Schools were also selected not only because they were located near large Indigenous populations in regions in which Canadian and American governments focused their assimilative educational projects but also because the archival and oral historical sources needed to make my analysis possible were largely available for each school.

My effort here, therefore, is not to let the lens of genocide shape case selection so that only the harshest schools in the United States, in their most aggressive periods, are compared with similar schools and periods in Canada. Understanding genocide as a process means that attention must be paid to those schools where destructive assimilation unfolded in an uncertain manner and where resistances might have been in place, at different points in the histories of the schools, with potential to derail some aspects of the genocidal process. The analysis presented in the next four chapters is thus an exercise in offering examples of how policies were applied, intensified, negotiated, resisted, and subverted at the local level.

Albuquerque Indian School

Plans to establish a school near Albuquerque surfaced as early as 1878, and the school opened in January 1881, housed in a one-story adobe building near the town of Durannes.[2] The school relocated in June 1884 to the Menaul campus in Albuquerque, where it remained until it was closed in 1982, when its students were transferred to SFIS. In 1884, a larger school building was erected to house 150 students.

FIG. 1. Albuquerque Indian School, ca. 1885

Initially, AIS operated as a "contract school" under the auspices of the Presbyterian Church, which received $130 per student, but the school was placed fully under federal government control on October 2, 1886.[3] Early reports show that AIS faced great resistance from the Pueblo when it came to enrolling their children, which, as we will see, resulted in some concessions made to the Pueblo on how their children were schooled. But AIS was also perceived among some Pueblo to hold the advantage that fewer Pueblo students would be removed and taken to faraway eastern boarding schools, such as Carlisle.[4] In the first year, AIS enrollment was forty-seven students, growing to eighty-one in the second year and 114 by the third year.[5] Student ages ranged from six to eighteen in these early years.[6] By 1888–89, enrollment at the school reached 219. At this time, instruction was offered in several trades, including harness making, shoemaking, cooking and baking, sewing, and laundering. The school went through several superintendents in its first decade and a half of operation, finding stability only once Reuben Perry assumed the position in 1908.

Across most of their histories, the most prevalent group at both the Albuquerque and the Santa Fe Indian Schools were the Pueblo. There are nineteen Pueblo communities, all located in northern, central, and eastern New Mexico.[7] Like the term "Indian," "Pueblo" is a European-assigned (in this case, by the Spanish) umbrella term that unites a diverse group of Indigenous cultures, with distinct cultural traditions and practices, yet also a common history of trade, cultural sharing, and military cooperation—most dramatically in the Pueblo Revolt of 1680, when the various Pueblos banded together to defeat the Spanish and keep them out of the region until 1692.[8]

Pueblo communities had long experience with colonial governments, and not just the Spanish, prior to initiation of the boarding school system. When Mexico became independent of Spain in 1821, the Pueblo communities came under Mexican rule. The Mexican government disavowed the Law of the Indies, under which the Spanish had governed Indigenous peoples, simply making the Pueblo and other Indigenous peoples citizens of Mexico. This move had later consequences for the distinct position of the Pueblo in relation to other Indigenous groups in the United States. When the United States secured control of the territory that would become the state of New Mexico in 1848, the Treaty of Guadalupe Hidalgo, which brought an end to the American-Mexican War, declared all Mexican citizens in the southwest to be American citizens. This led to confusion about the status of the Pueblo under U.S. governance, since it was also held that all Indigenous groups in the United States were wards of the state.[9]

One of the first superintendents at AIS, R. W. D. Bryan, who had been, among other things, the astronomer for Hall's Polaris expedition in search of the north pole prior to taking charge of the school, described the plight of the school with the Pueblo peoples as follows: "These Pueblo Indians had been living for centuries in the midst of a Spanish civilization and their improvement was scarcely appreciable. They were being rapidly surrounded by an aggressive American civilization and without the help of Christian education their extinction was inevitable. . . . It is impolite for a superior race to allow an inferior one to die out in their midst and it is unchristian in the extreme."[10] As was the case at the higher levels of government, benevolence offered a justificatory logic for those working in the schools, simultaneously confirming their sense of superiority while rationalizing their actions against Indigenous cultures.

In the late 1800s, when both AIS and SFIS opened their doors, federal boarding schools received a per capita grant of $167 per student. This did not mean that $167 per year was directed toward the survival of the individual student. Instead, schools like AIS also used these funds to cover costs such as transportation and student recruitment.[11] Moreover, under this model, schools felt compelled to maintain full or more than full enrollment and to attract as many nearby students as possible so as to minimize transportation costs. Therefore, especially in these early years, conditions were rather rough at AIS, and disease and hunger were common concerns that exacerbated Pueblo reluctance to enroll children.

But, as I will demonstrate below, AIS eventually managed to work with the Pueblo communities to ensure higher levels of enrollment. At its peak, over 1,000 students were present each year at the school. In addition, AIS survived longer than most other federal boarding schools, evading the closings that occurred from the 1930s to the 1950s. Indeed, in 1976, AIS was the first federal boarding school to morph into a tribally run institution, when the Pueblo took control of its operations.[12]

It would be a mistake to view AIS as solely a Pueblo school, however. Snapshots of its enrollment at various times show diversity within the student body. At the end of the school year in 1916, for example, AIS was home to seven Apache, one Chippewa, nine Hopi, five Mojave, 127 Diné, three Papago, two Pima, 265 Pueblo, and eleven Zuni.[13] At the end of the school year in 1920, the numbers were 399 Pueblo, ninety-two Diné, thirty-three Apache, two Mojave, one Hopi, one Creek, one Sioux, and one Seneca. Most of these students were in the fourth to tenth grades.[14] By 1925, school enrollment was up to 813, with 373 Pueblo, 279 Diné, fifty-one Apache, forty Zuni, thirty-four Hopi, and a handful of students from other nations.[15] In 1930, there were nearly as many Diné (290) as Pueblo (300) students in the school, though groups sometimes considered Pueblo, such as Zuni (forty-two) and Hopi (101), are listed separately in the annual report.[16] Apache students (seventy-three) also made up a significant portion of the school in 1930.

More information concerning day-to-day life at AIS is presented below.

But it is worth mentioning that the records for AIS are patchier than those available for some other schools. A 1910 campus fire destroyed many of the early records, and later, during the 1980s, multiple fires set by homeless persons finding shelter in the abandoned school would destroy more of its recorded history. Still, sufficient records have survived, and combined with oral testimony they provide a sense of life at the school.

Santa Fe Indian School

The Santa Fe Indian School traces its origins back to the first University of New Mexico, initiated by reverend Haratio Oliver Ladd, a Congregationalist minister. Ladd claimed that his proposal to launch an Indian school at Santa Fe was at the urging of Chief San Juan of the Mescalero Apache, who reportedly wanted Apache children to receive an education similar to that provided to white children. The Board of Indian Commissioners approved Ladd's proposal in 1884, and the school opened in 1885 after Ladd negotiated a $25,000 lump sum and $120 per student contract from the federal government.[17] The contract, however, was conditional on the people of Santa Fe providing the school with a permanent 100-acre site, subsequently made available to the school.[18]

The United States Industrial School at Santa Fe opened to all Indian students of the southwest in 1890 and became part of the federal boarding school system.[19] During that year, there were 150 students in attendance. SFIS then became an Indian normal school in January 1894. By the end of the nineteenth century, it had an enrollment of 250, with 106 acres of farmland, seventeen white employees, twenty-two Indian employees, and twenty-five paid pupil helpers. Students were trained, depending on their gender, in cooking, sewing, housekeeping, tailoring, shoemaking, blacksmithing, carpentering, laundering, farming, and gardening by irrigation.[20]

S. M. Cart was the first superintendent at SFIS, followed by Thomas Jones and Andrew H. Viets. The latter two were military men.[21] In 1891, Cart visited Pueblo, Apache, and Diné communities, and communicated with Indian agents, to try to secure students for the school. In many communities, he faced resistance; for example, the Jicarilla Apache were unwilling to send their children to the school until they could be sure that the children would be safe from smallpox while there.[22] In seeking to convince Indigenous parents to send their children to SFIS, Cart argued

> that this is a Government school and that the Indians should send their children here as a duty to the Government. . . . They should educate their children as a duty they owe to them; that they are better fed and clothed and cared for than they possibly could be at home; that they should patronize this school because it is a training school, where their children can learn a useful trade and acquire the habits and customs of American citizens; I have offered to pay them for bringing in their children (and in some cases have done so) at the same rate it would cost the Govt. by regular modes of travel; have invited the parents to visit the school, and have treated them kindly when they came; have pointed out the advantages that certain educated and trained Indians had over others in the way of earning a better living &c; have shown them the climate in Santa Fe is very healthful.[23]

But soon after, in the summer of 1891, the Jicarilla were disturbed to learn of the death of a girl from their community at SFIS. Two chiefs from the community insisted that they visit SFIS to check on the school's sanitary conditions before any further children would be allowed to attend.[24]

In these early years, SFIS followed a rigid military model. Harsh discipline and insufficient food were common. Yet, for the most part, students were located not too far from their home communities, since most of the Pueblo who allowed their children to attend the school were located within sixty miles of its campus. Thus, as at AIS, the Pueblo children had greater access to their home communities, especially during summers.[25] This arrangement was not typical of U.S. federal nonreservation boarding schools. This fact, combined with a general Pueblo reluctance to criticize authority and teachings that stressed the importance of following rules,[26] means that it is more difficult to locate student criticisms of even the most oppressive periods at SFIS and AIS.[27]

Northern Pueblo children typically remained at local day schools until they reached the age of eleven or twelve, when they were transferred to SFIS.[28] Grade eight was the highest level offered at SFIS until the 1920s. Promising students who completed this level were sent to another institution, such as

AIS or the Sherman Institute in Riverside, California.[29] At the end of 1924, SFIS housed 212 northern Pueblo, 127 southern Pueblo, sixty-three Diné, thirty Zuni, nineteen Ute, ten Pueblo Bonito, two Hopi, one San Juan Diné, one Jicarilla Apache, and eight independent students.[30] The school had a capacity of 450 students in the mid- to late 1920s, but this capacity was increased to 500 in 1928–29.[31] SFIS also housed a number of Indigenous employees, though not typically in higher-status positions. From 1918 to 1928, approximately 30 percent of SFIS staff members were Indigenous persons, and this number increased to 50 percent during the 1930s. Many of these staff members were from Pueblo communities, but several also came from other nations, such as the Cheyenne, Sioux, and Cherokee. These staff members served as tailors, laundresses, seamstresses, assistant cooks, gardeners, dormitory advisers, bakers, laborers, and night watchmen.[32]

By the 1930s, conditions at SFIS had improved noticeably. Under Superintendent Chester E. Faris, a Quaker from Indiana, greater effort was put into working with Pueblo communities to shape the school. Of his approach, Faris stated, "I always made a rule never to tell an Indian what to do. . . . I waited until he told me what he wanted, and then I helped him get it."[33] Under Faris, military drills were abolished, and a high school program was started. Vocational trades were expanded to include building trades and auto mechanics, and topics such as Indian arts, culture, and history were increasingly taught in the school. Moreover, the school was remodeled to reflect Pueblo architecture.

It was in the 1930s and 1940s that SFIS gained a reputation as an Indian arts school.[34] The 1932 hiring of Dorothy Dunn contributed greatly to this reputation, for Dunn encouraged students to take pride in their cultures and sought to guide them in further developing the artistic skills and crafts familiar to them from their home communities.[35] Such programs faced cuts after the onset of the Second World War, and the school reverted to more assimilative programs designed to encourage prescribed habits of U.S. citizenship. By 1957, vocations at SFIS had been abolished, and then in 1958 and 1959 students were transferred to other institutions, such as AIS, so that SFIS could become an arts and crafts school, renamed the Institute of American Indian Arts, as well as an institution for elementary-level students (primarily Diné, Ute, and Apache). Through such adaptations, SFIS avoided the federal chopping block, and it became the first Indian contract school under the Indian Self-Determination Act of 1975.[36]

Portage la Prairie Indian Residential School

There were two residential schools located in Portage la Prairie, Manitoba, one Methodist and one Presbyterian. The Presbyterian school, my focus here, began in the 1880s as a day school operated by the Women's Missionary Society of the Presbyterian Church. But the day school was thought to be insufficient because of the distance that a number of students had to trek each day. Indeed, though twenty-six Dakota Sioux students were enrolled in the day school, the average attendance was only ten per day.[37] The federal government was also reluctant to support a day or boarding school within the town's borders, expressing concerns that Indigenous people would be "a nuisance."[38] But after some persuasion, the government agreed to pay the teacher's salary in 1890. In 1891, it made the school part of the per capita funding system, and the boarding school was opened in a new building just outside Portage la Prairie.[39] The school went under various names over the course of its history, including the Portage la Prairie Sioux Boarding School (1896–1908), the Portage la Prairie Boarding School (1896–1927), and the Portage Indian Student Residence (1965–75).[40]

The Presbyterian Church erected the original PLPIRS building without financial contribution from the Canadian government. But, by 1910, the school was in such disrepair that it was suggested a new location be sought.[41] In 1913, the establishment of a new school became possible through the purchase of property owned by the estate of Margaret Cumming, property deemed to be suitable because (a) children could walk to the Knox Presbyterian Church and Sunday School from the campus; (b) it was on a road that led to the Long Plain Reserve (Anishinaabe-Ojibway), and parents could easily see their children; (c) it was close to parish lot number fourteen, where many Sioux had elected to reside; and (d) it was closer to the Sioux reservation than the former school.[42] The Department of Indian Affairs and Northern Development owned the new building. Soon after moving to this larger location, the half-day system was introduced, with PLPIRS students spending half the day in vocational training and half in scholarly pursuits, which made academic progress at the school very difficult for them.[43]

FIG. 2. Portage la Prairie Indian Residential School, ca. 1914–15

Around 1919, the school's principal, W. A. Hendry, in charge from the school's opening until 1909 and then again from 1911 to 1934, sought more land for the school as well as plots at the Portage la Prairie cemetery for students who passed away during their time at PLPIRS. But growth at the school was slow. PLPIRS did not reach ninety students until the early 1930s.[44] Its peak enrollments were achieved in the 1950s, when the school held between 115 and 180 students.[45]

In 1925, the Presbyterian Church fell under the auspices of the United Church, and the school was subsequently placed under the administration of the United Church's Women's Missionary Society (1926–65); it was transferred to the United Church Board of Home Missions in 1965 and then to the Department of Indian Affairs and Northern Development in 1969.[46] But the 1925 merger under the United Church was cause for concern at the time because it was uncertain whether or not the United Church would choose to maintain the school. In a letter written by several Sioux people, they requested the continuing survival of the school: "We have been told by Mr. W. A. Hendry the Principal of the Indians that all our children will be turn [sic] out of the school and sent to some other school. To this point we could not bear it and will not stand for it."[47] These fears were quickly dispelled, but Hendry also noted that he doubted the veracity of the letter or the legitimacy of its writers as spokespersons for their community, since, in his estimation, most of the Sioux already belonged to the United Church.

In June 1930, in the *Missionary Monthly*, Principal Hendry published an article titled "An Indian Training Ground." In it, he wrote that "our chief recruiting ground is the Long Plain Reserve which is sixteen miles to the west of the school. More than half of our pupils come from this reserve. The Indians of the Sioux village are being moved to it, which will make it the largest reserve in southern Manitoba." He also spoke of the advances made in Indian education at the school, suggesting that most Indian students were able to speak English and were learning how to farm. But, he added, "if we continue giving to him, ever giving, we may be working toward an ever-fading objective, and at the same time creating in the Indian what is sometimes called, 'lethargy of expectancy.'" In short, the Indian Problem framed his concerns for the school, and Hendry considered his project to be that of making the Indian into an independent and resourceful actor who would need less from the government.[48] At a time when some U.S. boarding schools were being guided by the Meriam Report to be more respectful of Indigenous cultures, the assimilative push in schools such as PLPIRS was still evident.

In the 1940s, most of the students at PLPIRS came from local Dakota or Anishinaabe-Ojibway communities such as Roseau River, Sioux Valley, Long Plain, and Swan Lake. However, a few Cree students were transported to the school in the later years of the decade. The age range for students at the school was from six to fifteen during this period. For girls, the industrial training offered was primarily in the form of kitchen or laundry work, though a few girls pursued sewing, housekeeping, or nursing. For boys, farming was the most prominent form of training, with animal husbandry and poultry care the main activities during winter months.[49] To facilitate this work, the school possessed 175 acres of farmland on which the students grew wheat, oats, barley, corn, potatoes, and sweet clover.[50] For both boys and girls, work training began as early as nine years of age.[51]

By 1957, the PLPIRS residence was used primarily to house students enrolled at city schools, and from 1959 to 1963 the school rented some of its classrooms to the Mount Pleasant School District. PLPIRS closed its doors in 1975. The building still stands on the former campus site and is now a resource center for the Long Plain First Nation.

Fort Alexander Indian Residential School

In a March 1900 letter, the archbishop of St. Boniface requested that a boarding school be established at the Fort Alexander Reserve (now known as Sagkeeng, an Anishinaabe-Ojibway community). He argued that the existing day school, in operation since 1880, was too far away for parents (a five-mile walk for some), that the Winnipeg River was difficult to cross for those located on its opposite bank, and that the parents were very poor. Therefore, he believed, a boarding school was better suited to the area. He also noted that Sagkeeng parents were willing to send their children to St. Boniface but preferred a school closer to their reserve for the younger ones.[52] Fort Alexander Indian Residential School, also referred to as Fort Alexander Boarding School (1905–25) and Fort Alexander Residential School (1925–68),[53] was subsequently opened on September 15, 1904. Situated ninety miles north of Winnipeg, it was run by the Oblates of Mary Immaculate, an order of the Roman Catholic Church.[54] The school was approximately one mile from the Fort Alexander Reserve and located on the south bank of the Winnipeg River. The school possessed about 145 acres of land.[55]

Fort Alexander began as a small mission-based school. Indeed, it was not until 1910 that the school saw its first significant gain in enrollment from forty to sixty pupils. At this time, the majority of students were grant earners, meaning that they were eligible for government per capita funding. However, this minor growth in the student population presented a challenge in terms of providing living and learning space in the existing building. Ventilation was a particular problem.[56] Later, in 1914, concern was also expressed about heating the building, described as "none too warm," especially in the brutal winter months experienced in Manitoba.[57] Heating the school continued to be a concern until at least 1923, when a new heating plant was added, but the acetylene machine, which powered the school's lighting, continued to raise concerns about the possibility of an explosion, especially since both it and the boiler were housed in the main building.

By 1929, eighty-five students were enrolled at the school. This number increased to 100 in the 1930s. The highest enrollments occurred between

1949 and 1958, when an average of 130 children attended.[58] As of the 1940s, most of the children at FAIRS were drawn from Sagkeeng, with the remainder from other Anishinaabe-Ojibway reserves such as Roseau River, Peguis, and Brokenhead. The ages of these children ranged from six to sixteen, and they attended grades one through nine. In their daily work, the boys engaged in trades that included driving horses and tractors, care of cattle, carpentry, painting, shoe repair, and gardening. The girls worked in sewing, knitting, embroidering, cooking, housekeeping, dairying, and painting. In 1949, a day school was built beside FAIRS, and the two schools operated side by side. This school was amalgamated into FAIRS in 1954.[59]

In 1958, the majority of students at FAIRS were from Sagkeeng. Twenty-four were from the east side of the Winnipeg River (eleven of whom came from a broken home or had no home) and fifty-eight from the west side of the river (twenty-seven of whom came from a broken home or had no home). In addition, the school housed three children from Berens River (Anishinaabe-Ojibway), three from Norway House (Cree), seven from Brokenhead, and three from Roseau River. As well, FAIRS also ran a day school at this time, which enrolled forty-seven children (forty-one treaty and six nontreaty). The school also kept data on the number of Roman Catholic children in the area. As of 1920, the Indian Act set denominational boundaries among Canadian Indigenous peoples, ascribing each child's faith at birth based on that imputed to parents and the community. This restricted other denominational schools from enrolling those children perceived as belonging to a specific church and made it necessary for churches to keep close tabs on children whom they thought belonged to them.[60]

As of 1969, the FAIRS student residence was considered unsafe for occupancy.[61] Fort Alexander closed its doors on June 30, 1970. The building has since been demolished. Only rubble is left in the space where it once stood.

Other Schools: Cooperation and Competition

Although the settler colonial project took distinct shape at each of these schools, it is not possible to assess each solely as an isolated entity. Certainly, each school was under the influence of macrolevel visions of social engineering via dominant conceptions of the Indian Problem as well as part of a broader governmental network that brought to bear on the schools the influence of other institutional efforts to resolve the Indian Problem, such as those taking place through law, policing, and health. However, in addition, these schools were situated within organizational networks, at what I have referred to in chapter 1 as the lower mesolevel of the settler colonial mesh. Here patterns of conflict and cooperation among various schools helped to form local school conditions.

As well, local schools fed back into negotiations at higher levels of the system. Indigenous boarding schools were not simply nodes within a network of schools, passively drawing resources and ideas from above, but also sites of assimilative innovation and reform within this broader network. In some instances, perspectives drawn from the schools influenced progressive changes in Indigenous educational policy, such as when SFIS superintendents John DeHuff and Chester Faris, inspired by the artistic efforts of their students, encouraged the government to make more space for Indigenous arts within Indian education.[62] In other cases, as discussed in chapters 5 and 6, new techniques were introduced to more effectively regulate and transform Indigenous students. The influence of the microlevel on higher levels is also reflected in how schools often dealt with local issues beyond those of assimilative education. Questions of land, health, citizenship, and religion were filtered at times through American and Canadian boarding school systems, with school officials often intervening in conflicts or concerns arising from these issues, lending government officials their opinions on land claims, reserve health services, and spiritual practices of local communities, as they saw fit. Indeed, for periods of time, superintendents at AIS and SFIS possessed powers of oversight well beyond the remit of their schools. For example, between 1931 and 1935, the superintendent of SFIS was also in charge of the Northern Pueblos Agency and thus responsible for matters of general governance related to these Pueblo.[63]

In Canada, there existed a great deal of competition among the Christian denominations that oversaw boarding schools, especially Roman Catholic and Protestant schools.[64] Such competition was also evident in the United States, also between Catholic and Protestant denominations, in the late nineteenth century, but it became less prevalent when denominational contract schools lost their funding.[65] But in Manitoba, competition for students was prominent in the early stages of residential schooling and remained so for years. For example, in response to a request from James Mann that his son Cornelius be removed from the Anglican-run Rupert's Land School to the Catholic School at St. Boniface, the principal of Rupert's Land School wrote to the government to express his concern about this transfer. He argued, among other things, that Cornelius had been baptized into the Church of England and therefore belonged in Rupert's Land School. As well, he presented his suspicions that the Catholic Church was working to convert Indians belonging to other Christian denominations.[66] Such suspicions had long been expressed, for each denomination tended to view others as predatory toward its converts. But more than just a competition for souls was at stake. As English Canadian power was consolidated throughout much of Canada, French Catholic groups such as the Oblates had to assert themselves to ensure their continued relevance, not just to Indigenous education but also in multiple domains.

The competition among Christian denominations adds a degree of complexity to the Canadian residential school system largely distinct from twentieth-century American boarding schools. This competition was particularly heated prior to a 1920 amendment to the Indian Act, which guaranteed Roman Catholic and Protestant schools secure access to Indigenous children recorded as belonging to their respective faiths. This amendment was intended to resolve conflicts such as that expressed in a petition from the chief and councilors of Peguis, Fisher River, Berens River, and Bloodvein to His Royal Highness, Victor Christian William, on January 27, 1919. In the petition, concerns were expressed about how boarding school funding arrangements produced conflict among churches, which competed with one another for converts. Such competition, it was suggested, caused divisions within communities. As well, the control that religious denominations had over the hiring of teachers was believed to result in the hiring of incompetent teachers who "do as they like." The petition recommended that education be handled entirely by the government in a manner consistent with treaty promises.[67]

Despite the concerns expressed by the chiefs and councilors in this instance, competition was not solely a source of disruption in Indigenous communities. As J. R. Miller has demonstrated, it could also offer a source of power to Indigenous people, who could demand from competing denominations more sensitivity to matters such as use of Indigenous languages in schools.[68] For this reason, the Canadian government perhaps had another motivation to clarify denominational jurisdiction over Indigenous souls. But, as we will see in later chapters, among the groups discussed in this volume, the Pueblo were best positioned to make good use of such competition among various schools to advance their interests within the American boarding school system.

None of this is intended to suggest that the U.S. system did not display some degree of competition among schools. Competition was most notable between contract and federal boarding schools, at least in the early years of the system. With respect to SFIS, the main sources of competition were the St. Catherine's and Ramona Indian Schools—the former a Roman Catholic school and the latter a Protestant school. These schools eventually lost the federal funding that they had received under the contract program, phased out in the late 1800s. However, St. Catherine's continued to operate beyond this time thanks to the personal wealth of Katherine Drexhall, who brought a considerable inheritance with her when she joined the order of nuns. The Ramona school, in contrast, when its funding was removed, was closed, transferred to SFIS, and placed under the oversight of Superintendent Thomas Jones.

In discussing the challenges and objections that he faced in trying to enroll Pueblo, Apache, and Diné students at SFIS, Superintendent S. M. Cart drew on an anti-Catholic sentiment widespread in 1891: "Undoubtedly the Catholic influence is against all other Government schools. The Superintendent of St. Catherine's School has said that it was of no use for us to visit the Pueblos for the purpose of securing children," implying that this Catholic mission school felt a certain degree of ownership of the (syncretically) Catholic Pueblo.[69] Indeed, on a September visit to Taos Pueblo, Cart found the community unwilling to send their children to any but a Catholic school, and he learned that the superintendent of St. Catherine's had visited Taos Pueblo before him to deliver this message to the Pueblo.[70] Likewise, Cart suspected that the superintendent of the Ramona school had influenced criticisms of SFIS by a Mr. Graves (whom Cart described as a man on trial for murder). Graves had charged that students at SFIS were dirty, dissatisfied, and "do as they please." Cart did not entirely refute these criticisms, and he used the opportunity to note the school's need for a new tailor. He also reduced the claims of dissatisfaction to nothing more than the complaints of a single disgruntled student. Cart offered reasons why the students might have appeared less than orderly. But the primary cause of his concern was that the Ramona school was seeking to disparage SFIS in the battle for Indigenous students.[71]

After the loss of funding to religious contract schools, and closing of the Ramona school, St. Catherine's continued to be a source of conflict and competition for superintendents at SFIS. In October 1895, Superintendent Jones wrote to the commissioner of Indian Affairs to complain that nine children enrolled at his school from the Tesuque Pueblo, who had been allowed to return home, had subsequently been sent to the St. Catherine's school: "The point I wish you seriously to consider is the example such a precident [sic] sets to these ignorant parents, for surely the Govt. after its liberal expenditure of money has some rights, which these should be taught to respect."[72]

However, competition in the United States was not simply a matter for religious and federal boarding schools. The nonreservation federal boarding schools also competed among themselves, as well as with day and reservation schools, for students. AIS and SFIS faced threats from schools such as Phoenix or Carlisle when these more distant schools came to New Mexico in search of students. As well, day and reservation schools were reluctant at times to transfer their more talented students up the ladder to nonreservation schools, the proposed system from the late nineteenth century on.[73] Moreover, even though AIS and SFIS frequently worked in cooperation with one another to share knowledge and ensure their mutual survival, and their superintendents met regularly, moments of competition arose between them. For example, in 1893, Superintendent Cart voiced his displeasure to the Indian agent at Sacaton, Arizona, when children were sent from the reserve to AIS and not SFIS, despite the latter's previous requests for pupils.[74]

This competition among schools in the U.S. system returns us to a key difference between American and Canadian boarding school networks. In the United States, there were greater attempts to fashion an integrated boarding school system. Cooperation among day, reservation, and nonreservation schools was fostered initially under Thomas J. Morgan's leadership as commissioner of Indian Affairs (1888–93; see chapter 3).[75] Commissioner Francis Leupp (1905–9) sought to reform Morgan's system to place more emphasis on day schools rather than federal nonreservation boarding schools, and he managed to reduce boarding school attendance by 10 percent while increasing day school attendance to 47 percent.[76] But Morgan's system persisted, both through Leupp's years and even as emphasis was placed more squarely on community-based day schools at the onset of John Collier's tenure as commissioner of Indian Affairs in 1934. As noted in the previous chapter, under Morgan's system, day schools and reservation boarding schools were considered feeder schools for the nonreservation schools, allowing children to stay close to their home communities until they were believed to be old enough for separation. Because of this system, some of the experiences of the Canadian residential school system, such as the disorienting assault on culture and language that occurred when very young students were removed from their parents and placed in residential schools, did not occur all at once for many American students. But day schools still confronted the children with assimilative demands. Frank Tenorio recalls that, "at the outset, I was in day school before I went to the Indian School. Speaking your native language was definitely frowned upon. They told us that wasn't the way to learn English. So we had to almost forget everything that you had at home and try to blend into a situation that was definitely alien to you."[77]

In the 1912 SFIS annual report, a plan to work in greater cooperation with day schools was noted: older students would be transferred from the latter once they completed the day school's course of work.[78] Indeed, since the day schools in the Southern and Northern Pueblos Agencies were under the supervision of the superintendents at AIS and SFIS, respectively, these schools formed an integrated network to some extent, though one still prone to snags, as when day school teachers were reluctant to advance competent students to boarding schools because they feared the effects of losing their best and brightest on their classrooms. This network faced other challenges. When boarding school superintendents felt the threat of potential closure, as various commissioners of Indian Affairs placed greater emphasis on day schools for educational or budgetary reasons, it was not uncommon for them to disparage the efforts of day schools. On one such occasion, Superintendent Perry from AIS wrote to the commissioner of Indian Affairs in response to a BIA proposal to increase the time that Indigenous children spent at local day schools: "The day school does not do as much for the child as the boarding school does. I believe the Indian child will be better qualified for seeking and obtaining employment and in proving himself proficient if the 5th and 6th years of his school life are spent in boarding school. . . . There is not much opportunity to assist a child in a day school to select a life vocation."[79]

Only in the later years of the Canadian system did there seem to be an attempt to organize various school types into one system. For example, in 1937, there is evidence of an attempt to be systematic when assessing the applications of Dorothy and Isabel Cameron, aged seven and nine, from Swan Lake. Their father, Sam, who signed their application forms, requested that they be admitted to PLPIRS. Both girls up to that point had attended the Swan Lake day school. Dorothy had minor trachoma and a slightly cold temperature but was otherwise described as healthy and well nourished, and Isabel was reported to be fully healthy. However, Philip Phelan, chief of the training division, wrote to J. Waite, the Indian agent, on January, 7, 1938 that he was unsure why these girls should be admitted, since their parents were alive and they were already attending day school. The agent responded that there was no special reason why they should be admitted into residential school, and the girls were rejected for attendance at PLPIRS.[80] However, Waite later wrote to the secretary of Indian Affairs (on November 22, 1938) to say that the situation in the home of Dorothy and Isabel had changed and that their mother, who had tuberculosis, needed to be shipped to a sanatorium, leaving their father to care for three small boys. Therefore, he recommended that the girls be admitted to PLPIRS. Phelan responded favorably but also noted that the grant for PLPIRS would not be extended beyond ninety pupils.[81] A few years later, Isabel and Dorothy were both attending PLPIRS, as were two of their brothers. By this point, their mother was dead, and their father had enlisted in the army and was fighting in France. Isabel was due to be discharged, but Principal John A. McNeill wrote to the government to say that he wanted to keep her longer since there was no one back home to care for her other than her aged grandparents.[82] The government agreed, and the extension was approved. One can see an effort here to utilize rationally the various types of school based on criteria such as whether or not perceived competent parents were present to care for children while they attended a day school, reserving boarding schools for children without requisite levels of parental supervision; however, such negotiations among Indian agents, schools, and government officials continued to be haphazard and did not necessarily follow a codified logic.[83]

Finally, information sharing and cooperation did not simply occur within the organizational frameworks of each respective nation (see also chapter 3). Rather, communication also existed between Canadian and American officials about boarding schools. Occasionally, school staff would draw on events in the other country when negotiating with government managers. Principal W. A. Hendry from PLPIRS, for instance, felt great concern about what he interpreted to be a government plan in 1930 to lower the discharge age from eighteen to sixteen—the actual proposal extended compulsory schooling from fifteen to sixteen, and under both the previous and the amended versions the government was empowered to encourage students to stay until eighteen. In building a case against this perceived move, Hendry drew selectively from the Meriam Report:

> The Meriam report of the USA . . . uses very strong language about overworking children in their schools. They say "that no industrial work should be done by children until they reach their 15th year and that it is done because the small amount of money allowed for food and clothes makes it necessary to use child labour" (page 375) and their grant is $270.00 per capita against our $160.00. The report further states, "The labour of children as carried on in Indian Boarding Schools would, it is believed, constitute a violation of child labour laws in most states" (Page 376).[84]

Hendry's concern here, ignoring the wider criticisms presented in the Meriam Report, was that the work necessary to maintain the school would need to be done by younger children if the discharge age was lowered, thereby leaving the school prone to the same criticisms offered in the Meriam Report.

More formal instances of information sharing also occurred. On June 23, 1941, Willard Beatty, director of education for the U.S. Department of the Interior, sent a letter to R. A. Hoey, superintendent of welfare and training for the Department of Mines and Resources. In it, Beatty thanked Hoey for sending him a pamphlet of addresses of Canadian Indians. In return, Beatty sent Hoey the report of the U.S. Department of the Interior for 1939, which also contained the annual report of Indian Affairs. As well, Beatty included a list of publications for use in Indian schools that had been produced by the American education division, which he noted they would be happy to supply to Hoey at "minimal cost." Hoey responded by offering to share some Canadian materials, including a story about protection of fur-bearing animals.[85] One should not overstate the degree of mutual influence demonstrated by such exchanges; however, it is clear from the Davin Report onward that the two systems were aware of one another and at times cooperated with the goal of improving their respective systems.[86]

Staff, Parents, Communities, and Students

The primary actors in negotiating the experience of Indigenous boarding schools were the staff, parents, community members, and students. At each school, staff interpreted and even reframed government policy, seeking to enlist parents, Indigenous communities, and students in what was often a locally nuanced response to the Indian Problem.

STAFF

In other regional contexts, the point has been made that some staff members mediated the harsh experiences of assimilative schooling. Paige Raibmon, for example, uses the figure of George Raley, the principal at Coqualeetza Indian Residential School, to demonstrate that principals possessed a degree of autonomy in overseeing their schools, which allowed them to lessen or increase the intensity of what I have referred to as the settler colonial mesh. Raibmon writes that "Raley's attempts to improve the institutional environment at Coqualeetza are evidence of the considerable, although not unlimited, room to maneuver within the parameters of the social values of the day and of the Canadian residential school system. Still more significantly, Raley's actions demonstrate that the way an individual used this latitude made a great deal of difference to the children with whose residential school experience he was entrusted."[87] Raibmon does not deny the connection of a school like Coqualeetza to the settler colonial project, but her work does show how snags in the settler colonial mesh could arise when those charged with responding to the Indian Problem were not fully invested in the project and brought with them different sets of motivations and intentions.[88] Likewise, the settler colonial mesh could tighten and intensify for students when superintendents, principals, and staff fully embraced this project and even sought to go beyond the call of duty in their efforts to impose assimilation. In short, though such individuals were located within a multilevel mesh that weighed on Indigenous peoples regardless of individual actions, the individual actions of staff members could have impacts on softening or hardening residential school experiences. This was true for both the American and the Canadian Indigenous boarding school contexts.

In the early days of SFIS, school superintendents laid claim to Indigenous children, and they believed that their claims superseded any stake that parents had in their offspring. As Superintendent Jones of SFIS wrote in one letter, "it is full time that these Indians be forced to learn what they can, and what they cannot do, after the vast expenditures made for them."[89] In this instance, the government's investment in Indigenous children was viewed to override Pueblo parental desires that children be allowed to remain home during harvesting or return home from school to attend ceremonials and festivals. Such power struggles between school staff and Pueblo communities were frequent in the late nineteenth century, and even erupted occasionally in the twentieth century, as superintendents confronted Pueblo communities and sought means to access more of their students.[90] However, superintendents at AIS and SFIS soon learned that they had to be more flexible in their negotiations with Pueblo communities and parents if they wanted to ensure a steady stream of Pueblo enrollments. Simply put, parents would not send their children (and might send them instead to one of the contract schools) unless superintendents accommodated Pueblo requests. For this reason, Superintendent Rueben Perry at AIS, and various superintendents at SFIS, learned that they needed to be more flexible with respect to issues such as student home visits. Indeed, a particularly urgent demand was made by Pueblo parents that they be permitted to see their children, and early on the first superintendent of SFIS, S. M. Cart, began the practice of allowing parents to visit their children at the school. Likewise, both Cart and later Perry at AIS used promises of summer vacations spent at home as means to entice Pueblo students to join their schools. Such vacations were largely available only to Pueblo students, had to be funded by parents, and were sustained only as long as the students returned to the school at the start of the fall semester.[91] Later, at SFIS, Superintendent Crandall began his twelve-year tenure by trying to limit summer vacations for students, only to concede this issue eventually under pressure from the Pueblo community.[92] Such concessions, however, should not be taken as evidence that Crandall or other superintendents completely relented in their pursuit of assimilation. Throughout his career, Crandall was consistent in his view that Indigenous children needed to be adapted to Euro-American society. For example, in a 1924 discussion with SFIS superintendent John DeHuff concerning the latter's desire to transfer a few Santo Domingo boys to AIS, Crandall, now superintendent for the northern Pueblo, commented that "Santo Domingo is a reactionary pueblo. It will take fifty or one hundred years under our present process to bring this people up to any degree approaching the standard of our American civilization."[93] But his efforts to "uplift" the Pueblo had to be measured against the willingness of parents to send their children to schools, since Pueblo resistance made it potentially more difficult to populate these schools.

Without links to an upper mesoinstitutional framework such as the church, U.S. superintendents were responsible to the civil service bureaucracy of which they were a part. However, in a somewhat isolated region such as New Mexico, at times it meant that resources to compel schooling, such as sufficient police or military forces, were less readily at hand, especially when it came to trying to pursue Navajo children in their vast territory. But this distance also provided New Mexican superintendents with some freedom in managing their schools. For example, John DeHuff, superintendent at SFIS from 1916 to 1924, likely influenced by his wife, Elizabeth, who possessed a keen interest in Indigenous arts, was able to allow practices such as Pueblo dancing to occur on campus for many years before his superiors took notice.[94] However, one cannot say that DeHuff

FIG. 3. Pueblo leaders visiting officials of the Albuquerque Indian School, ca. 1912

used his degree of autonomy solely to soften the schooling experience
for students, since he was also liberal with the strap, especially when
students were discovered to have engaged in romantic trysts with members of the opposite sex. On several occasions in his journals, DeHuff
recounted how he had administered severe beatings to male students who
had violated the sexual mores of the school—despite government circulars
prohibiting corporal punishment in boarding schools.[95] DeHuff could be
a stern and punitive superintendent, increasing the violence of the settler
colonial mesh in certain circumstances, yet in others expressing doubts
and questions about the efficacy of the boarding school system. Indeed,
on March 31, 1919, DeHuff included in his journal entry a reflection on
Francis Saunders's 1912 book *The Indians of the Terraced Houses*, in which
the author commented critically on U.S. government policy on changing
the Pueblo, questioning how "large boarding-schools are maintained and
paid for by the taxpayers of the United States, where white education, in
part literary and in part industrial, is crammed down the young Pueblo
throat in steam-heated rooms and in an atmosphere often foul to suffo-
cation."[96] Although DeHuff did not agree with Saunders's arguments in
their entirety, he noted that "I too have been thinking for some time past

that perhaps the boarding school, like the one of which I am superintendent, has some seriously objectionable features, although there is much
to recommend it."[97] Such ambivalence and self-doubt from the leader of
a boarding school suggests that his commitment to the settler colonial
project wavered at times. Indeed, in 1924, DeHuff was let go from his
position, in part because he permitted Indigenous dancing, when the
BIA assumed once again a strict assimilative posture, this time under the
leadership of Commissioner Charles Burke.

In Canadian regions where there was competition among denominational
schools, parents could find leverage for improving the conditions under
which their children were taught by threatening to withdraw them from
one school and place them in another.[98] However, this influence was less
evident at the schools under consideration here, at which staff had greater
power. At Long Plain, one of the reserves closest to PLPIRS, parents were
reluctant to let their children attend the school, in part because they believed
that their treaty did not oblige them to have their children educated off
reserve. Inspector Swinford complained about this fact:

> Ever since the Treaty was made, the Indians of the Long Plain reserve
> in the Portage la Prairie Agency have resisted all efforts to place a Mis-
> sionary or Day-school on their reserve. Neither would they consent to
> their children being sent to a Boarding or Industrial school. But lately a
> change has apparently come over a few of them and Principal Hendry of
> the Portage la Prairie Sioux Boarding School, assisted by Indian Agent
> Logan has succeeded in getting four pupils of school age from that reserve,
> very much against the wishes and efforts of the old Indians there.[99]

W. A. Hendry, the long-serving principal of PLPIRS, used Long Plain resistance, and his success at admitting these four pupils from the community,
as grounds to approach the federal government for an enrollment (and per
capita) increase so that he would not be forced to return these students
to the reserve, even though they put the school above its limit. Moreover,
rather than negotiate with Long Plain to better accommodate their concerns, Hendry worked on individual families, and used local authorities,
to secure students.

Despite the zeal with which he sought to increase enrollments, there is little archival or TRC testimonial evidence that Hendry was especially heavy-handed in the day-to-day running of the school.[100] The same is not true for later principals at PLPIRS under whose leadership, reportedly, there was frequent use of the strap by both principal and staff.[101] In a 1949 statement, Rowena Smoke said of her teachers and the principal at PLPIRS that "Mrs. Ross hits us on the head with her fists. . . . We ran away because we do not like Mrs. Ross. . . . Mr. Jones [the principal] cut my hair off last year because I ran away. I ran away last year because I was treated badly by Mrs. Ross. Mr. Jones whips us when we say anything back to Mrs. Ross."[102] Several other girls complained of their treatment by Mrs. Ross, the school matron, and Mr. Jones, the principal. Ross responded by pointing out that she sometimes pulled hair, and rapped the girls on the head with her knuckles, but not out of anger.[103] Jones requested, through the Indian agent, that he be permitted to punish one of the girls further, by cutting her hair, so that she might serve as an example to the other students. However, at that moment, Indian Affairs reined him in, and he was told to practice punishment like "a kind, firm and judicious parent in his family."[104] Jones was later removed as principal of PLPIRS.[105]

The incidents with Mrs. Ross represent a rare instance in which violence at one of the Manitoba schools considered here was discussed in any detail in the official archive, and this occurred largely because complaints from the children forced a response from the government. In contrast, much of the violence at PLPIRS and especially at FAIRS, revealed by testimony given to the Truth and Reconciliation Commission, received no official mention, demonstrating how little, if at all, staff violence was discussed. The abuse meted out by Ross and Jones also illustrates the frequency with which teachers at Canadian residential schools were poorly qualified if not downright incompetent. J. R. Miller writes of "a tendency to use the residential schools as a dumping grounds for missionary workers who were a problem for the evangelical bodies."[106] Into the 1950s, churches were responsible for hiring teaching staff. The Catholic Church, for instance, typically hired staff from female religious orders, "whose recruits were often young women from rural backgrounds."[107] Examples of teaching incompetence are frequent in the testimony of former students at PLPIRS and FAIRS, but the federal archival record is a poor source of information on teaching staff at these schools. For example, criticism of teaching staff at FAIRS is rare in Canadian government records. Nonetheless, one does see on occasion mild concern expressed by inspectors who uncovered that certain teachers lacked requisite skills or training.[108]

In the United States, David Wallace Adams writes, "the average teacher appears to have been a single woman in her late twenties. Between 1892 and 1900, out of 550 teachers, assistant teachers, and kindergartners appointed under civil service rules, some 312, a modest majority, were women. A dramatic shift was taking place, however, and by 1900 the Indian Office reported that of the 347 teachers employed, 286 were women."[109] But despite similarities in terms of gender and demographics, bonding did not always occur among teachers. Indeed, given the amount of time that employees spent among one another, and the fact that they were, for the most part, perfect strangers, there often existed tensions among members of the school workforce.[110] This is yet another reason why we cannot simply treat teachers or staff as an undifferentiated group, since in many cases disagreements arose based on personalities or school practices.

At all schools, Canadian and American, insufficient staff salaries presented a problem for recruitment and retention of qualified people. The 1920 AIS annual report noted that "the best people are not attracted by the meager salaries offered while the best employees in the service are constantly resigning to accept better positions outside."[111] Still, this did not mean that there were no caring or helpful teachers among U.S. boarding school staff. Indeed, young women recruited to fill the roles of teachers sometimes brought their own feminist beliefs, whether maternal, antimodernist, or liberal in orientation, to their interactions with students in the schools.[112] And some teachers served as inspirations and sources of cultural affirmation for students. The aforementioned Dorothy Dunn at SFIS was one teacher who appeared to be reluctant to subscribe to the broader assimilative project of the schools. As a student from SFIS recalled, "well, Dorothy didn't actually interfere with the culture of the Indian people. She was very careful not to pressure anybody into painting what their elders didn't want them to paint. She just told us we had freedom of our own thoughts, and whatever we painted was all right with her as long as it was pertaining to learning and also a few rules in the lessons that she put out and guidelines."[113]

Likewise, though not typically part of the teaching staff, Indigenous staff at the schools served as sources of succor and even resistance against the assimilative pull of the settler colonial mesh. In his memoir of life at FAIRS, Theodore Fontaine recalled the presence of Mrs. B., a Sagkeeng woman who helped in the laundry and kitchen and whose own children attended the school. Mrs. B. was restricted in her interactions with the students, but a glance from her could reinforce a sense of common community, yet it could also remind the children of their distance from that community.[114] Moreover, Fontaine later wondered if the theft of bread, which students engaged in to offset hunger induced by meager and poor-quality food at the school, was made possible by Mrs. B.'s placing bread strategically where they could reach it.[115] But in all the schools considered, Indigenous staff were relegated most often to subservient roles and had to wield such assistance from the margins rather than the positions of teacher, principal, or superintendent.[116]

Although not formally members of the boarding school staff, Indian agents in both the United States and Canada negotiated among the interests and influences of a variety of actors, including Indigenous groups, governments, churches and missionary societies, and business and corporate entities. They were also in frequent communication with superintendents and principals at Indigenous boarding schools, often serving as intermediaries between the government and schools. Indian agents played a role as well in offering inducements for children to attend boarding schools, either through threats (e.g., withdrawal of rations) or rewards (e.g., touting the health benefits of schools), and they assisted in evaluating the suitability of and preparing travel arrangements for children targeted for school admission. More generally, in Canada, the *Field Manual for Agency Superintendents* described their responsibilities in relation to residential schools as follows: "to assist in every way, the Principal of the residential school in the performance of his duties. He should co-operate with the principal in matters of repair and maintenance of the school, the attendance of children at the school, and the general administration of the educational unit."[117] The agent could also suggest that poorly performing teachers be relieved of their duties and had oversight of student admissions and dismissals.

However, the power of Indian agents was tempered by the influence of other parties involved in the schools. In Canada, for example, the Catholic Church sought to influence the choice of Indian agents near their schools for fear that Protestant agents would favor sending children to Protestant schools. Moreover, even when agents were aware of physical and sexual abuse in the schools, and inclined to intervene, they found themselves up against churches that preferred to handle these matters internally and a Department of Indian Affairs that ignored reports of harm against children.[118]

Likewise, the Indian agent in the United States was directed to encourage so-called progressives within Indigenous communities so that more traditional forces would not obstruct the progress of civilization. It was recorded in the regulations for the Indian service that "the chief duty of an agent is to induce his Indians to labor in civilized pursuits. To attain this end every possible influence should be brought to bear, and in proportion as it is attained, other things being equal, an agent's administration is successful or unsuccessful."[119] In addition to encouraging Indigenous persons to adopt agricultural and other means of livelihood, as well as discouraging behavior such as gambling or alcohol consumption, Indian agents fulfilled this requirement by influencing parents to send their children to day or boarding schools and by rounding up children truant from or refusing to attend said schools.[120] Margaret Jacobs details how Indian agents used a variety of inducements to strongly encourage schooling for children. These inducements included bribery, coercion, force, threat, trickery, claim of obligation, moral suasion, and withholding rations.[121]

PARENTS AND COMMUNITIES

On both sides of the border, Indigenous parents sought schooling for their children. Indigenous communities negotiated schools in treaty agreements and often viewed education as a means to adapt to the foreign culture overtaking their lands. However, the schooling offered seldom matched Indigenous visions of learning and adaptation.[122] When governments instead sought to mobilize schooling as an assimilative practice, Indigenous leaders and parents sometimes adapted to this maneuver by instructing their children to take what they could from the schools while preserving a sense of who they were.[123] This was true for Indigenous children in the American Southwest, who were often told to make such strategic use of European knowledge. In an interview transcript paraphrased by the interviewer, Herbert Talehaftewa remembered how his uncle warned him that,

> "when [the] time comes, you may be dragged to school, but there is one reason why we object to your going to school. We will give our consent to have only two Hopis educated. Everything will come in time; these two will be educated to talk for people; and if more Hopis learn to speak white man's tongue then there will be a lot of fighting." And he also said to me, "you'll be growing up in the midst of white people, but be careful—don't grab everything—you don't . . . have to take it. We'll have to pay it back."[124]

Contained in his uncle's warning is advice to learn the "white man's tongue" as a means to support the community. But young Herbert was also cautioned against fully embracing the "gift" of education, a gift accompanied by the symbolic violence of obligation to the federal government.[125]

Parents and communities resisted boarding schools in a variety of ways. They sometimes refused to send or return their children to the schools. They sent delegations to the schools, to Indian agents, or even to government centers to advocate their interests or protest what they thought was unfair treatment. They also wrote and signed petitions. For example, difficult conditions at FAIRS left Sagkeeng parents unhappy with the school. John L. Ross, a barrister and solicitor hired by Sergius Bruyere, a member of the Sagkeeng community, wrote in October 1920 to the superintendent of Indian Affairs to report that, for parents who sent their children to FAIRS, "their complaint is that there is very little or no book teaching at the . . . school. The priest or teacher compels the children to work all day in his garden, digging potatoes and in the threshing." He added that "their principal complaint appears to be with the teacher in charge of the school as they think that he is incompetent and is not a fit and proper person to be in charge of children."[126] Inspector J. R. Bunn, however, offered the government grounds to dismiss these complaints, saying that he had seen students doing good work at the blackboard. Moreover, he dismissed the source of the complaint: "Sergius Bruyere is rather a bright man, but his energy is directed along the complaining line. I have met him, and I have told him it would be better if he would help the school by helping the staff to maintain good discipline."[127]

School officials sought to overcome parental resistance through various strategies. They included withholding funds and resources as well as threats of arrest. In order to take his daughter from SFIS in the summer of 1905, Richard Tafoya was required to sign before witnesses a statement that read "I hereby promise to return SERAFINA TAFOYA to the U.S. Indian Industrial School, Santa Fe, New Mexico, promptly, Sept. 1, 1905, without cost to the Government, and failing to do so, I authorize the Superintendent, or his agent, to take said child above mentioned, and place her in said school, and I will offer no resistance or objection, delegating full guardianship and care of said child to the Superintendent of the Santa Fe U.S. Indian Industrial School." Serafina was returned to SFIS on September 1, just as promised.[128] And when in 1914 the governor of San Felipe Pueblo, Jose Domingo Valencia, came to power and promised the community that he would rid it of its day school and return it to traditional ways, he was placed under arrest by the superintendent of Pueblo day schools, P. T. Lonergan, who added to the charge his suspicion that the governor was permitting "immoral practices" to occur at fiestas, apparent, he claimed, by the number of children born nine months after the annual fiesta on May 1.[129]

All schools under consideration here thus engaged in practices intended to mitigate the influence of parents. At FAIRS, the proximity of the school to the reserve, and thus to parents, was construed as a problem by school staff. Inspector R. H. Cairns reported that "interference by the parents and guardians . . . is the chief source of trouble experienced by the school staff in maintaining discipline. The parents want to visit and talk to their children in a free and easy manner, and it is difficult to make them understand that they are causing trouble."[130] A year after this remark, Sagkeeng leaders attempted to gain access to and inspect FAIRS as well as another school to which their children had been sent. A letter of February 28, 1923, from Chief William Mann requested that the Department of Indian Affairs "kindly tell us if Chief and Councilors of the Band of this Reserve has any rights to see if the schools are well conducted by the teachers or the Principals."[131] J. D.

McLean, secretary of the department, responded on March 6, 1923, that the schools were under the auspices of the Roman Catholic and Anglican Churches, respectively, and chief and councilors possessed no authority to direct policy in this regard. If they had complaints, then they should bring them to the attention of Indian Affairs through the Indian agent. McLean noted in his last sentence that "it is the duty of yourself and the councilors to assist the principal and teachers in any way that you can in encouraging the Indian parents to send their children to school."[132]

Under these circumstances, Sagkeeng had fewer resources available to influence schooling than were available to the Pueblo, since their demands and threats often fell on deaf ears. Unlike the Pueblo, however, other Indigenous groups whose children attended AIS and SFIS showed similar signs of frustration at their powerlessness with respect to their children's education. Around 1884, a group of Utes from the northern part of New Mexico came to AIS to see their children just after the school had moved from its adobe buildings. Erna Fergusson alleged many were drunk as they occupied the dining room of the school and demanded better quarters for their children. The Indian agent from Santa Fe, who happened to be at AIS at the time, jumped up on a table and exhorted the men in Spanish, explaining to them that he represented the government and that the government would do terrible things to them if they did not cease their protest.[133] The risk of government violence was likely real to the Utes, engaged in conflict with the U.S. government between 1849 and 1923. At the time of their protest at AIS, they were still under close scrutiny in the aftermath of the 1879 killing of Indian Agent Nathan C. Meeker in White River, Colorado, who had threatened to call in the army on the Utes unless they submitted to assimilation.[134] The words of the Indian agent from Santa Fe thus possessed real force for the Utes.

For the Diné, access to children sent to school in New Mexico was made difficult by the distance and difficulty of travel. Therefore, the most potent resource that parents had was their ability to hide their children from school officials and police officers in their vast territory, thereby preventing child removals. Several Diné participants in the Doris Duke American Indian Oral History interviews spoke of how their parents hid them from the Navajo police, who were supposed to capture and send them to boarding schools. John Charlie, for example, recounted that "this is the way a lot of us think about ourselves, and today for myself I think of myself, I wish I went to school. I didn't went to school because of my parents. During the time when the school started, my father and mother used to hide me from the policemen. The policemen used to pick us up, they used to look for us. . . . Policemen used to look for children that are not in school."[135] His desire to attend boarding school notwithstanding, his parents kept him from apprehension.

In contrast, the Pueblo were able to use their proximity to the schools, experience with negotiating with three different colonial powers (Spanish, Mexican, and American), somewhat sedentary lifestyle, and agricultralism to present themselves as closer to civilization than other Indigenous groups and therefore more worthy of input into the lives of their children. As well, the Pueblo had an unusual status in their relations with the U.S. government. As full citizens of the United States under the Treaty of Guadalupe Hidalgo, the Pueblo could buy and sell land, and the U.S. government treated them as sovereign peoples. Given that they owned their land (albeit collectively rather than individually), the Pueblo presented a conundrum for the government in that they were already citizens and, to an extent, civilized Indians, making it difficult to apply to them laws created for those perceived as uncivilized Indians. This positioning was of some practical value when it came to placing demands on local boarding schools. But the exceptional status of the Pueblo also opened them to potential taxation. In 1904, a New Mexican court ruled that Pueblo persons could be taxed; however, Congress prevented the application of this ruling in 1905 when it created a legislative tax exemption for the Pueblo Indians. This legislation was enacted at the behest of the All Pueblos Council and its supporters, who feared that taxation would place many poor Pueblo farmers at risk of losing their lands for not being able to pay their taxes. Thus, it was only in the early twentieth century that Pueblo Indians, like other Indigenous groups in the United States, became wards of the state.[136] Nonetheless, the perception that the Pueblo were more civilized in the eyes of many whites likely granted them greater influence when interacting with the schools. As such, they were able to provoke reactions such as the following from Superintendent Andrew Viets at SFIS:

FIG. 4. Pueblo members visiting officials of the Albuquerque Indian School, ca. 1885

For instance, in all of my years of working with Indians before coming here I found without almost a single exception, that the Indian parent demands three things of the school and only three things. These demands are as follows, (1) My boy must be well fed. (2) He must be well clothed. (3) He must not be punished. Here they expect these three things and enforce their expectations emphatically with a resounding, continuous howl when these three points of etiquette are not complied with; but they demand more. When inspecting the industrial departments their criticisms are certainly just, if they are not generous. These huts which we call shops are not at all to their liking.[137]

Although Viets drew strategically on the concerns of Pueblo parents to try to obtain further resources from the government to improve his shops, that he credited these parents with a voice was remarkable at the time.

However, even groups who lacked the influence of the Pueblo in schooling matters sought recourse in acts of rebellion and violence, when all other pathways appeared to be closed. For example, one survivor who attended PLPIRS briefly in the late 1940s recalled that "I started school in Portage la Prairie in 1949. At the Portage Indian Residential School but after two months we got expelled because my Uncle went there and punched the principal because the principal had strapped his son [. . .]. And my uncle didn't like that, so he punched the principal, and all the family had to get out of the school. So that—after two months, I was out of that school."[138] Although such individual acts of resistance lack the force of collective action against the schools, they nonetheless further demonstrate that Indigenous parents and families did not meekly allow their children to be removed and abused by the schools.

STUDENTS

A variety of factors is said to have affected how individual students responded to their boarding school experiences. These factors include the background context, such as what they learned or knew about the schools prior to attending them; the student's perception of the reasons for attending the school, such as whether or not the student thought that he or she was being abandoned or singled out for a special purpose; the ways in which the student coped with or managed the experience while at the school; and the coping mechanisms available to the student after release from the school.[139] One means available for students to cope with and take ownership of the schooling process was through subtle and blatant acts of resistance.

Students resorted to similar forms of resistance and subversion on both sides of the border. Reports of food theft, whispered conversations in an Indigenous language, tricks, and practical jokes are equally pervasive among both American and Canadian boarding school narratives, and this resistance is reflected in the historical boarding school literature of both countries.[140] Subtle tactics, such as humor, dawdling, secret language use, and pranks, were deployed to resist the disciplinary structures of the schools. Other students rebelled and escaped from the schools using more dramatic strategies. A three-page list of misdemeanors from the 1928–29 school year at AIS includes offences such as automobile theft, shoplifting, truancy, intoxication, refusal to work, and one for "creating dissention among the students."[141]

Some scholars, such as J. R. Miller, Jacqueline Gresko, and Celia

Haig-Brown, emphasize how Indigenous children in Canada found such opportunities to challenge and subvert the authority of their captors. As well, they note how these children, with the education that they received, the networks that they formed, and their exposure to the settler world, were better placed to be the leaders of future generations of Indigenous peoples and to pursue justice for their communities.[142] Likewise, Sally McBeth identifies the same leadership phenomenon in U.S. schools, and scholars such as K. Tsianna Lomawaima, Clyde Ellis, and Brenda Child comment on the many ways that students found to resist assimilation.[143] Both Canadian and American authors note how, ultimately, boarding schools did much to reinforce Indigenous identity even though the intention was to destroy it. McBeth further argues that the schools served to reinforce rather than transform Indigenous identities as students associated with each other in terms of their Indigenous affiliations, and visits with family often reinforced such affiliations.[144]

For this reason, it is crucial to recognize in this discussion of genocidal processes that the targeted group, Indigenous children, did not passively submit to the settler colonial mesh. They sought to tear open this mesh to create gaps in which they could assert and perform their identities. And when all else failed, in both Canada and the United States, the most direct way for students to refuse their role in the assimilative project was to run away from school. In the following account, told by seventy-six-year-old Hopi-Hopi, a Diné from the Manuelito area, the runaways succeed in evading capture and being returned to the school. The account is recorded here in full detail to give an idea of the dramatic lengths to which some students went to try to escape the settler colonial mesh:

> While I was going to school at Santa Fe . . . I have done pretty good, I went as far as the fifth grade, . . . and then, there was some boys, talked me into run away from school. So that was what I had done, I ran away from school, . . . and I know which direction that I came from. I can go by the sun. I went around Mount Taylor and Sandia Mountain and on to Santa Fe. This is the way I know my way back to my home. . . .
>
> There was a big river running which they call the Rio Grande River, that runs through Albuquerque. . . . Before I ran away, I learned how

to swim at Santa Fe; I was practicing mostly every evening. Finally, I swim pretty good.

So then we made up our own minds, and we started out towards the mountains. We went the opposite way: we went towards west, towards the mountains. And we went up the mountain, and we circled around the school. That evening, we was still at the mountain, it was pretty warm, so we slept out. We didn't build no fire; we had some matches, but we were afraid to build a fire because we thought that they would catch us easy. We went about two miles that morning, circling around the Santa Fe school. We went on the north side of the school, and then we went right straight to the mountains from there on. To San Felipe Mountains. It took us pretty near a day to reach the mountains, and then from there on we follow the river down. We got to the river, and the river was pretty strong.

We walked a little ways without any clothes, just naked, and then we went into the woods. . . . There we untied our bundle, and where the wet part was, we had to dry it out in the sun and the wind. . . . We let it wait for about two or three hours. . . . We stayed on the hot sand without any clothes for two hours, and then we put our clothes back on. And then we still went southwards, along the side of the river. . . . It was on the other side of the dam, along towards our home side. So we went on, and I think they had a blood hound on our trail, but we went towards the mountain, for three or two days. . . . The bloodhound find our trail going the other way, towards the mountain, Santa Fe Mountains. They track us around I think.

We walked all day long; finally, we found the village what our friends told us that it was called Zia. . . . We got to Zia that evening, and we came to another house, another Indian house. There the Indian was very kind. . . . They talked to us in a kindly way. . . . So we stayed around there . . . for a night again, we told the truth, we said that we ran away from school. We heading back to the Navajo reservation. They told us that the Navajo reservation was not too far off from there. . . . It was just about sixty miles right straight, and I think it was Torreon what they were talking about.

People was good to us. . . . We was our own people then. Now we were in Navajo territory, they told us that there were more Navajos living from here on up to Tohatchi, so we were safe. . . . We wouldn't starve to death; so then we went on, that morning all we done was just walk right straight to the Tohatchi Mountain, there was nothing to be afraid of, no fences. . . . So we went on, we follow the Torreon Mountain all the way down towards the west. . . . We walked about a little better than twelve miles or ten miles, we rest there, and we took a nap. . . . It was warm, and then I think we slept about two or four hours, we feel a lot better then. We went on down alongside the mountain for about another ten miles. And then finally we found another camp then. From the morning, where we start from we walk about twenty miles. Taking our time, that was as far as man would make a day walking twenty miles.

It was past one week since we left Santa Fe, we got into Lake Valley, there was another Navajo village there. We stayed there for at least one whole day. From there on, there was nobody living between up to Tohatchi. So we had some relations of ours, that live at Lake Valley, that is why we stayed over a day, it was nine days there. [Then] we went that morning from there on, early in the morning, we went right straight to Tohatchi Mountain. We went across the flat all day long, and then it was moonlight, it was a full moon then, and we decided to walk the rest of the night back home, we went on, and that evening . . . the moon was shining pretty good with the moonlight. We was near the mountain there, and we know where we live, it was on the foot of the Tohatchi Mountain, and we walked from there. . . . And then we went on. . . . We was back home, where our real home was, around between 10:30 that we got back home that night.

We stayed around home, and then in the next four or five days we went from my aunt's place up to Tohatchi Mountain, way on top, top of the mountain. And I think the policeman came around, but we wasn't there, I think they told them that we wasn't back home yet, in the next fifteen days the policeman came again, and we told him that they were back, but we don't know where they are. . . . They just left here again. So we don't know just what their parents told the policemen. . So we were out at my aunt's place for two good months, and then three months, four months, five months, six months.

We stayed there at my aunt's place for six months, and one day we went back home to where our mother lives, and they said that the policemen never did show up again. And about the end of six months, was just about school out, and so we stayed around home from there on, we were not afraid of no police because I think they forgot us, they let us go. So we stayed around all that summer long.[145]

In this remembrance, the children evade capture thanks to both their own cunning and the assistance of strangers and family members. Their determination to stay at home and among their people is more than just a game or a temporary absence from their school. They are thorough and tactical in ensuring that they will not be returned to SFIS. Moreover, such efforts were not without risk, for children died, lost limbs to frostbite and other ailments, and faced other dangers when they ran away.[146] In the case of Alejandro Colaque, a boy from Jemez Pueblo who died while running away from SFIS in 1919, the cause of his death was unclear. He ran away with two other boys but fell behind when he complained of a sore knee. He was later found dead in the middle of the road, and it was suspected that he had perished from a combination of exhaustion and exposure to the elements.[147]

However, at times, running away was not resistance to the entire notion of schooling but resistance to one particular aspect—the restriction on movement. On occasion, students simply longed for time at home, after which they would return to school:

> Yeah, I remember the times when some of my friends (especially when we went to the Albuquerque Indian School when they transferred us)—some of my friends just took off because they couldn't get interested to the new school even though it was still an Indian school. . . . Personally, I took off a couple of times, just to see my family. I wanted to see my mom and dad. In those days I think things were kind of rough with everyone, including my family. But I didn't run away to get away from school. I ran away to see the family.[148]

In this case, personal matters related to family life and loneliness motivated escape as much as a desire to be away, once and for all, from the school. Such statements have led some to suggest that Pueblo students most often deserted the school simply to return home for special events or ceremonies and saw continuity between school and home community.[149] However, this claim is not entirely supported by archival documents. For example, in 1928–29, fifty students deserted AIS, and only five of them returned. Although a few of them were in their twenties, and therefore likely to be let go by school staff, the majority were between twelve and nineteen and would have been expected to return to school.[150]

Running away was also a frequent response to hardship at Canadian boarding schools. As noted above, on January 29, 1939, four senior girls ran away from PLPIRS. During their journey, their feet were badly frozen. They had run away in response to abuse by their matron, Mrs. Ross, and the principal, Mr. Jones, which included the matron's practice of hitting the girls on the head and the principal's practice of whipping them. In discussing the runaways with Indian Affairs, A. G. Hamilton reported Jones's complaints that the four girls had become heroes among the other children. He added that one of the four, Annie Assiniboine, had run away in 1948 as well. He then noted that Jones wanted to punish her by cutting her hair. Hamilton was unsure whether or not this was allowed, but Jones had argued that a lack of punishment led to further runaways.[151] Jones was directed not to exact too harsh a punishment on the girls, but revisiting this example reminds us that violence and suffering in the schools were powerful motivators for escape. After this point, students continued to run away from PLPIRS with great frequency. In 1950, the principal described running away as an "epidemic," and by 1964, it is estimated, 20 percent of students housed at PLPIRS ran away.[152]

In this chapter, four schools have been introduced as the foci for microlevel analysis. These schools have been placed at a lower meso-, or organizational, level of the settler colonial mesh and examined both as stand-alone schools and in their interactions with other schools. In addition, the principal actors at the microlevel in the schools—staff, parents and communities, and students—have been considered with respect to the variety of ways in which they engaged with forced assimilation. Some found ways to resist enrollment in this project and to lessen the genocidal violence of the settler colonial mesh, whereas others committed fully to assimilation. In the next three chapters, I will take a closer look at how these four schools enlisted various techniques and other actors in the project of assimilation and at how these techniques and other actors intensified, or lessened, the destructive impacts of these schools.

With this brief introduction to various lower meso- and microlevel actors from the settler colonial mesh, we gain a better sense of the complexity involved in carrying out settler colonial destruction. Local factors conditioned and transformed how the Indian Problem was addressed and resulted in novel applications of settler colonial violence as well as resistance. In the next three chapters, I will provide more specific examples of the techniques and actors enlisted in both carrying out and subverting settler colonialism's benevolent experiment in genocidal education.

5 | Discipline and Desire as Assimilative Techniques

This chapter and the next two continue the examination of meso- and microlevel factors that impacted the efficacy of the settler colonial mesh as it contracted and expanded across North America through the use of Indigenous boarding schools. In this chapter and the next, my focus is on a sample of the specific assimilative techniques used in these schools.[1] I borrow the term "technique" from the work of Michel Foucault, who, based on the Greek word *techne*, often used it interchangeably with "technology" to describe practical logics or rationalities directed toward specific ends.[2] In the context of this chapter, these rationalities took shape within the administrative space of a specific school and were thus adapted to a local resolution of the Indian Problem. These techniques were also responses to policy directions formulated at higher levels of the settler colonial mesh, and the general intent underlying such policies was typically the destruction of Indigenous groups as groups. However, as these tactics mutated to fit local circumstances, they were occasionally revised in response to the individual perspectives of school staff, or the vagaries of local conditions, or they were implemented in ways that produced opportunities for resistance and subversion. Such resistance and subversion allowed Indigenous peoples to overcome, to a degree, the assimilative force of government policy and to find spaces of what Gerald Vizenor refers to as "survivance," a term that combines the words *survival* and *resistance* to demarcate processes through which Indigenous peoples have countered assimilative pressures while also changing and adapting.[3]

The techniques discussed in this chapter include harsher interventions such as rigid discipline (e.g., martial, monastic, etiquette, work, and gender). However, the chapter also draws attention to subtler, desire-based means by which boarding schools sought to lure Indigenous children into an assimilated life. These "softer" techniques mobilize what Foucault refers to as a *technology of the self* rather than a *technology of domination*, and they are often read as being the products of Indigenous agency. The implication is that resistance from students and parents forced schools to find gentler means for educating Indigenous children.[4] Such a claim is not without merit. However, gentle techniques, perhaps initiated in response to Indigenous resistance, were also enlisted or redeployed in an effort to advance the project of Indigenous assimilation.

Discipline

"One of the primary objects of discipline is to fix; it is an anti-nomadic technique."[5]

Foucault's description of discipline as an "anti-nomadic technique" is apt when applied to Indigenous boarding schools. The perception among settler colonizers that Indigenous peoples ranged too freely over the land, preventing its acquisition and development by white settlers, was, as we have seen, at the core of the late-nineteenth-century and early-twentieth-century conceptualization of the Indian Problem. Indigenous boarding schools were one strategy among many for making Indigenous peoples more sedentary, limiting their movements, and reformulating their relationships to their territories.[6]

Foucault's use of the term "discipline," however, is different from that common in the Indigenous boarding school literature, where it is used to discuss corporal punishment.[7] In contrast, and in keeping with Foucault, I use the term here to describe the techniques employed in schools to shape behavior and provoke the embodiment of "civilized" habits.[8] This broader notion of discipline is captured in claims that borrow from sociologist Erving Goffman to describe Indigenous boarding schools as "total institutions."[9] Such institutions are isolated and enclosed spaces in which the institutionalized are subjected to near-complete control of their day-to-day lives.[10] But perhaps more evocative is the notion of "despotic discipline," which Foucault uses to describe the prison as a space in which an omnipresent discipline operates on the bodies of prisoners.[11] This is an "unceasing" discipline directed toward transforming "all aspects of the individual, his physical training, his aptitude for work, his everyday conduct, his moral aptitude, his state of mind."[12] Under such despotic discipline, reference to these assimilative institutions as schools, or their targets as "students," seems to grossly minimize the power operating therein. However, it is worth noting that throughout European history, schools have exhibited multiple disciplinary forms that overlap with those of other carceral institutions such as the workhouse, the orphanage, and the seminary. With this understanding in mind, no single categorization—e.g., prison, camp, or school—is going to adequately capture the cruel admixture of disciplinary forms present in boarding "schools;" instead, we must take a closer empirical look at how they manifested in particular settings.

But we must also recognize that visions of order—such as attempts to fit the Indigenous child within European society—are pursued and achieved by methods other than strict discipline. For this reason, I couple the concept of discipline in this chapter with that of desire. I do so to capture more than the use of reward as a disciplinary tool.[13] Rather, the emphasis on desire can show how pleasure and excitement were deployed, and operated in conjunction with discipline, as techniques to co-facilitate Indigenous assimilation.[14] I also consider gender discipline separately below, since the gendering practices of the schools were distinct and important and therefore deserve independent treatment.

Although deriving from a place of mutual influence, Indigenous boarding schools in the United States and Canada were erected on somewhat different disciplinary models. Whereas Lieutenant Richard Pratt's militarism influenced U.S. boarding school design and internal organization in the late 1800s,[15] only to be gradually replaced in the early decades of the twentieth century by managerial technologies of governance more typical of the professionalized and expert-driven Indian bureaucracy, monastic (or religious) modes of discipline were prominent and lasting in the Canadian schools.[16]

Monastic and martial forms of discipline share many similar qualities: both attempt to use the distribution of space and time to work on their subjects; each focuses on the minutiae or details of the body, including its presentation and movement; and they bring to bear on their subjects a variety of tactics intended to shape character. However, there are also subtle differences. Of monastic discipline, Foucault writes that its "function was to obtain renunciations rather than increases in utility and which, although they involved obedience to others, had as their principal aim an increase of mastery of each individual over his own body."[17] In contrast, of martial discipline, he notes that "the soldier has become something that can be made; out of a formless clay, an inapt body, the machine required can be constructed; posture is gradually corrected; a calculated constraint runs through each part of the body, mastering it, making it pliable, ready at all times, turning silently into the automatism of habit."[18] There are two obvious differences here. First, the monastic model is directed toward developing an internalized sense of bodily regulation. The harshness of monastic discipline was therefore intended to reconstitute the Indigenous subject as a self-governing member of the flock who would thereafter require only the gentle nudge of the shepherd. In contrast, the martial model creates the disciplined body through externally imposed habituation trained through the orders of the superior officer. Second, martial discipline works to produce a subject who is usable (e.g., in war), whereas monastic discipline responds more to religious doctrine than to any readily discernible utility.[19] Thus, the two disciplinary styles do result, at times, in different emphases or tactics within a project such as Indigenous assimilation. As well, each disciplinary model rests on a different institutional structure (i.e., organized religion and the military), and these structures were important with respect to how boarding schools operated in the United States and Canada.

Nonetheless, these different disciplinary styles often resulted in similar treatment of Indigenous students: loss of all emblems of cultural identity upon entry into the school, prohibitions against the use of Indigenous languages, a regimented timetable with days split between education (often religious and including debasement of Indigenous cultures) and manual labor, and severe punishments for perceived indiscretions. Basil Johnston captures well the total of discipline in Indigenous boarding schools: "Bells and whistles, gongs and clappers represent everything connected with sound management—order, authority, discipline, efficiency, system, organization, schedule, regimentation, conformity—and may in themselves be necessary and desirable. But they also symbolize conditions, harmony and states that must be established in order to have efficient management: obedience, conformity, dependence, subservience, uniformity, docility, surrender. In the end it is the individual who must be made to conform, who must be made to bend to the will of another."[20] Whether primarily martial or monastic in origin, the disciplinary systems in both Canadian and American Indigenous boarding schools operated to impose a working order on the students assembled within their walls. This was partly because techniques of ordering were required when contending with such large numbers of students.[21] However, more importantly, in order to be shaped into non-Indians, the students had to be made pliable.

In the early years of the schools, disciplinary strategies were motivated by a perception that Indigenous children lacked discipline.[22] According to Samuel C. Armstrong, the superintendent of the Hampton Institute, military discipline was necessary in the schools because it "enforces promptness, accuracy and obedience and goes further than any other influence could do to instill in the minds of the students what both the Negro and Indian sadly lack, a knowledge of the value of time."[23] Likewise, monastic forms of discipline were perceived to be necessary to save the souls of Indigenous students. As late as the 1940s, the Catholic Hierarchy of Canada argued that "we are of the opinion that the daily discipline in force in our residential schools, which calls for rising at a given hour, spiritual exercises also at a stated time, plus breakfast, dinner and supper, intermingled with hours of class-work and recreation, have in themselves more power to stabilize the nomadic habits of our Indian brethren than any other system of education."[24] In this manner, nomadism was viewed as a form of indiscipline that could only be corrected through sedentarization wrought by militaristic or monastic means.[25]

The spiritual component of this disciplinary timetable was important to the denominations running Indigenous boarding schools in Canada, and it was particularly a point of emphasis for Roman Catholic schools. This emphasis occurred most when the state sought to intervene and reduce the amount of religious training that took place in the schools. In this respect, in 1964, the federal government requested changes to religious instruction at FAIRS. In response, Principal Jalbert took issue with the notion that the period of catechism should be moved from 9 a.m. to 3 p.m., at the end of the school day, so that it would not interfere with the hours of education. Jalbert argued that "religion is the most important subject in the school programme. It should get priority. The Department stresses the need of vocational guidance. This is good. But vocational guidance without a good religious foundation produces people who evaluate everything in dollars and cents."[26]

The role played by the timetable in disciplining Indigenous children in the schools is clear in the quotations above, and it was a notable commonality in both American and Canadian boarding schools. Although the content of the timetable could differ, in both countries emphasis was placed on the strict temporal regulation of student activities. Such temporal regulation is a component of any educational environment, but in Indigenous boarding schools this organizational strategy was intended not simply to arrange the Indigenous students for effective management but also sought to reorient them to European notions of time. Whereas prayer and catechism were prominent in Canadian Roman Catholic–run school timetables, the 1914–15 calendar for AIS shows a more militaristic orientation:

Daily Programme a.m.

Reveille 6:00
Morning Roll Call 6:35
Breakfast 6:45
Care of Rooms 7:20
Industrial Departments —
Instructive Work 7:30
Productive Work 7:30
Athletics for Morning Pupils. 7:30
Academic Departments Open 8:45
All Departments Close 11:30
Dinner 12:00

Daily Programme p.m.

Industrial Departments—
    Instructive Work 1:00
    Productive Work 1:00
    Academic Departments Open 1:15
    Academic Departments Close 4:00
    Athletics for Afternoon Pupils 4:10
    Industrial Departments Close 5:00
    Supper 5:30
    Band Practice 6:00–7:00
    Evening Work 7:00–7:45
    Bugle to Retire 8:00
    Taps . . . . 8:30[27]

The student's day was punctuated by those familiar moments of military life: reveille, roll call, the making of beds, athletics, and the bugle to sound the end of the day.

Likewise, Pratt's initial experiment in Indian education at Fort Marion was an exercise in martial discipline, with the students treated like army recruits, even to the point that they wore Civil War Union blue uniforms and were drilled in marching.[28] Pratt continued this practice at Carlisle, where he noted that

> our 185 boys are divided into three companies, having a first sergeant, three sergeants, and four corporals for each company. In suitable weather, they are instructed in the primary movements and setting up process of army tactics. This is invaluable on account of health and discipline. A sergeant, a corporal, and four boys are detailed in their order daily for guard duty, but during the night they watch over our grounds as protection against fire and improper coming and going.[29]

Superintendent Cart at SFIS agreed with Armstrong, Pratt, and others with respect to the need for military discipline at Indigenous boarding schools. On May 27, 1891, he wrote to the commissioner of Indian Affairs and requested that he be sent a copy of "The New Drill Regulations for

FIG. 5. Class of boys in uniform at Albuquerque Indian School, ca. 1900

the Army," for "I consider any kind of military drill an aid in disciplining a school."[30] In 1910, Superintendent Crandall at SFIS would write to the Office of Indian Affairs to request that rifles be made available for his pupils to use when drilling.[31] Similarly, military discipline was evident in the early years of AIS. A reporter's description of movement among classes at AIS in 1885 is telling of the discipline that existed there: "Classes are constantly moving about from room to room at regular intervals with the orderly precision of squads of marching soldiers. They are governed by bell taps, and there is not near so much scramble and confusion in their movement as there are among white children of our public schools."[32]

This emphasis on military forms of discipline did not mean that monastic discipline was absent from Indigenous boarding schools in New Mexico. At SFIS, the Annual School Calendar for 1918–19 shows that students were scheduled to practice the Christian faith, whether Catholic or Protestant, on Sunday mornings as well as during a Monday evening hour of religious instruction. Time was also made for Catholic students to attend confessional on Saturdays.[33] But daily life at these schools, at least in their early years, was set by a military rather than monastic rhythm.

This militaristic discipline also served to ready students for involvement in the U.S. military. Students from AIS and SFIS enlisted in the U.S. Army in large numbers during both the First and the Second World Wars. It was thought that the discipline of the schools made the transition to soldiering easier for them.[34] In 1918, Superintendent Rueben Perry at AIS expressed his pride at how well AIS students fared as soldiers when he commented on how "the training in boarding school has been very helpful to them."[35] In later years, several students also suggested that their time at boarding schools had prepared them for military service.[36] Moreover, hearing about the experiences of returning Indigenous soldiers, and their earlier experiences at boarding schools, often enticed Indigenous youth to attend the schools. Diné children were said to have been inspired to enroll in school by soldiers returning from the Second World War who told the children stories of their adventures and convinced them that there was much to learn in the world.[37] And militaristic discipline was part of the attraction of boarding schools for some children. Sally Hyer notes that "many Pueblo students admired the cooperative, unified effort of hundreds of students moving together. As at home in the Pueblos, teamwork and collaboration were more important than individualism."[38]

Yet the military model in U.S. boarding schools did not have the backing of an upper mesolevel institutional matrix to support its continuation. Although several principals and school workers had military backgrounds, the military itself was not a primary actor in delivering education. Therefore, managerial technologies of control came to replace militaristic forms since this organizational logic of the civil service was much more entrenched at the mesolevel of the American Indian bureaucracy. Advances in state understandings of how to best govern and manage various populations circulated among government departments and found their way into the Bureau of Indian Affairs. Under this managerialism, self-regulatory schemes held great appeal since they removed the constant demands of staff supervision by enlisting students in their own governance. For example, in the 1920s, student councils were formed at AIS and SFIS to replace more punitive systems of student discipline. As well, students were assigned tasks such as hallway patrol and grounds supervision to ensure that both spaces were kept neat and orderly.[39]

But this transition from military discipline to managerial governance happened more quickly at some schools than others in the American Indigenous boarding school system. For example, AIS abolished its military system in 1924, eight years before it was formally discontinued by the BIA, and replaced it with a model of student self-governance.[40] However, often such councils were still disciplinary and mimicked the harsh tones of military school regulation. For example, when the Isleta Boys and Girls Council met on April 14, 1932, to consider the case of Andy Abeita, whose offence was to go home every Friday and appear back at school late on Monday, council members gave him a stern lecture. They expressed a great deal of resentment: "All of us would like to go home just as well as he does." But the students also made a point of reminding Andy of his responsibility to his school and his education. In the end, with the help of the principal, Mrs. Harrington, the council decided that Andy alone, and not his father, was to blame for his actions.[41]

Ted Jojola, an Isleta Pueblo scholar, argues that, "in Albuquerque, Pratt's approach was short-lived. Almost immediately, pueblo parents began keeping their children home. A lawsuit was filed on behalf of an Isleta boy who was prevented from leaving the school.[42] The parents prevailed and the school quickly softened its militaristic tone."[43] Yet militaristic discipline did not disappear entirely from the AIS campus; instead, it mutated into a new form. In 1932, Superintendent Perry responded to a letter from the commissioner of Indian Affairs asking about reports that military parades were practiced on Sundays at AIS. Perry retorted that the Sunday program could hardly be considered military. It consisted of the pupils lining up at 2:30 p.m. for a doctor's inspection, during which fingernails and clothes were inspected—but for hygienic rather than disciplinary purposes. During the inspection, the school band played; after the inspection, students marched to the athletic field, where they practiced drills for five minutes. The entire program, Perry noted, lasted only forty-five minutes.[44] Although perhaps technically nonmilitary, such inspections continued to enact the "normalizing gaze"—the ritual of observation and correction—that is the form and function of the military parade.[45]

FIG. 6. Students standing at attention at Albuquerque Indian School, ca. 1910

Given this transformation of military discipline into medical discipline, as well as the new techniques designed to foster regulation through self-governance, it can be tricky to precisely mark the end of military discipline in New Mexican Indigenous boarding schools. However, abundantly clear is that monastic models of discipline were far more persistent throughout the history of the Indigenous boarding schools in Manitoba under consideration here. The Christian denominations charged with the delivery of schooling in Canada formed an institutional matrix with vested interests in the continuation of schooling and the delivery of religious teaching through the schools. This is evident in moments of crisis or concern at specific schools, when one sees higher-echelon church administrators intervening on behalf of staff at the school in order to preserve monastic practices. For instance, when the federal government rebuked Superintendent Jones at PLPIRS in 1949 for his heavy-handed punishments of Rowena Smoke and the other girls discussed at the end of chapter 4, Reverend Dorey, secretary for the United Church Board of Home Missions, wrote to the superintendent of

Indian education and argued that, "if some of the officials of the Department had to manage the schools, with the difficult children that come to them, the chances are that they would have more rather than fewer restrictive measures," and he suggested that "too much weight" was being given to pupil testimony.[46]

Thus, while martial discipline gradually faded from U.S. boarding schools during the 1920s and 1930s, monastic discipline continued well into the 1950s and 1960s in Canada. At the Oblate schools, for example, the strictures of the Durieu system were still felt. As Miller describes this system, "this regime, named after Oblate Paul Durieu, employed methods of total control over mission Indians for the purpose of effecting a permanent conversion to Christian religious values and practices. The Durieu system aimed at eradicating all unchristian behaviour by means of strict rules, stern punishments for transgressors, and use of Indian informers and watchmen as proctors to ensure conformity and inflict punishments as necessary."[47] This emphasis on monastic discipline, however, does not suggest that martial strategies of discipline were absent at Canadian schools,[48] only that they were secondary to religious forms of discipline.

Monastic ideals of silence were observed in Canadian schools, especially the Roman Catholic schools. In particular, meals were taken without chatter.[49] Silence was enforced at other times and at Presbyterian schools. Gladys Hearns, who attended PLPIRS in the later 1930s and early 1940s, remembered one instance: "Like my sister we were ironing in the laundry and, you know, talking and having fun and the supervisor said, 'no talking, no having fun. You're not supposed to do that.' My sister was a chatterbox, she kept on. She came in and taped her mouth with masking tape. I wanted to murder that woman."[50]

As well, at a Catholic boarding school like FAIRS, prayer and confession were regular parts of the disciplinary regime. Reflecting on his time at FAIRS in the 1930s, Joseph Boubard reported that he "went to school so early [in life], [I] don't remember much about depression days. Didn't learn much at school. Lot of praying."[51] Likewise, Leo Morrisseau, who attended FAIRS in the 1940s, remembered that "pray, pray, that's all I used to learn in that school, is praying."[52] School inspector B. Warkentin noted the continuance of monastic discipline at FAIRS into the early 1940s: "What has been wrong, if I may presume to criticize, is that church authorities have been and are concerned about saving the Indian's soul. . . . Instructors shall not destroy the excellence of the Indian character by ill-advised behavior or by the teaching of incomprehensible and disputed dogma. Our aim always should be to build on the existing foundation rather than to substitute a new basis."[53] Warkentin's assessment should be taken as a rebuke not of assimilative discipline in Indigenous boarding schools but of the monastic nature of this discipline.

At FAIRS, Roman Catholic control over the school, sustained by isolation from regular inspection, as well as reinforcement from Catholic institutional networks, meant a much longer experience of monastic discipline than was the case for martial discipline in New Mexico. This is evident when one looks at levels of tolerance of Indigenous dances on both sides of the border. During the 1920s, a period when Superintendents Perry (AIS) and DeHuff (SFIS) called on the BIA to be more tolerant of Indian dances and fiestas, the principals of Roman Catholic boarding schools demanded that the Canadian government remain vigilant regarding the prohibition of Indian dancing: "Several people have desired us to countenance the dances of the Indians and to observe their festivals; but their habits, being the result of a free and easy mode of living, cannot conform to the intense struggle for life which our social conditions require. This has to be kept in mind for the training of new generations."[54]

The discussion of dancing also demonstrates how discipline was not simply contained within the regulatory space of the boarding school but also emanated out from it, seeking to find purchase in Indigenous communities. As Foucault notes, this has long been the objective of the Christian school, but it found new purpose when adopted within the project of assimilation: "Thus the Christian School must not simply train docile children; it must also make it possible to supervise the parents, to gain information as to their way of life, their resources, their piety, their morals. The school tends to constitute minute social observatories that penetrate even to the adults and exercise regular supervision over them."[55] In this respect, Indigenous boarding schools implemented a variety of technologies designed to extend discipline past the school gates to reach Indigenous parents and communities: record keeping on the parents' religion and employment; visits to the community to observe students and their homes during periods when school was not in session; severe admonishment when parents did not abide by the school schedule and returned their children late or asked that they be returned home during the school year; and encouragement that students take their lessons into their homes and communities and demand civilized behavior among their parents.

This proselytizing function of the schools was apparent not only in the more monastic Canadian schools. Indigenous students in the United States were also subject to efforts to ensure that they maintained their lessons of assimilation within and brought them to bear upon their home communities. For example, on November 8, 1897, Superintendent of Indian Schools William H. Hailman sent a circular to U.S. Indian agents stating the Department of the Interior's desire that "self-help" associations be formed for returning students and progressive Indians on each reserve.[56] Hailman noted that

> the chief objects of such associations should be the study of the resources of their respective reservations, to aid each other in the development of these resources by encouraging individual and joint enterprise, to seek profitable markets for the products of their labor and enterprise, to seek employment and settlement for their members in districts adjoining the reservation, to foster thrift by the establishment of savings institutions, to organize and encourage means for rational social entertainment, to encourage the formation of religious and ethical societies, to support one another in resisting the pressure of tribal customs and to receive and guide Indian youth that may from time to time return to the reservation from Indian Schools.[57]

In short, the goal was to delegate to former students the normalizing work of facilitating and reinforcing the lessons and objectives of the school within the home community. This externalizing ambition of the schools would continue throughout their histories on both sides of the border. For instance, in 1939, senior students at AIS were surveyed and asked to consider the question "what do you feel that you can bring to your people to improve their status?" One senior responded that "I would like to be among my own people so as to help them to improve their homes, clothes, and feed their families in a proper way."[58] This was the correct and expected answer to such a question.

Two areas in which the monastic and military disciplinary strategies also met and found common purpose were manners and work. In both American and Canadian Indigenous boarding schools, great efforts were made to reshape the bodies of Indigenous children, providing them with the habits of civilized life while also training their bodies for the farms and factories of the North American economy. With respect to embodying civilized habits, the "before" and "after" pictures manufactured by boarding schools in both countries were emblematic of this disciplinary quest. During their initial experiments with Indian industrial schooling, Armstrong and Pratt introduced such pictures to advertise the assimilative efficacy of their schools.[59] These photographic displays were later used in Canada as well to promote the transformative power of the schools. The photographs were intended to illustrate to all audiences that Indigenous children could be cultivated into European citizens through their immersion in assimilative education. In one of the most well-known Canadian photographs, the "wildness" of Thomas Moore as he posed soon after his entry into the Regina Indian Industrial School in 1874, complete with his toy pistol, traditional Cree dress, and leaning against an animal skin, is juxtaposed with the reformed Thomas Moore, a figure of European propriety in his formal attire and bodily comportment.

Horror was often expressed with respect to the everyday habits of Indigenous peoples, which were considered unclean and unsanitary. In particular, in the early days of Indigenous boarding schools in the American Southwest, there was frequent mention of the eating habits of Pueblo children, disparaged for dining on the floor and not using cutlery. Clemente Vigil, from Nambe Pueblo, recalled his introduction to European concepts of etiquette:

They never had much dance [during his time at SFIS, which he attended after several years at a day school], like they do now. . . . But one good thing that they had in Santa Fe . . . was [a] home economics . . . department where the girls learned how to cook, sew, and then every so often they would get about eight boys and about eight girls, and they would teach them how to use the table how to eat . . . you know with forks and knives. . . . Yeah, and that was lesson that would teach us that, . . . and we would learn how to eat at the table.[60]

But the attempt to shape Indigenous manners did not entirely disappear with transformations in the administration of the U.S. schools. Although the 1930s brought more respect for and understanding of Indigenous cultures to the BIA, boarding schools in New Mexico still worked on the habits of Indigenous students, an effort pursued with renewed vigor after the Second World War. Indeed, into the 1960s, discipline for citizenship and for the manufacture of an American moral habitus was still evident in the training offered at AIS. The 1962–63 Regular Academic Program lists "training for citizenship" as the number one goal of the institution. This goal is followed by concerns about academic and advanced training, but later in the list priority is given to the development of "worthwhile leisure-time activities" and "good helath [sic] habits and practices."[61]

Cleanliness was also a topic of education in Canada. John Milloy notes that in 1896 the following lesson plans characterized Canadian residential schools:

> In the first year, Standard I, pupils were to be taught "the practice of cleanliness, obedience, respect, order, neatness." In Standard II, they were to learn "Right and Wrong. Truth" and a "Continuance of proper appearance and behaviour." In Standard III, they would "Develop the reasons for proper appearance and behaviour" in addition to "Independence and Self-respect." Standard IV was "Industry, Honesty, Thrift," while Standard V introduced "Patriotism. . . . Self-maintenance. Charity. Pauperism. . . ." The final standard was the most sophisticated and aggressive. Pupils were to be brought to confront the differences in "Indian and white life, . . . [the] evils of Indian isolation, labour, the law of life, . . . relations of the sexes as to labour, . . . [and] home and public duties."[62]

In this passage, the advanced stages of schooling are more explicit in their lessons that disparage Indian ways of life, but even in the most mundane lessons on the practices of neatness and cleanliness is the implicit message that Indigenous practices are filthy, and it was not uncommon for returning children to experience a feeling of disgust toward the habits of their parents and other community members. This was true in both the United States and Canada.

At FAIRS, new students in some periods were acclimatized to the manners, styles, and discipline of the school by an older mentor. A student from the 1960s discussed this arrangement:

> I was immediately assigned a mentor to show me the ropes of living a firmly structured boarding school life. At first, not one of the older boys would volunteer to be my mentor, but finally one stepped forward and agreed. He was a good mentor. I remember him well, still today he's a good friend of mine. After fixing our beds, it was time to hit the showers. It was the first time I ever took a shower in this way—a whole bunch of us boys in our gitch in one big shower. Although it's somewhat strange, I enjoyed the shower very much. It felt good to be squeaky clean. After the shower, it was time to brush our teeth and comb our hair. My mentor would help me comb my hair, over to the side, as it was the proper fashion at the time. He also showed me how to brush my teeth properly.[63]

In such instances, each child would find his or her habits coordinated down to the finest detail, and the children were expected to internalize these habits to override those of their home communities, now cast as unclean.[64]

The training of the habits of civilization cannot be entirely separated from the training for work. Because Indigenous peoples were conceived through the Indian Problem to be obstacles to nation building, industry, and economy, the reformation of Indigenous children as citizens and workers went hand in hand. Their regulation by the timetable, as well as their training in practices of self-care, prepared them for entry into the workforce, where they would contribute to commodity production by day and then return home to ensure that their health and energy were guaranteed for the next day's work. However, in the United States and Canada, the ways in which Indigenous peoples were disciplined for work changed over time. Although in both countries there was some initial suggestion that Indigenous children were sufficiently malleable that they could eventually be readied for regular jobs, a racist pessimism eventually took hold, and the students were instead readied for more menial forms of labor thought to be more appropriate to their evolutionary level.[65]

Of course, student vocational training was ostensibly about preparation for the job market, since it served more often than not to provide the labor needed to maintain the boarding schools.[66] A school inspector at PLPIRS remarked on this fact in 1943:

> I am not satisfied with the present system of half-day classes in the senior room. I would be agreeable to this arrangement if I felt that the children were receiving vocational training during this time they are free but this is not the case. The girls are employed largely in scrubbing and the boys in farm chores and I question the value of this as educational training . . . but I suppose that due to the shortage of labor, it is necessary to employ the children on those matters which should rightly be done by hired labor.[67]

Despite this focus on school maintenance, work discipline was prominent in the industrial, domestic, and agricultural training of the students. As Miller notes, "the requirement that students carry out half a day's work would mould them for the Euro-Canadian world of work, in which clocks, whistles, and schedules were becoming dominant, while simultaneously subsidizing the operation of schools."[68]

But work discipline became more narrowly focused in the early twentieth century in the United States and soon thereafter in Canada as racist social evolutionary thinking became dominant among the respective Indian bureaucracies. Indigenous children were no longer viewed as blank slates on which civilization could be written; instead, they were understood to be bound by their indigeneity and therefore only able to move so far along the path toward civilization. For this reason, vocational training was prioritized in boarding schools, and this training was to be of a sort that would actually be useful to the purported needs of the Indian. Along these lines, in 1901, Superintendent of Indian Schools Estelle Reel sought to reform the U.S. boarding school curriculum to better equip and prepare Indian students for more limited future labor opportunities. Her curriculum placed heavy emphasis on disciplining the students for menial jobs. As Reel noted in her 1901 annual report, "I have just completed a course covering thirty-one subjects. Aside from the literary branches, the course embraces instruction in agriculture, baking, basketry, blacksmithing, carpentry, cooking, dairying, engineering, gardening, harness making, housekeeping, laundering, printing, painting, sewing, shoemaking, tailoring, and upholstering."[69] Literary and academic instruction was thus to be less favored under her new curriculum than training in basic forms of labor.

This revised curriculum found application at schools such as SFIS, where the 1913 annual report stressed that, "realizing the importance of farming, gardening, and the care of stock to the Pueblo Indians, special attention is paid to these industries, and so far as practicable most of the boys during their term at the school have an opportunity to learn much about these lines of work."[70] Here, rather than simply listing the sort of training on offer, the school superintendent focused on how this training matched the work that Pueblo communities were known to perform. Yet Reel's vision of Indigenous schooling, readily apparent in 1900 when Reel scolded the Chemewa, Oregon, boarding school for wasting time on piano lessons for an Indigenous girl,[71] did not permanently stamp out literary and artistic pursuits at all boarding schools. For example, in 1914, when Cato Sells was the Indian commissioner and still committed to the same principles as those that influenced Reel and her commissioner, Francis Leung, AIS was home to two literary societies and a twenty-six-piece band.[72] By 1917, there were four literary societies. The programs of these societies included songs, declamations, essays, orations, and debates.[73]

But this should not give one the impression that academic and artistic pursuits were placed on a level equal to that of labor discipline. Although the post–Meriam Report 1930s and 1940s brought to schools such as AIS and SFIS an increased appreciation for Indian cultures and arts, work discipline still featured heavily in school curricula. Students were required to spend much of the day learning trades and performing the labor that kept their school operational.[74] Katherine Augustine, who attended AIS in the 1940s, for example, recalled how work discipline overshadowed academic education while she was there: "What I really wanted to learn while I was at school was math, world history, geography, literature and more of the English language. However, our classes were structured so that half of our time was spent doing menial tasks—farming and dairy work for the boys, kitchen and dining-room chores for the girls."[75]

In both the United States and Canada, Pratt's outing program was utilized to expand work discipline. In Manitoba and New Mexico, the program was directed less toward familiarizing students with civilized life than toward availing them to the white community as a source of cheap labor. For example, at AIS, the outing program engaged students in paid work on weekends and during summer vacations. In 1910, fifty male pupils were sent to work in the beet fields of Colorado over the summer.[76] Female students, in contrast, were hired for domestic work. Once the girls accepted such work, it was difficult for them to extricate themselves and return to their communities. Rosalie Archulet and Virginia Montoya wrote to Superintendent DeHuff on August 11, 1918, and requested that they be allowed to return home "for a rest."[77] DeHuff responded tersely that the girls had promised to work for their employer the entire summer and that they needed to respect her needs. He added, "I frankly can't see any reason why you should go home at all this vacation. I understand, of course, how much your people would like to have you with them; but you are making a little money and are doing all right. I would suggest that you arrange to spend all of the next long vacation at home."[78] Moreover, after Rosalie managed to convince her employer to let her return home, DeHuff remarked that "the girl has simply gotten restless, like all other Indians do sooner or later. They can't stick to a job to save their lives, unless they are kept away from their home environment long enough to forget it."[79]

What can be taken from the above illustrations of assimilative discipline is that the Canadian system was less open to innovations and adaptations when it came to student discipline. Various degrees of monastic discipline characterized most periods of the Canadian Indigenous boarding schools under consideration here, whereas the American schools that I reviewed witnessed movement from militaristic to managerial forms of regulation. However, in both the United States and Canada, and in particular in New Mexico and Manitoba, disciplinary strategies around work and the habits of European civilization and citizenship did not disappear entirely from Indigenous boarding schools, for the basic purpose of schooling as a disciplinary institution for the production of workers and citizens was always imposed on Indigenous students. However, just as this discipline was ever present, so too was resistance to it. As the story of Rosalie Archulet and Virginia Montoya above attests, students did not necessarily become docile bodies for martial, monastic, civilizing, or work discipline. Instead, they sought ways to disrupt the imposition of techniques such as monastic silence or the order of the timetable. In such a context, running away, or even suicide, were ultimate responses to the boarding school project of despotic discipline. In other cases, however, students responded by adapting to this discipline, such as those pleased to have the opportunity to work and earn money through the outing system, even if that system was designed to exploit student labor and impose work discipline.[80]

Desire

Foucault notes that, "in discipline, punishment is only one element of a double system: gratification-punishment."[81] Here he refers to the coupling of reward and penalty in shaping behavior; however, in a context of assimilative discipline, reward is only one element of the tactic of gratification. Indeed, schools sought to play on the wants of and instill desires within Indigenous children.[82] Discipline was complemented by a regulated desire. Limited tactile, social, aural, athletic, and other pleasures were made available to attract students to the school environment. Along these lines, Superintendent of Indian Schools Estelle Reel wrote, in her 1904 annual report, of the girls at AIS who were so desperate to weave that they converted chairs and other objects into looms. Rather than discourage such traditional practices, Reel argued that this knowledge of the pleasure that the Indian girl took in weaving could be used to foster her insertion into American life: namely, by encouraging her to use her traditional arts, and the pleasures associated with the textures and creativity of weaving, as a means to earn income. Reel wrote that "the arts and crafts of the Indian have a far greater value than is generally known, and in many sections of the country they become efficient aids to him in earning a livelihood."[83] Earlier, in an 1896 address to the Mohonk Indian Conference, Merrill Gates, then the president of Amherst University, and the future chairman of the Board of Indian Commissioners,[84] similarly remarked that

> we need to *awaken in him wants*. In his dull savagery he must be touched by the wings of the divine angel of discontent. Then he begins to look forward, to reach out. The desire for property of his own may become an

FIG. 7. Young girls attending sewing class at Albuquerque Indian School, ca. 1910

intense educating force. The wish for a home of his own awakens him to new efforts. Discontent with the tepee and the starving rations of the Indian camp in winter is needed to get the Indian out of the blanket and into trousers,—and trousers with a pocket in them, and with a *pocket that aches to be filled with dollars!*[85]

For Gates, the pathway from reservation to civilized life was to be illuminated by cultivating Indigenous desires for all that civilized life had to offer. This sort of thinking about the seduction of Western culture occurred on both sides of the Canada-U.S. border, but it was placed more regularly into practice, and appears to have had greater resonance, in the melting pot of American acquisitive capitalism.

Before exploring the use of desire, I should note that discipline and desire are not oppositional categories. Discipline can both fulfill certain desires—for regularity, for order—and offer attractions—the cohesion of marching, the power of the uniform. Several students interviewed after their stints at Indigenous boarding schools spoke fondly of the discipline:

That school was just a strict school, it was like a military school. I like it that way because there is discipline, you just can't do anything wrong. . . . There was war going on at that time, probably that was the reason. We used to go out in the field in the morning before breakfast, rain or shine, we used to drill every morning, military training, like the soldiers do in actual combat zones, and we knew how to handle guns.[86]

As well, some students had their desires met simply through the busy schedule of the school. Lillian Kennedy, who had attended FAIRS, recalled positively how she had always been active while at the residential school:

I'm glad I went to residential school. Like I said, I learnt lots from there. And the, the, I like the priests and the nuns and the teachers that I had over there, they were good to me. And I was, I enjoyed everything in the school; at the residential school. We went for rides during the summer, or in the winter we went for walks. We never just sat around, we did everything all the time. We weren't bored. To this day I don't know what bored means 'cause we did everything. We, we never sat around.[87]

Jacqueline Fear-Segal is among the few scholars to identify the role that desire, or seduction, played in Indigenous education. Drawing from Stephan Lukes, she notes that, "in an intimidation/seduction dialectic, the subject is made aware of implied force yet is often seduced into connivance or even admiration—simultaneously belittled and impressed, he or she internalizes oppression."[88] Indian reformers, politicians, and school supervisors were not unaware of the power of desire to draw students in, even while the schools operated to devalue and alter their cultural identities. David Wallace Adams also alludes to the role of desire in his description of ritual in American Indigenous boarding schools. Religious activities were often introduced to replace, with a new set of rituals, the spiritual lives of Indigenous peoples. Students attended church, prayed, received religious instruction, and were present at various religious ceremonies. As well, secular holidays such as Columbus Day and Thanksgiving were part of the school calendar, and through them new myths and stories about Indigenous/non-Indigenous relations were circulated.[89]

But more than just the rituals of religion were required to draw students toward assimilation. From their first interactions with the schools, students in New Mexico faced various inducements intended to encourage their enrollment in identity transformation. An anonymous interviewee from Jemez Pueblo noted what had motivated his desire to attend AIS:

I was taken to the Albuquerque Indian School, which is the government boarding school, when I was in the fifth grade, I started in the fifth grade down there. . . . I went voluntarily there, and they didn't force me to go, and then the kids that were there told such exciting stories about movies every Saturday night and this government gravy and beans, you know, and how they drilled, and that there were many other Indians besides Jemez. I was also aggressive, I was never shy. . . . I was outgoing, never became homesick.[90]

For children from often extremely poor communities, the riches of the schools were attractive. Mr. Warner (Diné) spoke of begging his parents to let him go to school:

During the time of my childhood . . . my mother and father used to say, "herd sheep, we don't want you to go to school." So, that was for many years . . . I was trying to . . . get into school. I see boys and girls have nice clothes and clean way of living. Every time or every chance . . . I tried to ask my mother and father if I can go to school, they always turn me down.[91]

In addition to economic and poverty-related motivations for entering schools, students were attracted by a sense of adventure.[92] They heard stories from siblings and relatives about the better parts of life at the schools: seeing new places, meeting new people, and participating in clubs, dances, and sports. These stories often made life on the reserve seem more mundane and heightened desires to leave it to join the schools.[93] And once the young person was enrolled, desire was played upon to motivate certain behaviors and secure obedience. Mrs. Walter K. (Suzy) Marmon, from Laguna Pueblo, told her interviewer about how she had been persuaded to allow her hair to be cut when she attended the Menaul School in Albuquerque:

Miss Clay wanted my long black hair cut off. So that combing and brushing of my hair would be easier. I wasn't sure whether I liked the idea, however, when the appropriate time came, Miss Clay, who was our matron, with a big red apple in her hand, I suspected a present, quietly approached me. With my faithful Lily as interpreter, . . . these comments so well remembered by me followed, "sister, Miss Clay wants to have your hair cut." I replied, "tell Miss Clay that my mother doesn't ever want my hair cut." Well, that big red apple did its intended trick of luring me, for soon my hair was like the rest of the girls.[94]

In other instances, schools provided desired objects, such as shoes, to entice students. As a former SFIS student from Jemez Pueblo recalled, "Oh, I was proud of my new shoes when I got up there! They gave me a new pair of shoes, and every time I always walked, I'd look at my shoes. I guess those were my new shoes for the first time because I wore moccasins around here."[95] Likewise, Hildegard Thompson, director of Navajo education from 1949 to 1952, who replaced Willard Beatty as director of education for the BIA in 1952, fondly recounted her efforts to expand education among the Navajo, recalling in particular her ability to cultivate desire among Diné children through the provision of ice cream: "One of the greatest satisfactions I had that related to nutrition was giving children in isolated communities ice cream twice weekly."[96]

Activities at the schools also offered students in New Mexico a sense of excitement and replacement for the cultural events that they were missing in their own communities. Although Indigenous ceremonials and festivals were often frowned upon by school staff and supervisors, especially in the first three decades of American boarding schools, dances and socials at the schools were occasions when it was deemed acceptable for students to exhibit regulated desires. Indian Office guidelines prescribed that "such occasions should be used to teach them to show each other due respect and consideration, to behave without restraint, but without familiarity, and to acquire habits of politeness, refinement, and self possession."[97] Thus, the socials and parties that took place at SFIS and AIS were not simply for the purposes of offering students freedom to interact with the opposite sex. In the AIS 1910 annual report, for example, the superintendent makes it clear that student conduct at the socials and parties was closely monitored to ensure that it met assimilative criteria: "The boys and girls meet at Saturday evening socials and at parties given by themselves, and their conduct on such occasions and all other occasions has been exemplary. The boys have acted as perfect gentlemen and the girls are always ladies."[98] Likewise, at SFIS, into the 1920s, desire and pleasure were regulated and deployed instrumentally. Ample leisure and social activities, it was believed, prevented students from congregating independently and in accordance with their Indigenous identities. Therefore, weekends were scheduled with events intended to communicate important dispositions of civilization. Dances, for example, brought together boys and girls from similar-ranking military regiments, rather than specific Indigenous communities, for supervised interactions and lessons in social modesty and manners.[99]

Sports were another opportunity for exciting experiences in the schools, though they also helped to discipline students to follow rules, work in cooperation, and embrace school spirit. But these lessons were complicated in terms of how they were received. Much has been written about how boarding school sports teams were sources of great pride for students and enabled them to affirm and solidify Indigenous identities, especially when top Indigenous teams defeated rivals from white communities.[100] Ray Yazzie, for example, identified sports as one of the top attractions at AIS: "Yeah, that was a good school. . . . They . . . teach us how to be in track and football players and boxing. . . . Oh, they teach us everything. . . . But I was taking part in wrestling, . . . and some guy was boxing. . . . Play football . . . big boys too . . . strong boys . . . and girls. They play basketball too."[101] Other school activities, such as choir, dance, and arts and crafts, also provided outlets for student expression and desire fulfillment within the stultifying disciplinary space of an Indigenous boarding school.

Together such activities contributed a degree of seduction to the assimilative project, offering students social and physical pleasures alongside an attempt to reshape their identities. However, loss of access to these pleasures served as a threat or punishment when students failed to obey school rules. For example, a student who attended AIS in the 1930s recalled that "a lot of times the thing that they dwelt on the most was restriction. It started from depriving you of some of the goodies they had. Like you couldn't go to the movies or to parties, or you had extra duty of some sort. At that time, there was no end of the penalties they could assess you, because we

FIG. 8. Albuquerque Indian School baseball team, ca. 1911

were living in a controlled situation to the extent that they tried to get the school self-sustaining."[102]

Desire was also at work in the Manitoba Indigenous boarding schools under consideration here, though it is less evident in the particular archives researched for this project. Sports teams and movies are particularly prominent in survivor testimony of the good times at the schools, although the movies were often of the "cowboy and Indian" genre, which also contributed to ongoing processes of cultural denigration in the schools. However, these schools tended to be less successful than the New Mexico schools in their use of desire as an assimilative technique, in part because the monastic discipline of these institutions resulted in more austere and spartan schools. As such, in 1946, upon arriving at PLPIRS, Principal A. C. Huston remarked on how unattractive the school was:

> An observant visitor to certain of our Indian Residential schools would ask why we have deliberately set out to make our residences such dull and unattractive places. I must confess that it might easily appear that we had done so intentionally. Some schools are as void of light illuminative colors as a medieval dungeon. Where an attempt has been made

to introduce color dark brown floors and battleship gray walls has been the answer. The whole appearance is in many cases depressing. Hades could not appear more colorless, drab or forlorn.

For Huston, the schools were failing to entice students into the civilized world: "An Indian child more than the average White child needs to be transplanted into the type of environment that is Spring like in its warmth and color and cheer. His morose and frustrated mind needs to be induced out of its shell and infused with color and light and cheer. Only then will it live above the dissipation of less worthy thoughts."[103] His concerns about PLPIRS also applied to FAIRS, where one student recalled that "it was like a dungeon, eh. Everything was dark."[104] Another noted the lack of entertainment available to students at FAIRS: "In school we didn't have much entertainment, not dances anyway, but we used to get picture shows and of course we had the hockey but at first we didn't go anywhere. The first time we went out was to Pine Falls [a nearby non-Indigenous community] to play in a covered rink."[105]

Religious ritual in Canadian schools sponsored an attraction that was often of great ornate and symbolic potency;[106] however, in general, the fact that the Manitoba-based schools were commonly remembered as more desolate, despairing, and brutalizing places than their counterparts in New Mexico was likely a result, in part, of their failure to incorporate techniques of desire into the assimilative project.

As well, it is important to note here, in terms of understanding such techniques as part of a genocidal process, that both discipline and desire can be used in the attempted destruction of Indigenous groups. The carrot and the stick of assimilation operated simultaneously in efforts to eliminate Indigenous cultures. However, techniques of desire, because they are less severe in their regulatory structure, also provide more opportunities for resistance and creative redeployment among students subject to these techniques. Therefore, it is not contradictory that former students remember these moments, when desires for connection, entertainment, excitement, and the like were fulfilled, as good times at the schools. In the often oppressive environs of the schools, both students and teachers could seek to subvert or own practices of regulated desire and use them to survive. Desire, as a technique of assimilation, though perhaps more subtle and reaching in its destructiveness, also represents a loosening of the colonial mesh whereby students sometimes found opportunities to bring their own readings and interpretations to the struggles represented by sporting events (Indigenous versus settler rather than school versus school) or films about cowboys and Indians, finding in these moments sources of pleasure and identification other than those intended to draw them away from their Indigenous cultures.

Gender

Discipline and desire were not solely wrapped up in reinventing Indigenous children as efficient workers and docile citizens. These tools were also used to ensure that students undertook appropriate gender performances, enabling not just the embrace of the worlds of work and nation but also the reproduction of the workforce and assimilated family through the home. Gender was therefore uniquely constructed in accordance with a division of labor complementary to, but separate from, the monastic and military forms of discipline prevalent in the schools in Manitoba and New Mexico. In these spaces, female and male students were divided into clearly separated spheres of activity, and Indigenous gender patterns were undone. This division of labor made possible maintenance of the schools, with boys performing agricultural and manual labor and girls undertaking domestic chores,[107] but it also disrupted how young Indigenous men and women understood their roles in their communities.

Gendered labor roles were evident at the schools under consideration here. At FAIRS, in 1914, Inspector J. R. Bunn reported that

all the pupils are being taught to read, spell and write, all in English, arithmetic, geography, and map drawing. . . . Examination tests showed very satisfactory advancement and proficiency in these subjects. In addition to these studies the girls are taught sewing, plain and fancy, cutting out and making up their clothes, darning, knitting, laundry work and scrubbing, and other domestic work, they show aptitude in the performance of these duties. The boys are taught outside work, doing small chores, assist in gardening and farming, the use of tools and how to use them. They are taught habits of tidiness and respectful manners.[108]

Similarly, the 1910 annual report for SFIS recorded the gendered division of labor there: "The girls of the school are taught those duties that will be useful to them later as housewives. Sewing, including cutting and fitting garments, darning and repair work. Laundry work, ironing, general housework, nursing and the general care of the sick, and last but not least, family cooking, which is taught in the domestic science department, and is looked upon by many as our most valuable branch of industrial training for girls."[109]

This gendered division of labor disrupted gender patterns for Indigenous peoples. For example, it did not align with the matricentered gender norms in Diné communities, where women possessed power because important cultural components, such as place of residence and clan, were determined through the female family line. Diné women also held primary responsibility for livestock, such as sheep and goats.[110] However, in the schools, Diné boys and girls learned that home properties and livestock were male possessions, under masculine control, which severely disrupted the intergenerational transfer of traditional roles. Then, in the 1920s, the Navajo Tribal Council was established as an all-male entity, further diminishing the communal power that women held through their familial networks and responsibility for herds. The boarding schools to which Diné were sent were party to the masculinization of power in Navajo communities because they groomed men for leadership roles and women for domestic submission.[111]

With gender roles firmly in place, gender was subsequently enlisted for punitive purposes at some schools. For example, at FAIRS, a former student recalled being forced to wear a dress because he kept trying to spend time with his sisters and thereby violated the school's rules of gender segregation. The nuns admonished him by saying "that's how much you want to be with the girls."[112] Through such taunts, male students learned that to be feminine was to be weak and that masculinity meant a specific set of performances: tough, fearless, and unemotional. Moreover, such punishments also shamed those who subverted mainstream gender performances, such as individuals who identified as two-spirited or the Diné *nádleeh*—a third gender comprised of biological males who performed female roles—who were treated as a shameful abomination rather than respected for offering another way of performing one's gender.

FIG. 9. Young women washing dishes at Portage la Prairie Indian Residential School, ca. 1950

FIG. 10. Class of young women at Albuquerque Indian School, ca. 1900

Gender expectations had spatial consequences. Young women and men were held in different spaces in the schools, and their interactions were restricted to certain occasions, when they learned to appropriately interact with one another, such as at dances. Space itself was gendered in specific ways. In the 1910 SFIS annual report, dorm room crowding was presented as more than just a problem of sanitation; it was also a problem of gender education. In particular, the superintendent worried that the crowded conditions were too similar to those of "Indian home life" and therefore failed to communicate the modesty and "womanly attributes" that the school hoped to convey.[113] This point captures the fact that the gendered division of labor was not solely intended for school maintenance but was also as a means to transform the Indian home.[114] In the United States, a circular of May 29, 1915, from the Department of the Interior made this point clear: "The Indian home must be the real basis of work for the civilization of the American Indian."[115] According to this circular, "the field matron, of all employees, comes into the closest and most intimate contact with the Indian homes and Indian women. The Indian woman's influence, as a mother, wife, and sister, is just as powerful among the Indian men as is the influence of the white women among the white men. . . . The field matron should be a tremendous force for the development of the moral welfare of the Indians and the reservation life."[116] Field matrons were encouraged to help monitor the health, cleanliness, independence, and efficiency of the home, bringing the gender lessons of the school directly into the community.[117]

In this manner, patriarchal relations were enforced within the space of the school, and beyond the schools in Indigenous communities, upsetting cultures in which matrilineal and matrilocal forms of social organization were prominent. As K. Tsianna Lomawaima writes, "the struggle to reform and reshape the Indian home targeted the education of young women. They would serve as the matrons of allotment households, promoting a Christian, civilized lifestyle and supporting their husbands in the difficult transition from hunter, or pastoralist, to farmer. Women's capacity to bear this burden was taken for granted by the Victorian vision of Woman as Mother, influencing society and shaping the future through her nurture of her children."[118]

However, girls did not simply passively embrace a performance of European femininity. Lomawaima uses the "bloomer story" from Chilocco to illustrate this point. In short, interviewees told Lomawaima about how they resisted the imposition that they wear bulky and uncomfortable gray sateen bloomers. Girls removed the bloomers and hid them soon after inspection, or they fashioned a set of bloomer legs to give the impression that they were wearing the entire garment.[119] As well, the women who served as teachers and matrons in the schools on occasion brought with them their own feminist ideals through which they reinterpreted and redirected government policy, thereby resisting gender discipline at the staff level rather than the student level. For example, some female instructors encouraged girls to continue their education and to pursue careers such as teaching rather than submit to the domestic roles often promoted through school policy.[120] Moreover, Indigenous communities at times resisted the schools' attempts to transform gender roles. In 1907, in meeting their enrollment quota, Santo Domingo Pueblo sent to SFIS only one girl for every four boys. The inspector and the Office of Indian Affairs viewed this as problematic. In a letter to Superintendent Crandall at SFIS, the inspector instructed him to "notify the Santo Domingo people that hereafter they will be expected to permit more of their girls to attend the Santa Fe School."[121]

Yet, despite these forms of resistance and subversion, whereby students, teachers, and communities found gaps in the disciplinary mesh of the schools to pursue different performances of gender, gendering policy remained relatively consistent across the history of the New Mexican schools, though it did vary in intensity. At AIS, even as late as 1962–63, the following goals were listed for the home economics program:

1. Train the girls in sufficient fields of employment.
2. Train the girls to have desirable personality traits that contribute to good family relationship.
3. To develop good working habits and desirable attitude toward work and school.
4. To develop some knowledge of food, its preparation, the serving and its use in the body.
5. To develop some knowledge of clothing construction.
6. To develop some knowledge in buying readymade clothes and how to care for them properly.
7. To develop the understanding of child behavior in order to guide their activities in a home.
8. To develop the ability to use good judgment in selecting a vocation.[122]

Despite acknowledgment that Indigenous women might choose to work outside the home, these young women were nonetheless tasked with primary responsibility for the social reproduction of the workforce as well as the expectation that they embrace gendered personality traits perceived to be the linchpin holding together the family unit. Gender relations, therefore, remained fixed, even as liberal feminist ideals of equal employment and citizenship rights began to filter into the schools.

Indeed, Indigenous gender relations particularly troubled school and government officials in both countries. This meant that sexuality was heavily regulated, and the female body was especially the target of a great deal of assimilative energy. As Lomawaima suggests, "beyond domesticity as subservience training for all women, the acute, piercing focus on Indian girls' attire, comportment, posture, and hairstyles betrays a deep-seated, racially defined perception of Indian peoples' corporal physical bodies as 'uncivilized.'"[123] The female body was subject to the rigors of European notions of beauty and modesty, and perceptions of slovenly or immodest comportment were subject to disciplinary action. In earlier years at FAIRS or PLPIRS, girls suffered physical punishment for violating ideals of femininity. The same was true for AIS and SFIS. Indeed, Superintendent DeHuff at SFIS was at his fiercest in punishing boys and girls when they were caught in acts of perceived sexual misconduct.[124] But most school staff felt great responsibility to ensure the moral welfare of Indigenous girls. Even those wanting to work with Indigenous girls through the outing program were compelled to protect their morality. At AIS, those wishing to be "furnished with an Indian girl" for housework needed to complete a form declaring that

> I agree to look after the physical and moral welfare of the girl; to see that she is not out late at night; that she is not out at all on Wednesday and Saturday evenings and never permitted to loiter about the depot; that should the girl have a male caller the fact and the boy's name shall be reported to the Superintendent or Matron, and if I (or we) leave home for more than a day, the girl above mentioned will be returned to the school until our return.[125]

Disciplinary and regulatory gendering strategies remained more intense at Manitoban than New Mexican boarding schools in later years, though these tactics would disappear in neither country. Control of the Manitoban schools by religious denominations meant that regulation of female sexuality and gendering practices would take specific shapes. For example, in the late 1940s, the Catholic Hierarchy of Canada proposed that special schools for girls aged sixteen to eighteen be created "to inculcate moral principles during these transitional years" and "to fit them for their future life."[126] Where these moral principles were in violation, and corrective action failed, schools often sought to expel immodest girls before their behavior influenced other girls. In 1961, Reverend L. Jalbert, the principal at FAIRS, sent a letter to E. Daggit, superintendent of the Clandeboye Agency, asking that a fourteen-year-old girl from Dogcreek be removed from the school and sent to a "special school" where they might be able to "redeem" her. The problem with the girl, according to Jalbert, was that she was "oversexed," likely as a result of having lived with a man over the summer.[127]

Female bodies, however, could also be used as sites of resistance to the assimilative process. For example, a letter of January 15, 1924, from Superintendent DeHuff to Superintendent Crandall at the Department of the Interior voiced the former's suspicions that young women from the Santo Domingo Pueblo were intentionally returning to the school pregnant after summer vacation:

> To my certain knowledge this is the fifth consecutive year in which a number of Santo Domingo girls have had to be released from school attendance or otherwise disposed of on account of pregnancy becoming very apparent about December or January. In every case the origin of the trouble was traced to the girls' stay in the Pueblo during summer vacation. Santo Domingo has always been opposed to school attendance on the part of its children, and there is no doubt in my mind that the plan of getting these girls into the family way has been adopted as a regular practice in that Pueblo in order to defeat the law and governmental requirements as regards school attendance.[128]

DeHuff proposed that, without a marriage contract, these girls should be kept at the school to give birth and that their children should be cared for within its walls. In response, Crandall recommended retaining Santo Domingo girls at the school over the summer. In this situation, resistance failed, for the attempt to use pregnancy to avoid boarding school resulted in a reaction by school authorities to target specific girls (those from Santo Domingo Pueblo) and deny them access to their home communities.

Similarly, masculine roles, reimagined from warrior to soldier and athlete, could be redeployed in acts of strenuous resistance against school staff, such as when male students physically challenged their tormentors in the face of potential punishment. In one instance at FAIRS, a student in charge of looking after younger children hit back at the nun when she struck him for failing to keep the children quiet:

And we were going up for bed at what, right after supper, and these kids were getting out of line in the back, back of the line, so I had to go back there and straighten them out, and when I came back up, they were running around again, and the nun told me to look at the back of the line, and when I looked back, she just slapped me right across the face. And out of the blue, man, I just bang, threw a punch at her, and I hit her right in the stomach, and she went running for the priest, screaming and everything, and the priest came there, grabbed me by the neck, and threw, took me upstairs to his office, and told me to take my pants down. And he grabbed, you know those old leather straps they used to have a long time ago? That's what he used.[129]

In sum, gender discipline, particularly its destructive attempts to transform Indigenous girls and boys and their roles in Indigenous communities, was both widespread across the course of Indigenous boarding schools in the United States and Canada and uneven in its efficacy. Gender was the site of intensive technologies designed to remake Indigenous men and women as European men and women, recoding their gendered habits. However, such interventions came up against efforts to signify gender in locally meaningful ways, whether by students and communities or even by teachers who possessed very different notions of gender propriety. Thus, as gender discipline enmeshed students in the boarding schools, these students sought gaps through which they could challenge the gender expectations of the assimilative project.

Discipline, whether military or monastic in orientation, and whether directed toward moral uplift, workforce preparation, or inculcation of Western habits of citizenship and gender, was prevalent in Indigenous boarding schools. The settler colonial mesh took disciplinary shape in the space of the schools. However, strategies of desire operated alongside discipline in an effort to simultaneously seduce and shape students. These forces of assimilation were not absolute and inevitably failed in the full transformation of Indigenous young people, although they did do much damage to Indigenous individuals and groups. They were not the only techniques operating in boarding schools, however. As I will discuss in the next chapter, knowledge and violence were also powerful technologies in the attempted destruction of Indigenous groups as groups.

6 Knowledge and Violence as Assimilative Techniques

Discipline is a fraught technique of governance. Although the ideal of train-ing bodies to perform as required within a settler colonial universe has an obvious appeal to the purveyors of civilization, it often came up against its limits—the children and families targeted for discipline did not simply fall in line. For this reason, other techniques were of strategic importance, especially when discipline failed. In such circumstances, efforts to better know, and through knowledge to better control, the Indian appeared to offer an antidote for the shortcomings of discipline. But when both knowledge and discipline failed, violence remained the ultimate recourse of the settler colonial state. In Indigenous boarding schools, the originary violence of settler colonialism, experienced in warfare and dispossession, was recali-brated as physical, sexual, cultural, and symbolic violence.

Knowing the Indian

Over the course of their histories in each country, Indigenous boarding schools applied a variety of administrative and managerial technologies to more effectively regulate students. Record keeping, data management, surveys, and other such devices were implemented as means to know "the Indian" in a manner reflective of Foucault's notion of power/knowledge. In short, knowledge of Indians was viewed as a means for increasing assimilative power over them, and in turn this power allowed schools to know and make legible Indigenous peoples in specific ways that furthered their subsequent management. These two moments were braided together in a constant cycle.[1]

Record keeping on Indigenous pupils existed from the early days of modern boarding schools. In the United States, record keeping began upon the student's entry into the school. In an initial survey, information was gathered with respect to his or her "tribe," "degree of blood," "reservation," "church preference," and "physical condition." These data were combined with data collected at the school, which included staff commentary on the student, a list of "special adaptabilities" (i.e., athletic, military, musical, and religious training), and a review of the student's academic performance and "deportment" in the "Record of Pupil in School."[2] In this manner, the student was transformed into a biopolitical subject, monitored with respect to both her physical and embodied characteristics and her or his adaptability to the demands of European education. The "Application for Admission to Non-Reservation School and Test of Eligibility" also contributed to the knowledge that the BIA possessed about the student and his or her family. In a 1931 version of the application, in addition to gathering the information present on the "Record of Pupil in School" form, detailed information was sought on the income of and property owned by the potential student's family, the number of siblings of school age, and whether or not they were currently in school, as well as the results of a detailed medical examination.[3]

Many of these practices began at the Hampton Industrial School, under the leadership of Samuel Armstrong, where a file was created for each student, containing information related to Indigenous blood quotient and previous education. Data were also kept on students after they left the school, recording information such as their "character" and "home record."[4] Such knowledge was intended to help perfect the assimilative power of the schools, feeding back into teaching and administrative practices. By at least 1901, the BIA adopted Hampton's practices and was tracking students as they graduated and returned to their reserves as well as evaluating the levels of citizenship that they had achieved. Superintendent of Indian Schools Estelle Reel reported that "the student who has returned from school continues to exercise a potent influence for good upon the reservation Indians, and statistics show that a large percentage of returned students (at least 76 per cent) make good average citizens."[5] The question of the returning student was of even greater concern once the schools started producing larger numbers of graduates. For the schools in the American Southwest, only in the 1920s did a more organized method for tracking graduated students within the files begin to appear. For example, when asked about returnees while preparing the SFIS 1925 annual report, Superintendent DeHuff simply stated that none of them was "doing badly."[6] More standardized forms detailing information on the occupations, incomes, and land ownership of returning students become noticeable after this point in time. Indeed, in 1926, Commissioner Burke wrote to all school superintendents, reminding them of their responsibility to keep folders on all students that remained active even after they returned to their communities.[7]

Knowledge also made it possible to identify Indigenous children eligible for schooling. The lack of information on Diné children enabled parents to evade having their children captured and sent to boarding schools. Therefore, these schools required cooperation from government census and administrative bodies to acquire adequate knowledge of the students available for enrollment. It was not until 1927 that the BIA began to overcome some of the challenges of identifying Diné children, which stemmed not just from the vastness and difficulty of traveling through Diné territory but also from the diversity of names used by Diné individuals to identify themselves. The 1927 system provided each Diné with a "census number" connected to his or her fingerprint, impressed on a card embossed on a brass medal that could be worn around his or her neck.[8] A former Diné student well understood the significance of this moment:

My parents was hiding me away during the early days when the Red Coat Indians, Navajo soldiers, and the Navajo policeman was looking for children to go to school, they hide us. In those days they didn't had no census number, because we are not known, we are alive and nobody is looking for us, but today we do all kinds of things like that, that we go by and we are known by. We have census number. They can tell us just how old we are and then they could send us to the Selective Service and sign us in, and then if we are old enough to go to the army they always draft us.[9]

Indeed, census data on Indigenous students became increasingly important as American and Canadian governments moved to compel Indigenous education. A February 14, 1920, amendment to the regulations concerning the enrollment of Indian children in school in the United States stressed the need to compile school censuses for the various districts or agencies to ensure maximum enrollment of Indian children in accordance with compulsory education laws.[10]

Around this time, one can also see that the annual reports for AIS and SFIS become much more detailed. In particular, statistical reports on issues such as employment, government property distribution, and health become regular features, though superintendents of the schools had trouble at times seeing the relevance of these measurements to their particular schools. Under this new reporting strategy, superintendents were encouraged to submit precise information on matters such as the value of farm equipment, the number of doctor visits per year, the number of employees, the number of desertions, the linens and towels possessed by the school, the number of letters written and received by the school office, and the faith of students at the school, among other pieces of data.

In these and other ways, the nature of record keeping and data management changed over time. As another example, whereas early formulations of the Indian Problem imagined a homogeneous Indian who could be known and educated *en masse* using a standard set of tools and approaches, those working in Indian education soon arrived at the conclusion that a more specific knowledge of particular Indians would increase the state's power (and ability) to transform Indian children. Superintendent Reel argued early on that

> teachers have been shown by circulars and personal talks about the great importance of studying the Indian character, and that all efforts for the education of the Indian child must be guided by this knowledge. They can be instructed to get in closer touch with their pupils and learn the mental and physical peculiarities of each individual and endeavor to overcome the natural shyness and timidity of the child upon entering school, to make him at home in his new surroundings and to win his confidence. The importance has been urged upon them of acquainting

themselves with the details of the child's life previous to entering school, using the knowledge thus acquired as a basis for intelligent development of his latent mental capacity and as a guide in unfolding his senses and quickening his perceptions. They have also been cautioned to bear in mind the difference in heredity and early home education between white and Indian children, and to remember that methods of teaching suited to the former must be materially modified in instructing the latter.[11]

In this passage, Reel avers both the individuality and the collective tendencies of the student, combining these specific qualities with more generalizing and racist assumptions about the capacities of Indigenous children.

In short, in both the United States and Canada, data collection techniques intensified as the schools became more established. However, the United States, likely because of its more managerial and centralized Indigenous boarding school system, especially after its militaristic era faded, showed greater usage of data collection at an earlier stage. This is particularly evident at the schools studied here. In Manitoba, student records and reporting practices do become more detailed, however, in the 1930s. This was after a mid-1920s shift in Canadian policy with respect to classroom records. In an October 19, 1923, letter from Russell T. Ferrier, superintendent of Indian education, written to the principals of Indian residential schools, he advised that "the Department wishes to arrange for a careful and accurate keeping of classroom daily registers. It has been found that many Indian residential schools do not observe this practice; and still others, in the classrooms of which the registers are carefully kept, make no reference to them when the quarterly return is being compiled. In this return there is a column for the purpose of showing the total number of days the pupils attended the classroom during the quarter, and this should be carefully filled in, after reference to the classroom daily register."[12] Such data collection also reflected the tension between denominational desires to maximize per capita funding by not reporting absences and the Canadian government's continuing desire to reduce costs and pay only for those students actually in attendance in classrooms.

Ferrier's letter did not magically clear up the data-gathering challenges in Canada with respect to student attendance. Nor were the broader data collection strategies thought to be adequate to the task of learning about the Indian so as to better assimilate him or her. In the 1940s, Inspector Warkentin complained of poor knowledge of Indians at FAIRS:

> We can justify our attempts at educating the Indian only when we display an understanding of his immediate needs and interests, and appreciation of his probable future, when we can find an approach to his heart and mind through which we can assist him in the process of being assimilated, and changing himself over into what the white man's world demands of him. From my limited observation I am sure that we can so assist him, that we can make him healthier and happier now and for the future, and that we can break down the resentment that is still latent in a good many of his brothers.[13]

In this instance, Inspector Warkentin recommended to his supervisors that more needed to be known about the Indian child to appeal to his or her desires and connect him or her to the school and, ultimately, European civilization. Yet what Warkentin himself claimed to know about Indians was based on broad stereotypes. In the same report, he recommended a more practical curriculum for Indian students, timetables to reflect the short attention span of Indians, and a more rigid separation of the sexes since "the Indian adolescent boy particularly is much disturbed in the presence of the opposite sex."[14]

Such stereotypical thinking was quite different from the knowledge about Indians gathered by the BIA under Commissioner John Collier. During his time, the BIA enlisted various professionals in order to better know the Indian student. In the New Deal America of the 1930s, and under the "Indian New Deal," the managerial capacity of the BIA was expanded through the hiring of more staff, the use of anthropologists and other social scientists to adapt policy to Indian cultures, and the embrace of progressive education within Indigenous schools.[15] These mechanisms resulted in some increased powers of self-government for and improved recognition of the cultures of Indigenous peoples in the United States, but they also expanded governance of Indigenous peoples, allowing the state to penetrate farther into Indigenous communities. In particular, indirect controls over Indigenous peoples multiplied as forms of administrative consolidation, conservation programs, and community education allowed the state (or its experts) to have greater oversight of Indigenous families and communities.[16] Of the Diné experience of this era, Thomas James writes,

> for example, they [experts] drew from their research to produce a written history of the tribe, subsequently used in the schools to inculcate a sense of the past. The stories and tables they collected entered the curriculum in schoolbooks developed by the Indian Bureau. Administrators and teachers received instruction from them in the folkways and values of the tribe. The crowning achievement of the social scientists was to devise a written form of the Navajo language that by the end of the 1930s was used to produce bilingual curriculum materials. As Willard Beatty acknowledged—in a statement that again reveals the duality of such preoccupation with native culture—the written form of the Navajo language "was developed, in large part, to meet the acute need of explaining, to thousands of illiterate older Indians who knew no English, the government program worked out in their behalf."[17]

James reminds his readers that these changes in the manner of Indigenous governance and education in the 1930s were not simply progressive improvements on past injustices; instead, they remained part of a coordinated intervention in Indigenous group life that still held as its end goal, albeit in attenuated form, an effort to know the Indian so that she or he might be changed.[18]

As such, knowledge acquisition is an important technique to consider when examining the destructive prospects of Indigenous boarding schools at the upper meso-, lower meso-, and microlevels. Shifts within the philosophy and practices of Indigenous education occurred alongside the emergence of administrative strategies that made possible new forms of understanding and transforming Indigenous children. These new strategies allowed for the expansion and tightening of the settler colonial mesh as more Indigenous children and communities were caught up in its informational twine and became less able to resist coming under the gaze of this system. But they also relied on local actors to implement these strategies as well as to provide and record correct information. Whether because of the desire of Christian denominations running schools in Manitoba to obscure federal government knowledge of their students, the refusal of school principals and superintendents to conduct the busywork of gathering seemingly unrelated data on Indigenous children and their communities, or the unwillingness of children and their parents to freely offer the information desired, the settler colonial mesh could tighten or loosen in such circumstances.

Physical, Cultural, and Symbolic Violence

The focus on disciplinary and managerial techniques in this and the previous chapter could lead one to forget that boarding schools, in both the United States and Canada, were incredibly violent places. Indeed, most prominent among memories of the schools, especially for survivors in Canada, are those acts of physical, cultural, and sexual violence with which the schools are indelibly associated. Other forms of violence could also be listed here, such as spiritual and emotional violence. However, spiritual violence tends to intersect with cultural violence, and emotional violence is addressed below only to the extent that it derives from other forms of violence and thereby affects tools of group formation such as trust and familial bonding, since my focus is less on individual experiences of trauma and more on the collective consequences of violence.

Beatings, cruel punishments, and sexual violence permeate Canadian boarding school memories. Survivors have frequently recounted the physical violence of residential schools in their statements to the Truth and Reconciliation Commission of Canada. As is often the case with survivors of physical and sexual trauma,[19] these episodes were seldom mentioned publicly while the schools were in existence or even during the 1980s after most schools had closed. For the survivor of physical and sexual torture, too much is at stake in recounting the experiences, and to have someone deny or doubt their occurrence threatens retraumatization and revival of past feelings of helplessness. Therefore, Phil Fontaine's revelation of his experiences at FAIRS to a national Canadian audience was an important moment for survivors. It was not that Fontaine was the first to say these things; rather, it was his status as head of the Assembly of Manitoba Chiefs that allowed him to confront mainstream Canada with these truths and not to be dismissed on suspicion of fabrication or exaggeration. The class action lawsuits that followed in the wake of Fontaine's testimony made it possible for more Indigenous people to tell about their experiences of school violence. In this sense, it is possible that there is more evidence of physical and sexual violence in Manitoban than New Mexican Indigenous boarding schools under consideration here simply because Canadian Indigenous peoples have had more opportunities to process and articulate their suffering at these schools. As well, the abuse, in general, was more recent for Manitoban residential school survivors than for their New Mexican counterparts, since federal boarding schools in the mid-twentieth-century United States did more to regulate violence than was typically the case for Canadian schools, though this was not universally the case, and instances of school-based violence continued in the United States into the second half of the twentieth century.[20]

Regulation of physical violence, in fact, occurred early in the United States. As of 1890, the government position was that corporal punishment should be resorted to "only in cases of grave violation of rules," and the superintendent of each school was charged with administering or overseeing all such punishments.[21] The remit of punishment was broader when applied to students aged twelve and older, who could be punished or sent to the guardhouse, in effect a school prison used to isolate students from their peers for nearly any sort of misbehavior.[22] However, use of the guardhouse also began to be discouraged around this time, even though such rooms continued to exist at most boarding schools.

In this manner, there was negotiation afoot early on about what was and was not acceptable in terms of boarding school punishment. In 1891, Superintendent Cart at SFIS found himself reprimanded by the Office of the Commissioner of Indian Affairs for his purchase of handcuffs. He defended himself thus: "You state that you do not approve of 'hand cuffing pupils and chaining them to the floor,' [and] I have the honor to report that no such thing has been done with pupils at this school. The hand cuffs were procured for the purpose of securing their return to the school, when captured, without danger of escape."[23] In other words, Cart thought that handcuffs were needed to apprehend runaways, and he mentioned two boys in particular who had stolen horses from the school to make their escape. As punishment, these boys were required to work all day and to sleep in the guardhouse at night.

In the attempts of government and school officials to develop a logical basis for punishment, one can hear echoes of eighteenth-century criminal justice reformers such as Cesare Beccaria, who pushed for the reduction of often harsh and arbitrary forms of state punishment and their replacement by a more rational and scientific model.[24] However, just as was the case for criminal justice reformers, the rational mode of punishment in boarding schools was quickly married to practices of disciplinary institutions that had long been used to shape human behavior (i.e., the military and monastic). A. O. Wright, supervisor of Indian schools in the United States, wrote in 1901 that

> certain things may be said in relation to punishment that are the result of experience, and apply to Indian schools as well as to any other. It is not the severity but the certainty of the punishment that makes it effective. Punishments should, as far as possible, be made to fit the offense and be naturally connected with it. . . . Military drill for the pupils is discipline in the best sense. It trains in habits of order, obedience, promptness, and accuracy. It teaches proper carriage of the body and concert movements. There is no reason why girls should not learn to march in unison as well as boys. It is hoped that arms will soon be furnished to the pupils by the government, but in the meantime the simple drill in the company movements without arms will be of great advantage.[25]

In this sense, physical punishment in American schools was frowned on not always because of its inherent wrongness but also, if not primarily, because the violence reflected a failure of discipline in Foucault's sense of the term. The goal was to train Indigenous children into a state of obedience and docility, and the educated opinion was that physical violence was not a surefire way to achieve this outcome. Indeed, Superintendent of Indian Education Daniel Dorchester delivered a similar message earlier, in 1892, when he stated that

> I have had occasion during the year to rebuke the harsh and barbarous methods of discipline resorted to in a few of the schools. Some superintendents and matrons have used heavy whips and small boards in subduing the pupils, and have even applied shackles to the ankles. . . .

Those officials have been told plainly that the Government does not tolerate such treatment, and that employés who are incapable of controlling the Indian pupils by the power of tact and kindness, with such privations as a wise, firm administrator can easily devise, are not wanted in the service.[26]

This is not to suggest that BIA authorities were fully effective in regulating violence in the schools. Superintendents and other school staff continued to resort to violence into the 1920s and beyond. Such instances of violence were most likely when students were perceived to be incorrigible or too unruly to convert to Western ways. Students prone to drunkenness, running away, theft, and other misdemeanors were often the ones to receive physical punishments. As mentioned earlier, Superintendent DeHuff at SFIS was particularly prone to violence when faced with students who had committed sexual indiscretions. But on May 4, 1920, it was thievery that raised his ire. DeHuff wrote of having "wore out 2 brand new buggy whips" on three boys, complaining that it seemed to be the only way to get results. He also noted that he typically did not whip first-time offenders, but he thought that the one boy in trouble for the first time had committed such an egregious offense (stealing from an employee and forging a check) that the punishment was warranted. On June 5, 1921, two other boys were whipped for "having kept an assignation with a couple of girls." On December 2, 1922, DeHuff was personally reprimanded by Commissioner Burke for having put boys in leg irons, which DeHuff admitted that he had done.[27] But superintendents often believed that it was too difficult to manage their schools without recourse to physical violence and punishment. In the 1929 annual report from AIS, Superintendent Reuben Perry speaks to this challenge when dealing with troublesome students:

A boy who deserts once and knows he cannot be punished in any way other than adding of extra duty will run away again when inclination dictates his doing so or will walk away and refuse to perform the extra duty assigned. There is now no restraining influence to prevent his doing so and at present, about the only thing that can be done with a disobedient boy is to dismiss him and deny him the privileges of an education." He adds later in the report that "it is a sad commentary to have to state that more of our pupils have been in the city and county jails during the last 20 months than had been in the school guard house for a number of years.[28]

The disciplinary structures of the schools, therefore, failed to promote student obedience, and superintendents found themselves longing for more severe punishments to bestow on the worst offenders.

Despite years of discouraging corporal punishment in Indigenous boarding schools, on August 16, 1934, Secretary of the Interior Ickes thought it necessary to circulate a letter on school punishment to all superintendents, principals, and teachers in the Indian service: "Commissioner Collier has called my attention to a number of incidents which indicate that mediaeval forms of discipline have not yet been done away with in some Indian schools." He listed abuses such as beatings, hours of kneeling on concrete floors, and standing a quarter of a day with eyes fixed on a wall. As well, he noted that Collier had filed charges against five teachers who had been suspended and two others who had been dismissed from the service.[29] The fact that such a reminder was needed demonstrates the gap between federal policy and its application on the ground and the time lag experienced in attempts to reform Indigenous schooling.

When superintendents did try to steer clear of physical punishment, they were left with strategies of forced isolation, drudgery, and the curtailment of desires. Dorothy Roman from Jemez Pueblo noted some of the punishments that she witnessed or experienced at SFIS: "Yeah, they used to lock them up. Well, for boys, they used to lock them up, and for girls they used to make us scrub floors on our knees and wash windows and things like that. And they get us out from shows or dances and all that, we have to stay home during the fiestas."[30] Others spoke of being required to stand or kneel for lengthy periods of time. But, in general, reports of physical punishment at the hands of teachers and superintendents decreased over time in the two New Mexican Indigenous boarding schools under consideration here. Of course, there are unique aspects to the situations of these schools, including the proximity of Pueblo communities as well as the watchful eyes of non-Indian reformers, such as Collier during his time at Taos Pueblo, that permitted this snag in the physical violence of the settler colonial mesh in New Mexico.

This is in stark contrast to the physical abuse in the Manitoban Indigenous boarding schools, where corporal punishment was used frequently until the 1960s.[31] At PLPIRS and FAIRS, there is little evidence of interaction between government officials and school principals regarding the use of physical violence.[32] Indeed, the institutional structure of the Canadian residential schooling system limited government oversight and created conditions in which local actors could implement horrific cruelties. Physical and sexual violence was prominent at FAIRS in particular. As Purvis H. Fontaine, who attended the school in the late 1940s and throughout the 1950s, recounts,

> I lost my innocence there, I was assaulted many times and beaten you know, by nuns. I remember this nun she was bad for this, you know and I don't know what it is, what she had against me but she use to carry a sole of a runner in her pocket and sometimes when you're sleeping in the morning. I don't know where or how her brain was working, off the covers would fly and she started beating me, beating and she didn't stop until she had you bawling, crying you know.[33]

Even in the 1960s, physical violence was present:

> And as soon as we got in there, the beatings started right away. You know when, like, well first it was humiliating, they'd cut your hair off, and put a bowl on your head, and told you take your clothes off, and they threw flea powder all over you, and then they'd tell you go up to have a shower right after that, and that was pretty humiliating. But right away, man, the beatings started 'cause most kids didn't know what the rules were or anything like that, eh. And if you didn't follow the rules, that was it, you'd get strapped with the strap.[34]

Beyond the physical punishments was the sexual violence. Several of those who attended FAIRS have recalled being sexually abused by staff members and fellow students at the school. The record of sexual violence is most glaring for the 1940s until the closing of the school, the period most widely covered by Truth and Reconciliation Commission testimony.[35] This makes it difficult to discern whether or not patterns of sexual abuse changed over the history of the school. It is also impossible to assess the degree of sexual abuse in the New Mexican schools under study here since the testimony drawn on for this project was unlikely to elicit stories of sexual violence from interview respondents.[36] In the final chapter, I will discuss in greater detail the different contexts of knowledge production and testimony that generally surround Canadian and American Indigenous boarding school experiences. However, my purpose here is not to enter into a discussion on "which was worse" but to examine as best I can the local unfolding of the settler colonial mesh at these particular schools.

In addition, I could spend many pages detailing the individual violent horrors suffered by Indigenous students at multiple American and Canadian boarding schools. However, my purpose is to focus on specific schools as points of local assault on Indigenous collectivities, or genocide, as well as resistance to these processes. In this respect, physical violence and sexual violence are discussed here not in terms of the long-term trauma that they have caused individuals, or with respect to the prevalence of such violence, but with an eye to the repercussions that this violence has had for group life. These repercussions take several forms.

First, physical and sexual violence disrupt relational patterns. In the immediate context of Indigenous boarding schools, sexual and physical violence often became the norm for students, fracturing hopes of solidarity and mutual support. As one former PLPIRS student recalled,

> I started experiencing abuse, sexual abuse from an older student. And I, here again, I was in shock again. I was wondering to myself why is this happening to me? Why is this person doing this to me? And you know I, I just couldn't understand why somebody like that would do such a thing to me. And I couldn't tell the supervisor because I was threatened. The person that did this to me threatened to beat me up, and the person was bigger, a stronger guy, you know.[37]

To be violated is often to lose one's sense of trust and connection, making it that much harder to form relationships with others. When a large portion of a group is made the object of such violence, and then patterns of violence become cyclical within its community, the group faces a tougher challenge with respect to forming the bonds that permit the continuation and thriving of group life. For example, children sent away to boarding schools found it difficult to trust their parents, who could not protect them from the abuse. Then, as spouses and parents in later life, the same individuals were often filled with a great deal of doubt about their ability to form healthy relationships with those whom they loved or tried to love.

Second, sexual and physical violence are an assault on one's personal autonomy and communicate the absolute power of the forces that one is up against. The fact that school staff did as they wished with Indigenous children's bodies sent the message to children that they were powerless in the face of colonial settler domination and that resistance was futile. This is to suggest not that Indigenous children ever stopped resisting but that the schools sought to demonstrate their ultimate submission to the assimilative force of settler colonization.

Cultural violence, too, served to devalue Indigenous cultures and assert the superiority of European ways. Names, clothing, language, and other links to Indigenous societies were attacked upon entry into Canadian and American Indigenous boarding schools. Once again the experience of this cultural assault appears to have been more consistent in the Manitoban schools over time compared with the New Mexican schools. In the early decades of American Indigenous boarding schools, long hair was sheared off, uniforms were required, old clothing was taken away, and names were changed. As well, students had to contend with poor quality and culturally unfamiliar facilities, the lack of traditional foods, hunger, forced European etiquette and disciplinary training, and the prohibition of their languages.[38] For many in the New Mexican Indigenous boarding schools, they had already faced these methods of cultural assault in the community day schools where they had begun their studies. In these schools, they were also encouraged to cut their hair, speak only English, and behave like European children. So it is possible that they were less shocked by their arrival at boarding school. Still, for those in the early years of the American system, whose first taste of schooling came through the boarding schools, as well as those among groups such as the Diné who were sent at younger ages to boarding schools because of the lack of local day schools in certain regions, having their names, hair, clothing, and language stripped away was a terrifying experience.

U.S. policy eventually softened with respect to names, since Indigenous names, when converted into an English first name–surname format, were deemed to meet the requirements of American law and property ownership and viewed as sufficiently individualized to not automatically connote an Indigenous attachment. However, even after policies of naming shifted, Indigenous names were sometimes belittled. For example, Emily Cook from the Bureau of Indian Affairs, in a talk that otherwise supported the preservation of Indigenous names, argued "why should Nancy Kills a Hundred be doomed to go through life with such a bloodthirsty patronymic, or Eunice Shoot at [H]ail with such an idiotic one?"[39] In addition, reports vary about the extent to which the speaking of Indigenous languages was forbidden at AIS and SFIS. Certainly, it seems likely that there was greater lenience about Indigenous languages into the 1930s and 1940s.[40] Moreover, the prohibition of Indigenous dancing was loosened in the 1920s. Prior to this point, Pueblo dances and feasts were viewed as immodest affairs "intended and calculated to stimulate the warlike passions of the young warriors of the tribe, and when the warrior recounts his deeds of daring, boasts of his inhumanity in the destruction of his enemies, and his treatment of the female captives in language that 'ought to shock even a savage ear.'"[41] This viewpoint shifted despite the preferences of Commissioner of Indian Affairs Charles Burke. As previously mentioned, Burke, in many respects, was an old school assimilationist. For this reason, Superintendent Perry at AIS took a moment in his 1928 annual report to defend Pueblo ceremonials: "The dances indulged in by Indians of this section of the country are generally harmless and more in the nature of fiestas or celebrations participated in periodically. It is my opinion that the authorities should ignore the dances unless there are times when vulgarities are indulged in. At the time of the dances it is well to guard against the sale of intoxicants to the Indians."[42]

One must note that Perry's permissiveness about Indigenous ceremonials is not equivalent to recognition of their value. They are perceived as little more than an indulgence and therefore harmless. Around the same time, Superintendent DeHuff at SFIS, often remembered as an appreciator of Indigenous traditions, reported that the 1927–28 school year was a very successful one since students appeared to take greater interest in their studies. One marker of this improvement, he argued, was that the students were less interested in returning home to attend dances and fiestas. He noted that it has been the custom of this school for years to permit a number of the children to attend dances and fiestas at their Pueblos on certain well established occasions during the year, and I found this year that not many of the children wanted to go home for these festivities. I think this speaks well for the advancement having been made. I would not have them give up these ancient customs entirely but I do not think some features of the dances should be encouraged.[43]

In this manner, even where school staff demonstrated an appreciation of Indigenous cultures, there was often a backhanded quality to it that communicated the sense that cultural practices were appreciated for being quaint or interesting rather than culturally integral.

Likewise, staff attempts to encourage students to do their best could also have this backhanded quality. Mr. Baca, from Laguna Pueblo, recalled that in 1914 a teacher at SFIS told him

you are going to make your own life, you will have to make your own life on earth, nobody is going to give you something for nothing. You will have to be your own man, so if you want to study or if you want to learn, learn quick because at your age, at your time in the Indian life, it is just so many years cause when you pass that stage you go to the blankets, you don't progress, you just stay there, you don't have no better judgment about what there is in the future, that entered my mind at that time, that is why I thought you know . . . there is something else that is more essential.[44]

This motivational speech, delivered one presumes with sincere concern for the future of the student, also denigrated Indigenous cultures by associating "going to the blanket" with failure. Thus, even as staff and students moved away from more blatant forms of cultural violence, subtle (and not so subtle) debasements of Indigenous cultures were often present.

At FAIRS and PLPIRS, more blatant forms of cultural violence were common throughout the histories of the schools. For example, there was no permissiveness around Indigenous languages. Angela Marie Bruyere (Sagkeeng), who attended Fort Alexander in the 1930s, recalled the punishments received for speaking Indigenous languages. The nuns would wash their mouths out with soap, as though speaking an Indigenous language was equivalent to cussing. Otherwise, the girls might be forced to stand in the same position for quite a while.[45] Similarly, a survivor who attended PLPIRS recounted how the school helped to disconnect her from her culture: "Like I said, I never got home. I never got parenting skills that I could have had, had I gone home. And the culture and language—I lost my language because of that and I lost my ties with my community, my culture. Because when I went to see my brothers later on in years, they spoke the language 'cause my dad spoke the language, I didn't—we didn't—the ones that went away."[46]

Students also suffered the transformation of their appearance well into the later years at school. As a student who attended FAIRS in the 1960s reported,

> I remember seeing my brother without no hair because he was, they apparently shaved it off because he was attempting to, he got caught attempting to run away and that's what they used to do—shave their hair off. Boys and Girls. I remember my cousins being uh, held down and then a couple of nuns holding one down, and the other nun shaving their hair off because they got caught running away. And they were just screaming and I remember running to a corner and just sitting in that one spot until everything was over.[47]

In this instance, appearance was altered as a punishment, but it is nonetheless clear that such punishments were designed to target specific aspects of cultural identity.

Punishment for using Indigenous languages also continued into the 1960s. Eva Harriet Woodford, a former PLPIRS student, remembered instances when she was caught speaking her language: "And three times I was caught speaking my language on the phone to my mother when umm when she was phoning me long distance. And you know the matron or one of the other staff happened to walk by and right after I got off the phone I was told to go to the superintendent's office in there, I got a strap!"[48] She added later in her statement that "I couldn't teach my kids the language because I did not want them to get strapped. So my kids do not speak the language. I have grandchildren, they do not—they do not speak the language and my great grandmother, I don't think they'll—that language is forever lost. You know, the legends that your grandfather told you. You cannot tell that to your children because they have to be told in your language."[49] Under such circumstances, we see the destructiveness of cultural violence at boarding schools as entire Indigenous languages disappeared from existence.

Cultural violence, therefore, could cinch the settler colonial mesh in circumstances in which Indigenous boarding schools had a free hand to attack pillars of cultural life. In other circumstances, Indigenous children and communities were able to find interstices for cultural preservation, whether through illicit acts such as secret language use or through officially permitted cultural practices, including attendance at dances and ceremonials. But even when the settler colonial mesh bound Indigenous children most tightly, resistance did not disappear entirely. In particular, children learned practices of cultural hybridity that would allow them to assume future leadership roles, to "walk in two worlds" or "code switch" between white and Indigenous ways of being in order to advance Indigenous rights.[50]

Symbolic violence differs from the brute force of physical or cultural violence.[51] Pierre Bourdieu defines symbolic violence as "gentle, invisible violence, unrecognized as such, chosen as much as undergone, that of trust, obligation, personal loyalty, hospitality, gifts, debts, piety, in a word, of all the virtues honoured by the ethic of honour."[52] Symbolic violence arises in situations in which the exercise of direct domination or exploitation is difficult or impossible and a softer approach to persuasion is needed to confirm or transform a particular vision of the world. It is a violence that emanates from the social and, in particular, symbolic power of the actor who uses it, who is able to achieve recognition of his or her worldview and to have the practices and rationalities that define this worldview accepted by the addressee as normal and taken for granted.[53] In this sense, symbolic violence takes the appearance of reason and, in being reasonable, disguises the interests that lie behind its force and even the fact that force is being used.

The extent of physical, sexual, and cultural violence in Indigenous boarding schools is so horrifying that symbolic violence is often neglected as a topic of consideration.[54] Or, in some instances, moments of symbolic violence appear in contrast to those of physical and cultural violence as humane but isolated moments in abusive boarding school contexts. Kind teachers, caring superintendents, gifts, and other such niceties might reflect well on the compassionate qualities of specific individuals working in boarding schools, but they are nonetheless actions within a context intended to provoke a specific violent outcome: the elimination of Indigenous identities. In this respect, the discussion of desire above overlaps with the notion of symbolic violence, since fulfillment of desire was often deployed as a "gift." But the violence of such gifts is that their distribution is conditional on obedience to the assimilative project undertaken in the schools.

The notion of symbolic violence thus offers a means for understanding positive experiences within the largely negative conditions of the boarding schools. Surviving students have sometimes faced difficulty in reconciling positive and negative stories about the schools. For example, Agnes Shattuck Dill, from Isleta Pueblo, who graduated from AIS in 1932, told a reporter that "you only hear the negative that people say about the schools now, but I have a great love and respect for Indian schools. . . . At that time they were needed. There was no way any Indian student could have received an education if it weren't for the boarding schools."[55] Her positive experiences are not to be discounted, for the schools that she experienced contrasted with a reservation system that left young people feeling restricted and isolated, but her sincerity should not lead us to ignore the symbolic violence at work in the schools. In this instance, Dill suggested that education was needed and thereby reinforced settler colonial claims that only assimilative education was of value and that only colonial education could provide hope to Indigenous peoples. To this extent, symbolic violence left her with the sense that there was no alternative to the form of assimilative education offered by the U.S. government, and in her resilience she made the best of it.

As early as 1892, Superintendent of Indian Education Daniel Dorchester spoke of how care and kindness were more effective means of control than corporal punishment. Discussing a school for which both Indigenous parents and children were said to feel affection, he wrote that "several of the girl pupils, some of them orphans, declined to go home, preferring to stay at the school during the vacation. Many, both boys and girls, went home under protest, because they had begun to appreciate the difference between civilization and barbarism."[56] In part, such a statement reflects a settler overconfidence that Western culture is so obvious in its superiority that it should gain immediate allegiance. But it also speaks to a strand of BIA thinking, which held that students could be converted to Western ways through the symbolic violence of kindness—through the gifts, caring, and concern that might be offered by a competent school staff.

The following section details one specific form of symbolic violence noticeable at both the Manitoban and New Mexican schools: resocialization. Although Indigenous boarding schools were directed to bolster an individualist spirit in the student, at the microlevel they also sought to connect with and keep students by providing them with substitute social units—families and communities—within the walls of the schools. These substitute families became vital aspects of the settler colonial mesh in these locales.

Resocialization

An often-noted key destructive aspect of Indigenous boarding schools was their promotion of individualism among students.[57] One must be careful, of course, not to assume that Indigenous peoples did not possess individual identities, despite the importance of their collective identities. But, in general, Indigenous boarding schools sought to cultivate European-style individualism, particularly with respect to fostering dispositions of acquisitiveness, self-sufficiency, and economic autonomy. This emphasis on individualism in the schools was the product of concern for Indigenous dependency, since dependence on the government was perceived to be part of the Indian Problem. As David Wallace Adams notes, "while students were being taught how to earn a living, they also were being taught a host of values and virtues associated with the doctrine of possessive individualism: industry, perseverance, thrift, self-reliance, rugged individualism, and the idea of success."[58] Indeed, for Richard Pratt, the boarding school was inadequate for creating the sort of individualism that he envisioned. He saw the outing program as a partial solution to the problem that schools did not sufficiently foster independence: "The order and system so necessary in an institution retards rather than develops habits of self-reliance and forethought; individuality is lost. They grow into a mechanical routine."[59] Whereas the school sheltered students, the outing system sent them into the white community and required them to adapt individually to the outside world.

Indigenous families were also perceived to be obstacles to rapid assimilation.[60] The home environment was understood to tempt students away from the lessons in civilization provided at the boarding schools. The archbishop of St. Boniface, Louis Philip Langevin, argued in the early twentieth century that Indigenous children needed to be "caught young to be saved from what is on the whole the degenerating influence of their home environment."[61] But drawing children away from their families and communities, and imposing on them European individualism, disrupted familial and social relations in Indigenous life. A child of survivors testified that "these people that raised us were basically raised by priests and nuns, and they were not taught by their own parents . . . how to be parents, so they didn't know how to be parents, and I don't blame my father for what he did to me."[62] In addition to losing out on socialization into the patterns of Indigenous parenting, the removal of children from families often resulted in resentment toward parents, who became suspect in the child's eyes because they were unable to offer protection from the schools. This contributed to severing the child-parent bond. Tony Lucero from Isleta Pueblo, who attended AIS but also a mission school, recalled, "well, I told my father when I got back home in the summer, I said, he asked me, and I couldn't talk Indian, he said, 'where do you want to go to school?' I said, 'I don't know.' They sent me away, and what could I say, I guess they didn't want me there, that's what I thought, they sent me away."[63] As well, staff at the Indigenous boarding schools sometimes promoted such disconnection from parents. As a survivor who attended FAIRS in the 1960s reported,

> I remember one of the nuns one day told me, told us not to call our mum "mum" because she's not your mum—she's your mum, but call her by her Christian name. And when you go home and once and a while we do call her, I did call her by her name a few times in the summer. And she used to get mad, she'd get upset and "call me, call me mama. I'm your mum, call me mama." Took me a while for me to call her mum.[64]

Likewise, Vincent Pierre, a survivor from FAIRS, recounted how he was taught to resent his parents:

At that point in my life, when I was going to residential school, I thought my life had ended because of the love that I had from my parents was taken away from me and we were not taught that in residential school. We were not told that our parents still loved us. We were told differently, that's why we were in residential school, that our parents didn't love us anymore. That we would have to stay there until we were adults and able to go back to our communities as educated people.[65]

Theodore Fontaine offers the following observation with respect to what his parents did not know when they dropped him off at FAIRS: "From this point on, my life would not be my own. I would no longer be a son with a family structure. I would be parented by people who'd never known the joy of parenthood and in some cases hadn't been parented themselves."[66] Parents immersed and socialized into a community of families and familial practices were replaced by teachers who did not have this parenting background. This transition from one family to another was initiated at the moment when parents dropped children off at the school or when children were taken from the reserve. At that moment, children wondered why their parents left them or let them be taken away. As Fontaine notes about the day that his parents dropped him off at school, "thus were born the abandonment issues I would struggle with for years henceforth."[67] And with abandonment came an abatement of the trust essential to human relationships. As one Manitoba-based survivor remarked about his experience of relationships after residential schools,

I called those people who ran the boarding school, "stone people." What did I learn from those stone people? I learned how to suppress my natural feelings, my feelings of love, compassion, natural sharing and gentleness. I learned to replace my feelings with a heart of stone. I became a non-human, non-person, with no language, no love, no home, no people, and a person without an identity. In this heart of stone grew anger, hate, black rages against the cruel and unfeeling world. I was lost in a veil reaching up to the black robes and priests and nuns trying to make sense of all of this anger and cruelty around me. Why were these people so cold? Did they not have parents somewhere who loved them? Why did they despise us so much? In the beginning, I was constantly confused and always, always lost to their ways. I even went so far as to find a woman to marry that had no family connections, literally an orphan, my wife was an orphan, she has no family so that way I didn't have these people touch me. I didn't love this woman and I told her I didn't love her because I didn't know how. It was a cold calculated act, like buying a car. She had to meet certain requirements and function properly, but I didn't love her.[68]

Norman Twoheart, who attended FAIRS in the 1960s, also explained the feeling of loss of familial love:

A typical day, I guess like, they separate the family. Like you know family like, things to do with your family, the way you grew up. And when you're being separated after and you don't know how to function with your life normally, how you grew up. Like love was gone, like love was not there no more. Love was kind of a, a strange, a stranger I used to know. Now like love is not there, you sort of just like, something like military camp; get up certain time and do a certain thing.[69]

Madeline Smith, a survivor from PLPIRS, shared this view. Reflecting on her time at the school in the 1950s, she discussed how her connections with family members were severed: "I keep all these things to myself because I got nobody to tell it to and especially family, I don't like to talk about family. Today, my brothers and sisters I just see them as people, I don't think of them as my brothers and sisters because I never grew up with them. All I know is they are my brothers and sisters and that's it. I don't know their personal life; I don't know anything about them."[70] Indeed, loss of connection and the ability to feel and communicate love are two of the most frequent remembrances of survivors who gave statements to the Truth and Reconciliation Commission of Canada.

In Manitoba and other parts of Canada, extended families were also fractured by competing religious denominations. In Fort Alexander, the Catholic and Anglican Churches divided the community, with the Anglicans claiming those Sagkeeng living closer to the town and the Catholics claiming the remainder. Marcel Courchene remembers the pain caused by the separation from his grandmother, considered Anglican: "But these priests, their [sic] the ones that were separating us—a religious thing. It was not right, their teaching was it was not right to associate with Anglican."[71] This division also had the broader effect of preventing community unity, since the teachings were that the other side was tainted by their particular faith: "That's what the church teachings were, 'You don't wink at a protestant girl or even smile at them—the Anglicans are going to hell and the Catholics are going to heaven'—that's what they said."[72]

Children were also separated and alienated from siblings at the Manitoba boarding schools. Opposite sex siblings were kept apart, while older same sex siblings were enlisted in disciplining their younger brothers and sisters. Muriel Katherine Morrisseau, who attended FAIRS in the 1940s, testified that

> my sister abused me in school, my older sister; she was very mean to me. And I figured maybe that was just the way of life. She was looking after me when I first went to school and the nuns ordered her to comb my hair and she'd braid my hair and bang my head against the sink if I didn't keep still. Very abusive! That's all I remember—is being abused. If you don't do things right, disciplined right away.[73]

Family was also the primary transmitter of culture for Indigenous young people. Removal from Indigenous families meant disconnection from the building blocks of culture, including language and stories. Part of the loss experienced through Indigenous boarding schools was the loss of collective identity as represented within stories. Stories carried the time and space, the knowledge, the lessons of the group between generations. As Andrea Benally (Diné) told her interviewer, "then when you go to a boarding school, you are gone for a whole year, almost a whole year, and you know you hardly ever hear the story, only about once and then only in the winter time, they don't talk about it in the summer."[74] Given the protocols of Diné storytelling, whereby certain stories can only be told at specific times of the year, children sent to boarding schools were often deprived of entire story cycles. The Diné also experienced the disruption of the family economy, since children who would traditionally help parents with livestock on the range were sent to schools and disconnected from both family and herd.[75]

In both Manitoba and New Mexico, Indigenous boarding schools facilitated the tightening of the settler colonial mesh by diminishing the

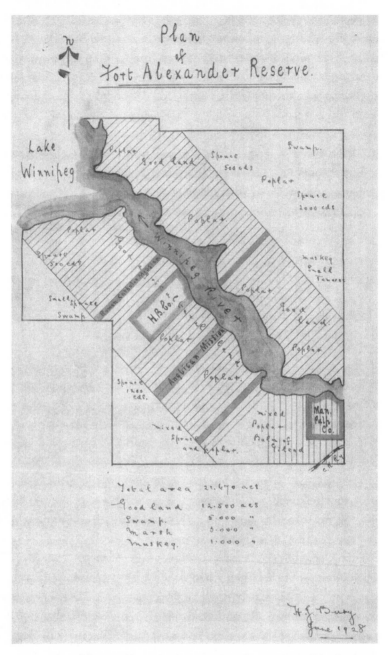

FIG. 11. Plan of the Fort Alexander Reserve. Note the positions of the Anglican and Catholic missions

relationship between children and their parents and community. But this separation did not serve solely to impose individualism on the student. Early on, students were confronted with the symbolic violence of resocialization.[76] Feeling isolated and alone in the schools, and suffering from terrible homesickness, students were naturally drawn to staff members, who became substitute families that would offer the occasional carrot of kindness to foster commitment to the assimilative project.[77] Ann Laura Stoler refers to this widely used colonial technique as "intimate colonialism," and Cathleen Cahill provides a close-up examination of how the BIA sought to form familial relationships between Indigenous students and school staff as a means to impart the habits of citizenship among these children.[78] Likewise, Brenda Child notes how Superintendent Johnson, in an 1896 speech before a group of educators, made the point that "the boarding school institution was capable of acting as a warm and maternal surrogate family to the young Indian girl." Johnson added that "the Indian girl is very affectionate. If we truly love her, she will truly love us, and will be as plastic clay in our hands. Her parents, too, will be as appreciative of our love for their child as we can wish, and knowing that we love her, and are kind to her, will trust her implicitly to our care."[79] In this statement, love is instrumentalized—it is a tool for achieving the successful assimilation of the child and for obtaining buy-in from parents. As well, love is assumed to be more effective with girls, who are given a special role in the assimilative project, since they are to serve as the future nurturers and socializers of Indigenous children into the European order.

Along these lines, Pratt represented himself as a firm but caring father figure at Carlisle. And the BIA employed thousands of women as "federal mothers" within the boarding school system.[80] Moreover, the BIA sought employment of Indigenous graduates from boarding schools, a practice less common in Canadian boarding schools. For example, in 1899, 45 percent of Indian School Service employees were former boarding school students.[81] Although this practice provided opportunities for school graduates, it was also intended to foster in current students a sense of connection to the schools as well as the notion that employment opportunities awaited them when their school days were done. It was thought important that these students not "return to the blanket" after graduation and thereby affirm the cynicism of those who doubted the assimilative vision. William Hailman, superintendent of Indian schools, remarked in 1884 that "the appointment of Indians as employees in all positions in which this is practicable should be not only recommended but consistently enforced. . . . By this policy the Government will afford to Indians fresh incentives for faithful work at school, additional reasons to love and foster the school, while at the same time it will make the school a practical object lesson of life in which the two races labor hand in hand toward a common purpose."[82] Of course, the jobs on offer were often at the lowest rungs of the service, and Indian agents in charge of local hiring did not always abide by government directives to hire former students. Moreover, the numbers of former students working in the Indian service dropped significantly after Estelle Reel replaced Hailman in 1898. Then, when Francis Leupp became commissioner of Indian Affairs in 1905, the proportion of Indian service employees drawn from former students dropped further to 25 percent.[83] In part, the experiment failed, because there was a perception among school leadership and the government that, rather than better connect students to schools, Indian employees had more influence in Indian communities than did their white superiors, a situation that the latter thought untenable. Similarly, the federal mothers employed by the BIA did not always follow the script of acting as role models of nurturance and maternal civilization.[84] Indeed, at times they brought with them critical perspectives on the patriarchal limitations placed on women in European societies.

On occasion, however, the desolate circumstances of boarding schools provoked resocialization of the sort that the colonial state desired. Theodore Fontaine remarks on his time at FAIRS that, "as young children, easily manipulated, we created new connections and rapidly bonded with some of our captors. Being malleable and wanting kindness and love, we slowly came to believe that there was kindness in those we were around every day and attached ourselves to those who looked after us."[85] Likewise, a sense of longing for home might lead a child to seek homelike connections within the school setting. As one former SFIS student recalled, "well, I was homesick for a while. But after a while, when I know there was someone that was taking care of me, I was happy here. At home I didn't have anybody but my dad."[86] Ozaawi Bineziikwe, who began school at FAIRS in 1949

FIG. 12. School employees of the Albuquerque Indian School, ca. 1910 (includes Indigenous employees)

or 1950, goes so far as to compare her time in residential school to adoption: "Now when I think about those times and the feelings I felt then, it was almost like being adopted into a white family. The clergymen were our fathers, the nuns were our mothers, and all the children at the school were our siblings."[87]

But in both Manitoba and New Mexico, children often fashioned relationships among themselves more so than with school staff, forging their own families despite their school's efforts to resocialize them into the new family of the school. Rather than bond with the school, nation, or a new religion, students found camaraderie among themselves, creating connections that, in many cases, would last a lifetime and networks that could be mobilized for later political involvements that attempted to weaken the settler colonial mesh.[88] At AIS, the introduction of student self-government, though it was often disciplinary in nature, in fact promoted student bonding and preserved relationships within specific identity groups. In "tribal councils" established after 1925, student representatives from different Indigenous groups met twice a month to govern the students from their communities.[89] In this manner, the school enrolled existing group identifications in order to facilitate better management of the student population. At the same time, however, this management came with the concession of reinforcing Indigenous identifications and potentially disrupted practices of resocialization and individuation that were the norm at boarding schools.

In other instances, school practices served to create divisions among students, leaving them more open to relationships with staff. Violence, for example, could disrupt student unity and lead to competition and aggression among students. As one former FAIRS student recalled,

> so I took it out on all the kids. If they insisted on telling the nun what, what was going on or, you know, then I'd take it out on them, too. And this went on for, I don't know for how long, for that whole year anyway. After awhile, they kids got so scared that they wouldn't even, they wouldn't even go against me or anything. The older ones I fought real hard, I fought 'em, and I totally won. I don't know, like, that really made it, really hardened me up. It made me mean and, you know.[90]

Violence among students occurred on an individual level, as in this instance, but battle lines were also drawn based on Indigenous group affiliations, pitting children from one Indigenous nation against those of another.

In addition to the family of the school, students were to become part of the family of the nation through citizenship training. The notion of citizenship first proffered in the United States through instruments such as the Dawes Act was simultaneously a form of individuation and resocialization. Through competent management of individually owned property, and through demonstration of individual skills, one proved one's worth within the family of the nation and earned rights of citizenship. Under the Dawes Act, this was a lengthy process, for one potentially had to wait until the twenty-five-year trust period had passed before assuming full ownership of the allotted territory. Other measures were subsequently implemented to expedite the process of Indigenous citizenship formation, for example by allowing land ownership to boarding school graduates or by conferring citizenship on Indigenous First World War veterans. But it was not until the 1924 Curtis Act that citizenship was bestowed on Indians in the United States.[91]

However, training for citizenship began long before the Curtis Act. In 1886, AIS students participated in a parade for Decoration Day (now known as Memorial Day). While the boys from the school marched in uniform, the girls rode on a float, wearing white aprons to reflect their newfound domesticity. On the side of the float were written four messages: "Anglo-Saxon civilization rules the world, we submit"; "Wise statesmanship demands a homogenous population"; "Patriotism precludes allegiance to civil powers, independent of the United States"; "We were free born; education confers knowledge and power to assert and maintain our freedom."[92] These mottoes carried the message of the new civic religion—submit yourself to our culture, blend within our nation, devote yourself to the nation, and embrace the regulated freedom we have on offer. Although likely directed outward to the parade's non-Indigenous observers to advertise the assimilative work under way at AIS, such messages also sought resonance with students. Such citizenship work was more frequent in the boarding schools in New Mexico than those in Manitoba. Nonetheless, in both contexts, examples can be found of the promotion of loyalty to one's country rather than one's "tribe."

Likewise, loyalty to one's school was actively encouraged. Techniques designed to bond students to the school and to foster "school spirit" are typical of any educational institution. But in the assimilative school, such bonding was often opposed to community attachments, presenting the school as a better alternative to Indigenous tradition. The pleasures of the school, in this respect, such as school songs, often placed the school as the model for a reformed community life. Take, for example, this song from the 1927 AIS school yearbook:

Sophomore Class Song

("Keep the Home Fires Burning")

From the hogan, from the 'dobe
From the mountain and the plain
Come the Red men, hear them marching
Marching to the glad refrain

FIG. 13. Class of boys with flags, Albuquerque Indian School, ca. 1885

We are learning, learning, learning
For ourselves and for our kin;
We are growing, growing, growing,
For the old school took us in.
Keep the old school going,
For the young are coming,
Keep the old school going
Till they all have come.
Repeat.

We're returning to the mountain,
To the mesa and the plain
With the knowledge we have gathered
Marching to the glad refrain,
We are going, going, going
And our lights afar will shine,
As we live the things you taught us,
Dear old school, old school of mine.[93]

Notice that the message of preservation is for the school, not for the Indigenous world, which is to be transformed by the knowledge-bearing child soldiers, who are marching back to mountain, mesa, and plain. Unlike their parents, perceived to be forever childlike in their state of wardship and savagery, Indigenous children were to grow up and become, as much as possible, Euro-American citizen-subjects.[94]

Indigenous boarding schools thus operated not only to disrupt families and foster individualism but also to confer new family-like attachments on Indigenous children. This is an example of symbolic violence, since through mechanisms such as trust and loyalty formation the student was wrenched from the world of family and community and encouraged to find succor in school, Christianity, and nation, those replacement institutions that promised the Indigenous child a new life and identity. These new attachments took specific localized form in New Mexico and Manitoba, with the former fostering a more secularized resocialization than was the case in the latter. Moreover, the potential for resisting or disrupting such enactments of the settler colonial mesh differed in each place; for example, Pueblo families were able to negotiate more time with, and therefore more influence over, their children. Resistance was never entirely absent, and Indigenous families persevered, albeit on occasion under extremely stressful and disruptive conditions.

I have discussed in this and the previous chapter a few techniques drawn on by Indigenous boarding schools to forcibly transform Indigenous children and to destroy Indigenous communities. Other techniques, such as policing and religious conversion, could also be assessed here. However, the goal of this chapter was not to present a comprehensive catalog of settler colonial techniques but to illustrate some of the ways in which the settler colonial mesh sought to tighten around Indigenous young people at the meso- and microlevels. In most cases, these techniques both responded to and provoked resistances that prevented the total assimilation of students into European ways. As Foucault notes, power begets resistance, though such resistance does not stand outside relations of power.[95] Therefore, in genocidal processes, one should not expect the complete absence of efforts among target groups to find a footing to prevent destruction and, as in our cases, disrupt the settler colonial mesh. But one also finds in Foucault's insight a sense that power needs resistance—the Indian is conceptualized as a problem, and this problematic character is reinforced when she or he resists. This power-resistance relationship then reinforces the need for institutions and techniques of assimilation and civilization. And each such instance, as it takes shape in local circumstances, sparks new, multiple, and diverse lines of resistance.[96] Such resistances can offset the structural force of the settler colonial mesh; nonetheless, at certain times and in certain places, the combined force of violence, discipline, desire, knowledge, and resocialization, not to mention other factors, made it extremely difficult for Indigenous children to maintain their connections to family and community, leaving them either isolated or seeking new forms of collective affiliation.

The techniques explored here range from those that fit common understandings of violence—that is, physical and sexual abuse—to those that target the Indigenous child as a cultural, embodied being. The argument is that the latter, more subtle forms of violence should not be ignored in discussions of genocide, since their subtlety is part of what makes them potentially effective means of cultural destruction. As one former FAIRS student noted, "I share these examples because . . . even the school curriculum perpetuates the myth that we are pagan, that we are not worthy of an education—we would not do it, and their hidden agenda of the day was not to educate us but assimilate us. I began to understand that later in my life and how it was done was so brutally subtle that we didn't even know the forces that were affecting us during [our time at school]."[97] But this subtlety of technique did not mean that Indigenous children did not find or later rediscover means of resistance. To close the chapter, the words of a FAIRS survivor capture this continuation of resistance many years after the experience of attempted elimination:

And when I look at our way of looking at life, we look at life in a holistic point of view. Everything is related, interrelated, and all creation. I looked at four things. First, what's most important in our lives is language. Second, is our land. The land means everything to us. Third, is our history. And the fourth and the last one is our way of life.

When I look at four of those, I begin to see a picture. They wanted
to completely elimina . . . —take us out of the picture of this country.
Eliminate. And try to make us something that we could never be. I
am Anishinaabe and I've always heard our elders of our past saying,
"You are Anishinaabe."[98]

7 | Local Actors and Assimilation

In addition to considering the techniques drawn on to assimilate Indigenous children, it is worth examining the roles of other, nonhuman actors in either advancing or resisting boarding school objectives. The previous two chapters noted the multiple assimilative techniques and lines of resistance enacted at the microlevel in relation to the settler colonial mesh. However, when discussing local interactions, especially in relation to genocide studies, there is a tendency to focus solely on human interactions, thereby ignoring a more complicated web of relations that exists between human and non-human actors. In this manner, this chapter takes a broad view of what it means to be an actor. Rather than presume that humans are the ones who act on an entirely passive world, this chapter attends to other participants in the shaping of social life. They include nonhuman actors allied to assimilative initiatives, such as food scarcity that helped to pressure Indigenous parents to send their children to boarding schools. They also include actors that refused to be enlisted toward destructive goals, such as territories that denied easy movement or diseases that spread in ways contrary to expectations and compromised a boarding school's health claims. To better understand human agency, one needs to look not only at the structural and institutional limits placed on such agency but also at the many local interactants that have consequences for how human agency unfolds. This chapter focuses on the microlevel interactions between human and nonhuman actors that gave distinct shape to the specific schools under consideration in this book. It reaches for a fuller understanding of how local nets of control are built, and succeed or fail, within the settler colonial mesh. And in so doing, it works to recognize and bring into the analysis Indigenous understandings of the world that do not simply assign a passive role to the nonhuman world.[1]

Space, Territory, and Time

Geography has too often been ignored in the field of genocide studies. In response to this lacuna, Ernesto Verdeja offers the following examples of its relevance: "Geography plays an important part in our understanding of the Armenian resistance in Musa Dagh, and elsewhere, in the abilities of Tutsi and Hutu to evade murder and the Khmer Rouge's unstable control over various national zones. Yet we still have no sophisticated explanation for the role of geography in genocide as such."[2] In most cases, genocide studies scholars conceive of geography in terms of how it might be used to isolate targeted groups from potential helpers or to deprive them of food and other forms of sustenance. In the context of Indigenous societies, mention is also made of how geography and space influenced the spread of disease.[3] But seldom is space itself treated as an actor within genocidal processes.[4] Space appears simply as a social product, utilized or violated, but not as a material participant in networks of relations. But, as Adrea Lawrence writes in her study of the day school at the Santa Clara Pueblo, "land—the physical geography, the flora and the fauna of a place—is a full-fledged participant in the story of how Santa Clarans, Hispanos, and Anglos learned their positions, roles, and strategies in the colonization of the place called 'New Mexico.'"[5] This point is true not just for Santa Clarans but also for all Indigenous groups faced with settler colonial pressures. Indeed, territory and space are at once the crucial stakes of settler colonialism, contributors to Indigenous collective identity, and actors enlisted in efforts to resolve the Indian Problem.

With respect to territory, at the upper mesolevel, the location of U.S. federal boarding schools in urban centers placed them directly in the sight lines of other institutional actors, such as health and legal professionals, as well as the general public, which included vocal Indian rights reformers.

Chains of authority flowed to these spaces through government agents rather than church bureaucracies; these chains were thus not, as was often the case in Canada, beyond the view of other observers, including Indigenous peoples and their advocates. In contrast, mission-based schools in Manitoba typically received government directives filtered through higher church authorities or Indian agents. Also, the distance of a school such as FAIRS from centers of government meant that, though policies continued to be developed by the government and circulated among schools, inspections were rare, and knowledge of conditions in the schools was less available to the public. As the Truth and Reconciliation Commission of Canada notes, "Indian Affairs regularly adopted various policies regarding health, discipline, and education, but these were not enforced consistently. At the outset, it had few school inspectors (and those it did have lacked educational qualifications). In later years, provincial school inspectors, who had no power to have their recommendations implemented, inspected the schools."[6] Thus, mesolevel institutional networks, and the ways in which they reached into boarding school spaces, had repercussions for how distant boarding schools were from potentially critical observations of the treatment of children at the schools.

But at the microlevel, territory and space played numerous, more regionally specific roles in the assimilative drama of the schools. First, the buildings and grounds of the schools were actors enrolled by governing authorities to transform Indigenous children but also subverted for purposes of resistance. School buildings were typically larger than any that Indigenous students had seen before and were meant to impart the superiority of European culture in both their grandness and their style.[7] And the space of the schools made a distinct visual and even olfactory impression on the students when they first arrived.[8] "Then all of a sudden we're transported to this institution here with strange buildings and high ceilings and everything varnished. I don't know why that shoe polish smell remains in my mind. Shoe polish and varnish!"[9] The size of the school also reinforced the student's isolation. Muriel Katherine Morriseau, a survivor who was at FAIRS in the 1940s, recalled that

I had a very lonely childhood. I was placed in boarding school when I was 5 years old. I remember my dad taking us there—big, empty building. I don't know, as a child I remember getting my hair cut first thing as I enter the residential school. I seen my cousin laying there in a bed, looked like a hospital or a dormitory—that's what they called it. And that's my first—I dunno it's such a lonely life.[10]

Vincent Pierre, another FAIRS survivor who attended from 1963 to 1970, recounted his first impressions of the school: "I was so amazed as a kid, I must've been five at that time, or four and a half, whatever. You know, I was amazed at this building, it was humungous. I was so blown away by this magnificent building in the middle of the bush! Walking up the stairs, I remember holding my grandma's hand, walking into the building and next thing we're in an office and seen a lot of these people dressed in black."[11] The foreignness and difference of the schools struck the students from their first day at school, signaling that their lives were about to change drastically. As well, agricultural lands around the school communicated the taming of nature. The land outside the school was not simply for play and in many cases lacked adequate play equipment. Instead, the school farm took place of priority on the grounds, since it was the source of food for the school (and often for sale on the market to supplement the school budget).

Moreover, the space of the school was used to separate children from opposite sex siblings, and to culturally disorient them, replacing the openness of Indigenous territory with the regulated and compartmentalized space of the classroom. Whereas large buildings loomed over the students upon their arrival at school, they soon found that they were restricted in their use of this space. Sally Hyer reports that the original Santa Fe Indian School was organized so that access to various parts of the school was limited, allowing for more strict supervision of the students as they made their way through the building.[12] In addition, guardhouses, principals' offices, and the school cemetery reminded students of the destructive and punitive power of the white man.[13] But these efforts to fashion regulatory space did not necessarily succeed, for students sought out and occupied its interstices—for example, secret places where food could be stored, conversations could go unheard, plans could be made, love could blossom, or tears could be shed.

In general, space was simultaneously large and compressed. For example, despite the size of some boarding schools, classrooms and dormitories were often crowded. As noted in a 1937 inspector's report on PLPIRS, "there are now 95 pupils enrolled. The Principal would like a grant for 100, but in my opinion he has not sufficient room to accommodate more than his allotment which I believe is 90. The dormitories are now very crowded and it is almost impossible to walk between the beds. If more pupils are allowed, more dormitory space will be required."[14] This overcrowding at PLPIRS would continue, contributing to heightened levels of teacher turnover and making education difficult, not to mention the risks that it presented for disease transmission. Over a decade later, the overcrowding problem at PLPIRS persisted: "I found a very unsatisfactory situation here with respect to the overcrowding of class rooms. Both rooms are badly overcrowded with the primary room in the worst shape with an enrollment of fifty-seven and the physical capacity for forty-eight. Nine small children are able to attend only part of the time as a result of this and the rest of the children cannot get proper instruction with such a large enrollment."[15] In both New Mexico and Manitoba, across most time periods, school admin-istrators sought to increase the sizes of their schools to accommodate more students (and, especially in the earlier periods, to obtain more per capita payments from their respective governments). But crowding also served a disciplinary function, for crowding eliminated personal space and thereby denied room for the flourishing of an individual Indigenous self, who might use personal space to resist or reject the compulsion of similar bodies all following the same regulatory demands.[16] In such instances, the contradictions of the individualizing and biopolitical tendencies in Indigenous boarding schools becomes clear: schools at which students were individuated through per capita funding policies, reporting criteria, and the school's ambition of fostering individual property ownership also grouped students in a manner to better facilitate control and prevent more rebellious forms of individuation.[17]

Second, despite such efforts to use crowding to prevent individual resis-tance, create surveillant spaces in the schools, or present an image of a fully controlled nature outside, a geography of resistance nonetheless persisted in relation to the schools.[18] In particular, space factored into how students and communities avoided forced attendance or changed the terms under which they were instructed. At AIS, Superintendent Bryan, whose tenure lasted from 1884 to 1886, was persuaded that Indian students should be drawn from nearby communities rather than brought from long distances, contrary to Pratt's vision of boarding schools. McKinney attributes this belief to Bryan's independence of thought, but Gram more convincingly demonstrates that the Pueblo communities did much to influence Bryan on these matters, mostly by using their proximity to the school to monitor conditions there as well as interschool competition to threaten to remove their children to mission schools unless AIS operated on terms more acceptable to the Pueblo.[19] As Joe Sando argues, Pueblo communities experienced life under three different colonial regimes—Spain, Mexico, and the United States. This history familiarized these communities with the art of negotiating with colonial powers. Moreover, because of their particular history, the Pueblo had retained their territory and were not subject to forced removals and community disruptions to the degree of other Indigenous groups. Therefore, their culture was strongly rooted in their territory, providing them with a basis from which to assert themselves in relationship with colonial society.[20]

Faced with the negotiatory power of the Pueblo, Bryan made compromises, but he also formulated his compromises so that they appeared to be consistent with assimilative goals:

> The ultimate object of the Indian schools is, as I understand, not so much the improvement of individuals as the gradual uplifting of the race. To this end it is important to guard against the formation of a wide gulf between parent and child, and to prevent the child from acquiring notions inconsistent with proper filial respect and duty. . . . I would recommend that at this school, therefore, the term consist of nine months, giving the children three months at their homes.[21]

In this instance, Bryan remained in line with the general objective of transforming Indigenous communities through their children, but he suggested that the Indian Problem would be better addressed by keeping children in some provisional contact with their communities. Moreover, Bryan appears to have had local support for this policy. An article in the *Sunday Post* approved of his move to allow child-parent visits:

The Zunis and Navajos having lost several children by death at Carlisle or immediately upon their return home will listen to no proposition to allow another child to go to the far East. The proximity of the Indian school at Albuquerque, N.M., rendering it possible for parents to visit their children, will overcome this prejudice. I am told when parents visit their children at this school they have no desire to interrupt them, but sit in the school room watching with the deepest interest the children recite or following the boys to the fields, and urge them to work like their teachers.[22]

Yet Bryan's perspective did not last past his exit from the superintendent's position in 1886. Indeed, in 1891 Charles Lummis, a journalist and Indian rights activist who lived at the time in Isleta Pueblo, was convinced by the Isleta to assist in facilitating the return of their children from AIS. Initially, this involved a letter to Commissioner Thomas Morgan that provoked the release of three children. But when Morgan refused to release any more, a writ of habeas corpus was filed on behalf of one Isleta man, Juan Rey Abeita, that charged the school with kidnapping his children. The judge ordered that his three children be returned, and the success of the case influenced the release of fifteen further children.[23] Subsequent superintendents at federal boarding schools in New Mexico thereafter had to manage their student populations in light of this case. Superintendent Crandall at SFIS, for example, noted that

our school is located so near the different Pueblos that the Indian parents visit their children once or twice during the school year. This in itself did not appeal to me at first, but I have come to believe that it is a benefit rather than a hindrance. In this way parents and children keep in close touch; when the child leaves the school he goes to his home and is thus prepared for his home life, and has not become estranged, forgotten his mother tongue, and does not feel that he is neither an Indian nor a white man.[24]

In addition to this concession to the Pueblo, AIS and SFIS superintendents often stressed how the environment and climate of their schools were similar to those to which Pueblo and Diné students were accustomed.[25]

Spatial and ecological similarities were used as selling points, both to the BIA hierarchy, who subscribed to the notion that shifting students from one climate to another made them more susceptible to illness, and to the Pueblo and Diné peoples, as an appeal that their children would not lose all connection to their territory. Of course, the health of their children was also of great concern to Pueblo and Diné parents, and community leaders, and they thought it necessary to keep a close eye on how their children were fairing in the boarding schools.

Complicating this picture of territory as a source of resistance is the fact that there was no single way in which space and territory factored into the boarding school experience. To illustrate this point, it is worth spending some time examining the specific ways that Diné territory intervened in attempts to stretch the settler colonial mesh across *Diné Bikéyah*. For the Diné, as with the Pueblo, territory is important, but it plays a different role in relation to boarding schools. Removal from territory, in particular through the "Long Walk" (1864–69), served as an initial threat to compel Diné assimilation. At the Navajo Museum and Cultural Center in Window Rock, Arizona, this infamous act of forced removal is described as the Navajo "holocaust," for it was experienced as a catastrophic severing of people from land, during which more than 2000 Diné perished. Diné oral histories often recall the scorched earth campaign or "fearing time" that preceded the Long Walk:

> General Kit Carson was not afraid, he went right into the heart of the Navajo country. The only way that . . . a Navajo can be whipped was destroying their gardens and the livestock, so that's what they done. Most of the crop was found in the canyon of Canyon de Chelley, way in the heart of the wall where most of the people raised corn, where nobody can get to it. The Navajo people didn't have enough ammunition and guns to fight the army, but they kept on. Finally, one day Kit Carson went in Canyon de Chelley in the canyon with his soldiers and destroyed most all camps that they had in the canyon, and they destroyed all the cornfields, and they turned their horses loose in the cornfields. For many days some of the Navajo people fought back, but the guns were too strong for them, so some of them just had to wander away. Kit Carson

destroyed all the corn up, burn some of them up. The soldiers was the ones that done all the damage, and then they came back. Kit Carson start to travel around in the country, in the Navajo country, looking for Navajo people, picking them up.[26]

The Bosque Redondo reservation (which was sited next to Fort Sumner, and named Hwéeldi or "place of suffering" by the Diné), in New Mexico, the place to which 9500 Diné were removed, is likewise referred to as a "prison camp" in the introduction to a volume of Diné descriptions of the Long Walk.[27] Indeed, it was an experiment in social engineering, as Diné were subjected to forced labor in an attempt to transform them into sedentary agriculturalists and pastoralists. The Diné leaders who negotiated their return from Bosque Redondo are venerated. Individuals such as Manuelito helped to convince the U.S. government to agree to the Treaty of 1868, which returned the Diné to their territory and set the boundaries for this territory, brought the tribe under the oversight of an Indian agent, promoted individual land ownership and farming among the Diné, and promised a variety of buildings and services in exchange for their obedience. Of specific interest, Article 6 of the treaty spells out a compulsory education requirement for the Diné:

In order to insure the civilization of the Indians entering into this treaty, the necessity of education is admitted, especially of such of them as may be settled on said agricultural parts of this reservation, and they therefore pledge themselves to compel their children, male and female, between the ages of six and sixteen years, to attend school; and it is hereby made the duty of the agent for said Indians to see that this stipulation is strictly complied with; and the United States agrees that, for every thirty children between said ages who can be induced or compelled to attend school, a house shall be provided, and a teacher competent to teach the elementary branches of an English education shall be furnished, who will reside among said Indians, and faithfully discharge his or her duties as a teacher.[28]

In this manner, the Treaty of 1868, and therefore the experience of forced removal through the Long Walk, were antecedent to the Diné federal Indian schooling experience. Although the treaty spared the Diné from isolation and immediate destruction, it was also a disciplinary document that sought to restrict the Diné to a delimited territory where they would be encouraged to abide by a fee simple property regime and settler citizenship standards. Thus, the Long Walk and Treaty of 1868 represent an attempt to tighten the settler colonial mesh around the Diné.

But territory also intervened to obstruct this assimilation. Diné territory is vast, and, during the first half century of assimilative schooling, the roads were poor to nonexistent. The U.S. government failed to provide local schools as promised under Article 6 of the Treaty of 1868, and the Diné resisted sending their children to boarding schools with the assistance of their territory. When trying to recruit Diné for SFIS in 1891, Superintendent Cart complained that "at the Navajo Agency the prospect is not encouraging. The Indians are scattered over such a vast extent of rough country that at this time of the year, they are almost inaccessible."[29] SFIS and AIS would gradually—and not without difficulty—increase the numbers of Diné students at their schools. In 1890, drawing from a population of 6,090 school-aged children, only eighty-nine Diné were enrolled in school. By 1918, this number increased to 1,881 children, which occurred after Commissioner Francis Leupp constructed more day schools in Diné territory—a mode of schooling more appealing to Diné parents.[30] Throughout the early 1900s, though, Diné parents resisted sending their children to boarding schools, which led the government to take drastic action to compel their attendance. For example, in 1932, Dana Coolidge testified before the Senate subcommittee investigating the conditions of Indians in the United States to report that "the children are caught, often roped like cattle, and taken away from their parents, many times never to return. They are transferred from school to school, given white people's names, forbidden to speak their own tongue, and when sent to distant schools are not taken home for three years."[31]

In the immediate aftermath of the Second World War, Diné education was perceived to be in crisis. The day schools set up under Commissioner John Collier were struggling, and a pair of BIA studies showed that the educational needs of many Navajo children were not being met. As well, Diné leaders such as Henry Chee Dodge, chairman of the Navajo Tribal

Council, called at this time for more reservation boarding schools for Diné students, since day schools were ineffective for a territorially dispersed Diné population. Dodge's request was ignored, and instead, in 1946, the BIA established the Special Navajo Education Program, implemented at Sherman Indian School in Riverside, California, where Diné children were to be prepared for life in the non-Indian world through training in basic academic and vocational skills. Diné students were also sent to other boarding schools, such as AIS, at this time. However, the program did very little to deal with the difficult economic conditions in Diné country, nor did it make a serious impact on Diné education. Thus, in 1950, the Navajo-Hopi Rehabilitation Act was implemented, appropriating $90 million over a ten-year period to foster economic opportunities for the Diné and allocating $25 million of this sum to hasten education among their children. Still, after four years under this act and its efforts to enroll Diné students in nonreservation schools, 13,000 school-aged Diné children were not in school. In response, Congress enacted the Navajo Educational Emergency Program, which provided for the construction of elementary and public schools, as well as the expansion of boarding schools, but also created what were referred to as "bordertown" dormitories so that Diné children could attend off-reservation public schools.[32]

Diné resistance to European-style schooling was a product, in part, of a different view of education, and, unlike Pueblo communities, Diné were generally less familiar with mission schools and other forms of European education. Education for the Diné involved learning by doing. Under observation by an adult, usually a family member, a child learned through experiencing the world. Even if this meant exposure to minor accidents, such as bites and burns, the children learned what was and was not safe to touch. They were respected as participants in the life of the community, with a voice to be heeded when decisions were made about their welfare.[33] The European schools offered an experience of education too opposed to Diné ways to seem particularly relevant. This is not to say that Diné were unwilling or unable to learn from and transmit knowledge to other cultures. Indeed, throughout their history, they had shared practices with Pueblo (dry farming), Spanish (sheepherding), and Mexican (silversmithing) neighbors.[34] But the schools demanded more than cultural sharing and, likely most salient to Diné parents, removed children from the life of the hogan and the family "outfit" (a matrilocal network), and the related duties of familial life, such as tending to livestock or the fields.

Diné resistance through territorial isolation would begin to unfurl in the 1920s, when an effort was made to reformulate Diné patterns of governance, resulting in a centralized form of tribal government rather than simply working through existing matrilocal networks. Based on this centralized unit, policy was more easily imposed on the Diné. Also in this period, perhaps not coincidentally, valuable mineral and oil deposits were discovered, and more efficient governance was needed to allow their exploitation.[35] This meant, of course, governance structures that facilitated negotiations for resource access. But this governmental change was further advanced through the culling of Diné sheep herds in the 1930s under Commissioner Collier's administration, since these practices also affected another traditional source of Diné social power, women's care of livestock.[36] At this time, Collier's pluralistic valuation of Indigenous cultures and his defense of Indigenous territories came up against his faith in ecological science, which suggested that the levels of grazing in Diné territory were unsustainable. This perceived fact led Collier to impose drastic stock reductions on the Diné in the belief that radical intervention was necessary to Diné survival.[37] But at the same time that he was culling Diné herds, he was also working to create community-based day schools that would both educate Diné children and provide a useful social and practical space for community members. However, many Diné were reluctant to embrace this revised form of education, in part because they lost all trust in Collier over his position on Diné grazing practices and his unilateral policy enforcement that ignored those practices, Diné knowledge, and the vitality of sheep to their culture.[38] Collier miscalculated the Diné connection to their animal herds, and the centrality of the herds to Diné ways of being, and his assault on the herds produced further resistance to his educational objectives.[39]

Thus, in the case of the Diné, the settler colonial mesh had great difficulty stretching across their vast territory, and various actors, including the Diné, but also their territory and livestock, interacted to prevent full capture within the mesh. In the face of such resistance, boarding school proponents sought to enlist a new set of technology-based actors to help overcome obstacles such as the physical distance separating students from schools. For example, the automobile and the train were of great importance in expanding school enrollments. The 1912 annual report for AIS boasts of the strategic value of the school's location: "[AIS] is in the very heart of Indian country and is the nearest of all Non-Reservation Boarding Schools to the Navajo Reservation where 5000 to 7000 children are without school accommodations. 4,500 Pueblo Indians reside within 70 miles of the school and within 2 ½ hours ride of same. The location and railroad facilities of the school make it easy for all Pueblos and Navajos to reach and render it almost unnecessary to solicit pupils."[40] In the 1940s and 1950s, therefore, as transportation increased in its capacity to circumvent territorial restrictions and gain access to Diné children, space was no longer as effective an ally for resistance among Diné families. Remote spaces could now be accessed with some effort, and Diné children became ever more likely to be sent to boarding schools, because day schools were said to be too costly or impractical in such regions. Moreover, they were more likely to be sent at a younger age and to be restricted in their ability to return to their home communities during holidays and the summer months.[41] It is no wonder, then, that one often finds among Diné oral histories more negative stories of experiences in boarding schools, running later into the twentieth century and more reminiscent of those heard in our Canadian case studies, than is the case for the Pueblo.

Students from Sagkeeng First Nation (formerly the Fort Alexander Reserve), like the Pueblo, appeared to be at an advantage in terms of their proximity to their boarding school with respect to the opportunities for resistance that it might provide them. However, territorial proximity alone was not sufficient for enlisting space to loosen the settler colonial mesh and facilitate greater Indigenous input into the schooling at FAIRS. As a Roman Catholic school in a relatively isolated region, FAIRS was part of a Canadian colonial network that exhibited fewer policy fluctuations than the American network. The location of the school, difficult to reach by roads, even though it was relatively close to towns such as Lac du Bonnet, Pine Falls, and Selkirk, also meant that there was less opportunity for inspection and less opportunity for Indigenous leaders to speak to officials beyond the school to voice their concerns. Isolation and the power of the Indian agent helped to ensure continued Indigenous enrollments without the Sagkeeng people, whose children were the majority at the school, increasing their negotiatory power.[42] But whereas FAIRS was isolated, PLPIRS had more pressure to serve as a demonstration school, since it was more likely to host visitors. In the words of Commissioner Graham, "I am particularly anxious that this school should always present a good appearance. It is in rather a public place and they always have a number of visitors, and people get a better impression [when] everything is up-to-date."[43] Under such circumstances, accessibility of the school resulted in concerns about impression management not characteristic of other Canadian boarding schools. However, it is not clear from the records that these concerns about impression management were acted on in any significant manner.

A third way that space interacted with the boarding school experience occurred when distance from territory was enlisted as part of an attempt to forge a radical break between Indigenous children and their communities. Of course, distance from territory alone was seldom sufficient to completely divorce children from their Indigenous cultures and territories. As Brenda Child argues, "distance caused hardship, distress, and unimagined miseries but failed to extinguish the very real influence parents and family continued to exert over the lives of students. . . . The power of home was so intense and comforting that few students left that world behind."[44] Child counters those who see distance as a pure break with the sociocultural world of the Indigenous community, but we must complicate her analysis and push it further to get to the variety of ways in which space, territory, time, and distance were involved in the negotiation of boarding school experiences. Distance could be catastrophic or overcome because it always interacted with other factors, such as access for and political power of the Indigenous group in question.

Child's insight speaks to another terrain of resistance: memory. It is through the use of memory that children were able to combat distance from their communities. Theodore Fontaine addresses this subversive tool in his memoir of FAIRS: "Early on, I discovered that I could escape from the loneliness and sadness of my life at Indian residential school by recalling and reliving my joyous life as a boy at home before school. . . . The practice of retreating into my mind and my memories became a lifelong survival skill."[45] Yet the disciplinary structure of the schools, and the disciplinary regimentation of time at the school, meant that it was often difficult for children to occupy this space of memory and to overcome imposed distance. Later in his book, Fontaine suggests that students regulated one another in a manner that made it increasingly difficult to recall home as one became more immersed in the world of the boarding school: "Memories of happy times surfaced a lot in my first year at school, particularly at night and in the dark. Eventually they came less and less often—perhaps mercifully, for whimpering and crying were reason for the older boys to belittle and abuse the younger ones—and later I thought perhaps they were only a dream."[46]

Physical distance was not always necessary to force a radical break between child and community. The proximity of a school such as FAIRS to the Sagkeeng First Nation did not automatically result in community empowerment, the retention of Indigenous traditions, or less loneliness for the children. Indeed, seeing a family member walk past the schoolyard fence, yet having no ability to make contact with him or her, intensified longing for home and created resentments for those community members outside the schools who had failed to protect the children from enrollment. "When I was at the residential school there, my home was only about a quarter mile away. I can see my home from the boarding school, like, when you, you know, I was lonely, wondering why I can't go home, or why people can't come and visit me."[47] In the early days of FAIRS, visits to home and family were more frequent; however, in 1917, Inspector J. R. Bunn thought that this privilege was being misused, and he reported to Deputy Superintendent D. C. Scott that

> I called the pupils together and explained to them that it was apparent that permission to visit their homes was being misused, by both parents and children, and that this leave would have to be stopped or changed from once a week leave, to once a month, and no oftener, and I so told the principal, as it was bound to have a bearing on the discipline of the school. This was rather drastic, but I am informed it has had a wholesome effect.[48]

This policy held stable for most years at FAIRS, and the school thus remained both separate from and within the community. This paradoxical location of the school is captured in the way that students both saw the school prior to attending it and yet did not discuss it with their parents, who were former students and wanted nothing more than to forget about their own experiences of residential schooling. As Mary Courchene remembered, "I knew where the school [FAIRS] was; we knew where the school was. It was five minutes away; I could see it, right. Step outside our door and there was the school, great big building. But, we never knew about it. My mom didn't talk about it. My dad didn't talk about it. It was just there."[49]

At PLPIRS, proximity to their home community also did not mean that students were able to leave the school: "As we — I remember the day we left, we travelled down that road to Portage and they left us there and that was the start of everything that came about in our lives. Stayed there — I didn't go home for the holidays. I stayed there from 6 years old 'til I was 18 and I never went home."[50] Reservation boarding schools, such as PLPIRS, could also taint the space of the reserve for survivors and their families. One intergenerational survivor tells of how her parents (PLPIRS survivors) moved away from their community to protect their children from ever needing to attend such a school: "And so they raised us off reserve for one of those reasons, for that particular reason, so that none of us would ever have to go to residential school."[51] In this manner, the location of the school on the reserve forged a final break between student and community, making it impossible for the student to remain in that space, not because the student had been successfully assimilated but because of the memories contained therein. Purvis H. Fontaine notes that "I left the reserve 'cause of what happened to me in the residential school. I couldn't stand the place. I hated the place so much I want to get out."[52]

In the United States, Pratt's boarding school model was meant to remove Indigenous children far from their traditional territories in order to accomplish such a break. Students were to be placed in white, English-speaking communities so that spatial proximity to European culture could be used to impart the habits and language of so-called civilization.[53] Yet, as mentioned above, AIS and SFIS violated this model. This does not mean that students at these schools were immune to homesickness, the physical manifestation of spatial distance — internalized, it was a source of infection. Especially early in their schooling days, students suffered much from this malady. Parents sought to alleviate homesickness by requesting that the students be permitted visits home, often only to be rebuked by AIS and SFIS superintendents. But, in most cases, the students adapted to and accepted their time at school.

According to Sally Hyer's research, Pueblo students at SFIS claimed that they were able to occupy the terrain of memory and preserve their heritage no matter what the school threw at them. Hyer, who admittedly interviewed only those students willing to talk about their past lives for a project intended to commemorate SFIS, argues that "Students were at school to learn the white man's way of life. But at the same time, their Indian identity was secure; they already knew who they were and who their parents were." She then quotes one student: "The attitude our parents gave us at home was, 'Don't ever forget your heritage. This is what you are, and you can't ever change because you are this. But you *must* learn this other [culture], which is necessary in this life.'"[54]

In his work, Patrick Wolfe has stressed that "whatever settlers may say—and they generally have a lot to say—the primary motive for elimination is not race (or religion, ethnicity, grade of civilization, etc.) but access to territory. Territoriality is settler colonialism's specific, irreducible element."[55] This raises a fourth connection between Indigenous boarding schools and space/territory: that between the schools and dispossession of Indigenous territories. Indigenous communities in both Canada and the United States did not necessarily oppose education. For example, despite general Diné reluctance to accept European education, Rex Becenti, Jr., a Diné from Tohatchi, New Mexico, argued that "they have done the right thing of educating the younger generation and some of the older people in the earliest days. It was right to be done, but not taking the land away from them, which we think as we should be the name of the government, we should get the best part of the money of our land today which we are not being treated right."[56] Here the disagreement is not with the education of Indian children but with the removal of land.

Yet land dispossession cannot be neatly separated from the schools. I already mentioned how the Dawes Act in the United States was conceived as a crucial stratagem within reformers' plans to advance assimilative education in the late 1800s. In this manner, Indigenous boarding schools sought to transform the relationships that Indigenous groups maintained with their places. In the United States, working in tandem with allotment policies, former students were encouraged to take allotments and to fence off these areas. As well, they were directed to make "improvements" to allotted terrain.[57] The Pueblo were also advised to build "more roomy and better houses" complete with "modern windows and doors."[58] But in reworking their communities, the Pueblo also found ways to maintain tradition within reformulated spaces, such as by hiding their kivas in new buildings, much as they had done for centuries.

For the Pueblo, their lands had already been bounded and defined by the Spanish; thus, in terms of revising Pueblo relationships to the territory, the focus was mostly on the individual dispersal and capitalization of the land, not on convincing them to become more sedentary on it. Indeed, government and school officials perceived the Pueblo to be different from other Indigenous groups. They were thought to be sedentary agriculturalists and pastoralists rather than mobile like the Diné and Apache.[59] Hyer contends that, "unlike the children from nomadic tribes who were students at other off-reservation schools, the Pueblos had been farming for hundreds of years. They were more experienced in local agricultural conditions than the farming teachers, who came from the east."[60] The 1910 annual report for SFIS confirmed this point, arguing that this agriculturalism set the Pueblo up for learning and improving their farming methods. But it also resulted in students being called on too frequently to help in their parents' fields, which, according to the report, was partly because Pueblo farming methods were archaic and resistant to modern influence. This was believed to be a problem but not as severe a problem as the fact that, like other Indigenous groups, the Pueblo still kept their land collectively, and this was viewed as a detriment to their civilization. The 1910 annual report for AIS noted that "the one incentive to put forth greater effort among the Pueblos would be the division of their lands and the allotment of them in severalty. This would be an inducement to each Indian to put better improvements on his land, better fences, and to cultivate it better and prepare it for irrigation and crops and would lead to its improvement."[61]

For most other Indigenous groups at the schools under consideration here, however, education was directed toward sedentarization.[62] The nomadic and seminomadic patterns of Indigenous peoples were viewed as a barrier to assimilation as well as an uncertainty in the face of capitalist expansion on the continent. Thus, much of the education at FAIRS and PLPIRS can be examined in terms of how it contributed to fitting Indigenous peoples into the mainstream Canadian economy, including its dominant land regime. Students were encouraged to embrace values of individualism, to view land as something to be owned, cultivated, and exploited, and they were instilled with European practices of farming and homemaking. The experience would not have been all too different for groups of Apache and Diné students at AIS and SFIS.

Finally, time, as a theme, runs throughout this book. Through the examples given, the objective is to show that government policies, institutional networks, and specific boarding schools were not stagnant across time—the settler colonial mesh expands and contracts, tightens and loosens, across historical time as contingencies arise and perhaps are overcome. However, time also factors into this discussion as an actor enrolled in the assimilative project. To begin, children in both the United States and Canada were trained in their boarding schools to follow the rigidity of the white man's clock. For example, as Indian Agent A. A. Muckle wrote in his report on the St. Peter's band in Manitoba,

> yet they do not progress as they should; one reason being that they take too many holidays. Time is of no value in their eyes. A great many of them would like to have council meetings two or three times a week. They think nothing of coming to my place and talking for half a day or more, in the middle of haying or harvest, about the most trifling affairs, but as there is no such word as time in the Indian language, it is hard to teach them that time is money, and I have been unable to find an interpreter who could do so.[63]

Time was no longer to be viewed as flowing, connecting generations and life beyond the present; instead, it was segmented, compartmentalized, and to be used with the greatest efficiency. This disciplinary use of time meant, among other things, that it was often difficult for children to think about their home communities, to sneak away to practice their languages in secret, and to conspire with fellow students to resist the school and its messages.

Time was also complicit in terms of the time of life when students were enrolled in schools. In general, students entered Indigenous boarding schools at younger ages in Manitoba compared with New Mexico. This meant that they were in schools and therefore separated from their communities for longer periods of time. For Indigenous students in the American Southwest sent to boarding schools at a young age, the experience was similar. Valencia Garcia, from Santa Ana Pueblo, remembers her time at AIS as time away from her family:

> No, I don't remember anything because when I was, I think when I was four or five years and then I went to school, that's what they told me. I was just a little kid then, so from there on I was in school. We never had a vacation from it, Christmas or something like they do now. Always had to be in school, until the summer time, June, when school is out. So I didn't have very much time to be among my people, you know, and during July and August we all go back. All winter long, so that's the way I went to school.[64]

The length of time over which a community engaged with boarding schools and European education is another factor that must be considered in such comparisons. However, it is not one that plays out in any neat or consistent fashion. Consider, for example, that Pueblo communities began their experience with mission schooling much earlier than most groups. They first made contact with the Spanish when Fray Marcos de Niza visited the Zuni in 1539. Even at this point, the Pueblo communities were clustered around central plazas in what the Spanish perceived to be towns, hence the name Pueblo. The Spanish Franciscan Friars built mission churches where the Pueblo people received religious instruction and practical training, but this came to an end in 1680 when the Pueblo revolt chased the Spanish from their territory. The Spanish would return in 1692, followed by Mexican control in 1821 and then American rule in 1846.[65] But with respect to time, evident here is a lengthy period of negotiation and adaptation among the Pueblo and various colonial powers. With this length of time came experience, knowledge, customs, and practices that facilitated Pueblo interventions in the schooling lives of their children in later periods.

In the New Mexican schools, one also finds that over time, because relatives and other people known to the students had attended boarding schools, the schools became more normalized for Indigenous communities. As more and more generations of Indigenous children were sent to the schools, they became habituated to the idea that attending a boarding school was simply something one did. Older siblings or relatives might fill the heads of the young with stories of the schools that could make the schools seem both exotic and frightening. This was less so in our Manitoban cases, in which intergenerational experiences of residential schools resulted in multiple layers of trauma stretching across extended families, often inspiring silence rather than discussion of the schools among family members. Mary Courchene, whose story begins this book, recalled her excitement of going to school at FAIRS and the possibility of learning a new language. But at the doorway to the school, after the confrontation with her brother that left him crying, she turned to find that her mother had gone without even saying good-bye. [66] Because the Manitoban schools were less differentiated across time—and survivors of multiple generations experienced the same patterns of discipline, violence, and cultural degradation—time in the Manitoban context had a much more destructive impact on Indigenous communities and militated against the habituation to schooling across generations.

Space and time are thus actors that can be enlisted to play a variety of roles in Indigenous boarding schools, though they do not always play the roles assigned to them. The crowded space of the dorm room could also serve as a cover for mischief, the fields and yards occasionally presented chances to act without staff eyes seeing, and territories that were wide ranging and unbounded so as to provide hiding spaces could be delineated and bounded as means to enable capture. Thus, though the ideal formulated in the centers of government, and among opinion leaders on the Indian Problem, might have suggested that time and space would be enlisted within the settler colonial mesh to entrap the child and sever him or her from Indigenous space and time, Indigenous places and concepts of time did not necessarily show fidelity to these plans. Instead, Indigenous children, parents, and families in some instances were able to draw on their relationships to space and time to force gaps in the settler colonial mesh and to resist its assimilative pressures.

Disease and Health

It has been noted that disease was the most destructive force unleashed on the Indigenous peoples of the American continent.[67] This is taken by some to suggest that natural (disease) rather than social (genocide) processes are most at fault for the near-catastrophic consequences of colonialism for many Indigenous groups.[68] But this separation between nature and culture is more artificial than it is real. As Bruno Latour notes, modern Europeans tend to construct separate poles of nature and culture, all the while allowing for the proliferation of hybrids that are amalgamations of nature and culture networked together in complex interface. This act of "purification"—that is, of keeping nature and culture separate—allows moderns to stack the deck in their favor, assigning events and objects to either the nature pole or the culture pole when it suits their interests.[69] Taking Latour's argument out of its science studies context, one can examine how this practice of purification operates within debates about what is and what is not genocide, since the hybridity of destructive processes—for example, the slow genocide of HIV/AIDS spread through rape or the destruction caused by (fully or partially) orchestrated famines designed to punish rebellious collectives—often complicates the picture of what is and is not part of a genocidal action. In short, we can separate hybrid and networked phenomena such as disease and famine into the category of "nature" (as distinct from "culture" or "society") not because this is what empirical evidence suggests but because we adhere to an intellectual orientation that holds nature and culture to be mutually distinct and uncoupled, despite their clear interconnections.[70] Thus, European diseases in many instances were permitted to ravage Indigenous communities largely unchecked and with a certain degree of indifference because these were not processes for which Europeans felt particularly responsible.[71] Although many health historians have been careful to show the intersections of health and culture in the destructive spread of disease in North America,[72] genocide scholars have too often contributed to the purification of these categories.[73]

The same health historians make clear that disease and health do not factor into Indigenous boarding schools in the United States and Canada in any straightforward or simple manner. Certainly, it was often the case that disease spread in schools because of the negligent actions of staff and government officials. In such instances, disease also served as a signal to parents that their children were at risk and that all was not right in boarding schools. However, in other cases, schools managed to advance health claims to present themselves as spaces more secure from disease than Indigenous communities. In still other cases, disease and health were enlisted as further means to fashion and regulate Indigenous bodies through boarding schools. As such, disease and health, as actors, had dynamic roles to play in boarding schools and the settler colonial mesh.

In the first few decades of Indigenous boarding schools in the United States and Canada, the drive to enroll students typically superseded concerns about health, placing many uninfected Indigenous students at risk of contagion once they entered boarding school.[74] Other factors, such as overcrowding, inadequate nutrition, lack of training, insufficient medical staff, scant medical supplies, sharing of linens and towels, loneliness, poor ventilation, and overwork and exhaustion, also made schools breeding grounds for disease.

In the United States, W. A. Jones, Indian commissioner from 1897 to 1905, pushed for increased enrollments at federal Indigenous boarding schools. A consequence of this push was that sick children were enrolled, thereby placing other students at risk.[75] Overcrowding combined with disease to create conditions that facilitated the spread of deadly illness. But even before this point, students were often in danger at the schools, especially those who were relatively unexposed to European living conditions and diseases. At AIS, half of the Ute children who attended in 1885 died because of disease.[76] And disease factored into the lives of students after Jones's tenure, as in the 1921–22 school year, when an influenza outbreak infected 392 AIS pupils.[77]

Parents were aware of the dangers of disease at the schools and therefore hesitant to allow their children to attend them. Oakie James, for example, told of how Diné parents sent their more sickly children to school for fear of losing their stronger children, needed around the hogan: "They were still afraid of boarding school, for they had seen how an epidemic of measles might kill off eight or ten children in the winter. When they chose the child who had to leave his family and live in this strange new place, they took one who had poor health and who could best be spared from work."[78] To deal with Diné resistance to sending their children, Supervisor of Indian Schools E. H. Hammond wrote to Superintendent J. D. DeHuff at SFIS in 1922 and requested that parents be provided with better and more prompt information on instances of illness, in particular tuberculosis, at the school, since the school's practice of simply returning ailing children to their communities unannounced was perceived to deter parents from sending their children to nonreservation schools. Two or three sick children who had been returned to Diné territory were reported to have died soon after arriving back at their homes.[79]

A review of student case files sheds light on the complex role of disease in a school such as SFIS. Anna de Jesus, a Jicarilla Apache, entered SFIS in 1917 at the age of sixteen. With her mother and father already passed away, her grandfather was her primary guardian. His concern for her health while in school was evident in 1917 when he wrote to request that she be returned home after he learned that she was not well. Superintendent DeHuff responded that the girl had "nothing more than a cold" and did not need to be returned.[80] In February 1920, however, her health took a more serious turn. Initially, Anna was diagnosed with double lobar pneumonia, which cleared up, but as the pneumonia disappeared it became apparent that she was suffering from tuberculosis. The latter condition progressed quickly, and she died on February 24, 1920.[81] During her bout with pneumonia, the school had considered sending her home. But Anna was not well enough for travel, though it was assumed that the return to her community would help her psychologically if not physically.[82] In this episode, one gains a sense of the role of disease in SFIS during this era. Concern about disease in the school was strong enough among Indigenous parents and guardians that Anna's grandfather felt compelled to keep a close watch on her health while Anna was ill at SFIS. Likewise, the school showed a commitment to fighting disease as a threat to its students. However, SFIS also used disease as a rationale for further control over the bodies of its students. When Anna was diagnosed to be only slightly sick, she was denied travel back home. When she became very sick, a trip home was considered acceptable yet impossible because of her poor health. Thus, whether she was perceived to be moderately or extremely ill, her ability to leave the school and return to her community still rested in the hands of the SFIS superintendent and his medical advisers.

Likewise, a Santo Domingo boy named Santana Aguilar was compelled by the superintendent overseeing his community to attend SFIS even though he was sick. The rationale was that the school had "an excellent hospital."[83] The boarding school was also portrayed as the best hope for the health of Petra Armijo from Jemez Pueblo. Superintendent DeHuff scolded her sister Lupe for requesting Petra's return to Jemez, suggesting that her ill health was the result of the substandard care that Petra had received in infancy, long prior to her attendance at SFIS. DeHuff also charged that family members had brought her unripe fruit to eat while she was in the hospital, adding that "the doctor and the nurse know better than anybody else what kind of food such a person should have."[84] In these cases, the authority of the school, and its claim on Indigenous children, rested on the supposition that the school was a place of superior health to the home community.

In Canada, the conditions for disease spread were particularly dire. Duncan Campbell Scott, while serving as deputy superintendent general of Indian Affairs, wrote that "it is quite within the mark to say that fifty per cent of the children who passed through these schools did not live to benefit from the education they had received therein."[85] John Milloy attributes these deadly conditions to the disorganization of the Canadian Indigenous boarding school system: "The reality was that, from the moment the school system was launched in the 1880s and 1890s, it drifted without a firm hand, without concerted intervention. And this was despite the knowledge that many children were held in dangerous circumstances and that the death rate was not only of tragic proportions but was, in addition, undercutting the whole purpose and strategy of the system."[86] Indeed, the Canadian system received strong warning about the deadly consequences of disease in Indigenous boarding schools. In a 1907 report, Dr. P. H. Bryce, chief medical officer to the Department of the Interior and Indian Affairs, noted widespread disease and death in Indigenous boarding schools: "It is apparent that it is everywhere the old-fashioned buildings, their very varied and imperfect methods of heating and an almost complete lack of a knowledge of the meaning of ventilation and the methods for accomplishing it in the different schools that are responsible for this most serious condition which has been demonstrated and which demands an immediate answer."[87] Based on Bryce's report, the government established for the first time health standards for the operation of residential schools. However, though the government did implement the most inexpensive of Bryce's recommendations, it also worked to remove Bryce from his position and limit his influence.[88] Thus, after his retirement from the civil service in 1921, an embittered Bryce felt compelled to publish a pamphlet titled "The Story of a National Crime: Being an Appeal for Justice to the Indians of Canada" (1922).[89] Here he noted that "24 per cent of all the pupils which had been in the schools were known to be dead, while of one school on the File Hills reserve, which gave a complete return to date, 75 per cent were dead at the end of the 16 years since the school opened."[90] Moreover, Bryce argued, indifference and neglect by government officials resulted in the continuing plague of tuberculosis for Indigenous peoples, leading to much higher than expected death rates and amounting to what he referred to as a "criminal disregard for the treaty pledges to guard the welfare of the Indian wards of the nation."[91]

Disease thus was not an entirely independent actor ravaging the hallways and dormitories of Indigenous boarding schools. Its passage was facilitated through a web of relations that included both human intervention and human neglect, which makes it worthy of consideration in any discussion of genocide. But the cooperation between human-created conditions and disease spread varied depending on the school, and the destructive capacity of human-pathogen interactions is an empirical question that requires further future investigation.

We must also take into consideration how death caused by disease was, at least on the surface, contrary to the assimilative project undertaken in Indigenous boarding schools. How could schools dedicated to transforming Indigenous children appear so blasé about their deaths? This question deserves more intensive investigation than is possible here, but one cannot help but wonder if, at least during certain periods of boarding school history, Indigenous children were not considered fully human prior to their supposed civilization. These students could be sacrificed to the abhorrent conditions during their time at the schools up to the point where they assumed the dispositions of European culture.[92] Yet the widespread presence of diseases such as tuberculosis among Indigenous peoples also reinforced among the white population the assumption that Indigenous peoples were genetically inferior and therefore more prone to such diseases.[93] In this manner, disease was also complicit in the racist degradation of Indigenous peoples and served as a further rationalization of and legitimation for policies of assimilation and aggressive civilization.

It is important to note here, however, that the role of disease and health was not one-dimensional in the history of Indigenous boarding schools. In both New Mexico and Manitoba, the same diseases presented concerns for school officials: tuberculosis, trachoma, measles, flu, and diphtheria. Depending on the period and the pattern of disease spread, disease could be a reason for parents to keep their children *from* school (if the school was feared as the source of infection) or to send their children *to* school (if the community was beset by disease and the school was perceived to have the health facilities required to provide prevention, care, and treatment). Therefore, disease and health care had complex roles to play in the histories of the schools.

Indeed, at times, schools in Canada and the United States sought to enlist the tools of health care and prevention in order to make their schools more attractive to Indigenous children. Cato Sells, commissioner of Indian Affairs from 1913 to 1921, was certainly aware of the contradiction in seeking to transform Indigenous children while exposing them to deadly conditions. He wrote in a circular to Indian service employees that "we can not solve the Indian problem without Indians. We can not educate their children unless they are kept alive."[94] Sells was not the first to arrive at this realization. The medical examination had already become a prominent aspect of student admission in both the United States and Canada. In most cases, prospective students were examined to determine whether they had any symptoms of spreadable disease as well as in terms of previous health records. In the United States, after the 1903 Indian Health Survey demonstrated to Commissioner Jones that the incidence of tuberculosis and other diseases was more prevalent than previously believed, it became mandatory for physicians to examine students before they entered the schools. After he replaced Jones in 1905, Commissioner Leupp established the first federal sanatorium for Indigenous students.[95] From this point forward, the Indian service waged an increasing battle against disease, even if the fight was often halfhearted, and economic pressures and other factors continued to contribute to school overcrowding. Data were increasingly collected on the health of children in schools. The goal remained to preserve the lives of students so as to change them. Disease and health information were thus enlisted as ways to know Indians, to observe their children and communities, and to assert further control over their bodies.

It was not simply the assimilationist goals of the schools that inspired an invigorated approach to health, however; because boarding schools were often located in non-Indigenous areas, the presence of disease among pupils was also perceived as a threat to non-Indigenous persons.[96] As well, it was widely known that Indigenous parents were reluctant to send their children to schools with high death rates from disease and other factors. Awareness of the poor impression caused by deaths in boarding schools led school administrators, in cases in which medical intervention had failed to prevent or stem disease, to remove children from the school and send them to a sanatorium or back to their home communities, where their deaths would have less impact on the school in terms of the spread of disease or elevation of the school's death rate.[97]

Boarding schools recruited modern medicine to displace the role of traditional healing practices in Indigenous lives. Although in both Manitoba and New Mexico Indigenous peoples tended to hold pluralistic beliefs about medicine, utilizing both Indigenous and Western traditions when and where they thought appropriate, settler colonial powers reduced Indigenous medicine to mere superstition and held that the embrace of Western medicine was entwined with processes of civilization.[98] Along these lines, C. Gorman (Diné) discussed how younger generations no longer sought the medicine man:

> I think that might have a lot to do with it, yes, . . . and this is because a lot of young people are going away from it, I say, that they don't really believe in it. . . . It's just that their parents, . . . in fact some of the people my age and younger now . . . have parents went to an Indian school, and so they weren't really, their childhood and adolescence weren't fostered to have a respect for these things, so that when they finally finished

their education and came back to the reservation then they really don't allow. . . . Like with me, my first reaction when something happens is to go to the medicine man.[99]

Converting children to Western health practices was part of a settler colonial effort to regulate and refashion Indigenous bodies, be it by altering their relationship to the natural environment, criminalizing traditional healing practices, changing their dietary patterns, or exposing them to unhealthy residential schools.[100] Indeed, schools targeted Indigenous children as embodied subjects, seeking to repattern the ways in which they dressed, ate, walked, and talked. Modern medicine provided a means for knowing and gaining control over Indigenous bodies as such. Children at Indigenous boarding schools came under Western medical control as the schools persisted into the 1920s and beyond. For example, reports on doctor visits, treatment records, and other such health data increased in the United States in 1925, when Commissioner of Indian Affairs Charles Burke distributed a circular requiring more complete medical records.[101]

In Manitoba, though it took longer for concern to be generated about disease at the schools, as is apparent by the hesitation to implement the full recommendations of the 1907 Bryce Report, more effort was eventually made to ensure the health of students. Here, too, however, the motivation was not solely the best interests of students. In the 1930s, faced with the fact that treaty Indians in Manitoba comprised just over 2 percent of the population, but one-third of all tuberculosis-related deaths, D. A. Stewart, the medical superintendent for Manitoba, described Indigenous reserves as "reservoirs of tuberculosis" and argued that disease spread among Indians was a serious threat to white populations. He further argued that such diseases would be present until the Indian population was entirely absorbed into settler society, thereby connecting the goals of assimilation and disease prevention. But to make this absorption possible, boarding schools had to be better equipped to prevent the spread of disease. Therefore, Stewart recommended that sanatoria and other tools needed to prevent the spread of tuberculosis be established.[102]

At FAIRS, the idea of constructing a "preventorium" on the campus arose in the late 1930s. In a April 26, 1937, letter from Dr. Harold McGill, director of Indian Affairs, to Reverend J. Plourde, superintendent general of the Oblate Catholic Indian Missions, McGill noted that the Roman Catholic Church proposed to build a hospital alongside FAIRS: "It is the Department's hope to enter upon a program for the control of Tuberculosis among the Indians of Manitoba with special reference to the elimination of this disease from the Indian Residential Schools."[103] Dr. McGill recommended that a sanatorium be created at FAIRS for Roman Catholic pupils from the Fort Alexander, Sandy Bay, and Pine Creek schools who were suffering from minor forms of tuberculosis. Plourde responded that the Catholic Church was interested, though he worried about the distance between Pine Creek and Fort Alexander and whether FAIRS had sufficient space for such an institution. He therefore requested permission for an addition that would serve as a preventorium.[104] Terms were negotiated, and it was agreed that FAIRS would cover the costs of renovation and that the government would provide furnishings. As well, the per capita payments for the thirty children sent to the preventorium would go to FAIRS for maintaining this institution. The preventorium opened in January 1938.

It did not take long, however, for the realization that a preventorium on campus, whereby tuberculosis-infected students interacted with children free from the disease, was a bad idea, since both the tuberculosis virus and the children refused to remain in their healthy and nonhealthy zones. On January 5, 1939, J. D. Adamson wrote to E. L. Stone, director of medical services at Indian Affairs:

> The obvious objection to the present situation is that the new cases sent in are potential spreaders and might possibly contaminate the children in the school with whom they freely associate except with regard to sleeping quarters. . . . Separate dining room, class room, and play grounds will be necessary, and these children should not be allowed to mix in any way with those of the larger school. . . . These suggestions came as a surprise to Dr. Bissett and Father Brachet who apparently up to now considered that the procedure would be similar to that which was in vogue last year.[105]

P. E. Moore, a medical doctor and the assistant superintendent of medical services, later warned that the arrangement at the preventorium was a clear danger to student health and that the unit should be entirely separated from the school.[106] The preventorium was closed at the end of the school year in 1939.

This episode illustrates the complex interactions of disease, health, and assimilation in the Manitoba schools under consideration here. Although at first disease was allowed to run rampant, almost unchecked, eventually greater concern was shown for managing the health of Indigenous students, if for no other reason than that healthy students would not threaten non-Indigenous populations with the spread of disease. Under such circumstances, health and disease prevention were viewed in some circles as outcomes of assimilation rather than as resources to make assimilation possible. Nonetheless, more effort was made to preserve Indigenous students, but such efforts were often ill conceived and came up against the refusal of diseases such as tuberculosis to abide by the preventive measures then in vogue.

In short, one could make a straightforward argument that deaths from disease at certain schools were high enough, and conditions in the schools were sufficiently characteristic of recklessness by school administrators and planners, that a genocide charge could be laid. However, in focusing solely on this physical component of destruction, one risks overlooking the more complicated role played by disease in patterns of attempted Indigenous destruction. Rather than simply acting as a physical risk to Indigenous children and communities, disease was also a means for controlling, regulating, and redesigning Indigenous bodies. It was enlisted at the microlevel of the settler colonial mesh in a variety of ways, and its destructive imprint was more than just its deadly outcome for too many Indigenous children. It was also enlisted in the competition between assimilation and resistance, often with novel outcomes, weakening or reinforcing the grasp of the settler colonial mesh. In this sense, efforts to enroll disease and health care occurred to intensify that mesh, but such enrollments were precarious, as the interactions among diseases, children, communities, and staff played out in locally distinct ways.

Hell and Damnation

Although all residential schools, at some point, warned children of the fires of hell, where Indians would burn for eternity lest they changed their pagan ways, the role of these metaphysical horrors was particularly pronounced in the Manitoban context. Here church and clergy, in their running of the schools, were a significant presence in Indigenous communities and a constant reminder of the possibility of damnation. Speaking of how his mother and father came to accept residential school as inevitable for their children, FAIRS survivor Theodore Fontaine writes that "it's unfortunate that Mom and Dad, because of their residential school experiences and the Church's presence in the community, became not only God-fearing but also *Church*-fearing. The respect and awe in which our people held the clergy was mostly based on fear of damnation and the devil. Clergy took advantage of it."[107] Another survivor from Sagkeeng, who went to a seminary rather than an officially recognized residential school, made a similar statement about his parents:

> To me, my dad was—and my mum, bless her soul—were brainwashed by the Catholic Church. And I firmly believe that still today. Anybody that suffered through the residential school, the parents were brainwashed by the priest, the parish priest that went into the communities. Cause if you did this, you'd go to hell, if you didn't do this you'd go to hell. But if you stayed on the straight and narrow path, you'd go to heaven. And I remember every morning we'd get up at 5 o'clock, we'd pray. We'd pray before we had breakfast, then we'd pray before we went to school.[108]

Damnation and hell, therefore, were often mobilized by Canadian proponents of assimilative schooling through techniques of cultural and spiritual violence as means to ensure obedience and to provoke behavioral change. Vincent Pierre, a FAIRS student from the 1960s, spoke of how the devil was enlisted in separating him from his language: "And they would tell us as a kid, you know, 'You speak the devil's language.' That would scare the crap out of me. I tried so hard not to speak our language and I tried so hard to speak English. But it was just natural, to speak the Ojibwa language."[109] Indeed, calling upon the devil and hell allowed schools to target student emotions, namely fear, in their efforts to resolve the Indian Problem. Whereas the physical space of the school offered its own terrors, the metaphysical space of Christian damnation was also vivid in the minds of students. Rose Hart, a survivor who spoke at the Winnipeg Truth and Reconciliation Commission statement gathering, explained that

I was always scared of going to hell or purgatory—was in between hell and heaven, is what I learned in residential school about my religious upbringing. It took me a long time to get rid of that fear, to get rid of the fear of God. I was always afraid of God because God was a judgmental God. I didn't like learning about God when I was young, you know, today I can't kneel because we used to have to kneel for hours and hours during lent, every day to pray, you know, say the rosary.[110]

Fear thus allowed for the intensification of monastic discipline at the microlevel of the settler colonial mesh, and heaven and hell were participants in ensuring the proper training of Indigenous young people. Other tools, such as Lacombe's ladder, were utilized to communicate the force of hell and the damnation associated with indigeneity. In this particular 1874 version of the Catholic ladder, Indigenous peoples were represented as facing a choice between two roads, one leading through civilization toward eternal salvation and the other leading through the ways of savagery toward damnation. Ozaawi Bineziikwe recalls being confronted with this device while at FAIRS:

> Every morning we had catechism. The priest hung this calendar in the classroom as a reminder of our unworthiness. This calendar was known as Lacombe's Calendar. I remember always worrying about meeting God and having to hear Him say, 'You were bad and you're an Indian so you go to hell,'—that is where the people who stood on the left hand side of God went. According to the priest and the nuns, we were standing on that left hand side of God. I struggled to memorize every prayer that the priest ever taught me.[111]

In both Manitoba and New Mexico, Indigenous boarding schools represented, to some extent, a battle between gods. Metaphysical forces were enlisted in the struggle to transform Indigenous children. In Manitoba, the conflict was all or nothing, with the supremacy of the European God meaning the destruction of Indigenous gods. In contrast, in New Mexico, a sort of truce formed between the gods, and Catholic saints and Pueblo Kachinas were blended in a syncretic mix. Although the latter were marginalized and weakened through the initial truce, they waited and reemerged as Pueblo beliefs revitalized. The Zuni Church of Our Lady of Guadalupe symbolizes this movement. Although its adobe structure, crosses, and bell tower are reminiscent of similar structures throughout New Mexico, the wall murals painted by Alex Seowtewa to depict the Zuni Kachinas fill the church's interior. On the north wall, for example, the mural is of Sha'La/ Ko', the largest annual Zuni celebration, held close to the winter solstice in late November or early December. The church, built in 1629, once featured an older painting of Kachinas that has long since faded. These Kachinas were there to discipline and warn the people to abide by the teachings of the church. In contrast, the new Kachinas represent a mixture of Zuni and Catholic teachings as well as the vitality and resilience of Zuni spiritual and cultural life.

But some Indigenous groups schooled in New Mexico faced a more difficult struggle to create a truce between gods. Among the Diné, whose relationship with the settler population has been shorter than is the case for the Pueblo, they have had less opportunity to combine their religion with that of the newcomers and therefore less opportunity for syncretic adaptation. Austin Begay, for example, summed up for his interviewer the struggle between white and Diné gods: "Today we know, your god is stronger than ours, but still we are not forgetting our own culture that we had for many years. . . . We like to keep it as long as our nation is living."[112] In Begay's evaluation, Diné gods are not defeated, since they survive in the memories of the people and therefore remain as actors who can be called upon to ensure the survivance of the Diné nation. Evidence of such survivance is clear as one travels through Diné territory, since Diné cer- emonials are equal to Christian holidays, and Diné identity continues to be negotiated through an interaction between traditional teachings and values and elements of the non-Diné world.[113] But in the schools, these gods, during most periods, were unwelcome. Such resilience is also evident among Indigenous groups that attended PLPIRS and FAIRS. For example, the Sagkeeng First Nation continues to recover, enhance, and transfer cultural practices through venues such as Turtle Lodge, a building erected in 2002 in which community members can share traditional knowledge, land-based spiritual teachings, ceremonies, and healing.

In this manner, though the metaphysical actors and spaces of Christianity were drawn on to motivate assimilative change among Indigenous groups, periods of resurging Indigenous spirituality often provided microlevel defenses against the force of these powers. This was true not only of the later years of the boarding school period in both Manitoba and New Mexico. The use of Indigenous spiritualities to resist the settler colonial mesh was indeed evident from the beginning of each country's boarding school system, such as the use in the 1880s of the sun dance among Plains peoples as an alternative form of education, just when realization dawned that boarding schools were designed to eliminate Indigenous cultures.[114] The battle of the gods therefore followed no single trajectory; instead, deities, ceremonies, rituals, damnation, salvation, and the like were pulled into the fight over Indigenous children with varying degrees of success at various moments.

Food and Poverty

Like the roles of many microlevel actors in the drama of Indigenous boarding schools, that of food and poverty was multidimensional. The hunger and poverty of students could be used through techniques of desire to motivate parents to send their children to boarding schools, where they were promised more adequate sustenance.[115] Yet the most common complaint heard from students at both American and Canadian Indigenous boarding schools was about the food. As well, clothing and lodgings were not always of better quality than those available in the home. So, once again, we need to look more closely at how these actors were allied either to facilitate or to resist the settler colonial mesh.

In a 1912 assessment of poverty and hunger in Pueblo communities, Superintendent Coggeshall at SFIS concurred with the Office of Indian Affairs that poverty was a potential means to motivate the Indian toward advancement: "It has seemed to me that the policy of the Office in encouraging the Indian in independence with respect to the necessities of life and in withholding gratuitous assistance except in rare cases of absolute necessity has been for progress in the development of self reliance in the Indian." For this reason, Coggeshall did not believe that Indian Affairs should be too quick to intervene in instances of Pueblo poverty; instead, if investment was to be made, he argued, it should be in the form of modern machinery and instruction in farming methods.[116] Poverty, he believed, was a means to force the Pueblo to adapt to and adopt European ways.

Indeed, in periods of great hardship, Indigenous boarding schools did appear to offer parents a means to ensure the survival of their children. Brenda Child writes with respect to the increasing numbers of students who attended boarding schools in the 1930s that this was not a sign of Indigenous acceptance of these institutions but "a sign that boarding schools had become familiar institutions and that, when economic or family problems beset Indian people, boarding schools could be useful to them. When the deprivation of Indian families became acute during the 1930s, the boarding schools filled with children. Depression-era records from Red Lake report a truckload of hungry children arriving from White Earth to be placed in their boarding school because their own families were unable to provide for them."[117] Moreover, this growth in the numbers attending schools occurred, in part, during the Collier years, when several boarding schools were closed down in order to promote day schools and integration into public schools. Based on this and other information, Child notes how boarding schools, though sources of resentment among Indigenous Americans, were also occasionally useful, providing sources of sustenance or preferred modes of education. As one former student from SFIS remarked, "if it wasn't for boarding schools, I would have been in a bad way, because my parents lost their job in Arizona. Then they went to California. And from California they came back to Arizona. There were very few jobs. So being in boarding school was a very good thing for my sister and myself."[118] Within the broader settler colonial mesh, reserve-based suffering, itself a consequence of settler encroachment on Indigenous territories and food-gathering practices, became a tool for driving children toward assimilative schooling.

Indigenous children's relationship with food was also a dispositional quality that assimilative education sought to transform. As Mary Ellen Kelm remarks,

> predicated on the basic notion that the First Nations were, by nature, unclean and diseased, residential schooling was advocated as a means to "save" Aboriginal children from the "insalubrious" influences of home life on reserve. Once in the schools, the racially charged and gendered

message that Aboriginal domestic arrangements threatened physical, social and spiritual survival was reinforced through health education. Children were taught to hate the food their mothers cooked and reject their standards of cleanliness. School officials told students that cultural alienation was to be welcomed as the first step toward healthful living and long life.[119]

As was the case with health, then, food was used as a means to effect change on Indigenous bodies. Indeed, several stories from New Mexico tell of pupils returning to their home communities only to be disturbed by family practices of eating on the floor. Mrs. Walter Marmon from Laguna Pueblo recounted the following about a pupil returning to his Pueblo community after time spent at Carlisle:

> Here's the story that one of the boys, the older boys, saw, after he returned and he had gotten used to seeing the big buildings back east, you know Pennsylvania and Philadelphia and all those places. And then he came back to the little homes, the little pueblo homes, looked very small to him, . . . and he said to his folks, "whose is this chicken house?" And his mother said, "why this is your home." Called him by his Indian name. And then they went into the next room, and there was his little brother in a cradle, . . . and he saw that his little brother was dark in color like himself, and he said, "whose is this Negro baby?"[120]

This story captures well the assimilative goal of making foreign the Indigenous community so that it was no longer recognizable to the assimilated student. When it was no longer recognizable, it would potentially no longer feel right to the student, who would then be more inclined to embrace and embody American citizenship.

The control of Indigenous children's bodies through food was forcefully brought to light in Canada in 2013 when a postdoctoral researcher at Guelph University, Ian Mosby, published a paper detailing the nutritional experiments that took place at certain Canadian residential schools and on specific Indigenous reserves in the late 1940s. During this period, hunger was common in residential schools in northern Manitoba as well as other parts of Canada. However, rather than treat this hunger as a problem that required immediate and drastic attention, health researchers viewed the schools as ready-made labs for the study of malnutrition where they could test whether or not certain vitamin supplements or enriched flour might help to offset nutritional deficiencies. They also investigated questions related to dental hygiene, such as the efficacy of the use of fluoride. These researchers argued that their findings would help to address the nutritional and health needs of Indigenous peoples, but the experiments were also tied to broader concerns with the Indian Problem in the hope that such nutritional interventions might make Indigenous peoples less of a burden on the government in the long term. But the experiments showed the deep disregard that existed for the rights of Indigenous persons to control their bodies, and what was put into them, since no parents or children were asked for their consent to participate in these tests.[121]

Students were also reoriented in terms of what they ate. At home, Pueblo children would eat corn, beans, squash, and chili stews; at school, they were fed porridge or hardtack biscuits.[122] Likewise, Anishinaabe, Cree, and Dakota Sioux students accustomed to game, berries, and foods derived from Indigenous agriculture were confronted with starch-heavy foods. In both circumstances, food portions were inadequate, and many students complained of hunger. Food was also poorly prepared and sometimes spoiled by the time that it was served to children. As one FAIRS survivor remarked, "the dogs eat better now than we did in them days."[123] Poor and insufficient food resulted in the emergence of an underground food economy in the schools. Opportunities to take extra food were sought, whether by working in the kitchen or in the fields. As well, students resisted imposed diets by hunting and trading small game caught on school grounds. Food was thus a valuable resource that allowed one to build alliances and accumulate owed favors, which could be turned toward survival in boarding schools.

Poverty and food were also enlisted as allies and weapons outside Indigenous boarding schools. It was a common practice, especially in the early days of American boarding schools, for agents to threaten to withhold funds, such as annuity payments or rations, when parents did not send their children to schools. However, not all Indigenous groups received resources from the federal government. The northern Pueblo, for example, did not receive annuities or rations, and in 1920 this fact led Horace J. Johnson, superintendent of the northern Pueblos, to reflect on the challenge of compelling school attendance for Pueblo children. With respect to the new school regulations of that year, which made Indigenous education a legislative requirement, Johnson noted his confidence that he could place eligible Pueblo children in schools as long as he received the necessary backing from the federal government. He added that "I have never done these things on 'bluff', however, and do not care to begin it here where there is every prospect of a bluff being called."[124] Thus, the power of the northern Pueblos, and their lack of dependence on government resources, granted them a degree of resistance to having rations and funds enlisted to force their children into schools. For this reason, the superintendent later stressed the need for a "show of force" by the government, which would allow him to "take care of the recalcitrants."[125]

Others would dangle rewards for compliance in front of extremely poor parents. Margaret D. Jacobs writes of how Indian Agent Plummer took the latter approach in his efforts to enroll Diné students in an on-reserve school: "Instead of wielding the stick—withholding annuities—he dangled the carrot. In 1893, he offered axes to any Navajo parents who sent their children to school. . . . Still, the Navajos did not rush to accept Plummer's generosity. Plummer added pails and coffee pots to the offer and tried playing various Navajo groups off one another."[126] In tough economic times, such as when wool prices hit their low point in the mid-1890s, his strategy was more effective and managed to convince some parents to send their children to school.

Use of poverty and hunger as tools to compel student enrollment was more persistent across time in the Manitoban case studies. Into the late 1940s, instances of threats to withhold funds from parents who refused to send their children to school were noted. For example, in a 1948 letter, B. E. Olson, superintendent of the Clandeboye Agency, remarked that denying parents their family allowance payments was one of the most effective means to ensure school attendance.[127] Likewise, Victoria Elaine McIntosh, who was at FAIRS in the 1960s, told of how her mother was forced to give her up to the school:

> I didn't realize that she carried all that guilt. She said, "I had to give you up." She said, "Or else, they told us we wouldn't eat." My grandmother

was standing there and this is what they told her. And I was angry with my mom for a long time because I thought she gave up on me but I realize now that she didn't have any choice at that time and when she gave this back to me I was—I forgave her and I told her that it wasn't her fault.[128]

Food was also enlisted within the schools as a means for staff to exhibit their control over students. Several survivors recall being forced to eat spoiled or bug-infested foods. For example, the same FAIRS survivor recounted that

there was an incident where I would not eat porridge and the first time I looked down and it was the bowl in front of me and I noticed there was worms in it and a nun came up behind me and she told me, "Eat it." And I wouldn't eat it. No. And she slammed my face in the bowl and picked me up by my arm and threw me up against the wall and she started strapping me.[129]

Another FAIRS student from the 1960s, Eugene Patrick Boubard, told of another such event:

I remember I couldn't eat. I was sick and I was being called a suck. And I remember going to the cafeteria and the macaronis were hard like it was hard and I couldn't eat it. I just couldn't eat it, I sat at the edge of the table and it was a huge cafeteria and I tried to eat and I couldn't eat and the nuns came and hit me in the back of the head and kept hitting harder and harder, "Eat! It will make you feel better!" I kept, "Nun, I can't eat." And they kept hitting harder and harder so I forced this food, I forced eat it and by the time I threw up on my plate I remember all the kids sitting near me pushed their chair back and I was telling the nun I was sick. Those nuns, what they did, they forced me to eat what I threw up.[130]

However, the boarding schools in Manitoba and New Mexico did not solely enlist food and poverty to bully students and assert control. Indeed, in New Mexico, as we saw with the technique of desire, the "carrot" continued to be deployed as a means to enlist Indigenous poverty in service to the settler colonial mesh. The discussions in the previous chapter about new shoes, or the food that children heard about from students returning from boarding schools, meant that food and poverty could be allied to desire to compel students toward assimilative education. Nonetheless, food and poverty are not one-sided in the history of boarding schools, since children also drew on their memories of local foods, prepared by beloved family members, to resist assimilation.

Blood

In the previous chapter, I examined the administrative techniques of Indigenous boarding schools with respect to how they were refined and extended to better know and control the Indian. However, at the core of such techniques across most eras was a concern with Indian blood. Blood, in terms of an imagined quantum of Indigenous blood, was to be measured prior to entry into school to ensure that those enrolled were not already of diluted racial stock, for it was assumed that those with less Indian blood would be naturally absorbed into the dominant society. This racist logic of the blood quantum allowed schools to define which children should attend boarding schools, thereby limiting government budgetary commitments to those viewed to be more Indian.[131] Thus, one sees at AIS and SFIS, for example, efforts by superintendents to prevent the attendance of Mexican students.[132] In one instance, Supervisor of Indian Schools A. O. Wright reported on the need to remove certain students because they were of insufficient Indian blood: "In obedience to special orders, I have also removed from the school at Albuquerque a large number of Mexican pupils. These had mostly sufficient Indian blood to be eligible under the rules forbidding the admission of 'white Indians,' but they were children of Mexicans, whose ancestors had long abandoned their tribal relations and had intermarried with whites."[133]

In discussions of genocide, there is often the expectation that blood will be spilled. In chapter 2, I argued that physical genocide is merely one means of genocidal destruction, and it is most often braided with forms of cultural and biological destruction. However, there is still a European sensibility that leads us to think that the spilling of blood is a more serious form of group destruction. Indeed, the European cultures that have dominated the conceptualization of genocide have been too long obsessed with blood. Genocide has occurred to preserve the purity of blood, and, in its aftermath, we have fixated on bloodshed. But the bonds of the group are more than blood. And it is not only when it is spilled that blood is relevant to discussions of attempted group destruction. As can be seen in the case of Indigenous boarding schools, blood was enlisted as a tool for making the targeted group legible within the settler colonial mesh.

Blood quantum calculations have thus had a role to play in schemes of Indigenous elimination. Utilizing arbitrary and racist definitions, such as the notion that one-quarter or one-half Indigenous blood makes one an Indian, and ignoring how cultural affinities require more than a mere biological lineage connecting one to the cultural group, Canadian and American governments have long tried (and continue to try) to define Indigenous peoples out of existence.[134] Indigenous boarding schools have played a role in this process. By accepting only those identified as having a significant degree of Indian blood, the schools concentrated their efforts on targeting those whom they believed most likely to stick to backward Indigenous ways. Moreover, by removing them from their communities, and forcing them to interact with non-Indigenous communities, either through the placement of the boarding school near a non-Indigenous community or through the outing program, it was hoped that Indigenous men and women might connect with and even marry into non-Indigenous communities. Richard Pratt, for example, founder of the Carlisle Indian School, believed miscegenation to be a key tool for converting Indigenous young people to white ways. He boasted that five of his students had married white wives—a controversial claim given that settlers had long accepted that white men might marry Indian women but still had misgivings about white women coupling with or wedding Indian men.[135]

The utilization of blood quanta is an ongoing theme in Canada, and it stretches well beyond the residential schools. The "sixties scoop," for example, refers to the mass forced adoption of Indigenous children into white families as part of a coordinated effort to socialize and absorb these children into the Euro-Canadian community.[136] Moreover, Indigenous women who married non-Indigenous men prior to the passing of Bill C-31 in 1985 faced the loss of their Indigenous status,[137] for the patriarchal assumption was that the woman would take on her husband's identity. Illegitimate children and adoptees were also denied status, resulting in an increasing number of Indigenous persons defined as non-status Indians.[138] Canada still assesses the legal identity of Indigenous peoples according to a blood quantum standard; thus, Bill C-31, though correcting the inequitable removal of status from Indigenous women who marry non-Indigenous men, continues to assess Indian status based on the expectation that Indigenous people will possess a certain degree of Indian blood.

But blood not only served to identify a target for assimilative schooling and a strategy for reducing the sheer number of Indians through biological absorption. Blood was also a message, a symbol of the school's power over the student. Survivors recall vividly those moments when they witnessed the blood of another child spilled by a school staff member's violence. As a survivor who attended FAIRS in the 1960s, Victoria Elaine McIntosh, explained,

> I've seen a lot of things in there that a little kid should never ever see. I've seen the other kids being beaten. I remember sitting in the class room, and them going around with the ruler and she hit the boy behind me and all I heard was a crack and a scream and I didn't dare turn around and I found out after she broke his nose and I remember seeing the blood on the floor. But you learn to—don't look at it. Don't look down.[139]

Blood was also perceived as an obstacle. Especially in the early twentieth century, when race "science" held sway among many associated with Indian policy in both the United States and Canada, blood, or biological inheritance, was what stood in the way of the Indigenous child's full assimilation. Throughout this book, and throughout the archives, one can find examples of government authorities, superintendents, principals, teachers, and other staff members bemoaning how difficult their task was in the face of the evolutionary limitations of the Indian. Whereas some within each country's Indian service believed that Indians could become "white men,"[140] others argued that each group held separate racial destinies. In the latter category were individuals such as Samuel Chapman Armstrong, superintendent of Hampton School, and Estelle Reel, superintendent of Indian schools from 1898 to 1910. Armstrong theorized that the idea of hard work was not in the Indian's "brains or blood,"[141] and he understood boarding schools to provide a necessary introduction to such work while also communicating the idea that Indigenous peoples were racially inferior. Reel was influenced by Armstrong's approach, and Hampton School became the model in terms of developing the *Course of Study for Indian Schools*.[142]

In sum, blood intervened in different ways in assimilative schooling in Manitoba and New Mexico. Although both regions showed a general inclination to organize and categorize Indigenous children in accordance with their blood quantum, and to exclude others on the same grounds, blood was not unproblematic in this endeavor. In the early twentieth century, blood was also an essence, a deep-rooted limitation on boarding school aspirations, and therefore required adaptation by educators so that boarding schools would prepare Indigenous children for futures more suited to their perceived evolutionary shortcomings. Yet, in the schools themselves, particularly in those periods characterized by heightened levels of physical violence, blood communicated the power of the school to spill Indigenous blood, to create gashes on Indigenous children's bodies, or to shame Indigenous girls for their menstruation.

Blood did not always carry out the tasks to which it was set by those in charge of Indigenous boarding schools, however. Some Indigenous peoples embraced Indigenous identities—also in terms of blood—regardless of their alleged mixed-race status. People still embrace indigeneity after years of having Indigenous identities legislated away. Others have sought ways to circumvent legislated elimination. For example, a survivor from Fort Alexander, who fell in love with a Métis man after she finished school, attempted to ensure that her children would not lose their Indian status by delaying her marriage until after they were born. But this maneuver did not satisfy the Canadian registrar, who sent her a letter once the marriage was made known:

> We moved from Manitoba to Saskatchewan and then I got a letter from the registrar. I'll never forget his name: H. H. Chapman. And the letter said, "Since you have married the legal father of the children, they are no longer entitled to be registered as Indians and I am striking them off the record. Period." I—well I lost it. How could they do that? They're betraying me. That's what I thought. This is betrayal. I followed the law and they say no now. I—I didn't know what to do then except cry, and I did.[143]

In this chapter, I have attempted to get beyond human-centric examinations of genocidal destruction by delving more deeply into the roles played by nonhuman actors in producing the intended and unintended consequences of forced assimilation. Territory, space, time, disease, hell, food, poverty, and blood were actors allied in either facilitating or resisting assimilative education, often in multiple and nonlinear manners. Other actors could have been mentioned, but those assessed here provide a sense of the complicated microlevel context of Indigenous boarding schools and the changes that occurred over time in terms of how these actors factored into the attempted resolution of the Indian Problem. These nonhuman forces in the shaping of local Indigenous boarding school experiences have been discussed here as actors, rather than simply as inanimate factors, because they did not simply bend to the will of those human agents who sought to enlist them.

Combining insights from this and the previous chapter, one gathers a sense of how the settler colonial mesh was uneven and unpredictable in its application. The Indian Problem, and the legislation, policy, and circulars designed to address this problem, informed techniques of assimilation implemented in particular schools. However, these techniques were also adapted to local problems, concerns, personalities, struggles, and other factors that made them less than perfect vehicles for settler colonial intention. As well, the efficacy of these techniques required negotiation among a variety of local actors, including boarding school staff, parents, children, and community members, but also nonhuman actors enlisted by these various parties to try to realize their objectives in specific boarding school circumstances. At times, these actors could be enlisted to fulfill assimilative purposes—for example, rail lines could be used to overcome territorial isolation and bring children otherwise untouched by assimilation to boarding schools. However, just as often, these actors contributed to unanticipated outcomes in boarding schools. Territory proved to be more complex than expected, allowing Indigenous peoples to evade enrollment of their children. Diseases found ways, often through sheer neglect, to spread among school populations, undoing claims made by school officials that the schools offered healthy environments for children. The gods and spirits of the Indigenous world proved to be more resilient than expected by those propounding the Christian faith. The food and clothing of Indigenous communities were less impoverished than the offerings found in boarding school dining halls and closets. And blood did not always obey the quantum model, since indigeneity survived and persisted despite efforts at its dilution through biological absorption.

8 | Aftermaths and Redress

Up to this point, the focus of this book has been on North American Indigenous boarding schools from a sociohistorical perspective. However, this history did not simply end with the closing of boarding schools or their transformation into Indigenous-run institutions. The legacy of Indigenous boarding schools continues to trouble contemporary times, and it is with this in mind that efforts have been made (or not made) to redress the harms of these institutions. The settler colonial mesh might have mutated, but it has not retracted from the North American continent.

Although microlevel analysis pointed to the futility of a strict national comparison between Canadian and American Indigenous boarding school experiences, the contemporary politics of redress in Canada and the United States do raise distinct national questions. How is it that Canada has arrived at an Indian Residential School Settlement Agreement (hereafter IRSSA, 2006), whereas redress measures in the United States are few and far between? Are the differences between the two countries and their deployment of Indigenous boarding schools enough to make the Canadian case for redress more compelling? Or are there more important factors that explain the lack of redress measures in the United States? This chapter provides discussion of the aftermath of boarding schools in each country to demonstrate the multiple, overlapping effects of boarding schools on Indigenous communities. It then analyzes the pathways (or lack thereof) to redress in each nation before focusing on the Canadian IRSSA and its limitations as a model for redress in the United States.

Aftermaths

In both Canada and the United States the deleterious effects of colonialism are on display. Some have advanced notions of "historical trauma" or "soul wound" to describe intergenerational forms of trauma that result from ancestral suffering and manifest themselves in problems such as abuse, addiction, and suicide in contemporary Indigenous communities.[1] Although one must be cautious not to treat all Indigenous peoples as necessarily traumatized regardless of their personal experiences.[2] Indigenous communities do continue to feel the reverberations of historical and contemporary settler colonial practices.

In Canada, the impact of Indigenous boarding schools is traceable to the cycles of violence and abuse that emanated from these schools. Because multiple generations of children attended the schools, where they faced similar experiences of abuse and cultural degradation, extended families were disconnected from cultural patterns of parenting and socialization.[3] And, with the breakdown of these patterns, many Indigenous individuals were left rootless and adrift from the bonds of family, culture, and language. Add to this situation the forms of violence and abuse learned in the schools, and conditions were ripe for the continuation of violence and abuse in Indigenous communities, particularly those that fed the most brutal schools. Community suffering was exacerbated by ongoing instances of child removal, such as those that occurred under the "sixties scoop," and they continue today in communities that lack the social services needed to prevent severe, government-sponsored reactions to family challenges.[4] A survivor from FAIRS (who attended in the 1940s) discussed dealing with her trauma:

> I found alcohol when I arrived in the city. I just—just became alcoholic. I didn't drink to enjoy it; I didn't even like the taste of it. I like what it did to make me forget. I thought. I came to a point where I'm landing in a psych ward from alcohol drinking too much. I landed in treatment centre twice. But I had a lot of help. I found out I didn't need to drink.

It was killing me. I became suicidal, slashed my wrists because I was so embarrassed what I did to my kids. Same thing happened [inaudible] that's exactly what my mom did to us. What I was doing.[5]

But such experiences of ongoing trauma must also be connected to the contemporary structural factors that leave many Indigenous Canadian communities with too few resources and struggling with poverty, high food costs, poor quality housing, inadequate health care, and a lack of social services.[6] To connect these experiences solely to the historical wrongs rather than current problems would be a disservice to ongoing demands for social justice in Indigenous communities.[7] And these demands are many. For example, for Aboriginal children under the age of fifteen, 27.5 percent live in low-income households, compared with 12.9 percent for non-Aboriginal Canadians.[8] This is the result of severe income, employment, and educational gaps between Indigenous and non-Indigenous Canadians.[9] In some communities, such as in parts of northern Canada, the cost of food is double that in urban settings, and health care and social services are limited in their availability. Indigenous Canadians also suffer much greater incidences of certain health and mental health ailments, such as diabetes and depression.[10] Under these conditions, prisons rather than schools appear to be the new institutional means for dealing with those Indigenous peoples perceived to be "problems," especially in Manitoba, where, though Indigenous persons make up only 13 percent of the population, they accounted for over 69 percent of people in custody in 2010–11.[11]

It is also the case that Indigenous peoples in the United States have experienced a great deal of suffering since Indigenous boarding schools shifted away from serving primarily as institutions of assimilation. Indigenous persons living on reservations in the United States are part of the poorest 1 percent of the American population. Many of these communities suffer under the same conditions of poverty, poor health, and marginalization that appear on Canadian reservations. American Indian and Alaskan Native peoples comprise only 1.5 percent of the U.S. population, though in contrast to other segments of the population they are younger and faster growing, possibly a sign of resurgence. However, their rates of poverty are more than double that of the rest of the population, with 27 percent of all families and 32 percent of families with children living in poverty. Their rates of employment and education are also significantly lower than those for other Americans. For example, only 71 percent possess a high school diploma in contrast to 80 percent for the rest of the country. As well, unemployment rates range from just over 14 to 35 percent in various reservation communities. Perhaps even more startling is the fact that American and Alaskan Native peoples have the highest per capita rates of exposure to violence and abuse as well as to other traumatic events, such as accidents resulting in loss of life. For these reasons, Indigenous young people in the United States are much more likely to witness or experience traumatic events. Exposure to such violence couples with disparities in health and mental health care, exacerbating the effects of the violence on Indigenous communities. Post-traumatic stress disorder, alcohol dependence, depression, and suicide all exhibit high levels on reservations.[12]

Some scholars have sought to tie these conditions on reserve directly to the history of settler colonialism, including boarding schools.[13] Other commentators have suggested that communally owned property is a major barrier to overcoming Indigenous poverty, reviving within a neoliberal environment several historical settler colonial rationalizations for Indigenous land appropriation.[14] Current studies refute the latter claim and show that Indigenous economic success is possible under a collective ownership model.[15] Nonetheless, one must be wary of how current redress policies in both Canada and the United States too often couple with ongoing attempts to dispossess Indigenous peoples of collective stewardship of their lands, if not their lands themselves.[16]

None of these data is presented to suggest that conditions are worse either in Canada or in the United States; indeed, such data fail to take into account the microlevel circumstances, and differential experiences of community resurgence and suffering, that have been the focus of this book. However, they do represent a blunt instrument for demonstrating grounds for a politics of redress to emerge in each nation—Indigenous communities have suffered, and in many cases continue to suffer, as a consequence of the settler colonial mesh. Yet, while pursuing this line, we must bear in mind that Indigenous boarding schools, and settler colonialism more generally, did not affect all Indigenous communities in the same manner.

John Gram, for example, argues that AIS and SFIS had less severe impacts on Pueblo students compared with other boarding schools:

> What accounts for the seemingly easier transition of Pueblo students to life in their home communities? Culture shock for returned students largely resulted from the effects of alienation from the home community, drastic changes in lifestyle, and drastic changes in worldview through introduction to foreign ideas, particularly Christianity. In facing each of these factors, most Pueblo students had distinct advantages. . . . First, from the very beginning the New Mexico boarding schools allowed Pueblo students to return home each summer, though not necessarily members of other tribes. Certainly spending nine months at a time away from home could be a jarring experience, but not as jarring as spending five years or more away without a break. Second, how school officials expected "good" Indians to live was not all that different from how Pueblos already lived.[17]

This book confirms some of Gram's findings, especially as they relate to the ability of the Pueblo to maintain connections to their communities during their time at boarding schools. However, I would also introduce a note of caution in overgeneralizing the ease with which Pueblo returned to their communities, since, depending on when they attended the schools, these students still experienced forms of physical, cultural, and symbolic violence that could negatively affect their return experiences.[18]

Recognizing regional and temporal differences in the experience of the American settler colonial mesh through schooling, or what has been described in these pages as an attempt at the genocidal destruction of Indigenous peoples, does not, however, enable us to account for differences in redress policies in Canada and the United States. Such regional differences can also be found within the Canadian context, whereby, for example, boarding schools were used with less frequency in some regions than others.[19] Nonetheless, in Canada, Indigenous survivors organized class action lawsuits to pursue justice for the abuses suffered in assimilative boarding schools and thereby eventually sparked the negotiations that led to IRSSA in 2007.

Policies of redress, such as IRSSA, are seldom the result of the good intentions of governments. Instead, they are products of the activism of victim groups and their allies, who together force governments to take action on past injustices.[20] So how is it that Canadian survivors and their allies were more able to mobilize for reparations than those in the United States? The United States is a litigious society, home to class action lawsuits seeking historical atonement from the government and other wrongdoers.[21] As well, the United States preceded Canada in trying to make amends for other acts that they shared in common, such as the internment of Japanese Americans and Canadians during the Second World War.[22] So one cannot argue that the United States is somehow more hostile to such claims or that the legal resources are not available to accommodate historical redress. Something else is at work here.

Pathways to Redress

In discussing the different pathways toward redress, Charles Glenn ventures a culturalist explanation: "It may be because Canada experienced neither the agonies nor the triumphs of the Black Freedom Movement of the 1950s and 1960s that coming to terms with its past relationship with Indians has played a larger role in the national consciousness than has the parallel relationship in the United States."[23] Leaving aside the fact that the U.S. attempt to come to terms with slavery leaves much to be desired,[24] there are more promising discursive, political, and structural factors to help explain this difference.

First, on the discursive level, contrasting perceptions of the histories of American and Canadian Indigenous boarding schools hold some explanatory power. In particular, the more uneven and varied nature of American boarding school policy and its application might lessen, for some, the sense of absolute injustice of these institutions. As noted in chapter 3, Canadian schools were generally relentless in their assimilative mission for a longer and less differentiated period than were similar institutions in the United States. Moreover, because they tended to be more under the watch of Indian reformers, many, though certainly not all, American schools were more likely to harness softer forms of power, such as those that I have discussed under the headings of desire and symbolic violence in chapters 5 and 6. And American Indigenous groups appear to have been more likely, in general, to establish a stake of ownership in these institutions. The cumulative effect of these perceived differences is that they potentially foster the appearance that justice claims in the American context are less pressing than those in the Canadian context. I am not declaring that this is in fact the case, only that the perception matters. Based on my conceptualization of genocide, which takes the group and its survival as its focus, softer mechanisms of assimilation are still mechanisms directed toward the destruction of Indigenous groups and still carry with them a type of force, albeit one more subtle than the outright violence that we are accustomed to hearing about in discussions of genocide.

More importantly, what we might refer to as a discursive opening has not yet occurred to allow American testimony on widespread physical trauma, violence, and sexual abuse to come more prominently into the public spotlight.[25] Although some believe that we live in a culture of victimhood, it is in fact very difficult for victims to bring forward their testimonies of suffering, especially in what is perceived as a potentially hostile environment. Some cases of violence have come before U.S. courts to seek compensation for sexual and physical harms at BIA-run Indigenous boarding schools, such as the 1979 and 1980 cases of *Begay et al. v. The United States*. In these cases, eleven female minors and their parents or guardians filed suit against the government for sexual assaults at the hands of male teachers at the Teec Nos Pos Boarding School in Diné territory.[26] Yet they have not received the public attention needed to create a space for more survivors to feel safe in providing their testimonies about boarding school wrongs.

In Canada, an injustice frame for public discussion of Indigenous boarding schools is well developed, and survivors of the Canadian Indigenous boarding schools possess multiple "templates," to use Ronald Niezen's term for the personal and painful framing mechanisms offered to survivors by Canada's TRC, with which to articulate their boarding school lives.[27] These templates are less well established in the United States, where narratives of boarding schools as benevolent institutions, as an antidote to the Indian Wars, or as spaces of Indigenous resistance have been more persistent. This is despite the U.S. "history wars" that centered on the quincentennial of the Columbian voyage to the Americas. At this time, authors such as Ward Churchill and David Standard advanced arguments about the genocidal nature of American colonialism, including boarding schools.[28] But the polemical and partisan character of such debates often resulted in such perspectives being dismissed as part of a radical fringe, and they produced little middle ground for negotiating redress options that would allow the government to address the past without radically altering the status quo.[29]

Keeping with the theme of historical discourses, there is also a tendency among some in the United States to interpret subsequent policy changes as forms of historical redress. This view is evident in debates about slavery reparations, in which the argument is made that the Civil War (reinterpreted as a war to end slavery), as well as subsequent policies of welfare and affirmative action, complete America's historical debt to African Americans.[30] Likewise, some might suggest that a raft of policies has helped to make amends for Indigenous boarding schools in the United States. Under such an interpretation, various eras of Indian policy reform, such as those that followed the Meriam (1928) and Kennedy (1969) Reports, would be lauded as efforts to make right historical wrongs. As well, the fact that self-identified Indigenous persons have held the leadership of the BIA since 1966 might be argued to reflect an effort to correct the government's relationship with American Indigenous peoples. More particular to the topic under consideration, the distinct pattern in the United States of Indigenous political and educational self-determination might be noted as a form of making amends.[31] Although this pattern is not evenly spread across the country, in the Southwest and elsewhere experiments began early with Indigenous-directed education and shifted the focus among Indigenous leaders seeking justice for the boarding school past toward institutional control rather than broader forms of material and symbolic redress. For example, in 1966, the Rough Rock Demonstration School was established, and in 1969 Navajo Community College began operations. Both of these Diné-run institutions were the culmination of years of attempts to address the challenges of Diné education, in which children were difficult to reach to send to boarding schools and resources were few for local schooling.[32] Such schools can teach Indigenous children to walk in two worlds—to adapt to European culture while maintaining their own Indigenous cultures. But the record for self-determined boarding schools, though better than that of federal schools, is not an unmitigated success, and such schools have not completely addressed the harms of the past. Indeed, even contemporary schools can be experienced as harmful to Indigenous children when they are spartan, understaffed institutions that remove children from their families.[33] Overall, victims of historical wrongs are seldom satisfied with a patchwork of policies that may or may not have been specifically designed to redress these wrongs. Therefore, the argument that efforts at redress have already been made is unlikely to convince those whose communities and lives have been damaged by boarding schools.

With respect to political factors, in both Canada and the United States, Indigenous boarding schools contributed to the creation of an Indigenous leadership who spoke a common language and possessed pan-Indigenous networks through which grievance articulation and political mobilization took place.[34] For example, in 1969, an exposé of the physical abuse suffered by students at Chilocco Indian Residential School and the release of the Kennedy Report, which declared that U.S. efforts to educate Indigenous Americans were a failure, a "national tragedy," and a "national disgrace,"[35] combined with an atmosphere of heightened political activism in the United States to spark a period of political mobilization on the issue of Indigenous education. More dramatic statements about rights to Indigenous self-determination bolstered this activism, such as through the occupation of the BIA central office by Indigenous protesters in 1972 and the Wounded Knee uprising in 1973. These confrontations helped to bring the termination era to an end and were catalysts for the signing of the Indian Education Act (1972) and the Indian Self-Determination and Education Existence Act (1975) into law.

Such reforms, however, served as an accommodationist means to dampen "red power" in the United States. Stephen Cornell argues that this dampening occurred in three ways. First, the most radical of Indian activists were suppressed and marginalized. Second, acts such as the aforementioned Indian Self-Determination and Education Existence Act, as well as the Indian Civil Rights Act (1968) and the Indian Child Welfare Act (1978), focused Indigenous communities more on local issues, such as federal recognition, and specific Indigenous nation concerns. Finally, the BIA itself was treated as the object of reform as a means to revise Indigenous-non-Indigenous relations, distracting from broader, societal-level transformations that had been demanded in the era of red power.[36]

For certain, the Indian Self-Determination and Education Existence Act was a pivotal piece of legislation for changing the nature of Indigenous activism in the United States. Under its terms, federally recognized American tribes could gain access to federal grants and programs for their peoples. This act was part of a move away from blood quantum approaches to determining tribal membership, giving tribes more oversight of how "Indianness" would be determined in their nations. But, with greater powers of self-determination and sovereignty, Indigenous groups in the United States turned their attention more directly to issues of immediate concern, such as economic development, criminal justice, and other such matters. Indeed, some have viewed American policies of tribal recognition, and the economic development opportunities that sometimes follow from this policy, such as the creation of casinos, to be forms of redress.[37] In addition, the 1946 Indian Claims Commission provided Indigenous Americans with the opportunity to seek compensation for the wrongful appropriation of land, offering a means for attending to one of the most deeply felt and widely shared senses of settler colonial injustice against U.S.-based Indigenous peoples. In addition to this process, Indigenous groups have been able at times to seek land restitution from the U.S. government.[38]

In short, pan-Indigenous political activism in the United States was fostered to some degree by leadership arising out of Indigenous boarding schools. This activism reached its peak in the 1960s and early 1970s, and contributed to the end of the termination era in the United States,[39] before the movement became more fractured and localized as Indigenous nations able to obtain federal recognition turned their attention to resurgence and pursuit of matters of justice specific to their communities. Likewise, in Canada, there was a heightening of pan-Indigenous activism in the late 1960s, much of it emerging through leaders who themselves attended residential schools, and especially in response to the Liberal government's tabling of the white paper of 1969, which sought to eliminate the Indian Act through the legislated absorption of Indigenous peoples into the Canadian polity.[40] However, despite the greater attention to land claims and self-governance negotiations that defined Canadian Indigenous policy following defeat of the white paper, there remained much cause for pan-Indigenous activism, since the common fate of Indigenous communities was still defined by the many onerous statutes of the Indian Act, and many Indigenous groups continued to wrestle against both specific and comprehensive land claims policies that either ignored or offered limited forms of Indigenous self-government.[41] Therefore, national bodies such as the Assembly of First Nations remained prominent in the Canadian political context and provided national resources and leadership to assist with survivor demands for residential school reparations.[42]

This is not to say that accommodationist pressures were not also present in Canada, since to engage in any government-sponsored justice process, from land claims to self-government negotiations, required an Indigenous group to leave outside the negotiation room their broader claims to Indigenous territory and sovereignty.[43] In this manner, though Canadian Indigenous policy has been somewhat less successful in mobilizing a divide-and-conquer strategy in relation to pan-Indigenous movements, it has nonetheless operated to moderate Indigenous demands by creating circumscribed redress mechanisms that require Indigenous groups to remain in "good face"—in other words, they must turn their attention to the practical relations of the treaty or self-government negotiation table.[44] This means focusing on matters of jurisdiction, resources, policing, education, and the like, without bringing up messier issues of attempted genocide or the extent of land and resources removed under settler colonization.[45]

In short, sparked by a continuing tradition of pan-Indigenous activism, moderate redress for various settler colonial harms has been a more prominent part of Canadian Indigenous policy than has been the case in the United States. But the settler colonial mesh has mutated in a manner whereby redress projects themselves have taken on status quo–affirming and assimilative characteristics.[46]

These political factors overlap with a third set of issues, the structural conditions for redress. Here one must consider the broader socioeconomic factors that motivate neoliberal governments to engage in practices such as redress for historical wrongs, in particular those that might inspire a government such as that in Canada to try to harness redress politics in the settler colonial mesh. The neoliberal era is commonly viewed to have taken hold in North America in the 1970s, when Keynesian welfare policies were perceived to be in crisis. Throughout this period of economic transformation, some economists argued that the social programs of the welfare state were cumbersome and that the regulatory controls of the nation-state were a burden to increasingly mobile and global capital.[47] The political rationality of neoliberalism, finding expression in the policies of Ronald Reagan, Margaret Thatcher, and other world leaders, sought to roll back welfare provisions and create regulatory regimes and workforces more flexible to the needs of capital.[48]

Under such structural and ideological conditions, in which social spending by the state is heavily curtailed, one would not expect governments to enter lightly into policies of redress. However, one should not confuse reparations with welfare policy. Whereas welfare is understood as a constant drag on neoliberal governments, redress offers the luxury of one-time payment, commemoration, and truth telling that can serve a number of state purposes, such as allowing the state to gain or restore legitimacy,[49] rehabilitate its institutions and operations,[50] preserve or redeem a national order,[51] govern the victim group to ensure both finality and certainty within the social order,[52] or distract the public from more fundamental issues, such as Indigenous sovereignty and the return of Indigenous lands.[53]

Nonetheless, despite the strategic potential available to states through engagement with policies of redress, states do not undertake such processes willingly. As noted above, they need to be pushed toward involvement through the activism of victim groups and their allies. Activists secure state participation in redress by creating risks related to state noninvolvement. All too often redress measures are acts of risk management designed to quell the uncertainty caused by the legal or public demands made by victim groups. In some cases, the state can face exclusion from the international community if it fails to make amends.[54] In others, legal challenges launched by the victim group convince the state that the costs are greater for avoiding redress than they are for making redress.[55]

The state's desire to eliminate risk, however, does present some challenges for policies of redress that aspire to a goal of reconciliation. Reconciliation, as a relational process, demands risk. It also requires reflexivity—the ability to reflect deeply on one's identity and one's position in the order of things.

In contrast, most redress processes import law, which is ultimately reductive and certainty oriented, to manage the risk perceived to arise from claims to past injustices.[56] As the neoliberal state seeks to shore up uncertainty, it is often unwilling to seriously participate in the transformation of social relations, since such transformative redress would make the world seem more rather than less uncertain. Moreover, the state is often reluctant to transform itself, which results in resentment among those receiving reparations, for they receive the impression that the state is simply trying to buy silence from and pay lip service to the past rather than engaging in a sincere attempt to change a "form of life" that made atrocities possible.[57] State projects of reconciliation, therefore, tend to be projects where the wronged group is asked to reconcile themselves to existing conditions, thereby producing stability and certainty.

Following this line of reasoning, it is not so much a matter that the injustice claims of Canadian Indigenous peoples were graver with respect to their experiences of boarding schools. Nor is it the case that Canadian neoliberalism is more enlightened than that of the United States. It is rather the case that Canadian Indigenous boarding school survivors' justice claims were perceived to be riskier than those made in the United States, in particular because of the legal strategies mobilized by Indigenous groups to make the Canadian position on the residential schooling past less certain and therefore unsustainable.

In 1990, after Phil Fontaine, grand chief of the Assembly of Manitoba Chiefs, came forward with his experiences of abuse at FAIRS, leaders of the Assembly of First Nations discussed abuses in residential schools publicly for the first time. Moreover, in 1991, the former principal at Williams Lake Indian Residential School, Bishop Hubert O'Connor, was charged with two counts of rape and two counts of indecent assault for incidents that took place between 1964 and 1967.[58] Several other school staff members have since been charged for their crimes. As well, in 1996, survivors from the Alberni Indian Residential School brought forward the first class action lawsuit against the United Church of Canada and the federal government. Soon more survivors added their names to class action lawsuits. According to the federal government's National Resolution Framework, as of 2004, more than 12,000 survivors of IRS physical and sexual abuse had filed for compensation from the federal government.[59] The threat of an avalanche of settlements forced the government to undertake an alternative strategy to resolve the injustices of residential schooling.

One of the government's first moves was to consider an apology. Other groups involved in residential schooling had already offered apologies. The United Church issued an apology in 1986, followed by the Oblates of Saint Mary in 1991, the Anglican Church in 1993, and the Presbyterian Church in 1994. The federal government offered its first attempt at apology in 1998, with Minister of Indian and Northern Affairs Jane Stewart presenting a statement of regret to residential school survivors. However, this statement was thought by critics to be insincere because it focused almost exclusively on those who had suffered physical or sexual abuse in the schools, eliding broader issues of cultural loss and community disruption.[60] The statement was accompanied by *Gathering Strength: Canada's Aboriginal Action Plan*, which, among other things, directed $350 million toward creation of the Aboriginal Healing Foundation to facilitate community-based healing projects.[61]

The government's statement of regret and the Aboriginal Healing Fund did not quell the lawsuits. In 2002, the federal government sought to expedite the process through its introduction of the Indian Residential Schools Resolution Framework. The key to this framework was to settle legitimate claims outside the courts in an alternative dispute resolution (ADR) process, which the government claimed would handle up to 18,000 claims over a seven-year period in an equitable and just manner.[62] But the ADR process was quickly and roundly criticized. The Assembly of First Nations (AFN) estimated that ADR settlements would be too stingy to satisfy residential school survivors. In addition, the AFN noted that the ADR program focused solely on physical and sexual abuse, ignoring the residential school assault on Indigenous cultures, languages, and families.[63] An example of how these narrow definitions excluded specific traumatic experiences was given by Flora Merrick, a survivor from PLPIRS, to the House of Commons Standing Committee on Aboriginal Affairs and Northern Development, convened in February 2005 to consider problems with the ADR program:

I cannot forget one painful memory. It occurred in 1932 when I was 15 years old. My father came to Portage la Prairie residential school to tell my sister and I that our mother had died and to take us to the funeral. The principal of the school would not let us go with our father to the funeral. My little sister and I cried so much, we were taken away and locked in a dark room for about two weeks. After I was released from the dark room and allowed to be with other residents, I tried to run away to my father and family. I was caught in the bush by teachers and taken back to the school and strapped so severely that my arms were black and blue for several weeks. . . . I told this story during my ADR hearing, which was held at Long Plain in July 2004. . . . I was told that my experience did not fit into the rigid categories for being compensated under the ADR. However, the adjudicator, Mr. Chin, after hearing my story at my hearing, awarded me $1500. The federal government appealed to take even this small award from me.[64]

Concerns were also raised that the ADR process would simply enrich lawyers and mediators, leaving very little in settlement for residential school survivors. For this reason, a push was made by several groups (including the AFN, the Working Group on Truth and Reconciliation and the Exploratory Dialogues, and the Canadian Bar Association) for the parties to negotiate a lump-sum compensatory scheme similar to that offered to Second World War Japanese internment camp victims as well as a Truth and Reconciliation Commission to make Canadians more aware of the harms of residential schooling.[65]

Such a deal was negotiated in 2005 and then signed by representatives for the federal government, former students, the AFN, Inuit, and churches on May 8, 2006, as the Indian Residential School Settlement Agreement. The term "settlement agreement" is important here because, unlike other redress processes that have arisen entirely from interparty negotiations, IRSSA was a court-approved settlement that brought an end to the *Baxter* and *Cloud* class action lawsuits against the federal government.[66] IRSSA has several components. First, the settlement provides "at least" $1.9 billion for "common experience payments" (CEP), or payments allotted to any individual having attended a residential school, regardless of his or her experience.

This includes a base of $10,000 for the first year and $3,000 for every year thereafter. Second, the settlement features an "independent assessment process" (IAP) for those who have suffered sexual or serious physical abuses "or other abuses that caused serious psychological effects." Amounts from this process can range between $5,000 and $275,000 or more if a loss of income can be demonstrated. These amounts are determined through a "point system," which involves an itemization of the types of harm suffered while in a residential school. Third, collective reparations were also made, adding another $125 million to the Aboriginal Healing Foundation, setting aside $60 million for a Truth and Reconciliation Commission, and allotting a further $20 million for community commemorative projects.[67] The TRC was designed to include seven national events at which survivors and others connected to the schools could deliver either public or private statements about their residential schooling experiences and feelings about reconciliation, supplemented by community-based events, more numerous than the national events and less rigidly structured, allowing communities to adapt these hearings to local practices and traditions.[68]

Outside IRSSA, but in many ways essential to the process of negotiation, the federal government also agreed to deliver another public apology to residential school survivors, which it did on June 11, 2008, this time in front of the House of Commons and without restricting its audience to survivors of physical and sexual violence. On this occasion, Prime Minister Stephen Harper stated that "the government now recognizes that the consequences of the Indian residential schools policy were profoundly negative and that this policy has had a lasting and damaging impact on aboriginal culture, heritage and language."[69]

As I will discuss below, the CEP and IAP are mechanisms of legal closure and not simply acts of justice for past wrongs. Therefore, they are outcomes of a legal rather than negotiated settlement, as is the TRC.[70] This is dissimilar to most reparation programs arising in countries transitioning from periods of authoritarianism, atrocity, and human rights violation to a more peaceable and democratic future. However, it is not entirely uncommon for victim movements to use courts to pressure the state into taking their demands for justice seriously, and such tactics can be useful means for creating uncertainty and pushing governments toward more earnestly engaging in redress processes.[71] Indeed, the United States, with mechanisms such as the Alien Tort Claims Act, has often been a hotbed for such legal cases.[72] So how come there have been so few lawsuits filed on behalf of Indigenous survivors of American boarding schools?

We can begin to address this question by looking at some of the cases that have come forward. For example, in 2003, Sherwyn Zephier filed a class action lawsuit against the federal government for the abuse that he suffered while attending St. Paul's Marty Mission in South Dakota. Thousands of other survivors added their names to the lawsuit.[73] He and five other members of the Yankton Sioux were the lead plaintiffs and recorded their experiences of physical and sexual violence at the mission school. The lawsuit alleged a violation of treaties, such as the Laramie Treaty of 1868, which included a "bad man" clause stipulating that any wrongful action committed by a white person or other individual subject to the authority of the federal government against Indians would result in the arrest of that person and compensation. The lawsuit also included a breach of trust claim. For the latter, the court decided against the plaintiffs, charging that they had failed to state this claim. With respect to the former, the court also decided against the plaintiffs, this time because they had failed to exhaust administrative remedies through the BIA prior to bringing the case to court.[74] The current status of this case is unclear, since it has been reported that the plaintiffs would pursue exhaustion of BIA administrative remedies.[75] However, there have been criticisms of the plaintiffs from within American Indigenous communities, since the case had major ramifications for the legal pursuit of boarding school redress yet the plaintiffs had not fully consulted with the Indigenous community or boarding school survivor groups.[76]

According to Andrea Curcio, there are several legal means through which Indigenous boarding school survivors can pursue claims.[77] These means include Tucker Act claims, like that noted in the Zephier case, which allow Indigenous people to pursue damages when "bad men" among the white population violate treaties. Acts committed by such "bad men" could include physical and sexual abuse or institutional neglect. As well, Curcio points to the Federal Torts Claim Act as another vehicle for the pursuit of justice, under which the government can be sued for its failure to protect children under its care in boarding schools. Finally, Curcio mentions various international human rights norms violated by American boarding schools that could be the basis for lawsuits seeking damages. Curcio understands that the purpose of such claims is not the pursuit of justice in the courtroom; rather, they are a means to seek fuller justice:

> Although the boarding school claims cannot completely remedy all the wrongs committed against American-Indian children and American Indian nations, they can serve valuable purposes. They can bring this issue into the open and raise public awareness of the atrocities committed by our government against young children. . . . The cases can also provide a starting point for the government to begin to address, and redress, the multitude of harms caused by its horrific treatment of American Indians. The cases may help those boarding school attendees involved understand that the problems they have suffered and continue to suffer are due to what happened to them rather than to anything that they have done or not done. Finally, this kind of litigation can be used as an example of how the law can or should redress large-scale human rights violations.[78]

The U.S.-based Boarding School Healing Project (BSHP), which came into existence prior to the Canadian IRSSA and has made demands for boarding school reparations that would provide collective benefits to Indigenous peoples in the United States in terms of healing, education, documentation, and accountability,[79] initially rejected the Canadian strategy of class action lawsuits, viewing them as too individualistic and their compensation as inadequately symbolic of the harms committed at Indigenous boarding schools. The BSHP is a coalition that includes the following bodies: "The South Dakota Coalition Against Sexual and Domestic Violence, Tribal Law and Policy Institute, Indigenous Women's Network, American Indian Law Alliance, First Nations North and South, Seventh Generation Fund, In-cite! Women of Color Against Violence, and the Indian Desk of the United Church of Christ."[80] Its efforts are ongoing, but like many other redress movements it has recently faced the challenge of seeking redress in an American economy suffering from a market downturn that has made the general public less open to claims for historical redress.

Slow progress is nonetheless being made with respect to an apology for colonial harms against American Indigenous peoples. Assistant Secretary of the Interior Kevin Gover formally apologized in September 2000 on behalf of the BIA for how his government had participated in "ethnic cleansing" and forced relocation.[81] Gover, a citizen of the Pawnee Nation, did not have his apology publicly endorsed by President Bill Clinton, and no compensation or restitution followed in the wake of the apology, leading some to question its significance. More recent efforts have therefore been directed at demanding an official apology from the president. For example, in 2009, a petition made its way from Chemawa Indian School in Oregon across the country, calling on President Obama to "join the leaders of Canada and Australia by apologizing to First Nations people here for what was allowed to happen to children at the schools, and for the scars of hurt and pain that it left on generations of Native American people."[82] President Obama did make an apology of sorts that year when he signed into law the Native American Apology Resolution on December 19. The bill that preceded the law, sponsored by Sam Brownback from Kansas, "apologized on behalf of the United States to all Native Peoples for the many instances of violence, maltreatment, and neglect of Native Peoples by citizens of the United States" and "urge[d] the President to acknowledge the wrongs of the United States against Indian tribes in the history of the United States in order to bring healing to this land."[83] However, signing of this bill into law was closed to the press, and the apology itself was not read publicly until May 20, 2010, when it was presented before leaders representing the Cherokee, Choctaw, Pawnee, Muscogee (Creek), and Sisseton Wahpeton Oyate.[84] The apology was thus perceived by some as largely an empty gesture received too long after the abuses occurred.[85]

With such limited recognition of the harms of settler colonialism in the United States, more scholars are looking toward Canada as a source of inspiration regarding what reparations in the United States might look like.[86] Curcio, for example, writes that "the United States government should look to Canada for ideas on how to begin to address this issue. For example, following Canada's example, the United States should first set up a Commission to study and report on what was done to the children in the American Indian boarding schools, and the impact that this has had upon the American Indian peoples. This would be a starting point for understanding the problems caused by the boarding schools."[87] Although the efforts of Canadian survivors to force the Canadian government to consider redress are instructive, the larger question is whether or not IRSSA represents a fitting model for redressing American Indigenous boarding schools, if the United States were to reach a stage where the government thought it too risky to continue avoiding meaningful redress. The next section evaluates this question through an examination of TRC testimony reflecting feelings about Prime Minister Harper's apology, the CEP, the IAP, and the TRC. Such testimony is valuable for identifying problems with redress policy, since it directs our attention to the contradictions, limitations, and compromises as perceived by those who are its intended recipients and who, through redress, remain the targets of government intervention.

Canadian Redress Efforts and the United States

Quotations used in this section were not restricted to those from FAIRS or PLPIRS, as was the case for previous chapters. The rationale for this shift is that this chapter returns to a national rather than regional comparison, since redress policies are developed and applied at the national level. The Truth and Reconciliation Commission of Canada database was searched for discussion of apology, compensation, and truth and reconciliation. The views presented below are reflective of the criticisms issued toward the IRSSA and apology. It should be noted that not all Survivors were critical of this process, and that positive statements were made with respect to certain elements of the IRSSA and apology, though the criticisms were more frequent.

In many respects, Prime Minister Harper's apology went further than earlier attempts to acknowledge the harms of residential schools. Whereas the 1998 statement of regret was limited to expressing remorse for physical and sexual abuse in the schools, the 2008 apology recognized the wider harms of residential schools to Indigenous communities. Some residential school survivors expressed a sense of appreciation that the apology made public and official (and therefore less deniable) their suffering. Nonetheless, survivors giving testimony to the TRC also expressed a healthy degree of skepticism with respect to this apology. For some, the apology was simply too little too late:

And I just want to say to the Prime Minister that apologized, shame on you yourself; shame on the government. And I, I didn't, I just will not accept that apology; it's just too late. And I'm not going to, I'm. . . . It's just too late for apologies, even for my family and everybody; and, like my dad, my stepmother. And then I thought, I can't really think like that either too, because they had gone to residential school themselves. So until then I don't know what's going to make things right, except to tell our story.[88]

Similarly, some thought that too much had happened since their time at residential schools and that mere words could not heal their wounds, especially since the harms are ongoing:

The ironic thing is that Harper, what's he, who is he, Prime Minister Harper, whom I couldn't stand to begin with, this sanctimonious nincompoop, anyway, did his big apology for the residential school. What, three, four months after Danny died. I was enraged by that too, as if some words are going to make up for all the lives that are, have been ruined. Yet really, it's not just my life, my other son's life has been ruined, my granddaughter's life has been ruined. And the cycle just keeps on generating. The trauma just goes on and on and on.[89]

Others bristled at the inconsistencies of the apology, contending that it acknowledged past harms without doing enough to change the contemporary treatment of Indigenous peoples in Canadian society. They viewed it to be superficial, self-contradictory, and more about preserving the Canadian status quo than fostering social transformation in settler-Indigenous relations:

Well, I think, I think the Canadian public really needs to be educated. I think they have to get a feel for this. They have to appreciate what occurred, understand the reasoning behind it, and to make sure it never happens again. And I think Canada could be one of the leading countries in the world in doing that. But we, we, we have to follow through with, with what we say we're gonna do. For example, the Prime Minister made the apology, and now the efforts, not only the Truth and Reconciliation Commission has to take place, like the Healing Foundation lost its funding, and that's really gonna affect our community. So, it seems

Canada says one thing, but then they don't follow through, and that's really disturbing and it's confusing for people 'cause we're saying we want to deal with it in a constructive way, but then Canada's bureaucracy, or whatever you want to call it, is acting a different way.[90]

What did Harper do since the apology? Well, now, he's starting to implement a system where they do [mandatory minimum] punishment, where he's gonna punish people. And who are the people that he's punishing? It's our people! But what about the healing process? Yes, they did Aboriginal Healing Foundation and they did a lot of support, but that kind of thing has to keep on. What Marie Wilson and the rest of the [TRC] Commissioners are doing—that's a step in the right direction. That's the healing process. It's gonna take a long time.[91]

To me, that is what I urge the Commission to really look at. And to hear us. We need to tell the Prime Minister that, yes, he apologized and he did say in his apology that the loss of language was one of the areas that was most tragic, but nothing has come down to our communities to help us have emergent programs. We don't [have] any money . . . to help them take them out. That should be in there. They spent 1.7 billion dollars for gatherings like this, but there's no money for our kids to learn the language. Who benefitted from most of that money? The lawyers.[92]

The second speaker, like several other speakers, viewed reconciliation and social healing as more likely to come about through giving testimony. As participants in the TRC process, they likely felt some hope that this forum will educate Canadian society and begin a process of change and relationship building for Indigenous and non-Indigenous peoples in Canada. However, the third speaker saw the TRC as a diversion from the help needed on the ground in Indigenous communities.

The TRC made a later start than expected, in part because of conflict among the initial commissioners. The first chief commissioner, Judge Harry LaForme, resigned in October 2008. It was reported that he had had a dispute with the AFN and the two other commissioners, believing that they were too beholden to truth seeking rather than reconciliation. LaForme viewed the survivor testimony component of the TRC events as potentially divisive and thought that it needed to be accompanied by something that would build unity.[93] The two remaining commissioners later resigned in June 2009. Justice Murray Sinclair took over as commissioner on June 3, 2009, and the TRC has moved ahead under his leadership.

This early dispute raised concerns that the TRC might, through an emphasis on reconciliation, become a project in nation building and governance through forced closure. There was also a sense that the federal government was seeking to exert control over the process, treating the TRC as another branch of government and not granting it financial independence or facilitating access to the archival resources needed to provide a full picture of the residential school system.[94] Although the initial power struggle was won by those seeking to direct the TRC toward prioritizing the stories and experiences of cultural harm and abuse in the boarding schools, questions remain. Will the TRC offer an adequate reckoning of the Canadian past? Will Canadians embrace its telling of their history even if it tarnishes a positively held Canadian national identity? Will the telling of the past be limited and circumscribed by political and legalistic concerns? Will the TRC be decolonizing and encourage structural transformations in the settler-Indigenous relationship?[95] These questions are central to evaluating the "reconciliation" sought through the TRC, and it is still too early to pass judgment on its success in meeting its goals. However, it is fair to say that public attention to the TRC needs to grow, as too many Canadians remained unaware of what is under way at various TRC-sponsored events and community meetings across the country. Moreover, restrictions on mentioning perpetrators' names, as well as the exclusion of day schools and nonrecognized residential schools from the process, threaten to shape the sort of truth that the TRC produces and impose closure despite the ongoing character of Canadian settler colonialism.[96]

With respect to the "common experience" and "independent assessment" compensation programs, some early evidence of problems associated with these instruments can be noted. The compensation offered is *settlement* in the true sense of the word, since it is conducted in a language intended to prevent further liability by the government and churches and to represent a full and final resolution to all Indigenous boarding school class action suits.[97] The common experience payment, therefore, merely marks the time that one spent in a residential school without addressing directly the cultural harm of this schooling experience. The most prevalent complaint about the CEP recorded in TRC statements is that, because of poor record keeping at the schools, survivors are often not given full compensation for the years that they attended.

> Before, before it, okay, there was a thing where they said you, you send for your records, so I did, I sent for my records right away, and they sent me 28 pages with my name on it. And from what I understood, each page represents a quarter, so I, I still have those, those 28 pages. And the sad part was, I was paid one year. They didn't pay me for the other five. They said they couldn't verify, and I said, like, I thought to myself, holy cripes, just like I'm victimized again. And I thought, well, no amount of money is gonna, is gonna heal me. You know they could pay me all the money they want, but it's up to me, though I did appeal it. . . . No money, amount of money is gonna, is gonna release what's inside that I have, you know, I'm going to do that in my own time, in my own way.[98]

> I went through the CEP, common experience process and I applied for twelve years of residential school and I got eight years back. And I was rejected four years, 'cause the government said I went to day school those four years from grade nine to twelve. So I was rejected, another form of rejection I thought and I was very angry about this and today I'm still angry over that, I still want to pursue it.[99]

After thinking that their stories have too long gone unheard and unacknowledged, it is not so much the lack of compensation that hurts survivors but the feeling that their suffering is going unrecognized yet again. As well, they sense that they are doubted and discredited, and these feelings bring back memories of how they were treated at the residential schools—as unreliable, untrustworthy, and tainted individuals.

Unlike the CEP, the IAP deals with specific instances of harm, though it does so in an actuarial manner that asks claimants to identify instances of physical, sexual, or psychological harm that they have suffered individually rather than collectively. In this manner, harm is itemized and made governable—it can be delineated, counted, measured, estimated, and compensated. Through such practices, the past is managed more than it is mastered, as deeply social and ontological damage perpetrated through forced assimilation is transformed into a discrete set of calculable and reparable acts. The IAP form is a twenty-eight-page document that demands a great deal of personal and descriptive information from the applicant. As well, various forms of verification or proof are required, such as a doctor's note to confirm that one is too ill to attend a hearing. The complexity of the application means that applicants in most cases will require the assistance of lawyers in filling out its details,[100] adding a further level of translation, as their personal experiences of harm are converted by professionals into the terms demanded by the form and by the process. Survivors often note the byzantine nature of the process and the expenses paid to lawyers to navigate it.[101]

> The waiting period takes too long, nobody explains anything to us. For instance, my IAP is going on three years now, in all those years I've had three different case workers looking at my file and my lawyer was never notified that one of the case workers, when she left her position it was sitting on someone's desk for about six months. Until I told my lawyer to look into it, then I find out another case worker took over, just as he was phoning. We get all this run around, he doesn't get no information, I didn't even get no information about this residential school until I read it through the newspaper.[102]

> But by the time I got my pay out of it all, and the lawyer fees taken off, the lawyer collected, for my case alone, just me, her portion of it was like ten thousand five hundred; for her. So I only came, came out of it with like, twenty-five thousand.[103]

Moreover, the process is very invasive, and this experience is magnified for survivors who have spent a portion of their lives in the surveillant spaces of residential schools. And, in the end, its calculus of suffering is difficult for survivors to negotiate, for they are left unsure how to parcel their pain into the categories of harm presented by the IAP forms.

> When I applied for the IAP, we were told to gather documents, everything, treatment, medical, high school, elementary, treatment centers,

our relationships if we were ever sexually abused and our education, if we took other courses. . . . Sometimes I think they're getting too personal when they do that especially with your marriage life. They don't need to know how many times I married or lived common law with people, that's none of their damn business. All I was there for was to talk about the abuse and physical abuse and the stuff I saw going [on] in the residential schools.[104]

The IAP is asking me. . . . Sorry. Is asking me to measure the amount of hurt and pain I have experienced in the residential school. What I find most difficult is trying to separate my whole life experience from what happened to me in the school and the events before and after the residential school. I feel there is a connection from when I lived on the reserve, when I left the reserve, and came home after being in the hospital for 10 years.[105]

The hearing for the IAP is also designed to contain suffering within terms convenient to governance. Survivors must here rehearse and learn to present their pain in a manner that fits state categories of suffering. But, ultimately, their pain is under evaluation, and institutional actors not so far removed from those who were its originators adjudicate the veracity of their suffering. This has the potential effect of furthering trauma.

I had my residential school survivor hearing recently and gave my testimony. It was hard, difficult and stressful. The hearings are designed to determine just how much abuse one has suffered and how much the government should pay that individual. . . . The only saving grace of this process is that there would be money set aside to pay for therapy. Though I must admit I was disheartened to learn that it would be perhaps another entire year before I get that paid for by the government. In the meantime, I have to continue to suffer through my pain while the government looks over my case to determine if I'm telling the truth. . . . They treated me as though I were only concerned about a large financial gain. A large financial gain would never, no matter how large it is, give me a normal life. My life and history would still be messed up. . . . Throwing money is just another way for them [the government] to wipe their hands of this country's botched history.[106]

Finally, the retelling of one's traumatic experiences in such an environment does not always have the cathartic effect of the "talking cure" that some hope will derive from such truth-telling occasions.

> And now after so many years, the last few years it starts coming out, the pain and there's nothing I can do except try and forget it, it will never happen again. But people always ask you to repeat it, repeat it in these IAP meetings that I had, three of them already. I'm going for my fourth one and it's still. They think it's easier talking about it but it isn't.[107]

> That's why I was always afraid of her. But I think there was a lot of shame in telling that story, too. Because I remember when she hit me, too, I wet my pants. And that, so I was very much ashamed. . . . So, when I, I wrote out the IAP, I wouldn't even mention that part of it, you know. There's a lot of shame in it. So, . . . you know, that, you wet yourself and everything, eh.[108]

Likewise, a survivor from PLPIRS spoke at her statement gathering of her desire to simply forget all that had happened. However, she was encouraged to unburden herself and convinced that such unburdening is a key step toward healing.

> *Survivor:* Oh, I just want to forget all this. I don't want any more memories. There [are] some things I can't tell ya, I can't remember them. I, I believe I blocked them out.
> *Support Worker:* Every time you share, you're healing, you know.[109]

By the end of the statement gathering, this survivor did seem to be buoyed by telling her story, but it is impossible to gauge whether this was a lasting or fleeting outcome of the so-called talking cure. But the overwhelming impression that one receives when reading and listening to statements made by survivors for the TRC is that the compensation (CEP and IAP) components of IRSSA and the apology are not advancing individual healing. If this is the case, then what benefit can one expect to be accrued by Indigenous groups in the United States through engagement in such a process? Redress policies often appear as the best imperfect solution available for those not currently receiving their benefits, but American Indigenous boarding school survivors would be wise to look critically at the Canadian process before embracing it as a gold standard.

In this chapter, I have suggested that both Canadian and American Indigenous peoples continue to suffer from the aftermath of Indigenous boarding schools as well as other (ongoing) and still mutating dimensions of the settler colonial mesh. Moreover, I have noted that basic legal channels are available in each nation for the pursuit of reparations. Therefore, the different pathways to repair taken in the United States and Canada require explanation. Here I have suggested that there are discursive, political, and structural reasons for these differences. The discursive differences have largely to do with the perception that soft powers were more prevalent in American Indigenous boarding schools. This is true, to some extent, as previous chapters attest. However, one can also expect that, if a discursive opening for abuse testimony were to occur in the United States as it has in Canada, whereby survivors could safely tell their stories with the security that they would be met with reactions other than doubt and dismissal, more stories of abuse in American boarding schools would likely become public. Whether or not such abuses are on par with those that occurred in Canada is an exercise in needless accounting, however, since in both cases are examples of attempts to destroy Indigenous groups as groups, and therefore each case is worthy of redress. On the political front, I have argued that, after the late 1960s and early 1970s, when pan-Indigenous movements reached their peak of intensity, these movements travelled in different directions in each country. Fracturing is a common concern for all pan-Indigenous movements, since as multination entities they are defined by a variety of distinct national interests.[110] However, in Canada, enough common interests remained to make national forms of collective action both desirable and necessary, and they worked within a Canadian policy context in which redress policy was used as a means to try to contain Indigenous justice demands. Finally, structural differences meant that Canadian neoliberalism felt more deeply the risk of nonsettlement, whereas the U.S. government has been able to simply ignore such demands—at least for the time being, until it too is placed in a position where the costs outweigh the benefits of nonsettlement.

The comments of survivors on aspects of IRSSA at the TRC are instructive in light of this last reason. One can see here their awareness of the self-serving nature of the state's involvement in redress, such as when survivors question the sincerity of Prime Minister Harper's apology in light of his other policies on Indigenous peoples or when they criticize compensation programs for their bureaucratic complexity, rigid formulae, and attempts to itemize suffering. In such instances, survivors appear to be all too aware of the government's desires to make their suffering legible, calculable, and manageable, so that it no longer represents a burden on the government. They also sense that they are meant to find closure through these apologies and payments and to no longer be "a problem" for the government. The government's cancelling of funding for the Aboriginal Healing Foundation prior to the end of the TRC process, despite its role in providing support and assistance to survivors as they relived their residential school experiences, the continued expansion of the criminal justice system, and recent moves toward reducing funds to Indigenous representative organizations signify that Canada's current neoliberal government still appears to be engaged in freeing itself from the Indian Problem, offering one-time payments with one hand while threatening with the might of police, prisons, and economic rollbacks with the other.[111] In such circumstances, redress is felt not as a decolonizing impulse pushing toward a new nonsettler society but as another form of what Lorenzo Veracini refers to as "transfer," using a variety of methods to remove Indigenous peoples as an obstacle to settler colonial political formation. In this case, redress transfers the legitimate justice demands of Indigenous peoples into tidy boxes of repair, removing them as a challenge to the legitimacy of the settler colonial nation and potentially hiding the violence of settler colonialism within a language of reconciliation.[112]

9 Conclusion

The "benevolent experiment" of Indigenous boarding schools in North America was an effort to destroy Indigenous groups as self-sustaining and self-defining entities. It is for this reason that I have brought the term "genocide" into the discussion in this book. However, my goal has not been to shock the reader with use of an overly politicized term, and I have not used it out of naive optimism that the term is somehow sufficient to mobilize public opinion toward a certain political issue. Instead, I approach this topic as a genocide scholar who seeks to recover, but also to develop and advance, Raphael Lemkin's insights into the harm of genocide. In particular, genocide is the purposeful destruction of a group, and if we are to take the survival of groups seriously then it is incumbent upon us to know something about how groups persist and survive in a world of almost constant change. I have argued that culture, as a fluid and negotiated quality of the group, or, as some might prefer, identity, is as pertinent to the discussion of the survival of groups as are other key elements of group life. Culture is what holds the group together as a group, even as the group adapts to new circumstances and encounters. To forcibly remove the tools of culture is to seek to eliminate the group as a group.

This effort was directed toward importing into genocide studies a notion of culture that is not simply "frozen in time" but interactive in that it is negotiated among members of a collectivity as they reproduce themselves

culture or
interactive

289

as a unit. Genocide, when it targets the cultural bonds of the group, disrupts such interaction. In this sense, Indigenous boarding schools, by disrupting lines of cultural transmission, by severing links between child and parent or child and community or child and territory, by attempting to invalidate the traditions and practices of the cultural group, by seeking to replace cultural affiliation with affiliation to non-Indigenous groups, and so on, sought to disrupt the interactions that make group life possible, thus making group claims to territory impossible. That this attempt at total destruction often failed, or came up against unexpected and powerful resistance, does not absolve settler colonialism of the charge of genocide. A collective action framework, built upon the notion of an Indian Problem, that guided a multiplicity of settler colonial interventions, including Indigenous boarding schools, operated toward the elimination of Indigenous peoples as obstacles to settler colonial designs on Indigenous lands and souls.

Some fear, however, that culture is too vast and diffuse a category to sustain the notion of genocide. An argument against including "cultural" genocide within the definition of genocide has been that the concept would become so broad as to be meaningless. Such a response has almost become a reflex among certain genocide scholars and members of the general public. But this stems from a positivist inheritance assuming that precision lies within the limited applicability of a concept. Like most limits, however, this one too is arbitrary, because it finds precision in elevating certain forms of attempted group destruction above others. It reinforces a hierarchy of genocide studies, and establishes a genocidal canon of cases worthy of research, by reifying destruction in the most narrow terms and excluding all other forms of potential group demise.[1] Moreover, such manufactured precision can obfuscate and oversimplify processes of actual genocide. Recent genocide scholarship has sought to trace the complex patterns of destruction that emerge in actual historical contexts, whereby genocidal actions do not unfold neatly in accordance with a fully articulated plan.[2] Instead, groups seeking to destroy other groups come up against contingencies, including resistance from those targeted for destruction, to which they must adapt. In this book, I have presented a model for examining such processes in a settler colonial context. Referred to above as the settler colonial mesh, this model describes various levels of netting, or networking, that link together actors whose participation must be negotiated for the process of destruction to unfold. These networks exist at different societal levels—the macro, meso, and micro—and stretch across time and space, tightening in some circumstances, loosening and creating more opportunities for resistance in others.

At the macrosocietal level, my focus has been on those late-nineteenth-century actors engaged in addressing the so-called Indian Problem in the United States and Canada. These efforts at problematization and solution are important because they provide a basic yet flexible collective action frame that informed lower-level efforts to institutionalize assimilation. In each country, a diverse group of political, economic, military, and religious actors, among others, engaged in this project of problem framing. However, in the United States, one sees more influence among a group of largely Protestant reformers who believed assimilation and civilization to be humanitarian responses to the poor condition of Native Americans, itself a product of government and settler intrusion upon their lives and lands. In Canada, the same humanitarian justification was mobilized, but the conversation about the Indian Problem was more squarely located in the halls of government, though other actors did provide input. Indeed, multiple motives and intentions were at work in crafting the Indian Problem, but what emerged, whether framed as benevolence or racial social engineering, was the idea that *the Indian as an Indian was a problem* for each country, and therefore the Indian had to be eliminated through assimilation and civilization. These two notions provided a flexible action framework for the various institutions and organizations engaged in solving the Indian Problem.

Implementation of this collective action frame required multiple forms of intervention. The intervention of concern in this book is the Indigenous boarding school first used by religious missions but given formal shape by Richard Pratt through his experiments at Fort Marion, Hampton (alongside Samuel Chapman Armstrong), and Carlisle. At the upper mesolevel of the settler colonial mesh, the Christian denominations that oversaw schooling in Canada formed an institutional matrix that mediated between the federal government and the boarding schools. The churches were invested in preserving their control over their schools and students, while the government prioritized that the schools be managed in a frugal manner. These two factors combined to produce spare and often brutal conditions in Canadian Indigenous boarding schools over most of their existence. In contrast, one sees larger shifts in the way that American Indigenous boarding schools were governed, since there was no mediating institutional matrix that resisted changes in governance at the schools. Add to this the fact that the Canadian Department of Indian Affairs saw less turnover among its personnel than was true for the American Bureau of Indian Affairs, and the more static nature of the Canadian Indigenous boarding school experience can be better understood.

This is not to suggest that boarding schools were experienced in a uniform manner in either the United States or Canada. When we move in closer to the schools, and focus on lower meso- and microlevels of analysis, we can observe how specific relations of cooperation and competition emerged among various school types (e.g., reservation, nonreservation, and day; mission based; federal) as well as how specific techniques and actor networks determined the local dynamics of each school. The bulk of the empirical evidence presented in this book has been directed at these lower levels of analysis. It is there that we see how schools in Manitoba and New Mexico dealt with their perceived competitors, secured the students that they required to ensure their per capita budgets, administered assimilation to the students, and contended with a variety of actors, including not only staff, students, parents, and Indigenous communities but also space, time, disease, food, blood, and hell. It is also at this level that we see how gaps emerged in specific segments of the lower meso- and microlevel nets, allowing Indigenous groups to resist assimilative pressures and to assert themselves on the schools, demanding better treatment of students, though they were not sufficiently empowered to overturn or decolonize their contexts. Because of the distinct characteristics of the schools in New Mexico, in contrast to those in Manitoba, one sees more such gaps forming; however, this is not to suggest that resistance was not evident at the Manitoba Indigenous boarding schools examined in this study.

The final chapter of this book addresses the different pathways to redress in each country. I have suggested that the shadow of Indigenous boarding schools is present in each country, as are the legal mechanisms necessary to force government redress. However, only in Canada have significant measures been taken toward redressing the boarding school past. I have argued that there are discursive, political, and structural factors that explain why the United States has not taken a path similar to that in Canada. These factors have to do with the perception that American boarding schools were not as malevolent as those in Canada, the more fractured nature of pan-Indigenous politics in the United States, and the fact that the U.S. government simply has not thought that it is too risky to continue to ignore this history. However, I have also raised the question whether or not the Canadian model of redress offers a viable basis for U.S. redress policies. Based on statements drawn from Truth and Reconciliation Commission testimony, there are limitations to the Canadian process that should be of concern to those seeking redress in the United States. In particular, there is the danger that redress policy might be enlisted as a new technique of assimilation and thereby become but another mutation of the settler colonial mesh.

For those who wish to read only a scholarly treatise on Indigenous boarding schools, genocide, and redress, this might be as good a place as any to end this book. My efforts up to this point have been to show rather than tell about my topic. Although as a critical scholar I have been putting forward an argument, I have refrained from prescribing or imposing an ethical course of action. In what remains of this conclusion, I briefly consider where I believe my analysis leads us (even if I still work to avoid rigid prescription). Such discussion might be unwelcome for some in a scholarly book, but as a member of a settler colonial society who continues to work on how the settler condition has shaped his own perspectives and privileged his position, I feel responsible at minimum to venture some small suggestions with respect to what my analysis means for a broader project of North American decolonization.

Genocide, Accountability, and Redress

Some fear that, if the genocide concept is not restricted in its application, it will not inspire political intervention. However, recent years have proven that the term does not have the cachet to mobilize political will through its mere utterance. Whether in Sudan, Syria, Rwanda, or Congo, the term "genocide" can become a distraction from rather than a trigger for intervention. As Henry Theriault has noted however, the term can serve another purpose by setting the stage for redress.[3] The term is thus not solely purposed to work as a legal category for prevention and punishment. Indeed, the value of the genocide concept is often in how it captures the potentially catastrophic nature of certain interventions in the life of a group and provides a framework for setting a path for how we might live differently, together. In the American and Canadian contexts, the term can alert us to the destructive path of settler colonialism, highlight the centrality of land dispossession and elimination to this process, and press us toward a project of *decolonizing redress* rather than projects of redress that merely affirm the status quo. It can also prompt us to reckon with both our past and our present. In writing about the challenge facing the Truth and Reconciliation Commission of Canada, Paulette Regan notes that, "in the public mind, there has been no epitomizing moment of genocidal crisis or mass human rights violations that would trigger a need for transitional justice mechanisms such as international criminal courts, tribunals, or truth and reconciliation commissions more commonly associated with so-called developing countries or despotic regimes."[4] Regan's statement captures settler North America's reluctance to see genocide as a problem in our midst; genocide, and therefore transitional justice, are problems out there, not of concern to North Americans. Because of this reluctance, history is an important part of moving forward, and this includes creating public awareness of the full meaning of the genocide concept and its applicability to settler colonial North America, including its present day mutations. Understanding genocide is a way to understand ourselves as inheritors and perpetuators of settler colonialism who have benefited from its ongoing processes of dispossession and assimilation.

As a legal concept, genocide directs our attention toward a perpetrator who has exhibited specific intent in seeking the destruction of a group. In contrast, the sociological and historical notion of genocide used in this book is less focused on the individual accountability of particular actors and more concerned with the collective responsibility that issues from a set of social relations that promoted the elimination of Indigenous groups. In particular, the impulse to assimilate and civilize Indigenous persons in North America, which rose to dominance as a framework for collective action in the late nineteenth century, is understood here as part of an ongoing and multidimensional attempt by American and Canadian settler societies to resolve the so-called Indian Problem. Here Indigenous boarding schools had a primary role to play as vehicles for the forcible transformation, and therefore attempted destruction, of Indigenous societies. These schools varied in their effectiveness, took on different forms and functions in different times and different places, and were subject to local resistance and adaptation to, or subversion of, their destructive project. Moreover, those who attended the schools, or those who ran them, possessed a degree of agency in shaping their interactions, and occasionally they succeeded in softening these interactions. None of this, however, takes away from the fact that they were a manifestation of a collective settler attempt to address the Indian Problem through the elimination of Indigenous groups. Even in a gentler or softer form, Indigenous boarding schools were part of an infrastructure, a settler colonial mesh, intended to remove Indigenous peoples from the North American landscape, absorbing them into a lower tier of the mainstream society, and opening their lands for unimpeded acquisition.

This collective rather than individual understanding of accountability requires us to consider collective rather than individual approaches to redress. This is not to take away from processes of individual reckoning (for perpetrators of residential school violence) or reparation (for survivors), which might be deemed important remedies by survivors, who are the only ones who can speak about their own needs. However, from a societal perspective, how we have lived together as collectivities, as much as individuals, has set us on such a damaging course. So it cannot simply be left to the courts, the government, or the TRC of Canada to correct the past (and present). Such auspices can only serve as initiators of the discussion necessary to, in Regan's apt phrase, "unsettle the settler within" and contribute to the co-production of a decolonizing Canadian society.[5] The larger project is for individual Canadians to recognize that, regardless of their own perceived status as good and caring people, their very lives are built upon complicity with a project of societal destruction that can only be brought to an end by a similar collective project, a reframing of what Canada and the United States could be if they were to do the hard work of unsettling their colonial pasts and forging relations of mutual respect, sharing, and a never-ending commitment to redressing not only those pasts (so that they might be left behind us) but also our common existence on Turtle Island with all peoples.[6] Such redress, however, requires that each settler society no longer interfere with Indigenous resurgence and well-being, so that thriving Indigenous nations can participate on an equal footing in reconciling and decolonizing our relations. Until then, too often our processes of redress mutate into forms of affirmative repair that simply reinvent and reinforce the old society in a slightly reformed guise.[7]

But settlers can begin processes of collective redress sooner rather than later. This requires that American and Canadian settler societies find ways to come to terms with the fact that our nations have been founded upon a form of life that, if we follow Patrick Wolfe's insight that settler colonialism is a structure (not an event), functioned to replace the Native with the settler.[8] The question thus becomes much larger than simply one of who should go on trial or how many dollars in compensation are owed. Instead, the question is how do we radically alter a way of life that has resulted in such attempts at Indigenous destruction and remains with us today? How do we redress the fact that we live and have benefited from our lives upon Indigenous lands? Indeed, that aspects of IRSSA have received such criticisms from boarding school survivors is a testament to the unfortunate fact that, in such circumstances, the current mode of redress is felt not as a decolonizing impulse pushing toward a new society but as another form of settler colonial administration and assimilation.

This is where I think that the term "genocide" can do its most important work. My effort in this book has not been to act as hanging judge for specific accused individuals, nor has it been to mobilize an oversimplified concept of genocide as a means to hammer a diversity of experiences into a single hole. Instead, my effort has been to add to the conversation an understanding of genocide as a complex process that, like most human processes, unfolds in an uneven manner. Such an understanding demands that we not simply look for scapegoats—bad men and women whom we condemn for past crimes. Instead, we must look closely at our own societies, born from a genocidal impulse and built upon destructive processes that can only be redressed through a long-term commitment to transforming ourselves and our nations.

Genocide, Redress, and Indigenous Education

When confronted with a host of social problems, the knee-jerk response is to call for more education. In Euro-Western societies, we tend to view education as innocent, as mere knowledge transmitted to those eager to learn. However, as I have argued in this book, particularly in an intercultural context of contesting sovereignties, education is anything but innocent. In its institutional form, it transmits not mere knowledge but culturally specific knowledges designed to facilitate citizenship of a certain type. The knowledge that we obtain, what Bourdieu would refer to as our cultural capital, is a resource that allows us to navigate the social fields of the dominant society. It is knowledge shaped toward a cultural context that allows us to refer to the "right" books, explore issues from the "right" perspective, and exhibit the "correct" rationality in our day-to-day lives. In this manner, education is always an intervention.[9] This is partly why I continue to refer to those who attended Indigenous boarding schools as "students" rather than opting for some other term, such as "prisoners." Using the former term is not intended to mollify the boarding schools but to remind readers of the dark side of schools, where students can be subjected to a great deal of violence. Schools can be spaces where brutal violence, techniques of destruction, and deadly alliances are introduced and assume genocidal proportions. At the same time, it is true that the term "school" is not enough to describe the disciplinary admixture that existed within Indigenous boarding schools, which was influenced by a variety of European carceral institutions, including the monastery, military, the workhouse, prisons, and the orphanage. These were hybrid and destructive spaces that demonstrate the violence "schools" can contain when designed under circumstances of asymmetrical power.

In a settler colonial context in which Indigenous education has been marred by genocidal processes, it is very difficult to reinvent education at the state or societal level. In Canada, where the education of young Indigenous people is still viewed as an answer to a problem, IRSSA has led to new questions about how Indigenous education should take place. Certainly, models such as the contemporary Santa Fe Indian School, or Children of the Earth high school in Winnipeg, represent innovative and locally guided efforts to deliver education in a manner that allows for survivance—both the adaptation and the continuation of culture. But the success of such schools depends not solely on the best intentions of those who work in and create programming within their walls. If these schools are still locked in a settler colonial mesh that continues to set expectations, place limits, and govern outcomes through a variety of institutional channels, then they might represent only fleeting moments of Indigenous control soon to be undone or mitigated by a settler colonial society that continues to deliver colonizing messages: you must assimilate if you want to succeed in the world of work; you must learn to speak, think, and present yourself like us to enjoy success; your culture is backward and impractical, and you must enter into the modern world; forget your claims to territory and self-determination.

To this extent, education is still part of a broader settler colonial mesh that continues to weigh on local efforts to educate and to achieve cultural and territorial survivance. And it is for this reason that educational reform is not sufficient to address the challenge of Indigenous-settler relations in North America. It is also for this reason that genocide is a useful lens for looking at these issues. As I have presented it in this book, "genocide" is not a term intended to mire us in the past. Nor is it a term intended to lock Indigenous peoples into the role of passive victims. It is a term, rather, that asks us to think deeply about destructive relations (and not just symbolic relations, but material relations as well) between groups. In particular, I have drawn attention to the ways that clashes between a dominant culture and multiple Indigenous cultures take shape in a manner whereby the former seeks to eliminate the latter, thereby threatening the very existence of the groups themselves. Comprehending the complexity of these destructive relations allows us to trace the mutations of this "logic of elimination," since it fits itself into the redress processes and educational reforms that we muster in attempts to correct this past.[10] Thus, genocide, not as a legal concept but as a tool for tracing destructive relations, offers us a means to seek a decolonizing path.[11] If we confront genocide as an aspect of our destructive relations, then our efforts at redress must find nondestructive forms of interaction and mutual existence, which we can only approach by working through the settler colonial foundational assumptions, economic conditions, and unspoken expectations that guide current interactions between Indigenous peoples and settlers.

The analysis above asks us not only to look at our Indigenous educational policies or our efforts at redress but also demands closer observation of settler colonialism at the local level. In the microcontexts of education and redress, settler colonialism and processes of Indigenous destruction are carried out in novel ways beyond the gaze of policy makers. Kindness in education, or inclusion of Indigenous stories or arts, are not of themselves emancipatory acts, especially if the kindness becomes symbolic violence directed toward assimilative change or the inclusion of Indigenous culture is superficial and geared toward the marketing of that culture. Likewise, an apology to survivors of Indigenous boarding schools is undercut when other nodes of the settler colonial institutional mesh tighten just as the government expresses its regret over the abuses of the former educational system, placing these abuses only in the past and ignoring their current mutations. More concretely, the apology means little if the government, while apologizing, works toward intensifying a carceral system that continues to capture more Indigenous peoples than any other group in the nation and withdraws money from social services intended to help Indigenous peoples in their everyday lives. Or as it makes further encroachments upon Indigenous territories in pursuit of wealth and profit (not to mention environmental devastation). As well, compensatory schemes that are so rigid and actuarial that they compartmentalize the past in order to make it more certain, and the need for the government to deal with this past finally, are unlikely to scratch the surface of contending with a settler colonial mesh that features but is not fully defined by assimilative education.

NOTES

I. INTRODUCTION

1. All information drawn from the testimony provided to the Truth and Reconciliation Commission of Canada is referenced either anonymously or by pseudonym, unless the speaker gave the TRC consent for public use of testimony.

2. Truth and Reconciliation Commission of Canada; 2011–2515; Pine Creek First Nation, MB; November 28, 2011 (TRC).

3. Truth and Reconciliation Commission of Canada; 2011–2515; Pine Creek First Nation, MB; November 28, 2011 (TRC).

4. In this book, I use the term "boarding school" to refer, in general, to all forms of dormitory-based schooling for Indigenous children. This term therefore encompasses residential and federal boarding schools, industrial schools, mission schools, on- and off-reservation schools, and other variations. I only use these other terms when making specific reference to these school types. As well, I will use the term "Indigenous" to refer to both Canadian Aboriginal and American Indian peoples, though I will use terms such as "Aboriginal" and "Indian" when appropriate to the historical or legal context of discussion.

5. I have not placed scare quotation marks around terms such as "Indian Problem" and "civilization" in this manuscript to avoid cluttering the page and creating confusion about whether or not someone is being quoted. However, I do not treat these terms as unproblematic. As well, both words in the Indian Problem are capitalized to communicate how the problematization of the Indian dominated settler colonial thinking since the onset of mass European settlement.

6. The expression "this benevolent experiment" is drawn from an earlier era of Indigenous education than that on which I focus in this book. In the 1858 *Report of the Special Commissioners Appointed on the 8th of September, 1856, to Investigate Indian Affairs in Canada,* the authors write, with respect to industrial schools at Alderville and Mount Elgin, that "it is with great reluctance that we are forced to the conclusion that this benevolent experiment has been to a great extent a failure." This phrase, however, captures well both the high modernist social engineering that was the basis for boarding schools (the "experiment") and the perceptions of "benevolent" intentionality often used as a counterpoint to those who refer to boarding school projects in the United States and Canada as genocide.

7. Patrick Wolfe, "Settler Colonialism and the Elimination of the Native," 388, reminds us that "whatever settlers may say—and they generally have a lot to say—the primary motive for elimination is not race (or religion, ethnicity, grade of civilization, etc.) but access to territory. Territory is settler colonialism's specific, irreducible element."

8. Indeed, Indigenous boarding schools were sites of actual experimentation. Ian Mosby, "Administering Colonial Science," has noted how federal food scientists viewed Canadian residential schools as "laboratories" in which the malnutrition of the children was treated as an experimental variable rather than an unmet need.

9. Caleb Bush, "Subsistence Fades, Capitalism Deepens," has developed a similar notion, which he refers to as the "net of incorporation," to understand how capitalism expands into new areas, capturing some individuals and economies, whereas others escape its grasp. My concept of the settler colonial mesh, though sharing similarities with that developed by Bush (which I came across only after this manuscript was drafted), is indebted to the work of Loïc Wacquant, *Punishing the Poor.* In contrast, Bush draws more from world systems theory.

10. See Woolford, "Discipline, Territory, and the Colonial Mesh." This earlier model was referred to as the "colonial mesh," but I refine it here as the "settler colonial mesh" since my concern in this book is specifically with the settler colonial era, whereas my previous work was positioned within a volume that examined colonial genocide in North America more broadly. The metaphor of the rhizome might have provided a more complicated picture of interconnections and heterogeneity across settler colonialism, but I found the images of the net and the mesh more evocative for describing how settler colonialism both tightens and loosens around Indigenous communities. The settler colonial mesh is also distinctly hierarchical, whereas the rhizome is "acentered" and "nonhierarchical." I preferred

this hierarchical character in a context of government social engineering. See Deleuze and Guattari, *A Thousand Plateaus*, 21.

11. Woolford, "Discipline, Territory, and the Colonial Mesh."

12. This model is built upon a Bourdieuian conceptualization of the social. See, for example, Bourdieu, *In Other Words*; Bourdieu and Wacquant, *An Invitation to Reflexive Sociology*; Wacquant, *Policing the Poor*.

13. I use the past tense throughout much of this manuscript, since my primary focus is historical. This is not intended to suggest that many of these processes are not ongoing.

14. See, for example, Callon, "Some Elements of a Sociology of Translation"; Latour, *Science in Action*. In this respect, the model incorporates insights from Actor-Network Theory (ANT), albeit in a limited manner. Generally, Latour dismissed what he perceived to be Bourdieu's "structuralism"; however, the introduction of elements of ANT at a microsociological level helps to expand the role of agency within Bourdieu's field theory, allowing it to better realize its goal of overcoming a false structure/agency divide. This also enables one to overcome the tendency in genocide studies to ignore the role of nonhuman actors in genocidal processes, whether as enlisted allies or as sources of resistance. See also Buzelin, "Unexpected Allies," for a fuller discussion of the potential overlap between Latour and Bourdieu.

15. For the distinction "in whole or in part," see the *United Nations Convention on the Prevention and Punishment of the Crime of Genocide* (1948) where it reads "genocide means any of the following acts committed with intent to destroy, in whole or in part, a national, ethnical, racial or religious group as such." As discussed in chapter 2, the UN definition is not used uncritically in this book since many of its components have potential Eurocentric implications without some degree of scholarly unpacking of its grounding assumptions. See also Powell, *Barbaric Civilization*; Powell, "What Do Genocides Kill?"; Woolford, "Ontological Destruction."

16. Reyhner and Eder, *American Indian Education*.

17. Churchill, *Kill the Indian, Save the Man*.

18. For an exception to this tendency, see James, "Rhetoric and Resistance."

19. A. Smith, *Indigenous Peoples and Boarding Schools*. For a narrative-based, critical, comparative analysis of Canadian and American schools, see M. Smith, "Forever Changed."

20. Glenn, *American Indian/First Nations Schooling*.

21. For example, Adams, *Education for Extinction*; Grant, *No End of Grief*; Miller, *Shingwauk's Vision*; Milloy, *A National Crime*; Reyhner and Eder, *American*

Indian Education; Szasz, *Education and the American Indian*; Trevithick, "Native Residential Schooling in Canada."

22. For example, Fontaine, *Broken Circle*; Fortunate Eagle, *My Life in an Indian Boarding School*; Johnston, *Indian School Days*.

23. For example, Child, *Boarding School Seasons*; Ellis, *To Change Them Forever*; Ellis, "'We Had a Lot of Fun, but of Course, That Wasn't the School Part'; Funke, "'Growing Up It Seemed I Lived in Two Worlds'"; Lomawaima, "Oral Histories from Chilocco Indian Agricultural School, 1920–1940"; Lomawaima, *They Called It Prairie Light*; Riney, *The Rapid City Indian School*; Trafzer, Keller, and Sisquoc, "Introduction"; Trennert, *The Phoenix Indian School*. For an overview of some of these works, see Davis, "American Indian Boarding School Experiences."

24. Miller and Danziger, Jr., "'In the Care of Strangers.'"

25. Lomawaima, *They Called It Prairie Light*; McBeth, *Ethnic Identity and the Boarding School Experience of West-Central Oklahoma Indians*. Bolt, *American Indian Policy and American Reform*, also points out that, despite American goals of assimilation, policies and actions often achieved quite the opposite effect.

26. Gilbert, *Education Beyond the Mesas*; Gram, "Education on the Edge of Empire."

27. Several other scholars have advanced arguments that colonial genocide has occurred in Canada. See, for example, Akhtar, "Canadian Genocide and Official Culpability"; Annett, *Hidden from History*; Bischoping and Fingerhut, "Border Lines"; Chrisjohn and Young, *The Circle Game*; Churchill, "Forbidding the 'G-Word'"; Davis and Zannis, *The Genocide Machine in Canada*; MacDonald, "First Nations, Residential Schools, and the Americanization of the Holocaust"; MacDonald and Hudson, "The Genocide Question and Indian Residential Schools in Canada"; Neu and Therrien, *Accounting for Genocide*; Paul, *We Were Not the Savages*; Woolford, "Ontological Destruction"; Woolford and Thomas, "Genocide and Aboriginal Peoples in Canada."

28. Such conceptualizations of colonial genocide have been further advanced through the work of Australian scholars. See, for example, Barta, "Relations of Genocide"; Curthoys and Docker, "Genocide"; Moses, "An Antipodean Genocide?"; Moses, "Empire, Colony, Genocide"; Moses, "Genocide and Settler Society in Australian History"; Palmer, *Colonial Genocide*; Tatz, "Confronting Australian Genocide"; Tatz, "Genocide Studies."

29. Kevin Whalen, "Finding the Balance," 124, articulates a similar ambition to address the question "how can scholars of Indian education illuminate Native approaches to boarding schools without underplaying the tremendous loss they inflicted on indigenous communities?" Unfortunately, in trying to hold settler colonial education to account, Whalen misrepresents the United Nations Genocide Convention, and Lemkin's thoughts on genocide, and latches onto

a qualified notion of cultural genocide. For Lemkin, no such qualification was necessary: genocide is genocide and involves intersecting physical, cultural, and biological processes.

30. Miller, *Shingwauk's Vision*, 10.

31. Lemkin's initial list of "techniques of genocide" also included political, social, economic, moral, and religious forms. See his *Axis Rule in Occupied Europe*, 79–95.

32. Fear-Segal, *White Man's Club*, xii; emphasis added.

33. Lemkin, *Axis Power in Occupied Europe*.

34. Chalk and Jonassohn, *The History and Sociology of Genocide*; Jones, *Genocide*; Owens, Su, and Snow, "Social Scientific Inquiry into Genocide and Mass Killing."

35. Reyhner and Eder, *American Indian Education*, 107.

36. Trevithick, "Native Residential Schooling in Canada." This view is not uncommon among historians who fear that the term "genocide" will lose its moral force if applied too widely. There is also concern that its use will unnecessarily politicize one's historical analysis, distracting from the complexity of colonial history. See Axtell, *Beyond 1492*; Clendinnen, "First Contact"; Hauptman, *Tribes and Tribulations*.

37. See Grant, *No End of Grief*.

38. Trevithick, "Native Residential Schooling in Canada," 68.

39. Lemkin, *Axis Rule in Occupied Europe*, 79.

40. Woolford, "Discipline, Territory, and the Colonial Mesh"; Woolford, "Nodal Repair and Networks of Destruction."

41. See Callon, "Some Elements of a Sociology of Translation;" Latour, *Science in Action*. Such nonhuman actors are often referred to in Actor-Network Theory as "actants" to demonstrate how material factors interact with human actors in shaping the social world. I have avoided use of this jargon for the sake of clarity.

42. Dadrian, "The Victimization of the American Indian," 519, suggests that "the cardinal fact which emerges is the notion that victimization was neither uniform, nor constant, but that it was confined by a set of variables reducing its incidence, scope and severity." Although he is correct about the nonuniform nature of Indigenous victimization in North America, he is too quick to judge it for having limited "incidence, scope and severity." Nonetheless, his statement alerts one to the complexity of assessing genocide within colonial contexts.

43. Tom Ration, Navajo, Doris Duke American Indian Oral History Collection, 1968–72, Tape 153, interviewed September 1968 (AIOHC-CSWR).

44. On "giving face," whereby one participant in an interaction seeks to avoid placing another in "bad face," or out of line, see Goffman, "On Face-Work."

45. In most cases, because of time constraints and the sheer number of interviews,

interview transcripts were read rather than listened to. This methodological shortcoming was a necessary result of the need to cover a great deal of documentary and oral historical territory in order to perform the multilevel analysis offered in this book.

46. Trevithick, "Native Residential Schooling in Canada."

47. For more information on collective action frames, see Carroll and Ratner, "Master Frames and Counter-Hegemony"; Snow and Benford, "Ideology, Frame Resonance, and Participant Mobilization"; Snow and Benford, "Master Frames and Cycles of Protest."

48. Alexander, "Toward a Theory of Cultural Trauma."

49. This politeness had limits. Diné and Pueblo were and are very outspoken and direct when faced with challenges to their cultures and ways of life.

50. For example, the Sagkeeng Cultural Education Centre Oral History Project Records (1989), Archives of Manitoba, Winnipeg.

51. For an analysis of this discursive landscape, as well as the "templates" and "exclusions" of testimony, see Niezen, *Truth and Indignation*, especially chapter 4.

52. This is based on my own observation of TRC events (both in person and through real-time video) as well as my reading of the transcripts. See also Niezen, *Truth and Indignation*.

53. Fort Alexander Indian Residential School IAP School Narrative, September 28, 2011 (TRC).

54. Gram, "Education on the Edge of Empire."

55. Indeed, no such emblematic schools exist.

2. SETTLER COLONIAL GENOCIDE

1. Curcio, "Civil Claims for Uncivilized Acts"; Herschkopf, Hunter, and Fletcher, *Genocide Reinterpreted*; MacDonald and Hudson, "The Genocide Question and Indian Residential Schools in Canada."

2. See Powell, "What Do Genocides Kill?"

3. Some social scientists place emphasis solely on how the target group is constituted by the perpetrator, such as when the Nazis imagined a homogeneous and dangerous "Jew" who needed to be destroyed. See, for example, Chalk and Jonassohn, *The History and Sociology of Genocide*; Owens, Su, and Snow, "Social Scientific Inquiry into Genocide and Mass Killing." My emphasis is instead on the attempted destruction of those groups who self-constitute as groups and face external interventions designed to disrupt their collective existence. A decolonizing approach to colonial genocide must recognize Indigenous collective identities and not operate solely from the perspective of how the perpetrator

imagines these groups. This is because a focus on perpetrator imaginings of Indigenous peoples fails to recognize Indigenous self-determination as the core of Indigenous group identity. However, I do acknowledge that both types of group (imagined and self-constituted) are worthwhile subjects of genocide studies research, since both are forms of collective life, whether the impetus to group formation is internal or external. Moreover, both types of group formation often combine in specific genocidal contexts: a group or set of groups might actively constitute a group identity (e.g., Sagkeeng or Diné), but they are also subject to external constructions of their groupness (e.g., as Indians). In such circumstances, the external construction of the group can also be understood as a first step in the process of its attempted destruction, since such imagining of the group enables potential perpetrators to act against an assumed homogeneous and undifferentiated target, creating policies and interventions intended to eliminate that target.

4. See Woolford, "Nodal Repair and Networks of Destruction."

5. See Greenwalt, "Rethinking Genocidal Intent." In venues such as the International Court of Justice, there has been recent attention to the role of the state as a collective actor in genocidal contexts; see Schabas, "Genocide and the International Court of Justice." However, in most genocide tribunals, individual perpetrators of genocide are the targets of genocide law. Moreover, destructive collective interactions of the sort discussed here, which manifest more as cultural than as physical destruction, are often ignored by such tribunals, except in instances in which cultural genocide is considered by judges as evidence of a specific intent to commit physical genocide. See *Prosecutor v. Krstić*, ICTY Case No. IT-98–33-T, [Trial] Judgment (August 2, 2001), para. 580, where the court states that "the Trial Chamber is aware that it must interpret the Convention with due regard for the principle of *nullum crimen sine lege*. It therefore recognizes that, despite recent developments, customary international law limits the definition of genocide to those acts seeking the physical or biological destruction of all or part of the group. Hence, an enterprise attacking only the cultural or sociological characteristics of a human group in order to annihilate these elements which give to that group its own identity distinct from the rest of the community would not fall under the definition of genocide." Quoted in Herschkopf et al., *Genocide Reinterpreted*.

6. Kuper, *Genocide*.

7. Kiernan, "The First Genocide."

8. See, more generally, Jones, *Genocide*.

9. Lemkin, "Acts Constituting a General (Transnational) Danger Considered as Offences against the Law of Nations."

10. For a more thorough retelling of this portion of Lemkin's life, see Lemkin, *Totally Unofficial*.

11. Power, *A Problem from Hell*.

12. Lemkin, *Axis Rule in Occupied Europe*.

13. Lemkin, *Axis Rule in Occupied Europe*.

14. Thomas Butcher, "A 'Synchronized Attack,'" 254, notes that Lemkin indeed "conceived of genocide in a fundamentally cultural manner, because the ultimate purpose of genocide (under his definition of the term) is to destroy a cultural unit."

15. Lemkin, *Axis Rule in Occupied Europe*, 76.

16. See Butcher, "A 'Synchronized Attack'"; Short, "Australia"; Short, "Cultural Genocide and Indigenous Peoples."

17. See Docker, "Are Settler-Colonies Inherently Genocidal?"

18. Lemkin, quoted in van Krieken, "Rethinking Cultural Genocide." One could also consider here policies of what Katherine Ellinghaus, "Biological Absorption and Genocide," refers to as "biological absorption," whereby it was hoped that Indigenous peoples would disappear through interracial sexual relations and reproduction. Ellinghaus's study covers such policies in the United States and Australia, but they were also evident in Canada, where Duncan Campbell Scott, former deputy superintendent of Indian Affairs, noted in 1920 that "the happiest future for the Indian race is absorption into the general population," which he thought would occur through "the great forces of intermarriage and education." Quoted in Titley, *A Narrow Vision*, 34. As such, assimilation was a strategy often entwined with absorption.

19. See Morsink, "Cultural Genocide, the Universal Declaration, and Minority Rights." See also Herschkopf et al., *Genocide Reinterpreted*.

20. Moses, "Genocide and Settler Society in Australian History."

21. *United Nations Convention on the Prevention and Punishment of the Crime of Genocide*, 1948.

22. Annett, *Hidden from History*; Churchill, "Forbidding the 'G-Word'"; Grant, *No End of Grief*.

23. van Krieken, "Rethinking Cultural Genocide."

24. Macgregor, "Governance, Not Genocide."

25. See McDonnell and Moses, "Raphael Lemkin as Historian of Genocide in the Americas."

26. Moses, "Empire, Colony, Genocide."

27. See Irvin-Ericson, "Genocide, the 'Family of Mind,' and the Romantic Signature of Raphael Lemkin."

28. For more detailed discussion on Lemkin and the issue of cultural genocide, see Short, "Australia"; Short, "Cultural Genocide and Indigenous Peoples."

29. Docker, "Are Settler-Colonies Inherently Genocidal?," 94.

30. See Butcher, "A 'Synchronized Attack'"; Powell and Peristerakis, "Genocide in Canada"; Woolford, "Nodal Repair and Networks of Destruction."

31. Barta, "Relations of Genocide"; Barta, "'They Appear Actually to Vanish from the Face of the Earth.'"

32. Michael Mann, *The Dark Side of Democracy*, 72, for example, refers to assimilation as a "lesser" form of "cleansing." See also MacDonald and Hudson, "The Genocide Question"; Ponting and Gibbons, *Out of Irrelevance*; Schissel and Wotherspoon, *The Legacy of School for Aboriginal People*; Wotherspoon and Satzewich, *First Nations*.

33. Evans, "'Crime without a Name.'"

34. Evans and Thorpe, "Indigenocide and the Massacre of Aboriginal History."

35. Schaller and Zimmerer, "Settlers, Imperialism, Genocide."

36. Chalk and Jonassohn, *History and Sociology of Genocide*; Fein, *Genocide*; Kuper, *Genocide*; Letgers, "The Soviet Gulag."

37. Fein, *Genocide*, 24.

38. Chalk and Jonassohn, *History and Sociology of Genocide*, 23.

39. For further definitions of genocide, see, for example, Charny, "Toward a Generic Definition of Genocide"; Dadrian, "A Typology of Genocide"; Horowitz, *Taking Lives*; Shaw, *What Is Genocide?* For a useful summary and discussion, see Jones, *Genocide*.

40. Powell, "What Do Genocides Kill?"

41. Feierstein, "Leaving the Parental Home."

42. Powell, *Barbaric Civilization*, 84.

43. Powell, *Barbaric Civilization*, 83.

44. Chalk and Jonassohn, *History and Sociology of Genocide*, 23.

45. Kohl, "Genocide and Ethnogenesis"; Straus, "Contested Meanings and Conflicting Imperatives"; in contrast, Jeff Benvenuto, "Revisiting Choctaw Ethnocide and Ethnogenesis," argues that regroupment and revival in the aftermath of genocide are common to many cases—destruction and creation are often entwined processes.

46. van Krieken, "Rethinking Cultural Genocide," 125.

47. Cited in Kuper, *Genocide*, 31. See also Clastres, "On Ethnocide."

48. Clifford, *The Predicament of Culture*.

49. Clifford, *The Predicament of Culture*, 338.

50. Such a notion of culture is consistent with certain Indigenous understandings of their cultures. See, for example, Isaiah Lorado Wilner's insightful discussion in "A Global Potlatch" of how Franz Boas, often credited as the founder of cultural relativism, was "civilized" by the Kwakw_ak_a'wakw, who taught him

their self-understanding of their culture as a fluid rather than static collective possession.

51. On the movement between tradition and change within oral cultures, see also Lord, *The Singer of Tales*; Vansina, *Oral Tradition as History*.

52. See Jacoby, "'The Broad Platform of Extermination'"; Madley, "Patterns of Frontier Genocide"; Paul, *We Were Not the Savages*; Sousa, "'They Will Be Hunted Down like Wild Beasts and Destroyed'"; Stannard, *American Holocaust*. For contrasting views on the extermination of the Beothuks in what is now Newfoundland, see Paul, *We Were Not the Savages*; Upton, "The Extermination of the Beothuks of Newfoundland." The Acoma Pueblo, one of the Pueblo groups considered later in this book, were also subject to genocidal violence in the history of their encounters with colonial powers. After Acoma warriors killed eleven Spanish soldiers in retaliation for their abuses of Acoma women, Juan de Onate led seventy-two men to the top of the Acoma mesa, where they slaughtered 800 women, men, and children. See Nichols, *Indians in the United States and Canada*.

53. Research carried out under the auspices of the Truth and Reconciliation Commission of Canada has cited at least 3,000 unnecessary deaths that occurred in the IRS system. The TRC has since estimated at least 6000 dead. See Canadian Press, "At Least 3000 Died in Residential Schools, Research Shows," *cbc News (online)*, 2013; accessed May 27, 2013: http://www.cbc.ca/news/canada /story/2013/02/18/residential-schools-student-deaths.html.

54. Akhtar, "Canadian Genocide and Official Culpability"; Annett, *Hidden from History*; Bischoping and Fingerhut, "Border Lines"; Chrisjohn and Young, *The Circle Game*; Churchill, "Forbidding the 'G-Word'"; Davis and Zannis, *The Genocide Machine in Canada*; Grant, *No End of Grief*; Grinde, "Taking the Indian out of the Indian"; McKegney, *Magic Weapons*; Neu and Therrien, *Accounting for Genocide*; Tinker, *Missionary Conquest*; Woolford, "Ontological Destruction."

55. Annett, *Hidden from History*; Grant, *No End of Grief*.

56. See Herschkopf et al., *Genocide Reinterpreted*.

57. Drawing on this sense of genocide and group protection for this analysis, I pressume that Indigenous collectivities did provide valuable and nonoppressive spaces of collective identity formation for their members. See Newman, *Community and Collective Rights*. The fact that group members value membership in the group, and the fact that the group does not aggressively infringe on the lives of other groups, are important moral philosophical considerations to take into account in this discussion of genocide. Since the group is a set of relations and processes of identity formation, it becomes possible to imagine a wide variety of groups. However, we would not want to secure the protection of all these groups. Indeed, some, such as Nazis and Hell's Angels, might be viewed as legitimate

targets for intervention and infringement upon their group status. In such cases, however, there are solid moral reasons for such infringement, since both groups present threats to other groups through their predatory activities. There are other cases in which a legitimate group that does not threaten other groups nonetheless fails to provide satisfaction to certain members, such as when it commits human rights violations against a despised segment of the group. In such circumstances, it might also prove desirable or morally necessary to act against such violations.

58. For this reason, mediation is required between genocide definitions that focus solely on how the perpetrator imagines the targeted group and those that emphasize how the group understands and imagines itself. See endnote 3 above.

59. Episkenew, *Taking Back Our Spirits*; Neu and Therrien, *Accounting for Genocide*. See chapter 3 for further discussion on this issue as it relates to Canada and the United States.

60. Paul, *We Were Not the Savages*, 319.

61. Kelman and Hamilton, *Crimes of Obedience*.

62. Theriault, "Against the Grain."

63. Powell, *Barbaric Civilization*; Powell, "What Do Genocides Kill?". However, Short, "Australia," contests this characterization of Lemkin's work.

64. For more on the ethical imperative to work toward reducing moral distance between self and other, see Bauman, *Modernity and the Holocaust*; Derrida, "Force of Law"; Levinas, *Ethics and Infinity*.

65. This is the emphasis of the framers of the UNGC, who in the *travaux preparatoire* for the convention made clear their focus on material destruction. See Herschkopf et al., *Genocide Reinterpreted*.

66. Moses, "An Antipodean Genocide?"; Moses, "Empire, Colony, Genocide"; Moses, "Genocide and Settler Society."

67. Lytman Letgers, "The American Genocide," 770, provides early reflection on this issue when he writes that "mass killing is not the only way to destroy a way of life or even to exterminate a people."

68. Short, "Australia"; Wolfe, "Settler Colonialism and the Elimination of the Native"; Woolford, "Ontological Destruction"; Woolford, "Transition and Transposition."

69. See, for example, Lewy, "Can There Be Genocide without the Intent to Commit Genocide?"

70. van Krieken, "Rethinking Cultural Genocide," 141.

71. As is clear in cases such as *Bosnia and Herzegovina v. Serbia and Montenegro*, which went before the International Court of Justice but only found the massacre of Muslim men at Srebrenica to be genocide. See *Application of the Convention on the Prevention and Punishment of the Crime of Genocide (Bosnia and*

Herzegovina v. Serbia and Montenegro), 2007 ICJ 140 (February 26, 2007), available at http://www.icj-cij.org/icjwww/idocket/ibhy/ibhyjudgment/ibhy_ijudgment_20070226_frame.htm. See also Schabas, "Genocide and the International Court of Justice."

72. Trevithick, "Native Residential Schooling in Canada."

73. Truth and Reconciliation Commission of Canada, *They Came for the Children*, 1.

74. Truth and Reconciliation Commission of Canada, *They Came for the Children*, 1.

75. Cooper, *Colonialism in Question*, 24, reinforces this notion of complex collective intentions: "Among colonizing elites—even if they shared a conviction of superiority—tensions often erupted between those who wanted to save the souls or civilize natives and those who saw the colonized as objects to be used and discarded at will. Among metropolitan populations, colonized people sometimes provoked sympathy or pity, sometimes fear—as well as the more complex sentiments that emerged during the actual encounters and political struggles in the colonies themselves."

76. See Snow and Benford, "Ideology, Frame Resonance, and Participant Mobilization."

77. Fear-Segal, "Nineteenth-Century Indian Education"; Fear-Segal, *White Man's Club*. In his discussion of cultural genocide in Australia, Robert van Krieken, "Rethinking Cultural Genocide," 299, writes that "civilization was colonialism's most central organizing concept, quintessentially what imperialism and the colonial project was meant to achieve and the degree of civilization spread over the globe the measure of its success or failure."

78. See van Krieken, "The Barbarism of Civilization." Such an understanding also encourages a move away from evolutionary understandings of civilization.

79. See Tatz, "Confronting Australian Genocide."

80. Woolford, "Ontological Destruction."

81. For an analysis that deepens and complicates the discussion of "good" and well-intentioned Euro-Canadians in the formation of settler colonial Canada, see Haig-Brown and Nock, *With Good Intentions*. In the United States, see Trafzer, Keller, and Sisquoc, *Boarding School Blues*.

82. Bays, *Indian Residential Schools*, 161. On the exclusion of such narratives from trc testimony, see Niezen, *Truth and Indignation*.

83. Browning, *Ordinary Men*.

84. Tinker, *Missionary Conquest*, 4.

85. See, for example, Bourdieu, *In Other Words*; Bourdieu and Wacquant, *An Invitation to Reflexive Sociology*.

86. See Barta, "'They Appear to Vanish,'" for a discussion on "intentions" as expressed in pursuit of "interests" as a model for the historical determination of genocide.

87. The processual approach used in this manuscript draws on the foundational work done by Barta, "Relations of Genocide"; Hinton, *Why Did They Kill?*; Moses, "An Antipodean Genocide?"; Moses, "Empire, Colony, Genocide"; Moses, "Genocide and Settler Society"; Levene, *The Rise of the West and the Coming of Genocide*; and Wolfe, "Settler Colonialism and the Elimination of the Native."

88. See Rosenberg, "Genocide Is a Process, Not an Event."

89. Verdeja, "On Situating the Study of Genocide within Political Violence."

90. Verdeja, "On Situating the Study of Genocide within Political Violence," 84. Mazower, "Review Essay," 1160, has also discussed the need to "reintroduce the role of historical contingency both in time—the catalytic impact of wars, civil wars, and other upheavals—and space—geopolitical location, the proximity of disputed borders," in understanding the deadly and often genocidal nature of the twentieth century.

91. Moses, "Empire, Colony, Genocide," 22.

92. The same holds true for settler colonialism. See Elkins and Pederson, *Settler Colonialism in the Twentieth Century*.

93. Especially Arendt, *The Origins of Totalitarianism*.

94. For example, Moses, "Empire, Colony, Genocide"; Zimmerer, "Colonialism and the Holocaust."

95. Zimmerer, "Colonialism and the Holocaust," 95–96.

96. See Bartov, "Genocide and Holocaust"; Melson, "Critique of Current Genocide Studies."

97. See Veracini, *Settler Colonialism*.

98. Wolfe, "Settler Colonialism and the Elimination of the Native"; see also Veracini, *Settler Colonialism*; Wolfe, *Settler Colonialism and the Transformation of Anthropology*.

99. Wolfe, "Settler Colonialism and the Elimination of the Native"; see also Letgers, "The American Genocide," for an early statement on the necessity of displacement to settler colonialism.

100. Moses, "An Antipodean Genocide?," 91–92; see also Finzsch, "'Extirpate or Remove That Vermine'"; Levene, "Empires, Native Peoples, and Genocide."

101. Researchers following the tenets of the "new Indian history," for example, have raised concerns about the tendency of genocide studies to focus on perpetrators and to ignore instances of Indigenous agency within colonial histories. For further discussion, see Jacoby, "'The Broad Platform of Extermination'"; McDonnell and Moses, "Raphael Lemkin as Historian of Genocide." For examples of recent histories that focus more on Indigenous agency, see Blackhawk, *Violence over the Land*; Denetdale, *Reclaiming Diné History*; Wasiyatawin, *Remember This!* However, I intend to overcome the tendency of genocide studies to ignore victim agency

by treating genocide, like Moses, "An Antipodean Genocide?," as an uneven and imperfect process susceptible to resistive and subversive interventions by those targeted for elimination.

102. Lomawaima, *They Called It Prairie Light*, 167.

103. Ellis, *To Change Them Forever*, 67. See also Littlefield, "The BIA Boarding School."

3. FRAMING THE INDIAN AS A PROBLEM

1. Robert Lorne Richardson (1860–1921) (compiler); Frederick Temple Hamilton-Temple-Blackwood, 1st Marquess of Dufferin and Ava (1826–1902); John George Edward Henry Douglas Sutherland Campbell, 9th Duke of Argyll (1845–1914); Henry Charles Keith Petty-Fitzmaurice, 5th Marquis of Lansdowne (1845–1927). "Facts and Figures," 28.

2. Bracken, *The Potlatch Papers*; Cole and Chaikin, *An Iron Hand upon the People*.

3. Woolford, *Between Justice and Certainty*.

4. Szasz, "'I Knew How to Be Moderate.'"

5. For treatment of the broader history of colonization and settlement in Canada and the United States, including coverage of the multiple colonial powers (British, French, Spanish, and Dutch) that competed for the trade and resources of Indigenous North America, see Nichols, *Indians in the United States and Canada*.

6. Ignoring, of course, the vast differences in funding between elite and Indigenous boarding schools.

7. Bourdieu, "Rethinking the State."

8. See also Albach and Kelly, *Education and the Colonial Experience*; Friere, *Pedagogy of the Oppressed*.

9. Miller, *Shingwauk's Vision*.

10. Sealey, *The Education of Native Peoples in Manitoba*.

11. House, *Language Shift among the Navajos*.

12. Fear-Segal, *White Man's Club*; Miller, *Shingwauk's Vision*.

13. Foucault, *Discipline and Punish*. See also Truth and Reconciliation Commission of Canada, *They Came for the Children*, 13.

14. Rothman, *The Discovery of the Asylum*.

15. Reyhner and Eder, *American Indian Education*.

16. Reyhner and Eder, *American Indian Education*.

17. Reyhner and Eder, *American Indian Education*.

18. Reyhner and Eder, *American Indian Education*; Szasz, *Indian Education in the American Colonies*.

19. Miller, *Shingwauk's Vision*; Nichols, *Indians in the United States and Canada*.

20. Nichols, *Indians in the United States and Canada*.

21. Miller, *Shingwauk's Vision*, 60.

22. Nichols, *Indians in the United States and Canada*, 169. See also Bowden, *American Indians and Christian Missions*.

23. Quoted in Bureau of Education, *Indian Education and Civilization*, 162.

24. Quoted in Bureau of Education, *Indian Education and Civilization,*, 163; see also Nichols, *Indians in the United States and Canada*; Prucha, *The Great Father*.

25. Quoted in Bureau of Education, *Indian Education and Civilization*, 163.

26. Lewy, "Can There Be Genocide without the Intent to Commit Genocide?"

27. Nichols, *Indians in the United States and Canada*.

28. Bureau of Education, *Indian Education and Civilization*.

29. Indian commissioner, quoted in Bureau of Education, *Indian Education and Civilization*, 167–68.

30. Fear-Segal, *White Man's Club*. See also Prucha, *The Great Father*, chapter 3. Robert H. Keller, Jr., *American Protestantism and the United States Indian Policy*, 208–09, provides an interesting discussion on the role that anti-Catholicism played in the demise of contract schools.

31. Carney, "Aboriginal Residential Schools before Confederation."

32. See, for example, Daschuk, *Clearing the Plains*.

33. Carney, "Aboriginal Residential Schools before Confederation"; Enns, "'But What Is the Object of Educating These Children, if It Costs Their Lives to Educate Them?'"

34. Nichols, *Indians in the United States and Canada*.

35. Carney, "Aboriginal Residential Schools before Confederation"; Miller, *Shingwauk's Vision*.

36. This school began to take in boarders in 1831.

37. Miller, *Shingwauk's Vision*.

38. See, for example, Daschuk, *Clearing the Plains*.

39. This influence did not disappear all at once and reemerged within specific contexts, such as when competition formed between British and American designs on the continent, allowing Indigenous groups to play one colonial force off against the other. This particular opening for Indigenous groups, however, closed with the War of 1812, especially for those groups west of the Mississippi, who could no longer use the British as a negotiating chip when fending off American encroachments upon their territories. See Nichols, *Indians in the United States and Canada*.

40. Scott, *Thinking like a State*.

41. Borrows, "Contemporary and Comparative Perspective on the Rights of Indigenous Peoples"; Carney, "Aboriginal Residential Schools before Confederation"; Fletcher, "Contemporary and Comparative Perspective on the Rights of Indigenous Peoples."

42. See Bourdieu, "Rethinking the State"; Wacquant, *Punishing the Poor*.

43. Goffman, *Frame Analysis*.

44. Prior to this time, a discourse of extermination appeared to be more prevalent in the United States, especially in the American west, though the ideas of assimilation and civilization preceded this period and were circulating among certain groups, such as missionaries and reformers. Indeed, according to Prucha, *The Great Father*, 146, the "seeds" of these ideas were "sprouted at the beginning of the nation's life." Prucha also refers to these assimilative and civilizing policies under the broader label of "paternalism," which he argues emerged as a policy trend in the United States during the nineteenth century, with the president in the role of the "Great Father." However, as Prucha further notes, xxviii, this paternalism became more intensive and potentially destructive in the century that followed the 1880s.

45. See, for example, Wood, *Some Aspects of the Indian Problem*.

46. For further discussion of residential schools and governance, see Smith, "The 'Policy of Aggressive Civilization.'"

47. Tobias, "Protection, Civilization, Assimilation."

48. Status Indians are those recognized by the federal government as registered under the Indian Act. Until 1985 and the passage of Bill C-31, Indian women who married non-Indian men lost their Indian status under the terms of the Indian Act. Others were never able to obtain such status if their ancestors had not been registered under the Indian Act. See Lawrence, "Gender, Race, and the Regulation of Native Identity in Canada and the United States."

49. Wolfe, "The Settler Complex." In this article, Wolfe notes that such practices of subjectivation are part and parcel of the settler colonial assimilative project: "Assimilation does not merely include (and, thereby, reciprocally exclude). It positively produces the occupants of those categories [of inclusion and exclusion] in the first place. To breed White is to make anew. Assimilation reverses the republican formula: rather than the people constituting the government, the government constitutes the people" (3).

50. See Tobias, "Protection, Civilization, Assimilation."

51. See Lawrence, "Gender, Race, and the Regulation of Native Identity."

52. On removal and reservations, see, for example, Bolt, *American Indian Policy and American Reform*, especially chapter 2; Prucha, *The Great Father*.

53. See Laderman, "'It Is Cheaper and Better to Teach a Young Indian than to Fight an Old One.'"

54. Walker, *The Indian Question*.

55. Walker, *The Indian Question*, 66.

56. Walker, *The Indian Question*, 133.

57. Otis, *The Indian Question*, 251.

58. The exorbitant costs of the Indian Wars were apparent to many in the U.S. government, including leaders from an earlier era, such as Henry Knox, George Washington's secretary of war, and Thomas Jefferson, who noted after hoping that U.S. forces would "drub the Indians well this summer" that "the expense of this summer expedition [1791] would have served for presents for half a century." See Nichols, *Indians in the United States and Canada*, 147.

59. Quoted in Prucha, *The Great Father*, 595.

60. Quoted in Milloy, *A National Crime*, 12.

61. Ryerson University's Aboriginal Education Council, "Egerton Ryerson, the Residential School System, and Truth and Reconciliation."

62. See *Report of the Special Commissioners Appointed on the 8th of September, 1856, to Investigate Indian Affairs in Canada*.

63. See Nichols, *Indians in the United States and Canada*, 176–77.

64. Adams, *Education for Extinction*; Hoxie, *The Final Promise*; Miller, *Shingwauk's Vision*.

65. Lorenzo Veracini, *Settler Colonialism*, 25, makes a similar point when he writes that "degradation and absorption are only apparently contradicting each other: as they both operate in the context of a progressive erasure of the indigenous presence (assimilating one part, and effacing the other in a variety of ways), they also refer to circumstances in which the settler colonial situation operates towards its ultimate supersession." See also Bauman, "Making and Unmaking Strangers," 2. Bauman borrows Lévi-Strauss's concepts to describe two historical approaches to eliminating strangers: "One was *anthropophagic*: annihilating the strangers by *devouring* them and then metabolically transforming them into a tissue indistinguishable from one's own. This was the strategy of assimilation—making the different similar: the smothering of cultural or linguistic distinctions, forbidding all traditions and loyalties except those meant to feed the conformity of the new and all embracing order, promoting and enforcing one and only one measure of conformity. The other strategy was *anthropemic*: *vomiting* the strangers, banishing them from the limits of the orderly world and barring them from all communication with those inside. This was the strategy of exclusion—confining the strangers within the visible walls of the ghettos or behind the invisible, yet no less tangible prohibitions of *commensality, connubium*, and *commercium*, expelling the strangers beyond the frontiers of the managed and manageable territory; or, when neither of the two measures was feasible—destroying the strangers physically." One can see these strategies often operating simultaneously in Canadian and American settler colonialisms.

66. Hoxie, *The Final Promise*. For examples of a shift toward an assimilative approach

to the Indian Problem in the press, see Hays, *Editorializing "the Indian Problem."* Indeed, the following quotation from a *New York Times* editorial captures both the Lockean sense that Indigenous peoples do not truly own their land and the view that they are obstacles to progress that must be dealt with in some fashion. The article calls for this to be done as humanely as possible: "When the Indian possessions are reached, the Indians are in the way. They must move on. Civilization and progress are coming and cannot be impeded in their course. Indians are not independent peoples, and their lands are not their own. The jurisdiction of the Government is over them and their territory, in spite of treaties and agreements. They must move on. This is Gen. Sherman's view. It is the view on which our Indian policy has all along been based, and it has led to continued misunderstanding and a settled sense of wrong and injustice on the part of the Indians." Quoted in Hays, *Editorializing "the Indian Problem,"* 78.

67. Adams, *Education for Extinction*; Miller, *Shingwauk's Vision*; Milloy, *A National Crime*; Szasz, *Education and the American Indian*.

68. Fear-Segal, *White Man's Club*.

69. Bolt, *American Indian Policy and American Reform*; Nichols, *Indians in the United States and Canada*. However, Bolt suggests that American Indian reformers were influenced by what they perceived to be a better system of Indian Affairs in Canada (87).

70. See Nock, "The Canadian Indian Research and Aid Society." One could also look at the influence of Indigenous rights societies in Britain, such as the Aborigines Protection Society. On the latter point, see Blackstock, "Trust Us."

71. However, one should be careful not to treat the views of reformers as uniform. They coalesced around a common set of ideas, such as the need for individual allotment of Indian lands, civilizing education, and inculcation of a Protestant work ethic, but there was room for much debate about issues such as the evolutionary potential of the Indian and the role that Indian languages might or might not play in assimilation. See Bolt, *American Indian Policy and American Reform*.

72. Adams, *Education for Extinction*. See also Deloria, Jr., "The Indian Rights Association"; Hagan, *The Indian Rights Association*.

73. Hoxie, *The Final Promise*.

74. Adams, *Education for Extinction*. William Barrows, *The Indian's Side of the Indian Question*, 6–7, writes of the act that it "opens a new era in this branch of our national work, and it is beyond doubt the best thing possible in the line of the government, so far as it goes. It embodies a discovery, which has cost the expensive and sad experiments of two centuries, that the Indian must be made and treated as an American citizen. It, however, does not contemplate the removal

or neutralization of the force which has made the most of our preceding laws and labors fruitless. In the diagnosis of this great national infirmity or malady, the main cause has been assigned to the red man, and the medicines have been given to him. Perhaps the bill goes as far as the government can go in its side of the work. What remains to make the new era a successful one, the people must do."

75. It is interesting to note here, given the focus on southwestern tribes later in this book, that the American Southwest went largely untouched by the Dawes Act and its imposition of land severalty. See Bolt, *American Indian Policy and American Reform*, 99. However, the Pueblo in New Mexico did face some threat later from the Bursum Bill of 1922, which sought to make them cede their lands along the Rio Grande to white settlers. The Bursum Bill was defeated by the collective efforts of the Pueblo and their non-Indigenous allies.

76. *Proceedings Mohonk Lake Conference October 12, 13, 14, 1886.*

77. *Proceedings Mohonk Lake Conference October 12, 13, 14, 1886.*

78. The Cherokee schools in the United States are something of an outlier in the general history presented in this chapter. Soon after the forced Cherokee removal, the Cherokee National Council began to institute schools, with twenty-one day schools and two boarding schools operating by 1851. Cherokee children thus often attended schools close to their home communities and even received lessons in their language. By the later part of the century, the Cherokee were also able to hire teachers for their sixty-four schools and even graduated teachers to teach at their own schools. See Abbott, "'Commendable Progress'"; Nichols, *Indians in the United States and Canada*.

79. Adams, *Education for Extinction*. See also Cooper, *Indian School*; Fear-Segal, *White Man's Club*; Hamley, "An Introduction to the Federal Indian Boarding School Movement."

80. Adams, *Education for Extinction*.

81. Quoted in Adams, *Education for Extinction*, 53.

82. It should not be assumed here that Pratt and Armstrong followed identical assimilationist models. Pratt was more determined to separate Indigenous children from their cultures, while Armstrong was more tolerant of the presence of some Indigenous cultural practices within his school. See Fear-Segal, "Nineteenth-Century Indian Education."

83. Fear-Segal, *White Man's Club*.

84. Fear-Segal, *White Man's Club*.

85. Macdonald was initially inspired to consider the U.S. model based on his concerns about unrest among the Métis. Joyce Katherine Sowby, "Macdonald the Administrator," 137–38, notes that "a thoughtful memorandum from the

Deputy Minister of the Interior in December 1878 drew Macdonald's attention to the need to attend to the problems of extinguishing the Indian land title of halfbreeds of the northwest and of assisting them to become self-supporting. Dennis [John Stoughton Dennis, deputy minister of the interior] suggested that the establishment of industrial schools, as in the United States, might be one way of helping them. This proposal captured Sir John's imagination and he asked Nicholas Flood Davin, an Ottawa barrister, to visit the Department of the Interior at Washington, to ascertain the costs and results of the American programme, and to discuss the possibility with clergy and other knowledgeable Winnipeggers. Meanwhile, Macdonald circulated Dennis' memorandum to influential men in the west, who knew the halfbreed situation, for comment. By the time Davin presented his report, which recommended residential schools for boys and girls, Indian and Métis, teaching farming and homemaking, Sir John had received conflicting suggestions from the west for dealing with the halfbreed question, and had lost his enthusiasm for solving the problem. The first industrial schools were not established until 1883, and then only for Indian children."

86. The "five civilized tribes" are the Cherokee, Chickasaw, Seminole, Creek, and Choctaw. They were considered more civilized by Euro-American settlers because they adopted European customs more readily than other Indigenous groups and largely maintained good relations with their neighbours.

87. Davin, *Report on Industrial Schools for Indians and Half Breeds*, 1.

88. Davin, *Report on Industrial Schools for Indians and Half Breeds*, 11.

89. Miller, *Shingwauk's Vision*; see also "A Report of the Committee of the Honourable Privy Council, Approved by His Excellency the Governor General in Council on the 19th of July, 1883," Indian Affairs RG 10, Volume 6001, File 1–1–1, part 1 (LAC).

90. See Sowby, "Macdonald the Administrator."

91. See Miller, *Skyscrapers Hide the Heavens*; Stonechild, "The Indian View of the 1885 Uprising."

92. Quoted in Milloy, *A National Crime*, 32.

93. Dyck, *Differing Visions*. Prior to the rebellion, Canada's embrace of assimilationist policy was already evident in legislation such as the 1869 Act for the Gradual Enfranchisement of Indians. See also Tobias, "Protection, Civilization, Assimilation."

94. During 1880, Macdonald also placed Lawrence Vankoughnet in charge of the Department of Indian Affairs, which would take over Indigenous issues from the Department of the Interior. For more on Macdonald's Indian policy, see D. A. Smith, "John A. Macdonald and Aboriginal Canada."

95. Department of Indian Affairs, "Report of the Department of Indian Affairs for the Year Ended 31st December 1880," Sessional Papers, Volume 14, No. 8, Third Session of the Fourth Parliament of the Dominion of Canada, 1880–81.

96. Department of Indian Affairs, "Report of the Department of Indian Affairs for the Year Ended 31st December 1884," Sessional Papers, Volume 18, No. 3, Third Session of the Fifth Parliament of the Dominion of Canada, 1885.

97. Department of Indian Affairs, "Annual Report of the Department of Indian Affairs for the Year Ended 31st December 1888," Sessional Papers, Volume 22, No. 13, Third Session of the Sixth Parliament of the Dominion of Canada (Ottawa: Maclean, Roger, 1889), ix–x.

98. See Keller, *American Protestantism and the United States Indian Policy*; Prucha, *The Churches and the Indian Schools*.

99. See Indian Commissioner Hayter Reed's report, "The Following Indian Industrial Schools in Canada and the United States: Mount Elgin or Mohawk, the Muncey, and the Carlisle," 57500 R216–245–8-E Black Series, RG10, File 57799 (LAC).

100. Milloy, *A National Crime*.

101. Quoted in Adams, "Beyond Bleakness," 63.

102. Adams, "Beyond Bleakness," 63.

103. Letter from Acting Commissioner T. P. Smith, Office of Indian Affairs, to Agents and Bonded Superintendents, April 29, 1897, RG 75, Records of the Bureau of Indian Affairs, Northern Pueblos Agency, General Correspondence and Reports 1877–1934, Box 6, Folder 124 (NARA).

104. Reel, *Report of the Superintendent of Indian Schools*, 1900, 13.

105. Reel, *Report of the Superintendent of Indian Schools*, 1900, 13, 15.

106. Letter of April 17, 1912, from AIS Superintendent Perry to the Chairman of the Committee on Education, Santa Fe, New Mexico, RG 75, Records of the Bureau of Indian Affairs, Northern Pueblos Agency, General Correspondence and Reports 1877–1934, ARC 2694602, Box 16, Folder 309 (NARA).

107. Circular from Commissioner Chas Burke, Department of the Interior, June 14, 1921, Amendment #1 to Regulations Concerning Enrollment and Attendance of Indian Children in School, Pursuant to the Act of February 14, 1920, RG 75, Records of the Bureau of Indian Affairs, Albuquerque Indian School, General Correspondence Files 1917–36, 001–003, Entry 29, Box 6, Folder 170 (NARA).

108. Miller, *Shingwauk's Vision*.

109. Miller, *Shingwauk's Vision*, 170.

110. An Act to Amend the Indian Act, c. 50, SC, S. 10, 1919–20.

111. See Christophers, *Positioning the Missionary*; Miller, *Shingwauk's Vision*.

112. See "A Report of the Committee of the Honourable Privy Council," Approved by

His Excellency the Governor General in Council on October 22, 1892, Indian Affairs RG 10, Volume 6001, File 1–1–1, part 1 (LAC).

113. Miller, *Shingwauk's Vision.*

114. "A Report of the Committee of the Honourable Privy Council," Approved by His Excellency on March 27, 1895, Indian Affairs RG 10, Volume 6001, File 1–1–1, part 1 (LAC).

115. Given that I am using the term "Indigenous boarding school" to refer generally to boarding schools in both the United States and Canada, regardless of size or location, I have refrained here from using the distinction between "industrial" and "boarding" schools and have instead substituted "reservation-based" for "boarding" to refer to those small-scale schools located closer to reserve communities. For the distinction between industrial and boarding schools in Canada, see Enns, "'But What Is the Object of Educating These Children.'"

116. Enns, "'But What Is the Object of Educating These Children.'"

117. Enns, "'But What Is the Object of Educating These Children.'"

118. Enns, "'But What Is the Object of Educating These Children.'"

119. Memorandum from Duncan Campbell Scott to Honorable Mr. Meighan, possibly from January 1918, Indian Affairs RG 10, Volume 6001, File 1–1–11, part 2 Headquarters-Schools-General, 1904–28 (LAC).

120. Fay, "A Historiography of Recent Publications on Catholic Native Residential Schools."

121. For examples of instances when the church facilitated an opening in the settler colonial mesh, see Carney, "Residential Schooling at Fort Chipewyan and Fort Resolution"; Gresko, "Creating Little Dominions within the Dominion"; Gresko, "White 'Rites' and Indian 'Rites.'"

122. Milloy, *A National Crime*, 52.

123. Miller, *Shingwauk's Vision*; Riney, "Review."

124. Nichols, *Indians in the United States and Canada*, 239.

125. Burnett, "Building the System"; Titley, *A Narrow Vision*. I am also thankful to Robin Jarvis Brownlie for drawing my attention to this point.

126. Letter from S. H. Blake, Mission Society of the Church in Canada, to the Superintendent of Indian Affairs, Indian Affairs RG 10, Volume 6001, File 1–1–1, part 1 (LAC).

127. Letter from Deputy Superintendent General to S. H. Blake, Indian Affairs RG 10, Volume 6001, File 1–1–1, part 1 (LAC).

128. See Prucha, *The Churches and the Indian Schools.*

129. It is also worth noting the different conditions from which students came to the schools. Canadian reserves were typically smaller than American reserves, which started out large even though they were frequently reduced through

various land grabs and other appropriations. Many of these communities in the United States were also more frequently subject to warfare and, in many cases, forced removals by the U.S. government. Although violence and forced removal were not absent from the Canadian context, they played a more prominent role in American Indigenous/non-Indigenous relations. See Reyhner and Eder, *American Indian Education*.

130. Commissioner Morgan also moved to develop a standardized curriculum as early as 1890. See Adams, *Education for Extinction*.

131. Reel, *Report of the Superintendent of Indian Schools*, 1900, 17.

132. One must be wary of accepting at face value the claim that these children were orphaned, since the claim was not always true, and the trope of "orphan" was often used to justify removal and further belittle Indigenous parenting cultures. See Jacobs, *White Mother to a Dark Race*.

133. Wolf Rob Hunt, Doris Duke American Indian Oral History Collection, 1968–72, Tape 134, n.d., (AIOHC-CSWR).

134. Lomawaima, *They Called It Prairie Light*.

135. Hoxie, *The Final Promise*.

136. Meriam, *The Problem of Indian Administration*, 348.

137. Meriam, *The Problem of Indian Administration*, 351.

138. Meriam, *The Problem of Indian Administration*, 358.

139. See chapter 6.

140. Szasz, *Education and the American Indian*.

141. Address by Dr. W. Carson Ryan Jr., Director of Education, Indian Service, over Station WRC and nation-wide network, Washington DC, November 14, 1932, RG 75, Records of the BIA, Albuquerque Indian School General Correspondence Files 1917–36, 001–003, Entry 29, Box 2, Folder 11 (NARA).

142. Bolt, *American Indian Policy and American Reform*, 109.

143. John Collier, "A Birdseye View of Indian Policy, Historic and Contemporary," n.d., John Collier Papers MF Archives Division, State Records Center, Santa Fe, New Mexico, 1969 (SAL).

144. See McDonnell and Moses, "Raphael Lemkin as Historian of Genocide in the Americas." For a view that challenges the idea that Lemkin was essentialist in his thinking, see Short, "Australia."

145. For more on Collier, also see Kelly, *The Assault on Assimilation*; Laukaitis, "Indians at Work and John Collier's Campaign for Progressive Education Reform"; Philp, *John Collier's Crusade for Indian Reform*; Rusco, "John Collier, Architect of Sovereignty or Assimilation?"; Schwartz, "Red Atlantis Revisited."

146. S. 3645, enacted by Congress on June 16, 1934.

147. Statements of John Collier, Commissioner of Indian Affairs, on the purpose

and operation of the Wheeler-Howard Indian Rights Bill, John Collier Papers MF Archives Division, State Records Center, Santa Fe, New Mexico, 1969 (SAL).

148. "Missionaries Oppose New Indian Bill," *Santa Fe New Mexican*, March 26, 1934, John Collier Papers MF Archives Division, State Records Center, Santa Fe, New Mexico, 1969 (SAL).

149. "Collier Raps Indian Rights Bill Critics: Selfish Interests Seek to Defeat Measure, He Says," *Washington Post*, March 30, 1934, John Collier Papers MF Archives Division, State Records Center, Santa Fe, New Mexico, 1969 (SAL).

150. Szasz, *Education and the American Indian*.

151. Quoted in Szasz, *Education and the American Indian*, 76.

152. "Memorandum for Secretary Ickes, Subject: The Program of Moving 2500 Indian Children from Boarding to Day Schools," John Collier Papers MF Archives Division, State Records Center, Santa Fe, New Mexico, 1969 (SAL).

153. Szasz, *Education and the American Indian*, 61.

154. Prucha, *The Great Father*.

155. Szasz, *Education and the American Indian*.

156. See Szasz, *Education and the American Indian*.

157. See Ames, "Rhetoric and Resistance."

158. Jenson, "Teachers and Progressives."

159. Jenson, "Teachers and Progressives."

160. Dyck, *Differing Visions*, 55.

161. Miller, *Shingwauk's Vision*.

162. Trevithick, "Native Residential Schooling in Canada."

163. Bull, "Indian Residential Schooling."

164. See Blackstock, "Reconciliation Means Not Saying Sorry Twice"; Jacobs, "The Habit of Elimination"; Jacobs, "Remembering the Forgotten Child."

165. Cornell, *Return of the Native*.

166. Furness, *Victims of Benevolence*.

167. Truth and Reconciliation Commission, *They Came for the Children*, 19.

168. Truth and Reconciliation Commission, *They Came for the Children*, 19. Of course, one should bear in mind that the government is often free in how it defines neglect.

169. Royal Commission on Aboriginal Peoples, *Report of the Royal Commission on Aboriginal Peoples*, 323.

170. Jacobs, "The Habit of Elimination."

171. Hawthorne, *A Survey of the Contemporary Indians of Canada*; King, *The School at Mopas*.

172. Miller, *Shingwauk's Vision*.

173. Truth and Reconciliation Commission, *They Came for the Children*, 19.

174. Truth and Reconciliation Commission, *They Came for the Children*, 19.

175. See Canada, *Information*.

176. Bolt, *American Indian Policy and American Reform*; Meriam, *The Problem of Indian Administration*; Szasz, *Education and the American Indian*. In 1900, there were only 246 Indigenous pupils in American public schools. In 1920, this figure would grow to 30,858 compared with the 25,396 in federal government-run schools.

177. Szasz, *Education and the American Indian*.

178. Szasz, *Education and the American Indian*.

179. Bourdieu, "Rethinking the State."

180. Marker, "After the Whalehunt."

181. Szasz, *Education and the American Indian*.

182. Szasz, *Education and the American Indian*.

183. Thompson, *The Navajos' Long Walk for Education*.

184. Jacobs, "Remembering the Forgotten Child."

185. Special Subcommittee on Indian Education, *Indian Education*; Szasz, *Education and the American Indian*.

186. See Echohawk, "The Kennedy Report." Echohawk calls for a "Tribal Sovereignty Education Act" (17) that more fully acknowledges and facilitates Indigenous self-determination in education.

187. Canada, Indian and Northern Affairs Canada. *Information: Indian Affairs in Canada and the United States*. Ottawa: Government of Canada, 1998.

188. Jorge Barrera, "Grassroots Unease over Harper Government's First Nations Education Bill," Aboriginal Peoples Television Network National News, April 28, 2014, http://aptn.ca/news/2014/04/28/grassroots-unease-growing-harper-governments-first-nations-education-bill/.

189. Quoted in Titley, *A Narrow Vision*, 50.

190. Pratt, "The Advantages of Mingling Indians with Whites," 261.

4. SCHOOLS, COMMUNITIES, AND STUDENTS

1. Memorandum to H. W. McGill, February 22, 1934, RG 10, Volume 6001, File 1–1–11, part 3 Headquarters-Schools-General, 1904–28 (LAC).

2. Erna Fergusson, "Old Albuquerque: Do You Remember the First Indian School?," *Albuquerque Herald*, July 9, 1923 (NC-CSWR).

3. McKinney, "History of the Albuquerque Indian School."

4. See Acting Commissioner E. J. Brooks to B. M. Thomas, U.S. Indian Agent, Pueblo Agency, nm, June 5, 1880, RG 75, Records of the Bureau of Indian Affairs, Northern Pueblos Agency, General Correspondence and Reports 1877–1934, Box 4, Folder 67 (NARA).

5. Superintendent Bryan, September 15, 1884, Richard W. D. Bryan Family Papers 1844–1939, MSS IBC, Box 1, Folder 1 (BFP-CSWR).

6. "Our Young Savages: Democrat Reporter Visits the Albuquerque Indian School," January 22, 1885, *Albuquerque Evening Democrat*, Richard W. D. Bryan Family Papers 1844–1939, MSS IBC, Box 1, Folder 1 (BFP-CSWR).

7. The Hopi in Arizona are sometimes referred to as western Pueblo; however, given their distance from AIS and SFIS, I will keep them separate for purposes of this study. For more on Hopi educational experiences, see Adams, "Schooling the Hopi."

8. Sando, *The Pueblo Indians*. For more on Pueblo experiences of acculturation and assimilation under the Spanish, see Archibald, "Acculturation and Assimilation in Colonial New Mexico."

9. Gram, "Education on the Edge of Empire."

10. Superintendent Bryan, September 15, 1884, Richard W. D. Bryan Family Papers 1844–1939, MSS IBC, Box 1, Folder 1 (BFP-CSWR).

11. Gram, "Education on the Edge of Empire." See also the letter from Superintendent Perry (AIS) to Commissioner of Indian Affairs, November 27, 1916, RG 75, Records of the Bureau of Indian Affairs, Northern Pueblos Agency, General Correspondence and Reports 1877–1934, Box 21, Folder 381 (NARA). Likewise, in Canada, per capita funds were used to pay staff salaries and cover heating costs, among other expenses. See Kelm, *Colonizing Bodies*; Miller, *Shingwauk's Vision*; Titley, *A Narrow Vision*.

12. Gram, "Education on the Edge of Empire."

13. 1916 Annual Report, AIS, M1011, Superintendents' Annual Narrative and Statistical Reports from Field Jurisdictions of the Bureau of Indian Affairs, 1907–38 (NARA).

14. 1920 Annual Report, AIS, M1011, Superintendents' Annual Narrative and Statistical Reports from Field Jurisdictions of the Bureau of Indian Affairs, 1907–38 (NARA).

15. 1925 Annual Report, AIS, M1011, Superintendents' Annual Narrative and Statistical Reports from Field Jurisdictions of the Bureau of Indian Affairs, 1907–38 (NARA).

16. 1930 Annual Report, AIS, M1011, Superintendents' Annual Narrative and Statistical Reports from Field Jurisdictions of the Bureau of Indian Affairs, 1907–38 (NARA).

17. Garmhausen, *Indian Arts Education in Santa Fe.*

18. Hyer, *One House, One Voice, One Heart.*

19. Garmhausen, *Indian Arts Education in Santa Fe.*

20. Summary of Santa Fe Indian School by Superintendent Andrew Viets, compiled

between September 1, 1898, and March 7, 1900, RG 75.20.36, Reel M1473, Roll 5, v. 9–11, Bureau of Indian Affairs RG 75, Records Created at the Santa Fe Indian School, Press Copies of Miscellaneous Letters Sent (SAL).

21. Garmhausen, *Indian Arts Education in Santa Fe.*

22. Superintendent S. M. Cart to Commissioner of Indian Affairs, January 14, 1891, RG 75.20.36, Reel M1473, Roll 1, v. 1–2, Bureau of Indian Affairs Records Created at the SFIS, Press Copies of Miscellaneous Letters Sent (SAL).

23. Superintendent S. M. Cart to Commissioner of Indian Affairs, April 1, 1891, RG 75.20.36, Reel M1473, Roll 1, v. 1–2, Bureau of Indian Affairs Records Created at the SFIS, Press Copies of Miscellaneous Letters Sent (SAL).

24. Superintendent S. M. Cart to Commissioner of Indian Affairs, June 18, 1891, RG 75.20.36, Reel M1473, Roll 1, v. 1–2, Bureau of Indian Affairs Records Created at the SFIS, Press Copies of Miscellaneous Letters Sent (SAL).

25. Gram, "Education on the Edge of Empire"; Hyer, *One House, One Voice, One Heart.*

26. Hyer, *One House, One Voice, One Heart.*

27. Pueblo historian Joe Sando, *Pueblo Nations,* 133, however, notes that "the process of forced assimilation nearly destroyed Pueblo culture."

28. 1914 Annual Report, SFIS, M1011, Superintendents' Annual Narrative and Statistical Reports from Field Jurisdictions of the Bureau of Indian Affairs, 1907–38 (NARA).

29. 1922 Annual Report, SFIS, M1011, Superintendents' Annual Narrative and Statistical Reports from Field Jurisdictions of the Bureau of Indian Affairs, 1907–38 (NARA).

30. 1924 Annual Report, SFIS, M1011, Superintendents' Annual Narrative and Statistical Reports from Field Jurisdictions of the Bureau of Indian Affairs, 1907–38 (NARA).

31. 1928 Annual Report, SFIS, M1011, Superintendents' Annual Narrative and Statistical Reports from Field Jurisdictions of the Bureau of Indian Affairs, 1907–38 (NARA).

32. Hyer, *One House, One Voice, One Heart.* For more discussion on Indigenous men and women working in American boarding schools, see Cahill, *Federal Mothers and Fathers;* Jacobs, *White Mother to a Dark Race.*

33. *One House, One Voice, One Heart;* see also Hyer, *One House, One Voice, One Heart,* 31.

34. For more discussion on arts and crafts among the Pueblo, as well as at SFIS, see Meyn, *More than Curiosities.*

35. Hyer, *One House, One Voice, One Heart.*

36. Szasz, *Education and the American Indian.*

37. The Dakota Sioux were expelled from the United States after the Dakota War of 1862, and several Sioux families relocated to Manitoba near the town of Portage la Prairie. Perceived as migrants, the relocated Sioux were viewed by the Canadian government to possess no territorial rights. The original Portage la Prairie day school was constructed with the aim of educating children from this group, thought to be potentially a disruptive presence in Portage la Prairie. See The Children Remembered, Residential School Archive Project, "Portage la Prairie Indian Residential School."

38. Quoted in The Children Remembered, Residential School Archive Project, "Portage la Prairie Indian Residential School."

39. Portage la Prairie Indian Residential School Narrative, July 21, 2004, IAP Collection (TRC). See also Bush, "The Native Residential School System and the Presbyterian Church in Canada."

40. Portage la Prairie Indian Residential School Narrative, July 21, 2004, IAP Collection (TRC).

41. Secretary, Department of Indian Affairs, to Reverend R. P. Mackay, May 10, 1910, RG 10, Volume 6273, File 583-1, part 1, Portage la Prairie Agency, PLPIRS—General Administration, 1895–1934 (LAC).

42. Principal W. A. Hendry to Secretary, Department of Indian Affairs, May 8, 1913, Roll 13800, RG 10, Volume 8449, File 511/23–5–017 (LAC).

43. The Children Remembered, Residential School Archive Project, "Portage la Prairie Indian Residential School."

44. Inspector Report for PLPIRS by A. O. Hamilton, June 12, 1934, Roll 13800, RG 10, Volume 8449, File 511/23–5–017 (LAC).

45. Portage la Prairie Indian Residential School Narrative, July 21, 2004, IAP Collection (TRC).

46. Portage la Prairie Indian Residential School Narrative, July 21, 2004, IAP Collection (TRC).

47. Letter from Sioux Indian Village signed by Peter Ross, John Posha, and John Chaske, February 17, 1927, RG 10, Volume 6273, File 583-1, part 1, Portage la Prairie Agency, PLPIRS—General Administration 1895–1934 (LAC).

48. Reverend W. A. Hendry, "An Indian Training Ground," Missionary Monthly, June 1930, RG 10, Volume 6001, File 1–1–11, part 2 Headquarters-Schools-General, 1904–28 (LAC).

49. PLPIRS Quarterly Return, RG 10, Volume 6273, File 583–2, part 1 Portage la Prairie Agency—PLPIRS—Presbyterian—Quarterly Returns 1941–50 (LAC).

50. Inspector Report for PLPIRS by A. O. Hamilton, June 12, 1934, Roll 13800, RG 10, Volume 8449, File 511/23–5–017 (LAC).

51. PLPIRS Quarterly Return, RG 10, Volume 6273, File 583–2, part 1 Portage la Prairie Agency—PLPIRS—Presbyterian—Quarterly Returns 1941–50 (LAC).

52. Archbishop of St. Boniface to Clifford Sifton, Superintendent General of Indian Affairs, March 31, 1900, RG 10, Volume 6264, File 579–1, part 1 (LAC).

53. Fort Alexander Indian Residential School Narrative, September 28, 2011, IAP Collection (TRC).

54. The Sisters of the Cross, or Filles de [la] Croix, from France, provided services at the school between 1905 and 1914. The Oblates signed on to manage the school in 1911 and filled staff positions from 1914 to 1970. Fort Alexander Indian Residential School Narrative, September 28, 2011, IAP Collection (TRC).

55. Inspector J. R. Bunn to Deputy Superintendent D. C. Scott, March 25, 1914, RG 10, Volume 8448, File 506/23–5–019 (LAC).

56. Inspection Report, Fort Alexander, 1910, Reel 13800, RG 10, Volume 8448, File 506/23–5–019 (LAC).

57. Inspector J. R. Bunn to Deputy Superintendent D. C. Scott, March 25, 1914, RG 10, Volume 8448, File 506/23–5–019 (LAC).

58. Fort Alexander Indian Residential School Narrative, September 28, 2011, IAP Collection (TRC).

59. Fort Alexander Indian Residential School Narrative, September 28, 2011, IAP Collection (TRC).

60. List of Pupils at Fort Alexander Indian Day and Residential Schools, 1958, RG10, Volume 8623, File 506/6–2–019, part 5 (LAC).

61. Fort Alexander Indian Residential School Narrative, September 28, 2011, IAP Collection (TRC).

62. Meyn, *More than Curiosities*, 65–66.

63. See Lawrence, *Lessons from an Indian Day School.*

64. See Carney, "Church-State and Northern Education."

65. See Prucha, *The Churches and the Indian Schools.*

66. James Mann requests that his son Cornelius be removed from Rupert's Land School to the Catholic school at St. Boniface, July 26, 1891, RG 10, Volume 3858, File 81,806, Clandeboye Agency—Fort Alexander Band—Indian Affairs (LAC).

67. Petition from the chief and councilors of Peguis, Fisher River, Berens River, and Bloodvein to His Royal Highness, Victor Christian William, January 27, 1919, RG 10, Volume 6001, File 1–1–11, part 2 Headquarters—Schools—eneral, 1904–28 (LAC).

68. Miller, "The Irony of Residential Schooling."

69. Superintendent Cart to Commissioner of Indian Affairs, April 1, 1891, RG 75.20.36, Reel M1473, Roll 1, v. 1–2, Bureau of Indian Affairs RG 75, Records

Created at Santa Fe Indian School, Press Copies of Miscellaneous Letters Sent (SAL).

70. Superintendent Cart to Commissioner of Indian Affairs, September 11, 1891, RG 75.20.36, Reel M1473, Roll 1, v. 1–2, Bureau of Indian Affairs RG 75, Records Created at Santa Fe Indian School, Press Copies of Miscellaneous Letters Sent (SAL).

71. Superintendent Cart to Commissioner of Indian Affairs, October 21, 1891, RG 75.20.36, Reel M1473, Roll 1, v. 1–2, Bureau of Indian Affairs RG 75, Records Created at Santa Fe Indian School, Press Copies of Miscellaneous Letters Sent (SAL).

72. Superintendent Thomas Jones to Commissioner of Indian Affairs, October 1895, RG 75.20.36, Reel M1473, Roll 3, v. 5–6, Bureau of Indian Affairs RG 75, Records Created at Santa Fe Indian School, Press Copies of Miscellaneous Letters Sent (SAL). A similar conflict is noted in W. A. Jones, Commissioner, Office of Indian Affairs, to Captain C. E. Nordstrom, Acting U.S. Indian Agent, Pueblo and Jicarilla Agency, Santa Fe, nm, October 20, 1897, Records of the Bureau of Indian Affairs RG 75, Northern Pueblos Agency, General Correspondence and Reports 1877–1934, Box 7, Folder 138 (NARA), which discusses the difficulty of dealing with a situation in which a student had been removed from the government school and placed at the St. Catherine's Indian School.

73. See, for example, Acting Commissioner T. P. Smith to Captain J. L. Bullis, Acting U.S. Indian Agent, Pueblo and Jicarilla Agency, Santa Fe, nm, May 19, 1896, Records of the Bureau of Indian Affairs RG 75, Northern Pueblos Agency, General Correspondence and Reports 1877–34, Box 6, Folder 124 (NARA). In this letter, the acting commissioner questions why students from the Cochita Day School are not being transferred to SFIS. Also of interest here is the acting commissioner's reminder to the agent that parental permission to transfer students is not required but should be sought as a first option so as to avoid "unnecessary friction" with parents.

74. Superintendent Cart to Commissioner of Indian Affairs, May 5, 1893, RG 75.20.36, Reel M1473, Roll 2, v. 3–4, Bureau of Indian Affairs RG 75, Records Created at Santa Fe Indian School, Press Copies of Miscellaneous Letters Sent (SAL).

75. Cooperation among schools was also fostered at this time through summer workshops and conferences, which allowed staff and superintendents to share their experiences and knowledge of the assimilative project with their counterparts at other schools.

76. Hoxie, *The Final Promise*.

77. Frank Tenorio, San Felipe, interviewed March 5–7, 1986, SFIS First 100 Years, attended AIS 1933–39 (CSWR-SFIS100).

78. 1912 Annual Report, SFIS, M1011, Superintendents' Annual Narrative and Statistical Reports from Field Jurisdictions of the Bureau of Indian Affairs, 1907–38 (NARA).

79. Superintendent Rueben Perry, AIS, to Commissioner of Indian Affairs, October 6, 1924, Records of the Bureau of Indian Affairs RG 75, Albuquerque Indian School, General Correspondence Files 1917–36, 001–003, Entry 29, Box 36, Folder 815.2 (NARA). Perry also took issue in this letter with plans to keep students in grades four through six in the classroom for longer days, thereby reducing their exposure to vocational training.

80. Philip Phelan, Chief of the Training Division, to J. Waite, Indian Agent, January 7, 1938, RG 10, Volume 6275, File 583–10, part 1 (LAC).

81. J. Waite, Indian Agent, to Secretary of Indian Affairs, November 22, 1938, RG 10, Volume 6275, File 583–10, part 1 (LAC).

82. J. McNeill, Principal, PLPIRS, to J. Waite, Indian Agent, October 30, 1944, RG 10, Volume 6275, File 583–10, part 1 (LAC).

83. Basil Johnston, *Indian School Days*, provides from outside Manitoba another example of the haphazard logic determining school placement. He describes his move from a day school to the residential school at Spanish in Ontario as a punishment rather than as a part of an integrated system through which capable students were advanced to the boarding school level.

84. Reverend W. A. Hendry to Secretary of Indian Affairs, October 7, 1930, RG 10, Volume 6273, File 583–1, part 1, Portage la Prairie Agency, PLPIRS — General Administration, 1895–1934 (LAC).

85. Willard Beatty, Director of Education, U.S. Department of the Interior, to R. A. Hoey, Superintendent of Welfare and Training, Department of Mines and Resources, June 23, 1941, RG 10, Volume 6001, File 1–1–11, part 2 Headquarters — Schools — General, 1904–28 (LAC).

86. See, for example, exchanges between administrators on both sides of the border, such as the letter from Superintendent, Department of the Interior, United States Indian Field Service, Turtle Mountain Agency, U.S., to Superintendent General of Indian Affairs, Canada, February 26, 1924, RG 10, Volume 6039, File 160–1, part 1 (LAC), or Indian Commissioner Hayter Reed's May 14, 1889, "Report on the Following Indian Industrial Schools in Canada and the United States: Mount Elgin or Mohawk, the Muncey, nd the Carlisle," RG 10, Volume 3818, File 57.799 (LAC).

87. Raibmon, "'A New Understanding of Things Indian,'" 96.

88. See also Raibman, "'In Loco Parentis.'" A similar example from the American Southwest concerns the different perspectives and values that female Indian service workers brought with them when they worked in Indigenous communities

and at boarding schools and how these varying views affected how they carried out their duties. See Jacobs, *Engendered Encounters.*

89. Superintendent T. J. Jones to Department of the Interior, September 22, 1897, RG 75.20.36, Reel M1473, Roll 4, v. 7–8, Bureau of Indian Affairs RG 75, Records Created at Santa Fe Indian School, Press Copies of Miscellaneous Letters Sent (SAL).

90. Gram, "Education on the Edge of Empire."

91. Gram, "Education on the Edge of Empire."

92. Gram, "Education on the Edge of Empire."

93. Superintendent C. J. Crandall, Northern Pueblos Agency, to Superintendent J. D. DeHuff, SFIS, May 27, 1924, Records of the Bureau of Indian Affairs RG 75, Northern Pueblos Agency, General Correspondence and Reports, 1877–1934, Box 23, Folder 424 (NARA).

94. For further discussion of Pueblo Indian dance controversy and the moderate role of the DeHuffs therein, see Wegner, *We Have a Religion*, chapter 3.

95. John David DeHuff Diary, MS 99 BC (EWDFP-CSWR).

96. Saunders, *The Indians of the Terraced Houses.*

97. John David DeHuff Diary, MS 99 BC (EWDFP-CSWR).

98. Miller, *Shingwauk's Vision.*

99. S. Swinford, Inspector of Indian Agencies, to Secretary of the Department of Indian Affairs, November 19, 1908, RG 10, Volume 6273, File 583–1, part 1, Portage la Prairie Agency, PLPIRS — General Administration 1895–1934 (LAC).

100. However, few survivors from Hendry's time at PLPIRS would have been alive to testify to the TRC of Canada.

101. The Children Remembered, Residential School Archive Project, "Portage la Prairie Indian Residential School."

102. Statement from Rowena Smoke, Long Plain Sioux, to Department of Indian and Northern Development, INAC — Resolution Sector — Indian Residential Schools Historical Files Collection — Ottawa, File 501/25–1–067, Volume 1 (LAC).

103. Mary B. Ross, Matron, INAC — Resolution Sector — Indian Residential Schools Historical Files Collection — Ottawa, File 501/25–1–067, Volume 1 (LAC).

104. Bernard Neary, Superintendent of Indian Education, to Inspector A. C. Hamilton, February 25, 1949, RG 10, Volume 6275, File 583–10, part 2 (LAC).

105. The Children Remembered, Residential School Archive Project, "Portage la Prairie Indian Residential School."

106. Miller, *Shingwauk's Vision*, 320.

107. Truth and Reconciliation Commission of Canada, *They Came for the Children*, 71.

108. For example, see Philip Phelan, Chief of Taining Division, to Reverend J. O.

Plourde, OMI, July 5, 1938, RG 10, Volume 8448, File 506/23–5–019 (LAC). Chapters 5 and 6 will address some of the ways that teachers responded to their students; at times, they would place themselves as substitute family members and offer encouragement to students, but more frequently in Canada they were sources of terror and fear.

109. Adams, *Education for Extinction*, 82.

110. Adams, *Education for Extinction*, 82.

111. 1920 Annual Report, AIS, M1011, Superintendents' Annual Narrative and Statistical Reports from Field Jurisdictions of the Bureau of Indian Affairs, 1907–38 (NARA).

112. Jacobs, *Engendered Encounters*.

113. Pablita Velarde (Santa Clara), interviewed October 2, 1986, SFIS: The First Hundred Years, attended 1929–36 (CSWR-SFIS100).

114. Theodore Fontaine, *Broken Circle*.

115. Theodore Fontaine, *Broken Circle*.

116. Robin Jarvis Brownlie, *A Fatherly Eye*, 124–25, notes how the Canadian Indian bureaucracy, though engaged in a "civilizing" process, clearly did not think that Indians could become assimilated enough to take on the role of inculcators of assimilation for the young. Brownlie recounts the case of Clifford Tobias, an Indigenous man who pursued postsecondary education but was deemed inappropriate for a teaching position at an Indian school in Ontario.

117. Quoted in Satzewich and Mahood, "Indian Agents and the Residential School System in Canada," 54.

118. Satzewich and Mahood, "Indian Agents and the Residential School System in Canada," 54. See also Brownlie, *A Fatherly Eye*.

119. 1884 regulations quoted in Prucha, *The Great Father*, 645.

120. Child, "Runaway Boys, Resistant Girls."

121. Jacobs, *White Mother to a Dark Race*.

122. Miller, *Shingwauk's Vision*.

123. Fear-Segal, *White Man's Club*.

124. Herbert Talehaftewa, Doris Duke American Indian Oral History Collection, 1968–72, Tape 563, interviewed July 18, 1967 (AIOHC-CSWR).

125. For Bourdieu's discussion of the gift as an instance of symbolic violence, see Bourdieu, *Language and Symbolic Power; Bourdieu, The Logic of Practice*.

126. John L. Ross to Superintendent of Indian Affairs, October 6, 1920, RG 10, Volume 6264, File 579–1, part 1 (LAC).

127. Inspector J. R. Bunn to Assistant Deputy and Secretary of Indian Affairs, October 21, 1920, RG 10, Volume 6264, File 579–1, part 1 (LAC).

128. Notarized letter from Richard Tafoya to SFIS, June 28, 1905, Records of the

Bureau of Indian Affairs RG 75, Northern Pueblos Agency, General Correspondence and Reports, 1877–1934, Box 7, Folder 168 (NARA).

129. Superintendent P. T. Lonergam to Commissioner of Indian Affairs, March 3, 1914, Records of the Bureau of Indian Affairs RG 75, Southern Pueblos Agency, General Correspondence Files, Box 118, File 413–14, (NARA).

130. Report by R. H. Cairns, Inspector of Indian Schools, to Deputy Superintendent D. C. Scott, February 16, 1922, RG 10, Volume 8448, File 506/23–5–019 (LAC).

131. Chief William Mann and Councilors, Fort Alexander, to Department of Indian Affairs, February 28, 1923, RG 10, Volume 6264, File 579–1, part 1, General Administration 1900–35 (LAC).

132. Secretary J. D. McLean to Chief William Mann and Councilors, March 6, 1923, RG 10, Volume 6264, File 579–1, part 1, General Administration 1900–35 (LAC).

133. Fergusson, "Old Albuquerque."

134. See Athearn, *An Isolated Empire.*

135. John Charlie, Doris Duke American Indian Oral History Collection, 1968–72, Tape 197, interviewed November 1968 (AIOHC-CSWR).

136. Lawrence, *Lessons from an Indian Day School.*

137. Annual Report of Superintendent Andrew Viets, SFIS, to Commissioner of Indian Affairs, August 30, 1899, RG 75.20.36, Reel M1473, Roll 5, v. 9–11, Bureau of Indian Affairs RG 75, Records Created at Santa Fe Indian School, Press Copies of Miscellaneous Letters Sent (SAL).

138. Testimony to the Truth and Reconciliation Commission of Canada; Brandon, Manitoba, October 12, 2011 (TRC).

139. Colmant et al., "Constructing Meaning to the Indian Boarding School Experience."

140. For Canadian examples, see Haig-Brown, *Resistance and Renewal;* Johnston, *Indian School Days.* For American examples, see Child, *Boarding School Seasons;* Lomawaima, *They Called It Prairie Light.*

141. Report of Mr. Johnson, Adviser to Boys, in 1929 AIS Annual Report, M1011, Superintendents' Annual Narrative and Statistical Reports from Field Jurisdictions of the Bureau of Indian Affairs, 1907–38 (NARA).

142. Gresko, "White 'Rites' and Indian 'Rites'"; Haig-Brown, *Resistance and Renewal;* Miller, "The Irony of Residential Schooling."

143. McBeth, *Ethnic Identity and the Boarding School Experience of West-Central Oklahoma Indians;* McBeth, "Indian Boarding Schools and Ethnic Identity." See also Child, *Boarding School Seasons;* Ellis, *To Change Them Forever;* Lomawaima, *They Called It Prairie Light.*

144. McBeth, *Ethnic Identity and the Boarding School Experience of West-Central Oklahoma Indians;* McBeth, "Indian Boarding Schools and Ethnic Identity."

145. Hopi-Hopi (Diné), Doris Duke American Indian Oral History Collection, 1968–72, Tape 362, interviewed January 1969 (AIOHC-CSWR).

146. The story of nine-year-old Duncan Stick's death after running away is recounted by Furniss, *Victims of Benevolence*.

147. Superintendent DeHuff, SFIS, to Mr. Jose Rey Chihuihui, Governor, Jemez Indian Pueblo, January 19, 1919, Bureau of Indian Affairs RG 75, Student School Folders 1910–34, Santa Fe Indian School, Abbious to Augustine, Entry 47, Frague, Francisco (NARA).

148. Wilfred Garcia of San Juan Pueblo, interviewed March 4, 1986, SFIS: The First Hundred Years, attended SFIS 1957–58 (CSWR-SFIS100).

149. Gram, "Education on the Edge of Empire."

150. List of deserters who have not returned, Records of the Bureau of Indian Affairs RG 75, Albuquerque Indian School, General Correspondence Files, 1917–36, 001–003, Entry 29, Box 36, File 824.1 (NARA).

151. Inspector A. G. Hamilton to Indian Affairs, February 21, 1949, RG 10, Volume 6275, File 583–10, part 2 (LAC).

152. The Children Remembered, Residential School Archive Project, "Portage la Prairie Indian Residential School."

5. DISCIPLINE AND DESIRE

1. These techniques could also be understood in the language of Actor-Network Theory as "semiotics." Given that chapter 7 seeks to identify some of the local actors, human and nonhuman, that animated the world of the Indigenous boarding school, I could have remained within the ANT lexicon and conceptual universe by referring to these techniques as semiotic strands that mediate relations between these actors. However, I borrow only lightly from ANT for the purpose of intensifying my analysis of the local. This project remains primarily rooted in a Bourdieuian ontology, with the addition of concepts from Foucault, ANT, and other scholars to correct some of the structuralist tendencies of Bourdieuian sociology. On semiotics, and the sort of semiotic-material relationality that forms discursive strands among various actors in a network, see Law, "Actor Network Theory and Material Semiotics."

2. See, for example, Foucault, "Technologies of the Self." In particular, he itemizes four specific types of technology: "(1) technologies of production; (2) technologies of sign systems, which permit us to use signs, meanings, symbols, or signification; (3) technologies of power, which determine the conduct of individuals and submit them to certain ends or domination, and objectivizing of the subject; (4) technologies of the self, which permit individuals to effect by their own means, or with the help of others, a certain number of operations on their own bodies

and souls, thoughts, conduct, and way of being, so as to transform themselves in order to attain a certain state of happiness, purity, wisdom, perfection, or immortality" (225). All four forms of technology can be witnessed in Canadian and American boarding schools, although my focus is predominantly on the latter two.

3. See Vizenor, *Survivance*.

4. See, for example, many of the chapters collected in Trafzer, Keller, and Sisquoc, *Boarding School Blues*.

5. Foucault, *Discipline and Punish*.

6. See, for example, James Daschuk's discussion in *Clearing the Plains* on how starvation was used to restrict Indigenous peoples on the Canadian prairies to their reserves.

7. For example, Adams, *Education for Extinction*; Miller, *Shingwauk's Vision*.

8. See Foucault, *Discipline and Punish*.

9. For example, Adams, *Education for Extinction*.

10. Goffman, *Asylums*.

11. Foucault, *Discipline and Punish*, 236. The similarities between prisons and boarding schools have not been lost on survivors. As Arthur Wilfred Kent suggests of FAIRS, "that place was just like Stony Mountain Pen [a Manitoban prison]." Quoted in C. C. Fontaine, *Speaking of Sagkeeng*, 46.

12. Foucault, *Discipline and Punish*, 235.

13. Foucault, *Discipline and Punish*, 235.

14. Beth Piatote, *Domestic Subjects*, chapter 4, writes of "disciplinary paternalism," whereby the relationship between substitute parent figure (e.g., the government or school as embodied by Indian agent, superintendent, or other such actor) and ward necessitates a degree of surveillance and violence underneath its benevolent guise.

15. It is also worth noting that military influence was strong in the boarding schools prior to Pratt's innovations as well as in the BIA. Until 1849, when it was transferred to the Department of the Interior, U.S. Indian Affairs was run by dedicated personnel from the War Department, with assistance from military commanders in the field. The "department" became formalized and more bureaucratized in 1834 with the establishment of a commissioner of the Indian Department, more detailed accounting practices, and further codification of Indian policy. This would begin a gradual process of demilitarizing and bureaucratizing the Indian service. See Prucha, *The Great Father*, chapters 6 and 11.

16. See chapter 3.

17. Foucault, *Discipline and Punish*, 137.

18. Foucault, *Discipline and Punish*, 135.

19. Of course, Canadian boarding schools, even with their emphasis on monastic discipline, were also not immune to trying to impose use value through discipline of students. See the discussion in this chapter on work discipline.

20. Johnston, *Indian School Days*, 43.

21. Adams, *Education for Extinction*.

22. Adams, *Education for Extinction*; Reyhner and Eder, *American Indian Education*.

23. Quoted in Coleman, *American Indian Children at School*, 42–43.

24. Catholic Hierarchy of Canada to Special Joint Committee of the Senate and House of Commons Appointed to Examine and Consider *the Indian Act*, RG 29, Volume 3388, File 804-1-7, part 1 (LAC).

25. Scott, *Thinking like a State*.

26. Reverend L. Jalbert, omi, Principal, FAIRS, Pine Falls, Manitoba, to M. Rehaluk, Supervising Principal, Clandeboye Indian Agency, Selkirk, Manitoba, Deschatelets Archives, Oblates of Mary Immaculate, Ottawa, HR 6681.C73R 99.

27. 1914–15 school timetable, AIS, Richard W. D. Bryan Family Papers 1844–1939, MSS IBC, Box 1, Folder 1 (BFP-CSWR).

28. Fear-Segal, *White Man's Club*.

29. Quoted in Fear-Segal, *White Man's Club*, 180.

30. Superintendent Cart to Commissioner of Indian Affairs, May 27, 1891, RG 75.20.36, Reel M1473, Roll 1, v. 1–2, Bureau of Indian Affairs RG 75, Records Created at Santa Fe Indian School, Press Copies of Miscellaneous Letters Sent (SAL).

31. Assistant Commissioner F. H. Abbott responded to this request with the answer "I doubt the advisability of furnishing arms to Indian pupils for drilling purposes." See F. H. Abbott, Assistant Commissioner, Office of Indian Affairs, to Superintendent Crandall, SFIS, January 14, 1910, Bureau of Indian Affairs RG 75, Northern Pueblos Agency, General Correspondence and Reports 1877–1934, Box 15, File 277 (NARA).

32. "Our Young Savages: Democrat Reporter Visits the Albuquerque Indian School," January 22, 1885, *Albuquerque Evening Democrat*, Richard W. D. Bryan Family Papers 1844–1939, MSS IBC, Box 1, Folder 1 (BFP-CSWR).

33. 1918–19 Annual School Calendar, SFIS, Bureau of Indian Affairs RG 75, Northern Pueblos Agency, General Correspondence and Reports 1877–1934, Box 23, File 424 (NARA).

34. See Tate, "From Scout to Doughboy."

35. 1918 Annual Report, AIS, M1011, Superintendents' Annual Narrative and Statistical Reports from Field Jurisdictions of the Bureau of Indian Affairs, 1907–38 (NARA).

36. Several such statements can be found in the interviews by Sally Hyers for the

SFIS: The First Hundred Years project, Center for Southwest Research, University of New Mexico, Albuquerque.

37. Thompson, *The Navajos' Long Walk for Education*.

38. Hyer, *One House, One Voice, One Heart*, 12.

39. Hyer, *One House, One Voice, One Heart*, 12.

40. Gram, "Education on the Edge of Empire."

41. Minutes of April 14, 1932, Isleta Boys and Girls Council, Bureau of Indian Affairs RG 75, Albuquerque Indian School, Student Case Files, Box 1, Abeita, Andy (NARA).

42. Jojola is here referring to a lawsuit filed by Charles Lummis against the Albuquerque Indian School for taking Isleta Pueblo children away from their families for great lengths of time. Lummis was successful, and thirty-six children were returned to the community from AIS. See http://www.charleslummis.com/biography.htm.

43. Quoted in Leslie Linthicum, "Gone, but Not Forgotten: Memories and Photographs Are All that Remain of the Albuquerque Indian School," *abq Journal*, August 11, 2002, B1 and B5, B1.

44. Superintendent Perry, AIS, to Commissioner of Indian Affairs, October 18, 1932, Bureau of Indian Affairs RG 75, Albuquerque Indian School, General Correspondence Files 1917–36, 001–003, Entry 29, Box 30, File 670 (NARA).

45. Foucault, *Discipline and Punish*, 184.

46. Reverend George Dorey to Colonel B. F. Neary, Superintendent of Indian Education, March 24, 1949, File 501/25–1-067, Volume 1, Residential School Records Office, DIAND (part of Portage la Prairie IRS Narrative, TRC).

47. Miller, *Shingwauk's Vision*, 91.

48. See, for example, Truth and Reconciliation Commission of Canada, *They Came for the Children*, 37.

49. See Bull, "Indian Residential Schooling"; Knockwood, *Out of the Depths*.

50. Gladys Hearns, Testimony to the Truth and Reconciliation Commission of Canada; 01-MB-26JY10–003; Long Plain First Nation, MB; July 26, 2010 (TRC).

51. Joseph Boubard, Sagkeeng Cultural Education Centre Oral History Project, August 5, 1987, C1623 (AOM).

52. Leo Morrisseau, whose story appears in C. C. Fontaine, *Speaking of Sagkeeng*, 58–61.

53. Inspector B. Warkentin to R. A. Hoey, Superintendent of Wlfare and Training, Department of Indian Affairs, June 23, 1942, RG 10, Volume 8448, File 506/23–5-019 (LAC).

54. Reverend Joseph B. Blanchin and Reverend F. Beys, outline of resolutions of a

1924 convention of Indian Catholic school principals, RG10, Volume 6041, File 160–5, part 1 (LAC).

55. Foucault, *Discipline and Punish*, 211.

56. In the U.S. context, Indigenous groups were often viewed to fall into two camps, progressives and traditionalists. Progressives were those willing to embrace European ways, whereas traditionalists were perceived to cling irrationally to the old, Indigenous ways.

57. Circular from Superintendent of Indian Schools W. H. Hailman, to U.S. Indian Agents, November 8, 1897, Bureau of Indian Affairs RG 75, Northern Pueblos Agency, General Correspondence and Reports 1877–1934, Box 6, Folder 124 (NARA).

58. Questionnaire on seniors completed by Eulalia Abeita, March 23, 1939, Bureau of Indian Affairs RG 75, Albuquerque Indian School Student Case Files, Box 1 (NARA).

59. Adams, *Education for Extinction*; Margolis, "Looking at Discipline, Looking at Labour."

60. Clemente Vigil, Doris Duke American Indian Oral History Collection, 1968–72, Tape 753, interviewed November 20, 1970 (AIOHC-CSWR).

61. 1962–63 Regular Academic Program, AIS, newspaper clippings from University New Mexico stacks (CSWR-NC).

62. Milloy, *A National Crime*, 35–36.

63. Truth and Reconciliation Commission of Canada, Fort Alexander Public Event, October 2, 2012 (TRC).

64. On dirt, cleanliness, exclusion, and civilization, see Douglas, *Purity and Danger*; Elias, *The Civilizing Process*.

65. Hoxie, *The Final Promise*.

66. Hoxie, *The Final Promise*.

67. Inspector Eldon Simms's report on PLPIRS, November 11, 1943, RG 10, Roll 13800, Volume 8449, File 511/23–5-017 (LAC).

68. Miller, *Shingwauk's Vision*, 252. Phil Fontaine, "We Are All Born Innocent," reports that, when he arrived at FAIRS in 1951, students were no longer required to work for half a day and instead spent their entire day in the classroom.

69. Reel, *Report of the Superintendent of Indian Schools*, 1901, 13.

70. 1913 Annual Report, SFIS, M1011, Superintendents' Annual Narrative and Statistical Reports from Field Jurisdictions of the Bureau of Indian Affairs, 1907–38 (NARA).

71. Hoxie, *The Final Promise*.

72. 1914 Annual Report, AIS, M1011, Superintendents' Annual Narrative and Statistical Reports from Field Jurisdictions of the Bureau of Indian Affairs, 1907–38 (NARA).

73. 1917 Annual Report, AIS, M1011, Superintendents' Annual Narrative and Statistical Reports from Field Jurisdictions of the Bureau of Indian Affairs, 1907–38 (NARA).

74. Hyer, *One House, One Voice, One Heart.*

75. Katherine Augustine, "I Can Tell You, Boarding School Was Bad," *abq Tribune*, July 18, 2002, C2.

76. 1910 Annual Report, AIS, M1011, Superintendents' Annual Narrative and Statistical Reports from Field Jurisdictions of the Bureau of Indian Affairs, 1907–38 (NARA).

77. Rosalie Archuleta and Virginia Montoya to Superintendent J. D. DeHuff, SFIS, August 11, 1918, Bureau of Indian Affairs RG 75, Santa Fe Indian School, Student School Folders 1910–34, Abbious to Augustine, Entry 47, Archuleta, Rosalie (NARA).

78. Superintendent J. D. DeHuff, SFIS, to Rosalie Archulet and Virginia Montoya, August 22, 1918, Bureau of Indian Affairs RG 75, Santa Fe Indian School, Student School Folders 1910–34, Abbious to Augustine, Entry 47, Archuleta, Rosalie (NARA).

79. Superintendent J. D. DeHuff, SFIS, to Mrs. Ben L. White, August 7, 1918, Bureau of Indian Affairs RG 75, Student School Folders 1910–34, Santa Fe Indian School, Abbious to Augustine, Entry 47, Archuleta, Rosalie (NARA).

80. See Whalen, "Finding the Balance," for examples of students who appreciated the opportunity to work and earn small amounts of income in tough economic times.

81. Foucault, *Discipline and Punish*, 180.

82. Beenash Jafri, "Desire, Settler Colonialism, and the Racialized Cowboy," 78, correctly notes that settler colonialism is a "project of desire" and how settlerhood can be presented as an object of desire through which colonial power relations are sustained. This was certainly the case in Indigenous boarding schools.

83. Reel, *Report of the Superintendent of Indian Schools, 1904*, 22.

84. The Board of Indian Commissioners was a body formed by Commissioner of Indian Affairs Ely S. Parker in 1869. The board was comprised of unpaid, independent members who were all wealthy philanthropists engaged in discussions on the Indian Problem and whose specific task was to provide oversight for Indian Affairs. See Bolt, *American Indian Policy and American Reform.*

85. Quoted in Adams, *Education for Extinction*, 23.

86. Jerome Brody, Zia Pueblo, started at SFIS in 1916, Doris Duke American Indian Oral History Collection, 1968–72, Tape 24, interviewed April 5, 1968 (AIOHC-CSWR).

87. Lillian Kennedy, Truth and Reconciliation Commission of Canada; 2011–2563; Bloodvein, Manitoba; January 25, 2012 (TRC).

88. Fear-Segal, *White Man's Club*, 20.

89. Adams, *Education for Extinction*.

90. Anonymous, Doris Duke American Indian Oral History Collection, 1968–72, Tape 446, interviewed December 4, 1970 (AIOHC-CSWR).

91. Mr. Warner, Navajo (Diné), Doris Duke American Indian Oral History Collection, 1968–72 (MSS 314 BC), Tape 298, interviewed August 1969 (AIOHC-CSWR).

92. See Trafzer et al., *Boarding School Blues*.

93. See Adams, "Beyond Bleakness."

94. Mrs. Walter K. Marmon, Doris Duke American Indian Oral History Collection, 1968–72 (MSS 314 BC), Tape 514, interviewed August 19, 1967 (AIOHC-CSWR).

95. Jemez interviewee quoted in Hyer, *One House, One Voice, One Heart*, 11.

96. Thompson, *The Navajos' Long Walk for Education*, 16.

97. Quoted in Adams, *Education for Extinction*, 177.

98. 1910 Annual Report, AIS, M1011, Superintendents' Annual Narrative and Statistical Reports from Field Jurisdictions of the Bureau of Indian Affairs, 1907–38 (NARA).

99. Hyer, *One House, One Voice, One Heart*.

100. For example, see Adams, *Education for Extinction*.

101. Ray Yazzie, Doris Duke American Indian Oral History Collection, 1968–72 (MSS 314 BC), Tape 199, Interviewed October 24, 1968 (AIOHC-CSWR).

102. Frank Tenorio, San Felipe, interviewed March 5–7, 1986, SFIS: First 100 Years, attended AIS from 1933 to 1939 (CSWR-SFIS100).

103. Principal A. C. Huston, PLPIRS, to J. Waite, Indian Agent, February 4, 1946, RG 10, Volume 6274, File 583–5, part 8 (LAC).

104. Leo Morrisseau, whose story appears in C. C. Fontaine, *Speaking of Sagkeeng*, 58–61.

105. Charles Courchene, whose story appears in C. C. Fontaine, *Speaking of Sagkeeng*, 11–16.

106. For example, on ritual in the Durieau system, see Miller, *Shingwauk's Vision*.

107. See Paxton, "Learning Gender."

108. J. R. Bunn, Inspector of Indian Agencies, to Deputy Superintendent General of Indian Affairs, 1914, RG 10, Volume 8448, File 506/23–5–019 (LAC).

109. 1910 Annual Report, SFIS, M1011, Superintendents' Annual Narrative and Statistical Reports from Field Jurisdictions of the Bureau of Indian Affairs, 1907–38 (NARA).

110. Weisiger, *Dreaming of Sheep in Navajo Country*.

111. Weisiger, *Dreaming of Sheep in Navajo Country*.

112. Edward Charles Bruyere, whose story appears in C. C. Fontaine, *Speaking of Sagkeeng*, 1–3.

113. 1910 Annual Report, SFIS, M1011, Superintendents' Annual Narrative and Statistical Reports from Field Jurisdictions of the Bureau of Indian Affairs, 1907–38 (NARA).

114. See Jacobs, *White Mother to a Dark Race*.

115. Cato Sells, Circular No. 992, "Duties of Field Matrons," Department of the Interior, OIS, May 29, 1915, Bureau of Indian Affairs RG 75, Albuquerque Indian School, General Correspondence Files, 1917–36, 001–003, Entry 29, Box 36, File 827 (NARA).

116. Cato Sells, Circular No. 992, "Duties of Field Matrons," Department of the Interior, OIS, May 29, 1915, Bureau of Indian Affairs RG 75, Albuquerque Indian School, General Correspondence Files, 1917–36, 001–003, Entry 29, Box 36, File 827 (NARA).

117. Jacobs, *White Mother to a Dark Race*; see also the work of Haskins, *Matrons and Maids*, on the "outing" matrons in Tucson, who were responsible for ensuring that Indian girls adopted proper gender dispositions while taking part in the outing program.

118. Lomawaima, *They Called It Prairie Light*.

119. Lomawaima, *They Called It Prairie Light*; see also Lomawaima, "Domesticity in the Federal Indian Schools."

120. See Jacobs, *Engendered Encounters*.

121. Acting Commissioner C. F. Larrabee, Office of Indian Affairs, to Superintendent Crandall, SFIS, June 20, 1907, Bureau of Indian Affairs RG 75, Northern Pueblos Agency, General Correspondence and Reports 1877–1934, Box 14, Folder 263 (NARA).

122. Albuquerque Indian School, 1962–63, Regular Academic Program (Guide), Center for Southwest Research (CSWR), Regular Stacks, Albuquerque.

123. Lomawaima, *They Called It Prairie Light*, 82.

124. John David DeHuff Diary, MS 99 BC (EWDFP-CSWR).

125. Form for those seeking to hire an Indian girl for housekeeping work, AIS, used in 1931, found in the student file of Abenita Abeita, Isleta Pueblo, Bureau of Indian Affairs RG 75, Albuquerque Indian School, Student Case Files, Box 1 (NARA).

126. The Catholic Hierarchy of Canada to Special Joint Committee of the Senate and House of Commons Appointed to Examine and Consider *the Indian Act*, RG 29, Volume 3388, File 804–1–7, part 1 (LAC).

127. Principal Reverend L. Jalbert, omi, FAIRS, to E. Daggitt, Superintendent, Clandeboye Agency, RG 10, Volume 10386, File 506/25–2, part 4B (LAC).

128. Superintendent J. D. DeHuff to Superintendent Crandall, Department of the Interior, January 15, 1924, Bureau of Indian Affairs RG 75, Northern Pueblos Agency, General Correspondence and Reports 1877–1934, Box 23, Folder 424 (NARA).

129. Truth and Reconciliation Commission of Canada; Long Plain; July 27, 2010.

6. KNOWLEDGE AND VIOLENCE

1. Foucault, *Power/Knowledge*.

2. 1918 Record of Pupil in School, Teresita Abeita, Bureau of Indian Affairs RG 75, Santa Fe Indian School, Student School Folders 1910–34, Abbious to Augustine, Entry 47, Archuleta, Rosalie (NARA).

3. 1931 Application for Admission to Nonreservation School and Test of Eligibility for Joseph Begay, Bureau of Indian Affairs RG 75, Albuquerque Indian School, Students Case Files, Box 1 (NARA).

4. Fear-Segal, *White Man's Club*.

5. Reel, *Report of the Superintendent of Indian Schools*, 1901, 11; see also Adams, *Education for Extinction*.

6. 1925 Annual Report, SFIS, M1011, Superintendents' Annual Narrative and Statistical Reports from Field Jurisdictions of the Bureau of Indian Affairs, 1907–38 (NARA).

7. Circular No. 2381, Commissioner Burke to Superintendents of All Schools, December 4, 1926, Bureau of Indian Affairs RG 75, Albuquerque Indian School, General Correspondence Files, 1917–36, 001–003, Entry 29, Box 36, File 828 (NARA).

8. Weisiger, *Dreaming of Sheep in Navajo Country*.

9. Dis-chie-ne Benally, Doris Duke American Indian Oral History Collection, 1968–72 (MSS 314 BC), Tape 177, interviewed November 1968 (AIOHC-CSWR).

10. Department of the Interior, June 14, 1921, Amendment #1 to Regulations Concerning Enrollment and Attendance of Indian Children in School, Pursuant to the *Act* of February 14, 1920, Bureau of Indian Affairs RG 75, Albuquerque Indian School, General Correspondence Files, 1917–36, 001–003, Entry 29, Box 34, File 801 (NARA).

11. Reel, *Report of the Superintendent of Indian Schools*, 1904, 10.

12. Russell T. Ferrier, Superintendent of Indian Education, to Principals of Indian Residential Schools, October 19, 1923, RG 10, Volume 6001, File 1–1–11, part 2, Headquarters—Schools—General, 1904–28 (LAC).

13. Inspector B. Warkentin's report on FAIRS, June 28, 1943, RG 10, Volume 8448, File 506/23–5–019 (LAC).

14. Inspector B. Warkentin's report on FAIRS, June 28, 1943, RG 10, Volume 8448, File 506/23–5–019 (LAC).

15. James, "Rhetoric and Resistance."

16. James, "Rhetoric and Resistance."

17. James, "Rhetoric and Resistance," 613.

18. James, "Rhetoric and Resistance."

19. For example, Holocaust survivors rarely discussed their experiences in the concentration camps prior to the late 1950s, when the first memoirs of the camps began to appear. See Novick, *The Holocaust in American Life.*

20. See *Begay v. United States* (Begay 1), 219 Ct. Cl. 599 (1979).

21. Quoted in Adams, *Education for Extinction*, 121.

22. Use of the guardhouse was not prohibited for American boarding schools until 1927. Bolt, *American Indian Policy and American Reform*, 223.

23. Superintendent S. M. Cart to Commissioner of Indian Affairs, April 10, 1891, RG 75.20.36, Reel M1473, Roll 1, v. 1–2, Bureau of Indian Affairs RG 75, Records Created at Santa Fe Indian School, Press Copies of Miscellaneous Letters Sent (SAL).

24. Beccaria, *On Crimes and Punishments and Other Writings.*

25. Wright, "Discipline in an Indian School," 85.

26. Dorchester, *Report of the U.S. Superintendent of Indian Schools 1891*, 11.

27. John David DeHuff Diary, MS 99 BC (EWDFP-CSWR).

28. 1929 Annual Report, AIS, M1011, Superintendents' Annual Narrative and Statistical Reports from Field Jurisdictions of the Bureau of Indian Affairs, 1907–38 (NARA).

29. Letter from Secretary Ickes on Indian school discipline, August 16, 1934, John Collier Papers, MF Archives Division, State Records Center, Santa Fe (SAL).

30. Dorothy Roman, Jemez, Doris Duke American Indian Oral History Collection, 1968–72, Tape 34, interviewed April 4, 1968 (AOIHC-CSWR).

31. Miller, *Shingwauk's Vision.*

32. The exception here is Superintendent Bernard Neary's advice that punishment be delivered like "a kind, firm and judicious parent in his family" noted in chapter 4 in relation to Annie Assiniboine, Rowena Smoke, and other students who ran away. See Bernard Neary, Superintendent of Indian Education, to Inspector A. C. Hamilton, February 25, 1949, RG 10, Volume 6275, File 583–10, part 2 (LAC).

33. Purvis H. Fontaine, Truth and Reconciliation Commission of Canada; 02-MB-16JUI0–150; Winnipeg, MB; June 16, 2010 (TRC).

34. Truth and Reconciliation Commission of Canada; Long Plain First Nation, Manitoba; July 27, 2010 (TRC).

35. See also other pieces of testimony recorded in C. C. Fontaine, *Speaking of Sagkeeng.*

36. See also Archibald, *Decolonization and Healing Indigenous Experiences in the United States, New Zealand, Australia, and Greenland,* viii.

37. Truth and Reconciliation Commission of Canada; 01-SK-18AU10–003; First Nations University, Regina, SK; August 18, 2010 (TRC).

38. Adams, *Education for Extinction.*

39. Cook, "What's in a Name."

40. Hyer, *One House, One Voice, One Heart;* Gram, "Education on the Edge of Empire."

41. Commissioner H. Price to Pedro Sanchez, U.S. Indian Agent, New Mexico, June 27, 1883, Bureau of Indian Affairs RG 75, Northern Pueblos Agency, General Correspondence and Reports, 1877–1934, Box 5, Folder 102 (NARA).

42. 1928 Annual Report, AIS, M1011, Superintendents' Annual Narrative and Statistical Reports from Field Jurisdictions of the Bureau of Indian Affairs, 1907–38 (NARA).

43. 1928 Annual Report, SFIS, M1011, Superintendents' Annual Narrative and Statistical Reports from Field Jurisdictions of the Bureau of Indian Affairs, 1907–38 (NARA).

44. Mr. Baca (Laguna), Doris Duke American Indian Oral History Collection, 1968–72 (MSS 314 BC), Tape 650, interviewed July 1970 (AOIHC-CSWR).

45. Angela Marie Bruyere, Sagkeeng Cultural Education Centre Oral History Project, interviewed July 16, 1987, C1614 (AOM).

46. Truth and Reconciliation Commission of Canada; Brandon, Manitoba; October 11, 2011 (TRC).

47. Truth and Reconciliation Commission of Canada; Winnipeg, Manitoba; July 5, 2011 (TRC).

48. Eva Harriet Woodford, Truth and Reconciliation Commission of Canada; 02-MB-16JU10–068; Winnipeg, Manitoba; June 16, 2010 (TRC).

49. Eva Harriet Woodford, Truth and Reconciliation Commission of Canada; 02-MB-16JU10–068; Winnipeg, Manitoba; June 16, 2010 (TRC).

50. My thanks to Margaret D. Jacobs for reminding me of this point. See also McBeth, *Ethnic Identity and the Boarding School Experience of West-Central Oklahoma Indians;* Tennant, *Aboriginal Peoples and Politics.* The language of "walking in two worlds" and "code switching" comes from my interviews with Indigenous leaders as part of a research project on inner-city social services in Winnipeg. See Woolford and Curran, "Community Positions, Neoliberal Dispositions"; Woolford and Curran, "Limited Autonomy, Neoliberal Domination, and Ethical Distancing in the Social Services."

51. By introducing "symbolic violence" in this manner, the analysis shifts from Foucault's conceptual universe back into Bourdieu's. This is because, overall, the underlying theoretical framework of this book is more influenced by Bourdieu than it is by Foucault, though it is difficult for a critical scholar of my generation not to be influenced by Foucault's theoretical corpus. Given their mutual interest in power and domination, the two scholars are not entirely incompatible, especially in observation of the ways in which power operates within social contexts.

52. Bourdieu, *The Logic of Practice*, 127.

53. Bourdieu, *Language and Symbolic Power*.

54. For an exception to this tendency, see Smith, "The 'Policy of Aggressive Civilization' and Projects of Governance in Roman Catholic Industrial Schools for Native Peoples in Canada, 1870–95."

55. Tony Davis, "Indian Leader Loves, Respects Boarding Schools," *abq Tribune*, January 25, 1987, C2.

56. Dorchester, *Report of the U.S. Superintendent of Indian Schools 1891*, 12.

57. See, for example, Chrisjohn and Young, *The Circle Game*, 84–88.

58. Adams, *Education for Extinction*, 154.

59. Quoted in Adams, *Education for Extinction*, 157.

60. See Byler, "The Destruction of American Indian Families."

61. Quoted in Royal Commission on Aboriginal Peoples, *Report of the Royal Commission on Aboriginal Peoples*, 314.

62. Truth and Reconciliation Commission of Canada; Beausejour, Manitoba; April 10, 2010 (TRC).

63. Tony Lucero, Doris Duke American Indian Oral History Collection, 1968–72 (MSS 314 BC), Tape 112, interviewed April 4, 1968 (AOIHC-CSWR).

64. Truth and Reconciliation Commission of Canada; Winnipeg, Manitoba; July 5, 2011 (TRC).

65. Vincent Pierre, Truth and Reconciliation Commission of Canada; 02-MB-18JU10–002; Winnipeg, Manitoba; June 18, 2010 (TRC).

66. Fontaine, *Broken Circle*, 20.

67. Fontaine, *Broken Circle*, 30.

68. John, who attended three schools between 1955 and 1959, quoted in Dalseg, "In Their Own Words," 76–77.

69. Norman Twoheart, Truth and Reconciliation Commission of Canada; 2011–2656; Winnipeg, MB; January 18, 2012 (TRC).

70. Madeline Smith, Truth and Reconciliation Commission of Canada; 02-MB-17JU10–074; Winnipeg, Manitoba; June 17, 2010 (TRC).

71. Marcel Courchene, whose story appears in C. C. Fontaine, *Speaking of Sagkeeng*, 22–30.

72. Chief Lawrence Morrisseau, whose story appears in C. C. Fontaine, *Speaking of Sagkeeng*, 51–57.

73. Muriel Katherine Morrisseau, Truth and Reconciliation Commission of Canada; 02-MB-18JU10–057; The Forks, Winnipeg, Manitoba; June 18, 2010 (TRC).

74. Andrea Benally, Doris Duke American Indian Oral History Collection, 1968–72, Tape 189, interviewed August 1968 (AIOHC-CSWR).

75. Weisiger, *Dreaming of Sheep in Navajo Country*.

76. Margolis, "Looking at Discipline, Looking at Labour." Margolis notes in his overview of boarding school photographs that very few of the images represent individual accomplishment; instead, the images almost universally depict the Indigenous young person's resocialization into new forms of group life (e.g., military).

77. For further discussion of maternalism within assimilative institutions, see Jacobs, *White Mother to a Dark Race*, chapter 7.

78. Cahill, *Federal Mothers and Fathers*; Stoler, *Carnal Knowledge and Imperial Power*; see also Jacobs, *Engendered Encounters*.

79. Philena E. Johnson, a superintendent in the Indian school system, quoted in Child, *Boarding School Seasons*, 79.

80. Cahill, *Federal Mothers and Fathers*; Jacobs, *White Mother to a Dark Race*.

81. Ahern, "An Experiment Aborted."

82. William N. Hailman, Superintendent of Indian Schools, 1894, quoted in Ahern, "An Experiment Aborted", 271.

83. Ahern, "An Experiment Aborted."

84. Cahill, *Federal Mothers and Fathers*; Jacobs, *Engendered Encounters*.

85. Fontaine, *Broken Circle*, 132. Experiences of resocialization are also noted in memoirs from survivors of other Canadian boarding schools. As Mary Fortier, *Behind Closed Doors*, 56, writes, "that first night in bed, I realized my individuality had been taken from me. My name was replaced with a number. My personal clothing was replaced with a uniform. My siblings were exchanged for a group of strange girls. My home was replaced by this strict cold setting. A cold nun replaced my mother's loving warmth."

86. Santanita Lefthand (Taos), interviewed May 28, 1986, SFIS: The First Hundred Years, attended 1919–24 (CSWR-SFIS100).

87. Bineziikwe, "Surviving the Storm," 12.

88. Lomawaima, *They Called It Prairie Light*.

89. Gram, "Education on the Edge of Empire."

90. Truth and Reconciliation Commission of Canada; Long Plain, Manitoba; July 27, 2010 (TRC).

91. Adams, *Education for Extinction*.

92. Albuquerque Indian School to Christian Hour, Omaha, Nebraska, July 2, 1886, Richard W. D. Bryan Family Papers 1844–1939, MSS 1BC, Box 2 (BFP-CSWR).

93. See, for example, the 1927 yearbook *The Powwow*, AIS RG 75, Records of the Bureau of Indian Affairs, Albuquerque Indian School, General Correspondence Files, 1917–36, 001–003, Entry 29, Box 3, File 041.3 (NARA).

94. de Leeuw, "'If Anything Is to Be Done with the Indian, We Must Catch Him Very Young.'"

95. See Foucault, *The History of Sexuality*, 95: "Where there is power, there is resistance and yet this resistance is never in a position of exteriority in relation to power."

96. See also Scott, *Thinking like a State*.

97. Truth and Reconciliation Commission of Canada, Fort Alexander Public Event, October 2, 2012 (TRC).

98. Truth and Reconciliation Commission of Canada, Fort Alexander Public Event, October 3, 2012 (TRC).

7. LOCAL ACTORS AND ASSIMILATION

1. See, for example, Basso, *Wisdom Sits in Places*; Hubbard, "'Kill, Skin, and Sell.'" This chapter borrows from Actor-Network Theory approaches but is unlikely to fully satisfy the strongest proponents of this perspective. See, for example, Law, "Actor Network Theory and Material Semiotics." Among other divergences, the actor-networks described in this chapter, which form around specific Indigenous boarding schools, are located in a broader Bourdieuian context of power and domination rather than viewed as an instance of fluidity and pure mutability. In this chapter, the Indian Problem is understood as an effort to bring into being a network of destruction to eliminate indigeneities, but the variability of local networks, borrowed from an ANT approach, provides a descriptive means to show how such destructive networks advance or fail to take shape.

2. Verdeja, "On Situating the Study of Genocide within Political Violence," 85.

3. Bischoping and Fingerhut, "Border Lines."

4. Tim Cole, *Holocaust City*, 17, 18, reminds us that destruction, in his case the Holocaust, is "implemented through space" and that "space is not simply passive but active." Space, however, is not simply material but also the product of social constructions and representations. In this manner, relations between humans and their spaces (or places, when one is speaking more of their representation or constructed status) are sets of ongoing, co-constitutive interactions. For

the sake of not bogging the manuscript down in the technical terminology of social geography, my focus is primarily on space in its material form as well as on competitions to assign meaning or "place" to these material relations. For a more theoretically driven approach to these issues, see, for example, de Leeuw, "'If Anything Is to Be Done with the Indian, We Must Catch Him Very Young'"; de Leeuw, "Intimate Colonialisms."

5. Lawrence, *Lessons from an Indian Day School*, 18.

6. Truth and Reconciliation Commission of Canada, *They Came for the Children*, 18.

7. de Leeuw, "'If Anything Is to Be Done with the Indian, We Must Catch Him Very Young'"; de Leeuw, "Intimate Colonialisms"; Smith, "The 'Policy of Aggressive Civilization' and Projects of Governance in Roman Catholic Industrial Schools for Native Peoples in Canada, 1870–95."

8. See Jacobs, *White Mother to a Dark Race*, 243–52, for a discussion on the "new sensory regime" faced by children when they entered assimilative schooling institutions.

9. Upton Ethelbah (Apache), interviewed June 24, 1987, SFIS: The First Hundred Years (CSWR-SFISIOO).

10. Muriel Katherine Morrisseau, Truth and Reconciliation Commission of Canada; 02-MB-18JUI0–057; Winnipeg, Manitoba; June 18, 2010 (TRC).

11. Vincent Pierre, Truth and Reconciliation Commission of Canada; 02-MB-18JUI0–004–002; Winnipeg, Manitoba; June 18, 2010 (TRC).

12. Hyer, *One House, One Voice, One Heart*, 5.

13. de Leeuw, "Intimate Colonialisms"; Fear-Segal, *White Man's Club*.

14. Inspector's Report on PLPIRS by A. O. Hamilton, January 21, 1937, RG 10, Roll 13800, Volume 8449, File 511/23–5–017 (LAC). For an example of overcrowding at U.S. schools, see A. C. Tommer, Acting Commissioner, Office of Indian Affairs, to Superintendent of SFIS, October 22, 1904, Bureau of Indian Affairs, RG 75, Northern Pueblos Agency, General Correspondence and Reports, 1877–1934, Box 14, Folder 263 (NARA).

15. E. F. Simms to Indian Affairs Branch, Department of Mines and Resources, Re: Overcrowding in Portage la Prairie Indian Residential School, November 19, 1949, RG 10, Roll 13800, Volume 8449, File 511/23–5–017 (LAC).

16. See Sofsky, *The Order of Terror*.

17. My thanks to one of my anonymous readers for pushing me toward this point.

18. And not only a geography of exclusion. See McFarlane, "Educating First-Nation Children in Canada," for application to residential schools of David Sibley's notion of "geographies of exclusion" and Scott Pile's, as well as James Scott's, work on the spatial dimensions of resistance. See also Pile,

"Introduction"; Scott, *Domination and the Arts of Resistance* ; Sibley, *Geographies of Exclusion*.

19. Gram, "Education on the Edge of Empire"; McKinney, "History of the Albuquerque Indian School."

20. Sando, *The Pueblo Indians*.

21. Bryan, quoted in McKinney, "History of the Albuquerque Indian School," 11.

22. *Sunday Post*, n.d., Richard W. D. Bryan Family Papers 1844–1939, MSS IBC, Box 2 (BFP-CSWR).

23. Gram, "Education on the Edge of Empire"; Jacobs, *White Mother to a Dark Race*.

24. Quoted in Lawrence, *Lessons from an Indian Day School*, 54.

25. See, for example, the AIS Annual Reports from the 1920s, M1011, Superintendents' Annual Narrative and Statistical Reports from Field Jurisdictions of the Bureau of Indian Affairs, 1907–38 (NARA).

26. Johnson, *Navajo Stories of the Long Walk Period*.

27. Rex Becenti, Jr., Doris Duke American Indian Oral History Collection, 1968–72 (MSS 314 BC), Tape 363, interviewed December 1969 (AIOHC-CSWR).

28. U.S.-Navajo Treaty, 1868, http://reta.nmsu.edu/modules/longwalk/lesson /document/treaty.htm#article1.

29. Superintendent S. M. Cart, SFIS, to Commissioner of Indian Affairs, April 1, 1891, RG 75.20.36, Reel M1473, Roll 1, v. 1–2, Bureau of Indian Affairs RG 75, Records Created at Santa Fe Indian School, Press Copies of Miscellaneous Letters Sent (SAL).

30. Jacobs, "A Battle for the Children."

31. Quoted in DeJong, *Promises of the Past*, 118.

32. Quoted in DeJong, *Promises of the Past*, 118.

33. Metcalf, "The Effects of Boarding School on Navajo Self-Image and Maternal Behavior."

34. It is important to avoid contributing to the stereotype that the Navajo were simply latecomers to and nomadic cultural borrowers within this region. As Jennifer Denetdale, *Reclaiming Diné History*, chapter 2, notes, such stereotypes have served the purpose of further subjugating Navajo peoples to settler colonialism and have ignored Navajo understandings of their history.

35. House, *Language Shift among the Navajos*; Weisiger, *Dreaming of Sheep in Navajo Country*.

36. Weisiger, *Dreaming of Sheep in Navajo Country*.

37. Claims were made about Navajo overgrazing in their territory, though these accusations have been questioned by Richard White, *The Roots of Dependency*, 231, who shows the interests of American capitalism at work in the forced livestock reductions: "The crisis the Navajos faced was not the result so much of a

pronounced increase in livestock, as of a decrease in grazing land that stemmed from Anglo cattlemen's successfully restricting Navajo access to traditional off-reservation ranges." For further discussion, see Parman, *The Navajos and the New Deal*; Roessel and Johnson, *Livestock Reduction*; Weisiger, *Dreaming of Sheep in Navajo Country*.

38. It is worth noting, as Weisiger does in *Dreaming of Sheep in Navajo Country*, 66, that the Navajo experienced the sheep cull as "an assault on . . . [their] sense of peoplehood." As such, we see here also that nonhuman group allies, such as sheep, can be understood as fundamental to group existence and thereby co-constitutive of the group. This is how many Diné "experienced stock reduction as genocidal" (70). See also Hubbard, "'Kill, Skin, and Sell.'"

39. James, "Rhetoric and Resistance."

40. 1912 AIS Annual Report, Section III Schools, M1011, Superintendents' Annual Narrative and Statistical Reports from Field Jurisdictions of the Bureau of Indian Affairs, 1907–38 (NARA).

41. House, *Language Shift among the Navajos*.

42. It also helped after 1920 that the Indian Act was amended to clearly define denominational proprietorship over specific Indigenous children, lessening the degree of competition among churches and preventing Indigenous groups from playing one church against another.

43. W. M. Graham, Indian Commissioner, to D. C. Scott, Deputy Superintendent General, January 29, 1929, RG 10, Volume 6273, File 583–5, part 4 (LAC).

44. Child, *Boarding School Seasons*, 27.

45. Fontaine, *Broken Circle*, 11.

46. Fontaine, *Broken Circle*, 91.

47. Truth and Reconciliation Commission of Canada; Long Plain, Manitoba; July 27 (TRC).

48. Report on FAIRS by Inspector J. R. Bunn, submitted to Deputy Superintendent D. C. Scott, May 18, 1917, RG 10, Volume 8448, File 506/23–5-019 (LAC).

49. Mary Courchene, Truth and Reconciliation Commission of Canada; 2011–2515; Pine Creek First Nation, Manitoba; November 28, 2011 (TRC).

50. Truth and Reconciliation Commission of Canada; Brandon, Manitoba; October 11, 2011 (TRC).

51. Truth and Reconciliation Commission of Canada; Long Plain First Nation, Manitoba; July 28, 2010 (TRC).

52. Purvis H. Fontaine, Truth and Reconciliation Commission of Canada; 02-MB-16JU10–150; Winnipeg, Manitoba; June 16 ,2010 (TRC).

53. Adams, *Education for Extinction*.

54. Hyer, *One House, One Voice, One Heart*, 8.

55. Wolfe, "Settler Colonialism and the Elimination of the Native," 388.

56. Rex Becenti, Jr., Doris Duke American Indian Oral History Collection, 1968–72 (MSS 314 BC), Tape 363, interviewed December 1969 (AIOHC-CSWR).

57. See Ratliff, "The Necessity of Teaching the Indian Boy to Improve the Allotment the Government Has Given Him."

58. 1911 Annual Report, AIS, M1011, Superintendents' Annual Narrative and Statistical Reports from Field Jurisdictions of the Bureau of Indian Affairs, 1907–38 (NARA).

59. Movement is a fundamental aspect of Diné culture. Ethnographer Gary Witherspoon, *Language and Art in the Navajo Universe,* notes that the Dine language has over 356,000 distinct conjugations of the verb *to go.*

60. Hyer, *One House, One Voice, One Heart,* 18.

61. 1910 Annual Report, SFIS, M1011, Superintendents' Annual Narrative and Statistical Reports from Field Jurisdictions of the Bureau of Indian Affairs, 1907–38 (NARA).

62. See Scott, *Thinking like a State.* Agricultural practices were not absent among the other groups targeted by the schools under consideration. The Ojibway at Long Plain First Nation, for example, had signed onto Treaty One in part because of a verbal promise that the government would provide the group with farm implements and cattle to supplement their farming efforts in the Portage la Prairie area. The Diné also had their own traditional agricultural practices.

63. Department of Indian Affairs, Report of the Department of Indian Affairs for the Year Ended 31st December 1885, 1886, 46.

64. Valencia Garcia, Doris Duke American Indian Oral History Collection, 1968–72 (MSS 314 BC), Tape 13, interviewed April 23, 1968 (AIOHC-CSWR).

65. Hyer, *One House, One Voice, One Heart.*

66. Mary Courchene, Truth and Reconciliation Commission of Canada; 2011–2515; Pine Creek First Nation, MB; November 28, 2011 (TRC).

67. For example, Mann, *The Dark Side of Democracy;* Nichols, *Indians in the United States and Canada.*

68. Lewy, "Can There Be Genocide without the Intent to Commit Genocide?"

69. Latour, *We Have Never Been Modern.*

70. Latour, *We Have Never Been Modern.*

71. See as well the work of Russell Thornton, who points to the ways in which colonialism facilitated disease spread. Thornton, *American Indian Holocaust and Survival;* Thornton, "Native American Demographic and Tribal Survival into the Twenty-First Century." One could also look more specifically at instances in which disease was a form of "biological warfare" against Aboriginal combatants. See Fenn, "Biological Warfare in Eighteenth-Century North America." As well,

the relationship between disease and social conditions, and the degree of responsibility that might be assigned to government actors, vary depending on a broad array of historical circumstances. James Daschuk, *Clearing the Plains*, for example, notes how the fur-trade era transmission of diseases such as small pox had more to do with factors such as the patterns of global trade and the attempt by several Indigenous and non-Indigenous groups to position themselves in relation to the market for furs. In contrast, the late-nineteenth-century policies of starvation used by the Macdonald government to pacify Indigenous peoples on the Canadian plains can be more clearly linked to the spread of ailments such as tuberculosis.

72. In Canada, see, for example, Burnett, "Building the System"; Daschuk, *Clearing the Plains*; Kelm, *Colonizing Bodies*; Lux, *Medicine that Walks*.

73. Lewy, "Can There Be Genocide without the Intent to Commit Genocide?" is most egregious on this score.

74. DeJong, "'Unless They Are Kept Alive.'"

75. Lawrence, *Lessons from an Indian Day School*. The same was true in Canada, where medical examinations prior to admission were often forgone in the early days of boarding schools (late eighteenth century to early nineteenth century), since the competition for students and per capita funding often outweighed concerns about the health of the student population. See, for example, Sproule-Jones, "Crusading for the Forgotten," 210.

76. Greenfield, "Escape from Albuquerque"; McKinney, "History of the Albuquerque Indian School."

77. Greenfield, "Escape from Albuquerque."

78. Oakie James (Johnny Begay), Navajo medicine man and storyteller, Doris Duke American Indian Oral History Collection, 1968–72, Tape 391, interviewed April 1969 (AIOHC-CSWR).

79. Supervisor of Indian Schools E. H. Hammond to Superintendent J. D. DeHuff, Northern Pueblos Agency, Bureau of Indian Affairs RG 75, Northern Pueblos Agency, General Correspondence and Reports 1877–1934, Box 23, Folder 424 (NARA).

80. Superintendent J. D. DeHuff, SFIS, to Jacob T. Wright, Superintendent, Jicarilla Indian School, January 4, 1917, Bureau of Indian Affairs RG 75, Santa Fe Indian School, Student School Folders, 1910–34, Anna De Jesus Folder (NARA).

81. Superintendent J. D. DeHuff, SFIS, to Commissioner of Indian Affairs, February 25, 1920, Bureau of Indian Affairs RG 75, Santa Fe Indian School, Student School Folders, 1910–34, Anna De Jesus Folder (NARA).

82. C. E. Faris, Superintendent, Jicarilla Agency, to Superintendent J. D. DeHuff, SFIS, February 17, 1920, Bureau of Indian Affairs RG 75, Santa Fe Indian School, Student School Folders, 1910–34, Anna De Jesus Folder (NARA).

83. Superintendent H. Marble to Santana Aguilar, September 11, 1922, Bureau of Indian Affairs RG 75, Albuquerque Indian School, Student Case Files, Box 1 (NARA).

84. Superintendent J. D. DeHuff to Miss Lupe Armijo, August 30, 1923, Bureau of Indian Affairs RG 75, Albuquerque Indian School, Student Case Files, Box 1 (NARA).

85. Quoted in Miller, *Shingwauk's Vision*, 133. The Truth and Reconciliation Commission estimates 6000 children perished in or soon after leaving the schools.

86. Milloy, *A National Crime*, 101.

87. Bryce, *Report on the Indian Schools of Manitoba and the Northwest Territories*, 19. Initially, Bryce was not overly critical of the idea of residential schooling or of the missionary societies responsible for administering the schools. In his early historical overview of residential schooling, he wrote approvingly of the efforts to transform Indigenous "savages" into "civilized" persons: "Restrained through diplomacy, force and the interests of trade by the great fur-trading companies, the widely distributed and wandering bands of Indians would still have been savages, had it not been for the heroic devotion of those missionaries who, attaching themselves to some band, moved with it in its wanderings, or travelled from post to post where the Indians were assembled while bartering their furs" (6).

88. Sproule-Jones, "Crusading for the Forgotten." For more on Bryce, see also Kelm, *Colonizing Bodies*, chapters 4 and 6.

89. Milloy, *A National Crime*.

90. Bryce, *The Story of a National Crime*, 4.

91. Bryce, *The Story of a National Crime*, 14.

92. In relation to this point, scholars might be tempted to examine boarding schools in light of Giorgio Agamben's concept of *homo sacer* in *Homo Sacer*. However, the direction of movement differs in the Indigenous boarding school from that of Agamben's "camp." Whereas the camp takes the human and transforms it toward bare life, in the school the staff assume that the Indigenous person already inhabits a state of bare life, and the goal is thus to transform him or her toward the human.

93. Sproule-Jones, "Crusading for the Forgotten."

94. Quoted in DeJong, "'Unless They Are Kept Alive,'" 256.

95. DeJong, "'Unless They Are Kept Alive,'" 256.

96. DeJong, "'Unless They Are Kept Alive,'" 256.

97. Adams, *Education for Extinction*.

98. On a similar process in British Columbia, see Kelm, *Colonizing Bodies*, especially chapter 6.

99. C. Gorman, Doris Duke American Indian Oral History Collection, 1968–72 (MSS 314 BC), Tape 268B, interviewed April 1969 (AIOHC-CSWR).

100. See Kelm, *Colonizing Bodies.*

101. Circular No. 2117, Department of the Interior, Office of Indian Affairs to All Superintendents and Physicians, May 11, 1925, RG 75, Records of the Bureau of Indian Affairs, Albuquerque Indian School, General Correspondence Files, 1917–36, 001–003, Entry 29, Box 32, Folder 700 (NARA).

102. Present views and facts regarding tuberculosis among Indians in Manitoba, RG 29, Volume 1225, File 311-T7–16 (LAC).

103. Dr. Harold McGill, Director of Indian Affairs, to Reverend J. Plourde, Superintendant General of the Oblate Catholic Indian Missions, April 26, 1937, RG 10, Volume 6266, File 579–25, part 1 (LAC).

104. Reverend J. Plourde to Dr. Harold McGill, June 12, 1937, RG 10, Volume 6266, File 579–25, part 1 (LAC).

105. J. D. Adamson to E. L. Stone, January 5, 1939, RG 10, Volume 6266, File 579–25, part 1 (LAC).

106. P. E. Moore to E. L. Stone, March 3, 1939, RG 10, Volume 6266, File 579–25, part 1 (LAC).

107. Fontaine, *Broken Circle,* 94.

108. Truth and Reconciliation Commission, Fort Alexander Public Event, October 2, 2012 (TRC).

109. Vincent Pierre, Truth and Reconciliation Commission of Canada; 02-MB-18JU10–004–002; The Forks, Winnipeg, Manitoba; June 18, 2010 (TRC).

110. Rose Hart, Truth and Reconciliation Commission of Canada; 2011–2620; Winnipeg, Manitoba; June 25, 2011 (TRC).

111. Bineziikwe, "Surviving the Storm," 13.

112. Austin Begay, Doris Duke American Indian Oral History Collection, 1968–72, Tape 159, interviewed August 28, 1968 (AIOHC-CSWR).

113. See, for example, Deyhle, *Reflections in Place.*

114. Nichols, *Indians in the United States and Canada.*

115. Jacobs, *White Mother to a Dark Race.*

116. Superintendent Coggeshall, SFIS, to R. G. Valentine, Commissioner of Indian Affairs, April 15, 1912, Bureau of Indian Affairs RG 75, Northern Pueblos Agency, General Correspondence and Reports, 1877–1934, Box 16, Folder 308 (NARA).

117. Child, *Boarding School Seasons,* 15.

118. Annie C. Reyna, San Juan, interviewed October 10, 1986, SFIS: The First Hundred Years, attended 1933–40 (CSWR-SFIS100).

119. Kelm, "'A Scandalous Procession,'" 52.

120. Mrs. Walter K. Marmon, Doris Duke American Indian Oral History Collection, 1968–72 (MSS 314 BC), Tape 16, interviewed June 26, 1968 (AIOHC-CSWR).

121. Mosby, "Administering Colonial Science."

122. Hyer, *One House, One Voice, One Heart.*

123. Chief Albert Fontaine, whose story appears in C. C. Fontaine, *Speaking of Sagkeeng*, 31–45.

124. Superintendent Horace J. Johnson to Commissioner of Indian Affairs, September 29, 1920, Bureau of Indian Affairs RG 75, Northern Pueblos Agency, General Correspondence and Reports 1877–1934, Box 23, Folder 413 (NARA).

125. Superintendent Horace J. Johnson to Mr. H. B. Peairs, General Supervisor, Indian schools, Lawrence, ks, September 18, 1921, Bureau of Indian Affairs RG 75, Northern Pueblos Agency, General Correspondence and Reports 1877–1934, Box 23, Folder 421 (NARA).

126. Jacobs, "A Battle for the Children," 50.

127. B. E. Olson, Superintendent, Clandeboye Agency, to Colonel B. F. Neary, Superintendent of Education, March 31, 1948, RG 10, Volume 8448, File 506/23-5-019 (LAC).

128. Victoria Elaine McIntosh, Truth and Reconciliation Commission of Canada; 02-MB-16JU10–123; Winnipeg, Manitoba; June 15, 2010 (TRC).

129. Victoria Elaine McIntosh, Truth and Reconciliation Commission of Canada; 02-MB-16JU10–123; The Forks, Winnipeg, Manitoba; June 15, 2010 (TRC).

130. Eugene Patrick Boubard, Truth and Reconciliation Commission of Canada; 02-MB-18JU10–004; Winnipeg, Manitoba; June 18, 2010 (TRC).

131. Jaimes, "Federal Indian Identification Policy."

132. Superintendent Crandall at SFIS sent a letter concerning the attendance of Mexicans at his school to Commissioner Valentine on March 1, 1910, to which he received the response that non-Indians could attend boarding schools as long as they paid a tuition no greater than that charged by state non-Indigenous schools and were of a "desirable class" so that their presence might be of "benefit" to the Indians in the sense that they would be a positive influence on the assimilation of Indigenous children. Commissioner Valentine to Superintendent Crandall, SFIS, April 6, 1910, Bureau of Indian Affairs RG 75, Northern Pueblos Agency, General Correspondence and Reports 1877–1934, Box 15, Folder 274 (NARA).

133. Wright, "Report of Supervisor A. O. Wright."

134. Lawrence, "Gender, Race, and the Regulation of Native Identity in Canada and the United States"; Lawrence, *"Real" Indians and Others*; Limerick, *The Legacy of Conquest*; Palmater, *Beyond Blood.*

135. Fear-Segal, *White Man's Club*, 175–76. See also Kellinghaus, *Taking Assimilation to Heart.*

136. Sinclair, "Identity Lost and Found." One should note that "scooping" has not come to an end. Sinclair discusses how the "sixties scoop" evolved into the "millennium scoop."

137. In Canada, the term "status Indians" refers to those Indigenous peoples formally recognized by the federal government as Indians and to whom the Indian Act applies.

138. Lawrence, *"Real" Indians and Others*.

139. Victoria Elaine McIntosh, Truth and Reconciliation Commission of Canada; 02-MB-16JUI0–123; Winnipeg, Manitoba; June 16, 2010 (TRC).

140. For example, Principal Isis Harrington at ais delivered a speech (in 1923?) titled "What Shall We Do with the Indian?," in which she made this precise argument. Bureau of Indian Affairs RG 75, Albuquerque Indian School, General Correspondence Files 1917–36, Entry 29, Box 3, Folder 45 (NARA).

141. Quoted in Fear-Segal, *White Man's Club*, 115.

142. Quoted in Fear-Segal, *White Man's Club*, 115.

143. Truth and Reconciliation Commission of Canada; Sagkeeng, Manitoba; October 2, 2012 (TRC).

8. AFTERMATHS AND REDRESS

1. See Brave Heart-Jordan and DeBruyn, "So She May Walk in Balance"; Duran, *Transforming the Soul Wound*; Duran and Duran, *Native American Postcolonial Psychology*; Terry, "Kelengakutelleghpat"; Wesley-Esquimaux and Smolewski, *Historic Trauma and Aboriginal Healing*; Whitbeck et al., "Conceptualizing and Measuring Historical Trauma among American Indian People."

2. See Gone, "Redressing First Nations Historical Trauma."

3. Bull, "Indian Residential Schooling"; Morrissette, "The Holocaust of First Nation People."

4. Blackstock, "Reconciliation Means Not Saying Sorry Twice."

5. Truth and Reconciliation Commission of Canada; The Forks, Winnipeg, Manitoba; June 18, 2010 (TRC).

6. See Edgerton et al., "Markers of Ethnic Marginalization."

7. See Kirmayer, Gone, and Moses, "Rethinking Cultural Trauma."

8. Collin and Jenson, *A Statistical Profile of Poverty in Canada*.

9. Wilson and Macdonald, *The Income Gap between Aboriginal Peoples and the Rest of Canada*.

10. See Reading and Wien, *Health Inequalities and Social Determinants of Aboriginal Peoples' Health*.

11. Dauvergne, "Adult Correctional Statistics in Canada, 2010/2011."

12. Sarche and Spicer, "Poverty and Health Disparities for American Indian and Alaska Native Children."

13. See Brave Heart-Jordan and DeBruyn, "So She May Walk in Balance;" Duran, *Transforming the Soul Wound*; Duran and Duran, *Native American Postcolonial Psychology*; Terry, "Kelengakutelleghpat"; Wesley-Esquimaux and Smoleski, *Historic Trauma*; Whitbeck et al., "Conceptualizing and Measuring Historical Trauma among American Indian People."

14. John Koppisch, "Why Are Indian Reservations So Poor? A Look at the Bottom 1%," *Forbes.com*, 2011, http://www.forbes.com/sites/johnkoppisch/2011/12/13/why-are-indian-reservations-so-poor-a-look-at-the-bottom-1/.

15. Cornell and Kalt, "Two Approaches to the Development of Native Nations"; Cornell and Kalt, "Where Does Economic Development Really Come From?"; Cornell and Kalt, "Where's the Glue?"; Taylor, *Determinants of Development Success in the Native Nations of the United States*. However, Cliff Atleo, Jr., *From Indigenous Nationhood to Neoliberal Aboriginal Economic Development*, has taken Cornell and Kalt to task for their use of neoliberal competitive language not in keeping with an Indigenous communal ethos.

16. Woolford, "Governing through Repair."

17. Gram, "Education on the Edge of Empire," 265.

18. In Leslie Marmon Silko's *Ceremony*, the character Rocky provides a vivid example of an individual whose immersion into the white world of AIS eventually led to his death and had severe repercussions for his family.

19. MacDonald, "First Nations, Residential Schools, and the Americanization of the Holocaust."

20. Ratner, Woolford, and Patterson, "Obstacles on the Path to Post-Genocide Repair"; Woolford and Wolejszo, "Collecting on Moral Debts."

21. See Torpey, *Making Whole What Has Been Smashed*.

22. Barkan, *The Guilt of Nations*; Brooks, ed., *When Sorry Isn't Enough*; Torpey, ed., *Politics and the Past*.

23. Glenn, *American Indian/First Nations Schooling*, 6.

24. See Martin and Yaquinto, *Redress for Historical Injustices in the United States*.

25. Andrea Smith, "Boarding School Abuses, Human Rights, and Reparations," 8, notes that until 1987 the BIA did not issue a policy on reporting sexual abuse.

26. Thus far, these and other cases have not resulted in a great deal of public attention to the issue of abuse and violence in American Indigenous boarding schools. See *Begay v. United States* (Begay 1), 219 Ct. Cl. 599 (1979), which dealt with physical and sexual abuse at the school but suspended proceedings for ninety days to exhaust required administrative remedies. Also see *Begay v. United States*

(Begay 2), 224 Ct. Cl. 712 (1980), which allowed the case to proceed under the "bad men" clause in the 1876 Navajo Treaty but dismissed the claim because the BIA found against the plaintiffs and was considered to have been neither arbitrary nor capricious in its decision.

27. Niezen, *Truth and Indignation*, 5 and chapter 4.

28. Churchill, *A Little Matter of Genocide*; Stannard, *American Holocaust*.

29. Elsewhere I have argued that governments tend to embrace processes of redress most when they believe that they can be used as a form of "affirmative repair": that is, as a means of affirming the dominant social order while offering only superficial redress for past wrongs. See Woolford, *Between Justice and Certainty*; Woolford, "Transition and Transposition."

30. Torpey, *Making Whole What Has Been Smashed*.

31. This is not to suggest that Canadian Indigenous groups have not increased their oversight of the schooling of Indigenous children. See chapter 3.

32. Although Szasz, *Education and the American Indian*, does not take the view that self-determination in Indigenous education can be interpreted as a form of redress, she does provide a useful discussion on the rise of such schools that could be read as an effort to correct past boarding school wrongs.

33. Colmant, "U.S. and Canadian Boarding Schools."

34. McBeth, *Ethnic Identity and the Boarding School Experience of West-Central Oklahoma Indians*; Tennant, *Aboriginal Peoples and Politics*.

35. Special Subcommittee on Indian Education, *Indian Education* (Kennedy Report), x.

36. Cornell, *Return of the Native*.

37. See the discussion in Mezey, "The Distribution of Wealth, Sovereignty, and Culture through Indian Gaming."

38. See Cornell, *Return of the Native*; Newton, "Indian Claims for Reparations, Compensation, and Restitution in the United States Legal System."

39. See Nagel, *American Indian Ethnic Renewal*.

40. Pan-Indigenous political mobilization in Canada began as early as the 1870s in regions such as British Columbia and Ontario but was quelled to some extent by Canadian revisions to the Indian Act that made such organizing difficult. Thus, the collective action that occurred to defeat the white paper can be viewed as a revitalization rather than an emergence of a pan-Indigenous movement. See Woolford, *Between Justice and Certainty*. The same is true of American pan-Indigenous movements, with groups such as the Society of American Indians forming in the early part of the twentieth century. See Hertzberg, *The Search for an American Indian Identity*.

41. See Woolford, *Between Justice and Certainty*.

42. The Idle No More movement has recently brought forward criticisms of the

perceived accommodationist tendencies of the Assembly of First Nations, and it will be interesting to observe the effects that these criticisms have on this body that represents First Nations (e.g., non-Métis and non-Inuit Indigenous peoples).

43. Woolford, *Between Justice and Certainty*.

44. Goffman, "On Face-Work."

45. Woolford, "Governing through Repair."

46. Woolford, "Genocide, Affirmative Repair, and the British Columbia Treaty Process."

47. See Friedman, *Capitalism and Freedom;* Hayek, *The Constitution of Liberty;* Stedman-Jones, *Masters of the Universe*.

48. For varying perspectives on neoliberalism, see, for example, Hardt and Negri, *Multitude;* Tickell and Peck, "Social Regulation after Fordism"; Wacquant, *Punishing the Poor*.

49. Moon, "Healing Past Violence."

50. Humphrey, "From Victim to Victimhood."

51. Corntassel and Holder, "Who's Sorry Now?"; Wilson, *The Politics of Truth and Reconciliation in South Africa*.

52. Woolford, "Governing through Repair."

53. Corntassel and Holder, "Who's Sorry Now?"

54. This was the motivation, in part, that drove Konrad Adenauer toward an unpopular reparations policy in post–Second World War West Germany. See Woolford and Wolejszo, "Collecting on Moral Debts."

55. For example, the governments of British Columbia and Canada were dragged into forming the BC Treaty Process both by the courts and by the uncertainty created through Indigenous roadblocks and other capital-disrupting strategies that eventually brought businesses on side with the battle for recognition of Aboriginal title in the province. See Blomley, "'Shut the Province Down'"; Woolford, *Between Justice and Certainty*.

56. Christodoulis, "'Truth and Reconciliation' as Risks."

57. Here I am paraphrasing the words of Jürgen Habermas, who, in response to revisionist German historians, remarked that, "as before, there is the simple fact that subsequent generations also grew up within a form of life in which *that* was possible. Our own life is linked to the life context in which Auschwitz was possible not only by contingent circumstances but intrinsically. Our form of life is connected with that of our parents and grandparents through a web of familial, local, political, and intellectual traditions that is difficult to disentangle—that is, through a historical milieu that made us what and who we are today. None of us can escape this milieu, because our identities, both as individuals and as

Germans, are indissolubly interwoven with it." See Habermas, *The New Conservatism*, 232 ff.

58. Furniss, *Victims of Benevolence*.

59. Indian and Northern Affairs Canada, *National Resolution Framework*.

60. For a discussion of sincerity in apology, see Tavuchis, *Mea Culpa*.

61. Corntassel and Holder, "Who's Sorry Now?"

62. Indian and Northern Affairs Canada, *Resolution Framework*.

63. Assembly of First Nations, *Residential School Briefing Note for National Chief Matthew Coon Come*. This was a consequence, in part, of the ADR process being built upon a narrow notion of harm derived from tort law. See Canadian Bar Association, *The Logical Next Step*.

64. Quoted in Regan, *Unsettling the Settler Within*, 128.

65. See Assembly of First Nations, *Residential School Briefing*; Canadian Bar Association, *The Logical Next Step*; Working Group on Truth and Reconciliation and the Exploratory Dialogues, *Healing and Reconciliation*. Similar suggestions can also be found in Royal Commission on Aboriginal Peoples, *Report of the Royal Commission on Aboriginal Peoples*.

66. Initial approval for the class-action settlement came in December 2006, when seven provincial courts approved the settlement. The settlement then came into effect in 2007, since survivors had until August 20, 2007, to decide whether or not they wanted to accept the settlement or opt out of it. *Cloud v. The Attorney General Canada* was filed on behalf of students who attended the Mohawk Institute Residential School in Brantford, Ontario. *Baxter* was a class-action lawsuit filed on behalf of all residential school survivors in 2002, at which time more than 8,000 abuse claims had been filed against Canada.

67. Indian Residential Schools Settlement Agreement, *Detailed Notice for the Indian Residential School Settlement*.

68. See Truth and Reconciliation Commission of Canada, *Mandate for the Truth and Reconciliation Commission of Canada*.

69. See Harper, "Prime Minister Harper Offers Full Apology on Behalf of Canadians for the Indian Residential Schools System."

70. Green, "Unsettling Cures"; Nagy and Sehdev, "Introduction"; Stanton, "Canada's Truth and Reconciliation Commission."

71. See Woolford and Ratner, *Informal Reckonings*.

72. See Torpey, *Making Whole What Has Been Smashed*.

73. David Melmer, "Boarding School Victims Want Reparation: Decades of Abuse Results in Court Action," *Indian Country Today*, April 28, 2003.

74. *Zephier et al. v. United States*, No. 03–7681 (Fed. Cl. April 9, 2003).

75. Curcio, "Civil Claims for Uncivilized Acts."

76. Smith, "Boarding School Abuses, Human Rights, and Reparations."

77. Curcio, "Civil Claims for Uncivilized Acts."

78. Curcio, "Civil Claims for Uncivilized Acts," 129.

79. See Smith, "Boarding School Abuses, Human Rights, and Reparations."

80. Smith, "Boarding School Abuses, Human Rights, and Reparations," 13.

81. Gover, "Remarks at the Ceremony Acknowledging the 175th Anniversary of the Establishment of the Bureau of Indian Affairs." See also Glauner, "The Need for Accountability and Reparation."

82. Quoted in Carol Barry, "Presidential Support Sought for Boarding School Apology," *Indian Country Today*, February 9, 2009.

83. Lise Balk King, "A Tree Fell in the Forest: The U.S. Apologized to Native Americans and No One Heard a Word," *Indian Country Today*, December 3, 2011, http://indiancountrytodaymedianetwork.com/opinion/a-tree-fell-in-the-forest%3A-the-u.s.-apologized-to-native-americans-and-no-one-heard-a-sound-65750.

84. Lise Balk King, "A Tree Fell in the Forest: The U.S. Apologized to Native Americans and No One Heard a Word," *Indian Country Today*, December 3, 2011.

85. Levi Rickert, "Apology to American Indians Unacceptable," *Native News Network*, December 20, 2012, http://www.nativenewsnetwork.com/apology-to-american-indians-unacceptable.html.

86. See Fear-Segal, *White Man's Club;* Smith, *Indigenous Peoples and Boarding Schools*.

87. Curcio, "Civil Claims for Uncivilized Acts," 126.

88. Truth and Reconciliation Commission of Canada; Fort Simpson, Northwest Territories; November 23, 2011 (TRC).

89. Truth and Reconciliation Commission of Canada; Enderby, British Columbia; October 13, 2011 (TRC).

90. Truth and Reconciliation Commission of Canada; Fort Good Hope, Northwest Territories; July 15, 2010 (TRC).

91. Truth and Reconciliation Commission of Canada; One Spirit Convention, Ottawa, Ontario; February 5, 2011 (TRC).

92. Truth and Reconciliation Commission of Canada, Fort Alexander Public Event, October 2, 2012 (TRC).

93. Petoukhov, "An Evaluation of Canada's Truth and Reconciliation Commission." LaForme also disagreed with the AFN about the appointment of the TRC's executive director. The position had been filled by Bob Watts, Phil Fontaine's (the AFN's former national chief) chief of staff, prior to LaForme's appointment. However, LaForme thought Watts inappropriate, since he believed that the TRC needed to establish clear independence from the parties to IRSSA. See also "Justice Harry S. LaForme Resigns as Chair of the Indian Residential Schools

Truth and Reconciliation Commission," October 2008, http://www.newswire
.ca/en/releases/archive/October2008/20/c7708.html.

94. See Petoukhov, "An Evaluation of Canada's Truth and Reconciliation Commission."

95. Nagy, "The Scope and Bounds of Transitional Justice."

96. See Chrisjohn and Wasacase, "Half-Truths and Whole Lies"; Henderson and Wakeham, "Colonial Reckoning, National Reconciliation?"; James, "A Carnival of Truth."

97. Brooks, "Reflections on Reparations."

98. Truth and Reconciliation Commission of Canada; Saskatoon, Saskatchewan; June 24, 2012 (TRC).

99. Truth and Reconciliation Commission of Canada; Winnipeg, Manitoba; June 18, 2010 (TRC).

100. There are reports that some lawyers have taken advantage of IAP applicants. For example, see Paul Barnsley and Kathleen Martens, "David Blott Violated Trust, Breached Settlement Agreement," *aptn National News*, June 6, 2012, http://aptn .ca/news/2012/06/06/judge-punishes-lawyer-for-loan-scheme-targeting-residential -school-survivors/.

101. In some instances, lawyers scrambled to access survivors as clients and favored cases likely to generate sizable settlements. See Niezen, *Truth and Indignation*, 48.

102. Truth and Reconciliation Commission of Canada; Winnipeg, Manitoba; June 16, 2010 (TRC).

103. Truth and Reconciliation Commission of Canada; Inuvik, Northwest Territories; September 28, 2011 (TRC).

104. Truth and Reconciliation Commission of Canada; The Forks, Winnipeg, Manitoba; June 16, 2010 (TRC).

105. Truth and Reconciliation Commission of Canada; Victoria Regional Event, British Columbia; April 13, 2012 (TRC).

106. Richard Courchene, "Letter to the Editor," *Winnipeg Free Press*, March 26, 2010, A13.

107. Truth and Reconciliation Commission of Canada; Winnipeg, Manitoba; June 17, 2010 (TRC).

108. Truth and Reconciliation Commission of Canada; Victoria Regional Event, British Columbia; April 13, 2012 (TRC).

109. Truth and Reconciliation Commission of Canada; Winnipeg, Manitoba; June 16, 2010 (TRC).

110. Ratner and Woolford, *Informal Reckonings*.

111. See Woolford and Nelund, "The Responsibilities of the Poor."

112. Veracini, *Settler Colonialism*.

9. CONCLUSION

1. Hinton, "Critical Genocide Studies."
2. See recent work by Levene, *The Rise of the West and the Coming of Genocide*; Mann, *The Dark Side of Democracy*; Moses, "An Antipodean Genocide?"
3. Theriault, "Against the Grain."
4. Regan, *Unsettling the Settler Within*, 10.
5. Regan, *Unsettling the Settler Within*, 10. The term "decolonizing" rather than "decolonized" is used here because of a belief that decolonizing, like justice or reconciliation, is an ongoing process that must be negotiated anew on a day-to-day basis rather than a final outcome that can be prescribed by a report such as this one.
6. Here I am inclined to take lessons from Anishinaabe cosmology and to include nonhuman peoples or nations, such as animal and plant life, in these reconciliatory efforts. See Simpson, *Dancing on Our Turtle's Back*.
7. Woolford, *Between Justice and Certainty*.
8. Wolfe, "Settler Colonialism and the Elimination of the Native."
9. Boudrieu, "Rethinking the State."
10. Wolfe, "Settler Colonialism."
11. There has been much recent discussion of decolonizing settler societies as well as academic knowledge production. For example, see Alfred, *Peace, Power, and Righteousness*; Alfred, *Wasase*; Mallon, *Decolonizing Native Histories*; Regan, *Unsettling the Settler Within*; Simpson, *Dancing on Our Turtle's Back*; Smith, *Decolonizing Methodologies*.

REFERENCES

PRIMARY SOURCES

Albuquerque Indian School. 1962–63. Regular Academic Program (Guide), Center for Southwest Research, Regular Stacks, Albuquerque, New Mexico.

American Indian Oral History Collection (AIOHC), 1968–72, Center for Southwest Research (CSWR), University of New Mexico, Albuquerque, New Mexico, MSS 314 BC.

Interview with Anonymous, Tape 446, 4 December 1970.

Interview with Mr. Baca, Tape 650, July 1970.

Interview with Rex Becenti Jr., Tape 363, December 1969.

Interview with Austin Begay, Tape 159, 28 August 1968

Interview with Andrea Benally, Tape 189, August 1968.

Interview with Dis-chie-ne Benally, Tape 177, November 1968.

Interview with Jerome Brody, Zia Pueblo, Tape 24, 5 April 1968.

Interview with Valencia Garcia, Tape 13, 23 April 1968

Interview with C. Gorman, Tape 268B, April 1969

Interview with Hopi-Hopi, Diné, Tape 362, January 1969.

Interview with Wolf Rob Hunt, Tape 134, no date.

Interview with Oakie James (Johnny Begay), Tape 391, April 1969.

Interview with Tony Lucero, Tape 112, 4 April 1968.

Interview with Mrs. Walter K. Marmon, Tape 514, 19 August 1967.

Interview with Dorothy Roman, Jemez, Tape 34, 4 April 1968.

Interview with Tom Ration, Navajo, Tape 153, September 1968.

Interview with Herbert Talehaftewa, Tape 563, 18 July 1967.

Interview with Clemente Vigil, Tape 753, 20 November 1970.

Interview with Mr. Warner, Diné, Tape 298, August 1969.

Interview with Ray Yazzie, Tape 199, 24 October 1968.

An Act to Amend the Indian Act (c. 50, S.C.), section 10, 1919–20 (Can.)

Application of the Convention on the Prevention and Punishment of the Crime of Genocide (Bosnia and Herzegovina v. Serbia and Montenegro), 2007 I.C.J. 140 (February 26, 2007). http://www.icj-cij.org/icjwww/idocket/ibhy/ibhyjudgment /ibhy_ijudgment_ 20070226_frame.htm.

Assembly of First Nations. *Residential School Briefing Note for National Chief Matthew Coon Come*. Ottawa: The Assembly of First Nations, 2004.

———. *Report on Canada's Dispute Resolution Plan to Compensate for Abuses in Indian Residential Schools*. Ottawa: Assembly of First Nations, 2004.

Barrows, William. 1887. *The Indian's Side of the Indian Question*. Boston: D Lothrop Company, 1887.

Begay v. United States (Begay 1), 219 Ct. Cl. 599 (1979).

Begay v. United States (Begay 2), 224 Ct. Cl. 712 (1980).

Bineziikwe, Ozaawi. "Surviving the Storm." *First Peoples Child and Family Review* 2, 1 (2005): 9–20.

Bureau of Education, Special Report. *Indian Education and Civilization: A Report Prepared in Answer to Senate Resolution of February 23, 1885 by Alice C. Fletcher under direction of the Commissioner of Education*. 48th Congress, 2d Session, Senate, Ex. Doc. No. 95. Washington: Government Printing Press, 1888.

Bryan Family Papers (BFP), Center for Southwest Research (CSWR), University of New Mexico, Albuquerque, New Mexico

Bryce, P. H. *Report on the Indian Schools of Manitoba and the Northwest Territories*. Department of Indian Affairs, Ottawa: Government Printing Bureau, 1907.

———. *The Story of A National Crime Being an Appeal for Justice to the Indians of Canada*. Ottawa: James Hope and Sons, 1922.

Canada. Department of Indian Affairs. Report of the Department of Indian Affairs for the Year Ended 31st December 1880. Sessional Papers, Volume 14, no. 8, Third Session of the Fourth Parliament of the Dominion of Canada, 1880–81.

———. Report of the Department of Indian Affairs for the Year Ended 31st December 1884. Sessional Papers, Volume 18, no. 3, Third Session of the Fifth Parliament of the Dominion of Canada, 1885.

———. Report of the Department of Indian Affairs for the Year Ended 31st December 1885. Sessional Papers Vol. 19, no. 4, Fourth Session of the Fifth Parliament of the Dominion of Canada, 1886.

———. Annual Report of the Department of Indian Affairs for the year ended 31st December 1888. Sessional Papers, Volume 22, no. 13, Third Session of the Sixth Parliament of the Dominion of Canada. Ottawa: Maclean, Roger, & co., 1889.

Canada. Indian and Northern Affairs Canada. *Information: Indian Affairs in Canada and the United States*. Ottawa: Government of Canada. 1998.

———. *National Resolution Framework*. Ottawa: Government of Canada, 2002. http://www.ainc-inac.gc.ca/ai/rqpi/info/nwz/2002/20021212_is-eng.asp (accessed 12 April 2010).

Canada. Indian Affairs and Northern Development. Working Group on Truth and Reconciliation and the Exploratory Dialogues. Healing and Reconciliation: Alternative Strategies for Dealing with Residential School Claims. Ottawa: Minister of Indian Affairs and Northern Development, 2000.

Canada. Indian Residential Schools Settlement Agreement. *Detailed Notice for the Indian Residential School Settlement*. Ottawa: Government of Canada, 2006. http://www.residentialschoolsettlement.ca/detailed_notice.pdf (accessed 12 April 2010).

Canada. Library and Archives Canada (LAC), Federal Archives Division, Ottawa, Ontario. RG-10, Records of the Department of Indian Affairs, Red Series, Black Series, and School Files.

> DIA Annual Reports.
>
> Inspectors Reports.
>
> Headquaters — Schools — General, 1904–28.
>
> Portage la Prairie Indian Residential School and Fort Alexander Indian Residential School Files.
>
> Quarterly Returns.

RG-29, National Health and Welfare.

Cook, Emily S. "What's in a name?" *Proceedings of the Congress of Indian Educators*, National Education Association, St Louis Mo, June 25 to July 1, 1904.

Davin, Nicholas Flood. *Report on Industrial Schools for Indians and Half Breeds*. Ottawa, 14 March 1879.

Deschatelets Archives, Oblates of Mary Immaculate, Ottawa HR 6681.C73R 99

Dorchester, Daniel. *Report of the U.S. Superintendent of Indian Schools 1891*. Washington: Government Printing Office, 1892.

Elizabeth Willis DeHuff Family Papers, (EWDFP) Centre for Southwest Research (CSWR), University of New Mexico, Albuquerque, New Mexico.

Fontaine, Craig Charbonneau, ed. *Speaking of Sagkeeng*. Trans. Allan Fontaine. Sagkeeng First Nation: KaKineepahwitamawat Association, 2006.

Fontaine, Phil. "We are all Born Innocent." In *Residential Schools: The Stolen Years*, ed. Linda Jaiane, 51–68. Saskatoon: University Extension Press, 1993.

Fontaine, Theodore. *Broken Circle: The Dark Legacy of Indian Residential Schools, A Memoir*. Victoria: Heritage House, 2010.

Fortier, Mary. *Behind Closed Doors: A Survivor's Story of the Boarding School Syndrome*. Bellville, ON: Epic Press, 2008.

Fortunate Eagle, Adam. *My Life in an Indian Boarding School*. Norman: University of Oklahoma Press, 2010.

Gover, Kevin. "Remarks at the Ceremony Acknowledging the 175th Anniversary of the Establishment of the Bureau of Indian Affairs." *American Indian Law Review* 25 (2000–2001): 161–63.

Harper, Stephen. "Prime Minister Harper Offers Full Apology on Behalf of Canadians for the Indian Residential Schools System." 11 June 2008. http://www.pm.gc.ca/eng/media.asp?id=2149 (accessed 1 October 2012).

Hawthorne, Harry B. *A Survey of the Contemporary Indians of Canada: Economic, Political, Educational Needs and Policies*. 2 vols. Ottawa: Government of Canada, 1966–67.

Knockwood, Isabelle. *Out of the Depths: The Experiences of MiKmaw Children at the Indian Residential School at Shubenacadie, Nova Scotia*. Halifax: Fernwood Publishing, 2001.

Meriam, Lewis. *The Problem of Indian Administration*. Baltimore: The Johns Hopkins Press, 1928.

National Archives and Records Administration (NARA), Rocky Mountain Region, Denver, Colorado.

Records of the Bureau of Indian Affairs, Record Group 75.

Albuquerque Indian School, General Correspondence Files, 1917–36.

Albuquerque Indian School, Student Case Files.

Northern Pueblos Agency, General Correspondence and Reports, 1877–1934.

Santa Fe Indian School, Student School Folders, 1910–34.

Southern Pueblo Agency, General Correspondence Files.

Superintendents' Annual Narrative and Statistical Reports from Field Jurisdictions of the Bureau of Indian Affairs, 1907–38.

Newspaper Clippings (NC) from the Center for Southwest Research Stacks (CSWR), University of New Mexico, Albuquerque, New Mexico.

Otis, Elwell S. The Indian Question. New York: Sheldon and Company, 1878.

Pratt, Richard H. "The Advantages of Mingling Indians with Whites." In *Americanizing the American Indians: Writings by the "Friends of the Indian" 1880–1900*, ed. Francis Paul Prucha, 260–71. Cambridge: Harvard University Press, 1973 [1892].

Proceedings of the Mohonk Lake Conference, October 12, 13, 14, 1886. Washington: Government Printing Office, 1887. http://www.maquah.net/Historical/Mohonk.html.

Prosecutor v. Krstić, ICTY Case No. IT-98-33-T, [Trial] Judgment (2 August 2001).

Ratliff, Russell. "The necessity of teaching the Indian boy to improve the allotment the government has given him." In *Extracts from Papers and Discussions at Summer Schools: Department of Indian Education and Congress of Indian Educators*. Detroit and Buffalo, 8–20 July 1891.

Reel, Estelle. *Report of the Superintendent of Indian Schools.* Washington: Government Printing Office, 1904.

———. *Report of the Superintendent of Indian Schools.* Washington: Government Printing Office, 1901.

———. *Report of the Superintendent of Indian Schools.* Washington: Government Printing Office, 1900.

Report of the Special Commissioners Appointed on the 8th of September, 1856, to Investigate Indian Affairs in Canada. Toronto: Steward Derbshire & George Desbarats, 1858.

Richardson, Robert Lorne, et al. "Facts and Figures: The Highest Testimony: What Lords Dufferin, Lorne and Lansdowne Say about the Canadian Northwest: Convincing Comparisons of Cost of Wheat Production, 25 Cents a Bushel: The Indian Problem Discussed." N.p.: n.p., 1886?

Royal Commission on Aboriginal Peoples. *Report of the Royal Commission on Aboriginal Peoples.* Volume 1. Ottawa: Canada Communications Group, 1996.

Sagkeeng Cultural Education Centre Oral History Project Records (1989), Archives of Manitoba (AOM), Winnipeg, Manitoba.

Interview with Joseph Boubard, 5 August 1987, C1623.

Interview with Angela Marie Bruyere, 16 July 1987, C1614.

Santa Fe Indian School, The First 100 Years Oral History Interviews by Sally Hyer (SFIS100), Centre for Southwest Research (CSWR), University of New Mexico, Albuquerque, New Mexico.

Interview with Upton Ethelbah, Apache, 24 June 1987.

Interview with Wilfred Garcia, San Juan, 4 March 1986.

Interview with Santanita Lefthand, Taos, 28 May 1986.

Interview with Annie C. Reyna, San Juan, 10 October 1986.

Interview with Frank Tenorio, San Felipe, 5–7 March 1986.

Interview with Pablita Velarde, Santa Clara, 2 October 1986.

Scott, Duncan Campbell. "The First People: Survival of Indian Life: Hail to 'Great Father.'" *The Times* (London, England), 15 May 1939.

Smith, H. C. "The Duty of the State to Her Indians." In *Extracts from Papers and Discussions at Summer Schools: Department of Indian Education and Congress of Indian Educators,* Detroit and Buffalo, 8–20 July 1901.

Special Subcommittee on Indian Education. *Indian Education: A National Tragedy—A National Challenge.* Report of the Committee on Labor and Public Welfare, United States Senate. Washington: U.S. Government Printing Office, 1969.

State Archives and Library (SAL), Santa Fe, New Mexico.

Bureau of Indian Affairs RG 75.

Santa Fe Indian School, Press Copies of Letters Sent and Received, reel M1473.

John Collier Papers.

Truth and Reconciliation Commission of Canada (TRC).

Statement-Taking Interviews

Anonymous Testimony; Beausejour, MB; 10 April 2010.

Lillian Kennedy, 2011–2563; Bloodvein, MB; 25 January 2012

Anonymous Testimony; Brandon, MB, 12 October 2011.

Anonymous Testimony; Brandon, MB; 11 October 2011.

Anonymous Testimony; Enderby, BC; 13 October 2011.

Anonymous Testimony; First Nations University, Regina, SK; 18 August 2010.

Anonymous Testimony; Fort Good Hope, NWT; 15 July 2010.

Anonymous Testimony; Fort Simpson, NT; 23 November 2011.

Anonymous Testimony; Inuvik, NT; 28 September 2011.

Gladys Hearns, 01-MB-26JY10–003; Long Plain First Nation, MB; 26 July 2010.

Anonymous Testimony; Long Plain First Nation, MB; 27 July 27 2010.

Mary Courchene, 2011–2515; Pine Creek First Nation, MB; 28 November 2011.

Anonymous Testimony; Sagkeeng, MB; 2 October 2012.

Anonymous Testimony; Saskatoon, SK; 24 June 2012.

Anonymous Testimony; Victoria Regional Event, BC; 13 April 2012.

Victoria Elaine McIntosh, 02-MB-16JU10–123; Winnipeg, MB; 15 June 2010.

Anonymous Testimony; Winnipeg, MB; 16 June 2010.

Eva Harriet Woodford, 02-MB-16JU10–068; Winnipeg, MB; 16 June 2010.

Anonymous Testimony; Winnipeg, MB; 16 June 2010.

Purvis H. Fontaine, 02-MB-16JU10–150; Winnipeg, MB; 16 June 2010.

Anonymous Testimony; Winnipeg, MB; 17 June 2010.

Madeline Smith, 02-MB-17JU10–074, Winnipeg, MB, 17 June 2010.

Vincent Pierre, 02-MB-18JU10–002; Winnipeg, MB, 18 June 2010.

Muriel Katherine Morrisseau, 02-MB-18JU10–057; Winnipeg, MB; 18 June 2010.

Anonymous Testimony; Winnipeg, MB; 18 June 2010.

Eugene Patrick Boubard, 02-MB-18JU10–004; Winnipeg, MB; 18 June 2010

Anonymous Testimony; Winnipeg, MB; 5 July 2011.

Rose Hart, 2011–2620; Winnipeg, MB; 25 June 2011.

Norman Twoheart, 2011–2656; Winnipeg, MB; January 18, 2012.

Anonymous Testimony; Long Plain First Nation, MB; July 28, 2010.

Anonymous Testimony; One Spirit Convention, Ottawa, ON; February 5, 2011.

Statements at Public Events

> Fort Alexander Public Event testimony, 2 October 2012
>
> Fort Alexander Public Event testimony, 3 October 2012

School Narratives

> Fort Alexander Indian Residential School IAP School Narrative, 28 September 2011
>
> Portage la Prairie Indian Residential School Narrative, 21 July 2004, IAP Collection

Truth and Reconciliation Commission of Canada. *Mandate for the Truth and Reconciliation Commission of Canada.* Ottawa: Government of Canada, 2009. http://www .trc-cvr.ca/pdfs/SCHEDULE_N_EN.pdf (accessed 12 April 2010).

United Church of Canada Archives. "Portage la Prairie Indian Residential School." *The Children Remembered, Residential School Archive Project.* http://thechildrenremembered .ca/school-locations/portage-la-prairie/.

United Nations Convention on the Prevention and Punishment of the Crime of Genocide. Adopted by Resolution 260 (III) A of the UN General Assembly on 9 Dec. 1948. Entry into force, 12 Jan. 1951.

United States–Navajo Treaty. 1868. http://reta.nmsu.edu/modules/longwalk/lesson /document/treaty.htm#article1 (accessed 6 June 2013).

Walker, Francis A. *The Indian Question.* Boston: James R. Osgood and Company, 1874.

Wood, Edward Frederick Lindley. *Some Aspects of the Indian Problem Being the Inaugural Massey Lecture Delivered before the University of Toronto on 27 April 1932 by The Right Honourable Lord Irwin.* London: Oxford University Press, 1932.

Wright, A. O. "Discipline in an Indian School." *In Extracts from Papers and Discussions at Summer Schools: Department of Indian Education and Congress of Indian Educators,* Detroit and Buffalo, July 8–20, 1901.

———. "Report of Supervisor A. O. Wright." Synopses of Reports of Supervisors of Indian Schools and Special Agents, Pacific Coast Institute, Newport Oregon, 17–22 August 1902. In Report of the Superintendent of Indian Schools. Washington: Government Printing Office, 1903.

Zephier et al v. United States, No. 03–768L (Fed. Cl. April 9, 2003).

PUBLISHED WORKS

Abbott, Devon. "'Commendable Progress': Acculturation at the Cherokee Female Seminary." *American Indian Quarterly* 11 (1987): 187–201.

Adams, David Wallace. "Beyond Bleakness: The Brighter Side of Indian Boarding Schools, 1870–1940." In *Boarding School Blues: Revisiting American Indian Educational Experiences,* edited by Clifford E. Trafzer, Jean A. Keller, and Lorene Sisquoc, 35–64. Lincoln: University of Nebraska Press, 2006.

————. *Education for Extinction: American Indians and the Boarding School Experience, 1875–1928.* Lawrence: University Press of Kansas, 1995.

————. "Schooling the Hopi: Federal Indian Policy Writ Small, 1887–1917." *Pacific Historical Review* 48, 3 (1979): 335–56.

Agamben, Giorgio. *Homo Sacer: Sovereign Power and Bare Life.* Stanford, CA: Stanford University Press, 1998.

Ahern, Wilbert H. "An Experiment Aborted: Returned Indian Students in the Indian School Service, 1881–1908." *Ethnohistory* 44, 2 (1997): 263–304.

Akhtar, Zia. "Canadian Genocide and Official Culpability." *International Criminal Law Review* 10 (2010): 111–35.

Albach, P. G., and G. P. Kelly, eds. *Education and the Colonial Experience.* New York: Longman, 1978.

Alexander, Jeffrey. "Toward a Theory of Cultural Trauma." In *Cultural Trauma and Collective Identity,* edited by Jeffrey Alexander et al., 1–30. Berkeley: University of California Press, 2004.

Alfred, Taiaiake. *Peace, Power, and Righteousness: An Indigenous Manifesto.* 2nd ed. Don Mills, ON: Oxford University Press, 2009.

————. *Wasase: Indigenous Pathways of Action and Freedom.* Toronto: University of Toronto Press, 2009.

Annett, Kevin. *Hidden from History: The Canadian Holocaust.* Vancouver: Truth Commission into Genocide in Canada, 2001.

Archibald, Linda. *Decolonization and Healing Indigenous Experiences in the United States, New Zealand, Australia, and Greenland.* Ottawa: Aboriginal Healing Foundation, 2007.

Archibald, Robert. "Acculturation and Assimilation in Colonial New Mexico." *New Mexico Historical Review* 53, 3 (1978): 205–17.

Arendt, Hannah. *The Origins of Totalitarianism.* New York: Harcourt, Brace, and Company, 1951.

Atleo, Cliff, Jr. *From Indigenous Nationhood to Neoliberal Aboriginal Economic Development: Charting the Evolution of Indigenous-Settler Relations in Canada.* Victoria: Canadian Social Economy Hub, 2008.

Axtell, James. *Beyond 1492: Encounters in Colonial North America.* New York: Oxford University Press, 1992.

Barkan, Elazar. *The Guilt of Nations: Restitution and Negotiating Historical Injustices.* New York: W. W. Norton, 2000.

Barta, Tony. "Relations of Genocide: Land and Lives in the Colonization of Australia." In *Genocide and the Modern Age: Etiology and Case Studies of Mass Death,* edited by I. Wallimann and M. N. Dobkowski, 237–52. Syracuse, NY: Syracuse University Press, 1987.

———. "'They Appear Actually to Vanish from the Face of the Earth.' Aborigines and the European Project in Australia Felix." *Journal of Genocide Research* 10, 4 (2008): 519–39.

Bartov, Omer. "Genocide and the Holocaust: What Are We Arguing About?" In *Gewalt und Gesellschaft: Klassiker Modernen Denkens neu Glessen,* edited by Uffa Jensen et al., 381–93. Gottingen: Wallstein University Press, 2010.

Basso, Keith H. *Wisdom Sits in Places: Landscape and Language among the Western Apache.* Albuquerque: University of New Mexico Press, 1996.

Bauman, Zygmunt. "Making and Unmaking Strangers." *Thesis Eleven* 43 (1995): 1–16.

———. *Modernity and the Holocaust.* Ithaca, NY: Cornell University Press, 1989.

Bays, Eric. *Indian Residential Schools: Another Picture.* Ottawa: Baico Publishing, 2009.

Beccaria, Cesare. *On Crimes and Punishments and Other Writings.* Edited by Aaron Thomas. Translated by Aaron Thomas and Jeremy Parzen. Toronto: University of Toronto Press, 2008 [1764].

Benvenuto, Jeff. "Revisiting Choctaw Ethnocide and Ethnogenesis: The Creative Destruction of Colonial Genocide." In *Colonial Genocide in Indigenous North America,* edited by Andrew Woolford, Jeff Benvenuto, and Alexander Laban Hinton, 208–25. Durham, NC: Duke University Press, 2014.

Bischoping, Katherine, and Natalie Fingerhut. "Border Lines: Indigenous Peoples in Genocide Studies." *Canadian Review of Sociology and Anthropology* 33, 4 (1996): 481–506.

Blackhawk, Ned. *Violence over the Land: Indians and Empires in the Early American West.* Cambridge, MA: Harvard University Press, 2006.

Blackstock, Cindy. "Reconciliation Means Not Saying Sorry Twice: Lessons from Child Welfare in Canada." In *From Truth to Reconciliation: Transforming the Legacy of Residential Schools,* edited by M. B. Castellano, Linda Archibald, and Mike Degagne, 163–78. Ottawa: Dollco Printing, 2008.

Blackstock, Michael D. "Trust Us: A Case Study in Colonial Social Relations Based on Documents Prepared by the Aborigines Protection Society." In *With Good Intentions: Euro-Canadian and Aboriginal Relations in Colonial Canada,* edited by Celia Haig-Brown and David A. Nock, 51–71. Vancouver: UBC Press, 2006.

Blomley, Nicholas K. "'Shut the Province Down': First Nations Blockades in British Columbia, 1984–1995." *BC Studies* 111 (1996): 5–36.

Bolt, Christine. *American Indian Policy and American Reform: Case Studies of the Campaign to Assimilate American Indians.* London: Allen and Unwin, 1987.

Borrows, John. "Contemporary and Comparative Perspective on the Rights of Indigenous Peoples: Indigenous Legal Traditions in Canada." *Washington Journal of Law and Policy* 19, 273 (2005): 168–311.

Bourdieu, Pierre. *In Other Words: Essays towards a Reflexive Sociology*. Stanford, CA: Stanford University Press, 1990.

———. *Language and Symbolic Power*. Cambridge, MA: Harvard University Press, 1991.

———. *The Logic of Practice*. Stanford, CA: Stanford University Press, 1990.

———. "Rethinking the State: Genesis and Structure of the Bureaucratic Field." *Sociological Theory* 12, 1 (1994): 1–18.

Bourdieu, Pierre, and Loïc Wacquant. *An Invitation to Reflexive Sociology*. Chicago: University of Chicago Press, 1992.

Bowden, Henry Warner. *American Indians and Christian Missions: Studies in Conflict*. Chicago: University of Chicago Press, 1981.

Bracken, Christopher. *The Potlatch Papers: A Colonial Case History*. Chicago: University of Chicago Press, 1997.

Brave Heart-Jordan, Marie Yellow Horse, and Lemyra DeBruyn. "So She May Walk in Balance: Integrating the Impact of Historical Trauma in the Treatment of Native American Indian Women." In *Racism in the Lives of Women: Testimony, Theory, and Guides to Anti-Racist Practice*, edited by J. Adelman and G. Enguidanos, 345–68. New York: Haworth, 1995.

Brooks, Roy L. "Reflections on Reparations." In *Politics and the Past: On Repairing Historical Injustices*, edited by John Torpey, 103–14. Lanham, MD: Rowman and Littlefield, 2003.

Brooks, Roy L, ed. *When Sorry Isn't Enough: The Controversy over Apologies and Reparations for Human Injustice*. New York: New York University Press, 1999.

Browning, Christopher. *Ordinary Men: Reserve Police Battalion 101 and the Final Solution in Poland*. New York: Harper Perennial, 1998.

Brownlie, Robin Jarvis. *A Fatherly Eye: Indian Agents, Government Power, and Aboriginal Resistance in Ontario, 1918–1939*. Don Mills, ON: Oxford University Press, 2003.

Bull, Linda R. "Indian Residential Schooling: The Native Perspective." *Canadian Journal of Native Education* 18 (1991): 3–63.

Burnett, Kristin. "Building the System: Churches, Missionary Organizations, the Federal State, and Health Care in Southern Alberta Treaty 7 Communities, 1890–1930." *Journal of Canadian Studies* 41, 3 (2007): 18–41.

Bush, Caleb N. "Subsistence Fades, Capitalism Deepens: The 'Net of Incorporation' and Diné Livelihoods in the Opening of the Navajo-Hopi Land Dispute, 1880–1970." *American Behavioral Scientist* 58, 1 (2014): 171–96.

Bush, Peter. "The Native Residential School System and the Presbyterian Church in Canada." *Presbyterian History* 48, 1 (2004): 1–8.

Butcher, Thomas. "A 'Synchronized Attack': On Raphael Lemkin's Holistic Conception of Genocide." *Journal of Genocide Research* 15, 3: 253–72.

Buzelin, Hélène. "Unexpected Allies: How Latour's Network Theory Could Complement Bourdieusian Analyses in Translation Studies." *Translator* 11, 2 (2005): 193–218.

Byler, William. "The Destruction of American Indian Families." In *The Destruction of American Indian Families*, edited by Steven Unger, 1–11. New York: Association of American Indian Affairs, 1977.

Cahill, Cathleen D. *Federal Mothers and Fathers: A Social History of the United States Indian Service, 1869–1933*. Chapel Hill: University of North Carolina Press, 2011.

Callon, Michel. "Some Elements of a Sociology of Translation: Domestication of the Scallops and the Fishermen of St Brieuc Bay." In *Power, Action, and Belief: A New Sociology of Knowledge*, edited by John Law, 196–223. London: Routledge and Kegan Paul, 1986.

Canadian Bar Association. *The Logical Next Step: Reconciliation Payments for All Indian Residential School Survivors*. Ottawa: Canadian Bar Association, 2005. http://www.cba.org/cba/Sections/pdf/residential.pdf.

Carney, Robert. "Aboriginal Residential Schools before Confederation: The Early Experience." CCHA *Historical Studies* 61 (1995): 13–40.

———. "Church-State and Northern Education: 1870–1961." PhD diss., University of Alberta, 1971.

———. "Residential Schooling at Fort Chipewyan and Fort Resolution, 1874–1974." *Western Oblate Studies* 2 (1992): 115–38.

Carroll, W. K., and R. S. Ratner. "Master Frames and Counter-Hegemony: Political Sensibilities in Contemporary Social Movements." *Canadian Review of Sociology and Anthropology* 33, 4 (1996): 407–35.

Chalk, Frank, and Kurt Jonassohn. *The History and Sociology of Genocide: Analyses and Case Studies*. New Haven, CT: Yale University Press, 1990.

Charny, Israel W. "Toward a Generic Definition of Genocide." In *Genocide: Conceptual and Historical Dimensions*, edited by George J. Andreopoulis, 64–94. Philadelphia: University of Pennsylvania Press, 1994.

Child, Brenda J. *Boarding School Seasons: American Indian Families, 1900–1940*. Lincoln: University of Nebraska Press, 1998.

———. "Runaway Boys, Resistant Girls: Rebellion at Flandreau and Haskell, 1900–1940." *Journal of American Indian Education* 35, 3 (1996): n. pag. http://jaie.asu.edu/v35/v35s3run.htm.

Chrisjohn, Roland, and Tanya Wasacase. "Half-Truths and Whole Lies: Rhetoric in the 'Apology' and the Truth and Reconciliation Commission." In *Response, Responsibility, and Renewal: Canada's Truth and Reconciliation Journey*, edited by Gregory Younging, Jonathan Dewar, and Mike DeGagné, 217–29. Ottawa: Aboriginal Healing Foundation, 2009.

Chrisjohn, Roland, and Sherri Young. *The Circle Game: Shadows and Substance in the Indian Residential School Experience.* Penticton, BC: Theytus Books, 1997.

Christodoulis, Emilios A. "'Truth and Reconciliation' as Risks." *Social and Legal Studies* 9, 2 (2000): 179–204.

Christophers, Brett. *Positioning the Missionary: John Booth and the Confluence of Cultures in Nineteenth-Century British Columbia.* Vancouver: UBC Press, 1998.

Churchill, Ward. "Forbidding the 'G-Word': Holocaust Denial as Judicial Doctrine in Canada." *Other Voices* 2, 1 (2000): n. pag. http://www.othervoices.org/2.1/churchill/denial.html.

———. *Kill the Indian, Save the Man.* San Francisco: City Lights, 2004.

———. *A Little Matter of Genocide: Holocaust and Denial in the Americas 1492 to the Present.* San Francisco: City Lights, 1998.

Clastres, Paul. "On Ethnocide." *Art and Text* 28 (1988): 51–58.

Clendinnen, Inga. "First Contact." *Australian's Review of Books* 9 (2001): B6.

Clifford, James. *The Predicament of Culture: Twentieth-Century Ethnography, Literature, and Art.* Cambridge, MA: Harvard University Press, 1988.

Cole, Douglas, and Ira Chaikin. *An Iron Hand upon the People: The Law against the Potlatch on the Northwest Coast.* Vancouver: Douglas and McIntyre, 1990.

Cole, Tim. *Holocaust City: The Making of a Jewish Ghetto.* New York: Routledge, 2003.

Coleman, Michael C. *American Indian Children at School, 1850–1930.* Jackson: University Press of Mississippi, 1993.

Collin, Chantal, and Hillary Jenson. *A Statistical Profile of Poverty in Canada.* Ottawa: Library of Parliament, 2009.

Colmant, Stephen. "U.S. and Canadian Boarding Schools: A Review, Past and Present." *Native Americas Journal* 17, 4 (2000): 24–30.

Colmant, Stephen, et al.. "Constructing Meaning to the Indian Boarding School Experience." *Journal of American Indian Education* 43, 3 (2004): 22–39.

Cooper, Frederick. *Colonialism in Question: Theory, Knowledge, History.* Berkeley: University of California Press, 2005.

Cooper, Michael L. *Indian School: Teaching the White Man's Way.* New York: Clarion Books, 1999.

Cornell, Stephen. *Return of the Native: American Indian Political Resurgence.* New York: Oxford University Press, 1990.

Cornell, Stephen, and Joseph P. Kalt. "Reloading the Dice: Improving the Chances for Economic Development on American Indian Reservations." In *What Can Tribes Do? Strategies and Institutions in American Indian Economic Development,* edited by S. Cornell and J. P. Kalt, 1–59. Los Angeles: American Indian Studies Center, University of California Los Angeles, 1992.

———. "Two Approaches to the Development of Native Nations: One Works, the Other Doesn't." In *Rebuilding Native Nations: Strategies for Governance and Development*, edited by M. R. Jorgensen, 3–32. Tucson: University of Arizona Press, 2007.

———. "Where Does Economic Development Really Come From? Constitutional Rule among the Contemporary Sioux and Apache." *Economic Inquiry* 33, 3 (1995): 402–26.

———. "Where's the Glue? Institutional and Cultural Foundations of American Indian Economic Development." *Journal of Socio-Economics* 29 (2000): 443–70.

Corntassel, Jeff, and Cindy Holder. "Who's Sorry Now? Government Apologies, Truth Commissions, and Self-Determination in Australia, Canada, Guatemala, and Peru." *Human Rights Review* 9 (2008): 465–89.

Curcio, Andrea A. "Civil Claims for Uncivilized Acts: Filing Suit against the Government for American Indian Boarding School Abuses." *Hastings Race and Poverty Law Journal* 45, 4 (2006–7): 45–129.

Curthoys, Ann, and John Docker. "Genocide: Definitions, Questions, Settler-Colonies." *Aboriginal History* 25 (2001): 1–15.

Dadrian, Vahakn N. "A Typology of Genocide." *International Review of Modern Sociology* 5 (1975): 201–12.

———. "The Victimization of the American Indian." *Victimology: An International Journal* 1, 4 (1976): 517–37.

Dalseg, B. A. "In Their Own Words: Manitoba's Native Residential Schools Remembered." MA thesis, University of Manitoba, 2003.

Daschuk, James. *Clearing the Plains: Disease, Politics of Starvation, and the Loss of Aboriginal Land*. Regina, SK: University of Regina Press, 2013.

Dauvergne, Mia. "Adult Correctional Statistics in Canada, 2010/2011." *Juristat*, Catalogue No. 85-002-X, 2012.

Davis, Julie. "American Indian Boarding School Experiences: Recent Studies from Native Perspectives." OAH *Magazine of History* 15, 2 (2001): 20–22.

Davis, Robert, and Mark Zannis. *The Genocide Machine in Canada: The Pacification of the North*. Montreal: Black Rose Books, 1973.

DeJong, David H. *Promises of the Past: A History of Indian Education in the United States*. Golden, CO: North American Press, 1993.

———. "'Unless They Are Kept Alive': Federal Indian Schools and Student Health, 1878–1918." *American Indian Quarterly* 31, 2 (2007): 256–82.

de Leeuw, Sarah. "'If Anything Is to Be Done with the Indian, We Must Catch Him Very Young': Colonial Constructions of Aboriginal Children and the Geographies of Indian Residential Schooling in British Columbia, Canada." *Children's Geographies* 7, 2 (2009): 123–40.

———. "Intimate Colonialisms: The Material and Experienced Places of British Columbia's Residential Schools." *Canadian Geographer* 51, 3 (2007): 339–59.

Deleuze, Gilles, and Félix Guattari. *A Thousand Plateaus.* Translated by Brian Massumi. London: Continuum, 2004.

Deloria, Vine, Jr. "The Indian Rights Association: An Appraisal." In *Aggressions of Civilization: Federal Indian Policy since the 1880s,* edited by Sandra L. Cadawalader and Vine Deloria, Jr., 3–18. Philadelphia: Temple University Press, 1984.

Denetdale, Jennifer Nez. *Reclaiming Diné History: The Legacies of Navajo Chief Manuelito and Juanita.* Tucson: University of Arizona Press, 2007.

Derrida, Jacques. "Force of Law: The 'Mystical Foundation of Authority.'" In *Deconstruction and the Possibility of Justice,* edited by D. Cornell, M. Rosenfeld, and D. G. Carlson, 3-67. London: Routledge.

Deyhle, Donna. *Reflections in Place: Connected Lives of Navajo Women.* Phoenix: University of Arizona Press, 2009.

Docker, John. "Are Settler-Colonies Inherently Genocidal? Re-Reading Lemkin." In *Empire, Colony, and Genocide: Conquest, Occupation, and Subaltern Resistance in World History,* edited by A. D. Moses, 81–101. Oxford: Bergham Books, 2008.

Douglas, Mary. *Purity and Danger: An Analysis of Concepts of Pollution and Taboo.* New York: Frederick A. Praeger, 1966.

Duran, Eduardo. *Transforming the Soul Wound: A Theoretical/Clinical Approach to American Indian Psychology.* Berkeley, CA: Folklore Institute, 1990.

Duran, Eduardo, and Bonnie Duran. *Native American Postcolonial Psychology.* Albany, NY: SUNY Press, 1995.

Dyck, Noel. *Differing Visions: Administering Indian Residential Schooling in Prince Albert 1867–1995.* Halifax: Fernwood Publishing, 1997.

Echohawk, John. "The Kennedy Report: Robert and Edward Kennedy Understood Trust Responsibility for Indian Education in 1969. NARF Director Shares How Far We Have Come." *NIEA News* 41, 2 (2010): 16–17.

Edgerton, Jason, Lance Roberts, Lori Wilkinson, and Andrew Woolford. "Markers of Ethnic Marginalization: Aboriginal Peoples in Canada." In *Markers of Ethnic Marginalization: Focused on Aboriginal People in Canada and on Roma in Czech Republic and Slovak Republic,* edited by Petra Vojtová, 36–174. Ceské Budejovice: University of South Bohemia, Faculty of Health and Social Studies, 2008.

Elias, Norbert. *The Civilizing Process: The History of Manners and State Formation and Civilization.* Oxford: Blackwell, 2000.

Elkins, Caroline, and Susan Pederson, eds. *Settler Colonialism in the Twentieth Century.* Abingdon, UK: Routledge, 2005.

Ellinghaus, Katherine. "Biological Absorption and Genocide: Comparison of Indigenous Assimilation Policies." *Genocide Studies and Prevention* 4, 1 (2009): 59–79.

————. *Taking Assimilation to Heart: Marriages of White Women and Indigenous Men in Australia and the United States, 1887–1937*. Lincoln: University of Nebraska Press, 2006.

Ellis, Clyde. *To Change Them Forever: Indian Education at Rainy Mountain Boarding School, 1893–1920*. Norman: University of Oklahoma Press, 1996.

————. "'We Had a Lot of Fun, but of Course, that Wasn't the School Part': Life at the Rainy Mountain Boarding School, 1893–1920." In *Boarding School Blues: Revisiting American Indian Educational Experiences*, edited by Clifford E. Trafzer, Jean A. Keller, and Lorene Sisquoc, 65–98. Lincoln: University of Nebraska Press, 2006.

Enns, Richard A. "'But What Is the Object of Educating These Children, if It Costs Their Lives to Educate Them?' Federal Indian Education Policy in Western Canada in the Late 1800s." *Journal of Canadian Studies* 43, 3 (2009): 101–23.

Episkenew, Jo-Ann. *Taking Back Our Spirits: Indigenous Literature, Public Policy, and Healing*. Winnipeg: University of Manitoba Press, 2009.

Evans, Raymond. "'Crime without a Name': Colonialism and the Case for 'Indigenocide.'" In *Empire, Colony, and Genocide: Conquest, Occupation, and Subaltern Resistance in World History*, edited by A. Dirk Moses, 133–47. Oxford: Bergham Books, 2008.

Evans, Raymond, and Bill Thorpe. "Indigenocide and the Massacre of Aboriginal History." *Overland* 163 (2001): 21–40.

Fay, Terence J. "A Historiography of Recent Publications on Catholic Native Residential Schools." CCHA *Historical Studies* 61 (1995): 79–97.

Fear-Segal, Jacqueline. "Nineteenth-Century Indian Education: Universalism versus Evolutionism." *Journal of America Studies* 33, 2 (1999): 323–41.

————. *White Man's Club: Schools, Race, and the Struggle of Indian Acculturation*. Lincoln: University of Nebraska Press, 2007.

Feierstein, Daniel. "Leaving the Parental Home: An Overview of the Current State of Genocide Studies." *Genocide Studies and Prevention* 6, 3 (2011): 257–69.

Fein, Helen. *Genocide: A Sociological Perspective*. London: Sage, 1993.

Fenn, Elizabeth A. "Biological Warfare in Eighteenth-Century North America: Beyond Jeffrey Amherst." *Journal of American History* 86, 4 (2000): 1552–80.

Finzsch, Norbert. "'. . . Extirpate or Remove That Vermine': Genocide, Biological Warfare, and Settler Imperialism in the Eighteenth and Early Nineteenth Century." *Journal of Genocide Research* 10, 2 (2008): 215–32.

Fletcher, M. L. M. "Contemporary and Comparative Perspective on the Rights of Indigenous Peoples: The Insidious Colonialism of the Conqueror—the Federal Government in Modern Tribal Affairs." *Washington Journal of Law and Policy* 19, 273 (2005): 271–311.

Foucault, Michel. *Discipline and Punish: The Birth of the Prison.* New York: Random House, 1975.

———. *The History of Sexuality: An Introduction.* New York: Vintage Books, 1990.

———. *Power/Knowledge: Selected Interviews and Other Writings 1972–1977.* New York: Pantheon, 1980.

———. "Technologies of the Self." In *Ethics, Subjectivity, and Truth,* edited by Paul Rabinow, 223–51. New York: New Press, 1994.

French, Laurence. *The Winds of Injustice: American Indians and the U.S. Government.* New York: Garland, 1994.

Friedman, Milton. *Capitalism and Freedom.* Chicago: University of Chicago Press, 1962.

Friere, Paolo. *Pedagogy of the Oppressed.* New York: Continuum, 1970.

Funke, Kristin. "'Growing Up It Seemed I Lived in Two Worlds': American Indian Responses to Government Boarding Schools, 1890–1940." *Native American Studies* 19, 2 (2005): 21–32.

Furniss, Elizabeth. *Victims of Benevolence: The Dark Legacy of the Williams Lake Residential School.* Vancouver: Arsenal Pulp Press, 1995.

Garmhausen, Winona. *Indian Arts Education in Santa Fe.* Santa Fe: Sunstone Press, 1988.

Gilbert, Matthew Sakiestewa. *Education beyond the Mesas: Hopi Students at Sherman Institute, 1902–1929.* Lincoln: University of Nebraska Press, 2010.

Glauner, Lindsay. "The Need for Accountability and Reparation: 1830–1976, the United States Role in the Promotion, Implementation, and Execution of the Crime of Genocide against Native Americans." *DePaul Law Review* 51 (2002): 911–61.

Glenn, Charles L. *American Indian/First Nations Schooling: From the Colonial Period to the Present.* New York: Palgrave, 2011.

Goffman, Erving. *Asylums: Essays on the Social Situation of Mental Patients and Other Inmates.* New York: Doubleday, 1961.

———. *Frame Analysis: An Essay on the Organization of Experience.* Cambridge, MA: Harvard University Press, 1974.

———. "On Face-Work: An Analysis of Ritual Elements in Social Interaction." *Psychiatry: Journal for the Study of Interpersonal Processes* 18 (1955): 213–31.

Gone, Joseph P. "Redressing First Nations Historical Trauma: Theorizing Mechanisms for Indigenous Culture as Mental Health Treatment." *Transcultural Psychiatry,* May 28, 2013. DOI: 10.1177/1363461513487669.

Gram, John. "Education on the Edge of Empire: Pueblos and the Federal Boarding Schools, 1880–1930." PhD diss., Southern Methodist University, 2012.

Grant, Agnes. *No End of Grief: Residential Schools in Canada.* Winnipeg: Pemmican Publications, 1996.

Green, Robyn. "Unsettling Cures: Exploring the Limits of the Indian Residential School Settlement Agreement." *Canadian Journal of Law and Society* 27,1 (2012): 129–48.

Greenfield, Philip J. "Escape from Albuquerque: An Apache Memorate." *American Indian Culture and Research Journal* 25, 3 (2001): 47–71.

Greenwalt, Alexander K. A. "Rethinking Genocidal Intent: The Case for a Knowledge-Based Interpretation." *Columbia Law Review* 99 (1999): 2259–94.

Gresko, Jacqueline. "Creating Little Dominions within the Dominion: Early Catholic Indian Schools in Saskatchewan and British Columbia." In *Indian Education in Canada I*, edited by J. Barman, Y. Hebert, and D. McCaskill, 93–109. Vancouver: UBC Press, 1986.

———. "White 'Rites' and Indian 'Rites': Indian Education and Native Responses in the West." In *Western Canada: Past and Present*, edited by A. W. Rasporich, 163–81. Calgary: University of Calgary Press, 1975.

Grinde, Donald A. "Taking the Indian out of the Indian: U.S. Policies of Ethnocide through Education." *Wicazo Sa Review* 19, 2 (2004): 25–32.

Habermas, Jürgen. *The New Conservatism: Cultural Criticism and the Historians' Debate*. Boston: MIT Press, 1991.

Hagan, William T. *The Indian Rights Association: The Herbert Welsh Years, 1882–1904*. Tucson: University of Arizona Press, 1985.

Haig-Brown, Celia. *Resistance and Renewal: Surviving the Indian Residential School*. Vancouver: Tillicum Library, 1988.

Haig-Brown, Celia, and David A. Nock, eds. *With Good Intentions: Euro-Canadian and Aboriginal Relations in Colonial Canada*. Vancouver: UBC Press, 2006.

Hamley, Jeffrey. "An Introduction to the Federal Indian Boarding School Movement." *North Dakota History* 61, 2 (1994): 2–9.

Hardt, Michael, and Antonio Negri. *Multitude: War and Democracy in the Age of Empire*. New York: Penguin, 2004.

Haskins, Victoria K. *Matrons and Maids: Regulating Indian Domestic Service in Tucson, 1914–1934*. Phoenix: University of Arizona Press, 2012.

Hauptman, Laurence M. *Tribes and Tribulations: Misconceptions about American Indians and Their Histories*. Albuquerque: University of New Mexico Press, 1995.

Hayek, Frederick. *The Constitution of Liberty*. Chicago: University of Chicago Press, 1960.

Hays, Robert. *Editorializing "the Indian Problem": The New York Times on Native Americans, 1860–1900*. Carbondale: Southern Illinois University Press, 1997.

Henderson, Jennifer, and Pauline Wakeham. "Colonial Reckoning, National Reconciliation? Aboriginal Peoples and the Culture of Redress in Canada." *English Studies in Canada* 35, 1 (2009): 1–26.

Herschkopf, Jayme, Julie Hunter, and Laurel E. Fletcher. *Genocide Reinterpreted: An Analysis of the Genocide Convention's Potential Application to Canada's Indian Residential School System*. Draft report prepared for the Truth and Reconciliation Commission of Canada. Winnipeg: Truth and Reconciliation Commission of Canada, 2011.

Hertzberg, Hazel W. *The Search for an American Indian Identity: Modern Pan-Indian Movements*. Syracuse, NY: Syracuse University Press, 1971.

Hinton, Alexander L. "Critical Genocide Studies." *Genocide Studies and Prevention* 7, 1 (2012): 4–15.

———. *Why Did They Kill? Cambodia in the Shadow of Genocide*. Berkeley: University of California Press, 2005.

Horowitz, Irving Louis. *Taking Lives: Genocide and State Power*. 4th ed. New Brunswick, NJ: Transaction Publishers, 1997.

House, Deborah. *Language Shift among the Navajos: Identity Politics and Cultural Continuity*. Tucson: University of Arizona Press, 2005.

Hoxie, Frederick. *The Final Promise: The Campaign to Assimilate the Indian, 1880–1920*. Lincoln: University of Nebraska Press, 1983.

Hubbard, Tasha. "'Kill, Skin, and Sell': Buffalo Genocide." In *Colonial Genocide in Indigenous North America*, edited by Andrew Woolford, Jeff Benvenuto, and Alexander Laban Hinton, 292–305 Durham, NC: Duke University Press, 2014.

Humphrey, Michael. "From Victim to Victimhood: Truth Commissions and Trials as Rituals of Political Transition and Individual Healing." *Australian Journal of Anthropology* 14, 2 (2003): 171–87.

Hyer, Sally. *One House, One Voice, One Heart: Native American Education at the Santa Fe Indian School*. Santa Fe: Museum of New Mexico Press, 1990.

Irvin-Ericson, Douglas. "Genocide, the 'Family of Mind,' and the Romantic Signature of Raphael Lemkin." *Journal of Genocide Research* 15, 3: 273–96.

Jacobs, Margaret D. "A Battle for the Children: American Indian Removal in Arizona in the Era of Assimilation." Faculty Publications, Department of History, University of Nebraska—Lincoln, 2004. http://digitalcommons.unl.edu/historyfacpub/3.

———. *Engendered Encounters: Feminism and Pueblo Cultures, 1879–1934*. Lincoln: University of Nebraska Press, 1999.

———. "The Habit of Elimination: Indigenous Child Removal in Settler Colonial Nations in the Twentieth Century." In *Colonial Genocide in Indigenous North America*, edited by Andrew Woolford, Jeff Benvenuto, and Alexander Laban Hinton, 189–207. Durham, NC: Duke University Press, 2014.

———. "Indian Boarding Schools in Comparative Perspective: The Removal of Indigenous Children in the United States and Australia, 1880–1940." In *Boarding School Blues: Revisiting American Indian Educational Experiences*, edited by

Clifford E. Trafzer, Jean A. Keller, and Lorene Sisquoc, 202–31. Lincoln: University of Nebraska Press, 2006.

————. "Remembering the Forgotten Child." *American Indian Quarterly* 37, 2 (2013): 136–59.

————. *White Mother to a Dark Race: Settler Colonialism, Maternalism, and the Removal of Indigenous Children in the American West and Australia, 1880–1940.* Lincoln: University of Nebraska Press, 2009.

Jacoby, Karl. "'The Broad Platform of Extermination': Nature and Violence in the Nineteenth Century North American Borderlands." *Journal of Genocide Research* 10, 2 (2008): 249–67.

Jafri, Beenash. "Desire, Settler Colonialism, and the Racialized Cowboy." *American Indian Culture and Research Journal* 37, 2 (2013): 73–86.

Jaimes, M. Annette. "Federal Indian Identification Policy: A Usurpation of Indigenous Sovereignty in North America." In *The State of Native America: Genocide, Colonization, and Resistance,* edited by M. Annette Jaimes, 123–38. Boston: South End Press, 1992.

James, Matt. "A Carnival of Truth: Knowledge, Ignorance, and the Canadian Truth and Reconciliation Commission." *International Journal of Transitional Justice* 6 (2012): 182–204.

James, Thomas. "Rhetoric and Resistance: Social Science and Community Schools for Navajos in the 1930s." *History of Education Quarterly* 28, 4 (1988): 599–626.

Jenson, Katherine. "Teachers and Progressives: The Navajo Day-School Experiment 1935–1945." *Arizona and the West* 25, 1 (1983): 49–62.

Johnson, Broderick. *Navajo Stories of the Long Walk Period.* Tsaile, Navajo Nation, AZ: Navajo Community College Press, 1973.

Johnston, Basil. *Indian School Days.* Norman: University of Oklahoma Press, 1988.

Jones, Adam. *Genocide: A Comprehensive Introduction.* 2nd ed. London: Routledge, 2010.

Keller, Robert H., Jr. *American Protestantism and the United States Indian Policy, 1869–82.* Lincoln: University of Nebraska Press, 1983.

Kelly, L. C. *The Assault on Assimilation: John Collier and the Origins of Indian Policy Reform.* Albuquerque: University of New Mexico Press, 1963.

Kelm, May-Ellen. *Colonizing Bodies: Aboriginal Health and Healing in British Columbia, 1900–1950.* Vancouver: UBC Press, 1999.

————. "'A Scandalous Procession': Residential Schooling and the Re/formation of Aboriginal Bodies, 1900–1950." *Native Studies Review* 11, 2 (1996): 51–88.

Kelman, Herbert C., and V. Lee Hamilton. *Crimes of Obedience: Toward a Social Psychology of Authority and Responsibility.* New Haven, CT: Yale University Press, 1989.

Kiernan, Ben. "The First Genocide: Carthage, 146 BC." *Diogenes* 51, 3 (2004): 27–39.

King, A. Richard. *The School at Mopas: A Question of Identity.* New York: Holt, Rinehart, and Winston, 1967.

Kirmayer, Laurence J., Joseph P. Gone, and Joshua Moses. "Rethinking Cultural Trauma." *Transcultural Psychiatry* 51, 3 (2014): 299–319.

Kohl, Seena B. "Genocide and Ethnogenesis: A Case Study of the Mississippi Band of Choctaw, a Genocide Avoided." *Holocaust and Genocide Studies* 1, 1 (1986): 91–100.

Kuper, Leo. *Genocide: Its Political Use in the Twentieth Century.* New Haven, CT: Yale University Press, 1981.

Laderman, Scott. "'It Is Cheaper and Better to Teach a Young Indian than to Fight an Old One': Thaddeus Pound and the Logic of Assimilation." *American Indian Culture and Research Journal* 26, 3 (2002): 85–111.

Latour, Bruno. *Science in Action: How to Follow Scientists and Engineers through Society.* Milton Keynes: Open University Press, 1987.

———. *We Have Never Been Modern.* Cambridge, MA: Harvard University Press, 1993.

Laukaitis, John J. "Indians at Work and John Collier's Campaign for Progressive Education Reform, 1933–45." *American Educational History Journal* 33, 2 (2006): 97–105.

La Violette, Forrest E. *The Struggle for Survival: Indian Cultures and the Protestant Ethic in British Columbia.* Toronto: University of Toronto Press, 1961.

Law, John. "Actor Network Theory and Material Semiotics." April 25, 2007. http://www.heterogeneities.net/publications/Law2007aNTandMaterialSemiotics.pdf.

Lawrence, Adrea. *Lessons from an Indian Day School: Negotiating Colonization in Northern New Mexico, 1902–1907.* Lawrence: University Press of Kansas, 2011.

Lawrence, Bonita. "Gender, Race, and the Regulation of Native Identity in Canada and the United States: An Overview." *Hypatia* 18, 2 (2003): 3–31.

———. *"Real" Indians and Others: Mixed-Blood Urban Native Peoples and Indigenous Nationhood.* Lincoln: University of Nebraska Press, 2004.

Lemkin, Raphael. "Acts Constituting a General (Transnational) Danger Considered as Offences against the Law of Nations." Unpublished manuscript, 1933. http://www.preventgenocide.org/lemkin/madrid1933-english.htm.

———. *Axis Rule in Occupied Europe: Laws of Occupation, Analysis of Government, Proposals for Redress.* Washington DC: Carnegie Endowment for International Peace, 1944.

———. *Totally Unofficial: The Autobiography of Raphael Lemkin.* Edited by Donna Lee Frieze. New Haven, CT: Yale University Press, 2013.

Letgers, Lyman H. "The American Genocide." *Policy Studies Journal* 16, 4 (1988): 768–77.

———. "The Soviet Gulag: Is It Genocidal?" In *Toward the Understanding and Prevention of Genocide: Proceedings of the International Conference on the Holocaust and Genocide,* edited by I. W. Charny, 60–66. Boulder, CO: Westview Press, 1984.

Levene, Mark. "Empires, Native Peoples, and Genocide." In *Empire, Colony, and Genocide: Conquest, Occupation, and Subaltern Resistance in World History*, edited by A. Dirk Moses, 183–204. New York: Berghahn Books, 2008.

——. *The Rise of the West and the Coming of Genocide: Part II of Genocide in the Age of the Nation State*. London: I. B. Tauris, 2013.

Levinas, Emmanuel. *Ethics and Infinity: Conversations with Philippe Nemo*. Translated by R. A. Cohen. Pittsburgh: Duquesne University Press, 1982.

Lewy, Guenter. "Can There Be Genocide without the Intent to Commit Genocide?" *Journal of Genocide Research* 9, 4 (2007): 661–74.

Limerick, Patricia Nelson. *The Legacy of Conquest: The Unbroken Past of the American West*. New York: W. W. Norton, 1987.

Littlefield, Alice. "The BIA Boarding School: Theories of Resistance and Social Reproduction." *Humanity and Society* 13, 4 (1999): 428–41.

Lomawaima, K. Tsianna. "Domesticity in the Federal Indian Schools: The Power of Authority over Mind and Body." *American Ethnologist* 20, 2 (1993): 227–40.

——. "Oral Histories from Chilocco Indian Agricultural School, 1920–40." *American Indian Quarterly* 11, 3 (1987): 241–54.

——. *They Called It Prairie Light: The Story of Chilocco Indian School*. Lincoln: University of Nebraska Press, 1994.

Lord, Albert B. *The Singer of Tales*. New York: Atheneum, 1965 [1960].

Lux, Maureen K. *Medicine that Walks: Disease, Medicine, and Canadian Plains Native People, 1880–1940*. Toronto: University of Toronto Press, 2001.

MacDonald, David. "First Nations, Residential Schools, and the Americanization of the Holocaust: Rewriting Indigenous History in the United States and Canada." *Canadian Journal of Political Science* 40, 4 (2007): 995–1015.

MacDonald, David B., and Graham Hudson. "The Genocide Question and Indian Residential Schools in Canada." *Canadian Journal of Political Science* 45, 2 (2012): 427–49.

Macgregor, Russell. "Governance, Not Genocide: Aboriginal Assimilation in the Postwar Era." In *Genocide and Settler Society: Frontier Violence and Stolen Indigenous Children in Australian History*, edited by A. Dirk Moses, 290–311. New York: Berghahn Books, 2004.

Madley, Benjamin. "Patterns of Frontier Genocide, 1803–1910: The Aboriginal Tasmanians, the Yuki of California, and the Herero of Namibia." *Journal of Genocide Research* 6, 2 (2004): 167–92.

Mallon, Florencia E., ed. *Decolonizing Native Histories: Collaboration, Knowledge, and Language in the Americas*. Durham, NC: Duke University Press, 2011.

Mann, Michael. *The Dark Side of Democracy: Explaining Ethnic Cleansing*. Cambridge, UK: Cambridge University Press, 2005.

Margolis, Eric. "Looking at Discipline, Looking at Labour: Photographic Representations of Indian Boarding Schools." *Visual Studies* 19, 1 (2004): 72–96.

Marker, Michael. "After the Whalehunt: Indigenous Knowledge and the Limits to Multicultural Discourse." *Urban Education* 42, 2 (2006): 1–26.

Martin, Michael T., and Marilyn Yaquinto, eds. *Redress for Historical Injustices in the United States: On Reparations for Slavery, Jim Crow, and Their Legacies.* Durham, NC: Duke University Press, 2007.

Mazower, Mark. "Review Essay: Violence and the State in the Twentieth Century." *American Historical Review* 107, 4 (2007): 1158–78.

McBeth, Sally. *Ethnic Identity and the Boarding School Experience of West-Central Oklahoma Indians.* Washington DC: University Press of America, 1983.

———. "Indian Boarding Schools and Ethnic Identity: An Example from the Southern Plains Tribes of Oklahoma." *Plains Anthropologist* 28, 100 (1983): 119–28.

McDonnell, Michael A., and A. Dirk Moses. "Raphael Lemkin as Historian of Genocide in the Americas." *Journal of Genocide Research* 7, 4 (2005): 501–29.

McFarlane, Kimberly Ann. "Educating First-Nation Children in Canada: The Rise and Fall of Residential Schooling." MA thesis, Queen's University, 1999.

McKegney, Sam. *Magic Weapons: Aboriginal Writers Remaking Community after Residential School.* Winnipeg: University of Manitoba Press, 2007.

McKinney, Lillie G. "History of the Albuquerque Indian School." MA thesis, University of New Mexico, 1934.

Melson, Robert. "Critique of Current Genocide Studies." *Genocide Studies and Prevention* 6, 3 (2011): 279–86.

Metcalf, Ann Hillyer Rosenthal. "The Effects of Boarding School on Navajo Self-Image and Maternal Behavior." PhD diss., Stanford University, 1975.

Meyn, Susan Labry. *More than Curiosities: A Grassroots History of the Indian Arts and Crafts Board and Its Precursors, 1920–1942.* Lanham, MD: Lexington Books, 2001.

Mezey, Naomi. "The Distribution of Wealth, Sovereignty, and Culture through Indian Gaming." In *When Sorry Isn't Enough: The Controversy over Apologies and Reparations for Human Injustice,* edited by R. L. Brooks, 298–303. New York: New York University Press, 1999.

Miller, J. R. "The Irony of Residential Schooling." *Canadian Journal of Native Education* 14, 2 (1987): 3–14.

———. *Shingwauk's Vision: A History of Native Residential Schools.* Toronto: University of Toronto Press, 1996.

———. *Skyscrapers Hide the Heavens: A History of Indian-White Relations in Canada.* Toronto: University of Toronto Press, 1989.

Miller, James, and Edmund Danziger, Jr. "'In the Care of Strangers': Walpole Island First Nation's Experiences with Residential Schools after the First World War." *Ontario History* 92, 2 (2000): 71–88.

Milloy, John S. "The Early Indian Acts: Development Strategy and Constitutional Change." In *As Long as the Sun Shines and the Water Flows: A Reader in Canadian Native Studies*, edited by Ian A. L. Getty and Antoine S. Lussier, 39–64. Vancouver: UBC Press, 1983.

———. *A National Crime: The Canadian Government and the Residential School System, 1879 to 1986.* Winnipeg: University of Manitoba Press, 1999.

Moon, Claire. "Healing Past Violence: Traumatic Assumptions and Therapeutic Interventions in War and Reconciliation." *Journal of Human Rights* 8, 1 (2009): 71–91.

Morrissette, Patrick J. "The Holocaust of First Nation People: Residual Effects on Parenting and Treatment Implications." *Contemporary Family Therapy* 16, 5 (1994): 381–92.

Morsink, Johannes. "Cultural Genocide, the Universal Declaration, and Minority Rights." *Human Rights Quarterly* 21, 4 (1999): 1009–60.

Mosby, Ian. "Administering Colonial Science: Nutrition Research and Human Biomedical Experimentation in Aboriginal Communities and Residential Schools, 1942–1952." *Histoire sociale/Social History* 46, 91 (2013): 145–72.

Moses, A. Dirk. "An Antipodean Genocide? The Origins of the Genocidal Moment in the Colonization of Australia." *Journal of Genocide Research* 2, 1 (2000): 89–106.

———. "Empire, Colony, Genocide: Keywords and the Philosophy of History." In *Empire, Colony, and Genocide: Conquest, Occupation, and Subaltern Resistance in World History*, edited by A. Dirk Moses, 3–54. New York: Berghahn Books, 2008.

———. "Genocide and Settler Society in Australian History." In *Genocide and Settler Society: Frontier Violence and Stolen Indigenous Children in Australian History*, edited by A. Dirk Moses, 4–48. New York: Berghahn Books, 2004.

Nagel, Joane. *American Indian Ethnic Renewal: Red Power and the Resurgence of Identity and Culture.* New York: Oxford University Press, 1997.

Nagy, Rosemary L. "The Scope and Bounds of Transitional Justice and the Canadian Truth and Reconciliation Commission." *International Journal of Transitional Justice* 7 (2013): 52–73.

Nagy, Rosemary, and Robinder Kaur Sehdev. "Introduction: Residential Schools and Decolonization." *Canadian Journal of Law and Society* 27, 1 (2012): 67–73.

Neu, Dean, and Richard Therrien. *Accounting for Genocide: Canada's Bureaucratic Assault on Aboriginal People.* Black Point, NS: Fernwood Publishing, 2003.

Newman, Dwight. *Community and Collective Rights: A Theoretical Framework for Rights Held by Groups.* Portland: Hart Publishing, 2011.

Newton, Neil Jessup. "Indian Claims for Reparations, Compensation, and Restitution in the United States Legal System." In *When Sorry Isn't Enough: The Controversy over Apologies and Reparations for Human Injustice*, edited by R. L. Brooks, 261–72. New York: New York University Press, 1999.

Nichols, Roger L. *Indians in the United States and Canada: A Comparative History*. Lincoln: University of Nebraska Press, 1998.

Niezen, Ronald. *Truth and Indignation: Canada's Truth and Reconciliation on Indian Residential Schools*. Toronto: University of Toronto Press, 2013.

Nock, David A. "The Canadian Indian Research and Aid Society: A Victorian Voluntary Association." *Western Canadian Journal of Anthropology* 6 (1976): 31–48.

Novick, Peter. *The Holocaust in American Life*. Boston: Mariner Books, 1999.

One House, One Voice, One Heart: Native American Education at the Santa Fe Indian School, Exhibition Catalogue. Santa Fe: Museum of New Mexico Press, n.d.

Owens, Peter B., Yang Su, and David A. Snow. "Social Scientific Inquiry into Genocide and Mass Killing: From Unitary Outcome to Complex Processes." *Annual Review of Sociology* 39 (2013): 69–84.

Palmater, Pamela. *Beyond Blood: Rethinking Indigenous Identity and Belonging*. Saskatoon, SK: Purich Publishing, 2011.

Palmer, Alison. "Colonial and Modern Genocide: Explanations and Categories." *Ethnic and Racial Studies* 21, 1 (1998): 89–115.

———. *Colonial Genocide*. Adelaide: Crawford House, 2000.

Parman, Donald L. *The Navajos and the New Deal*. New Haven, CT: Yale University Press, 1976.

Paul, Dan. *We Were Not the Savages: Collision between European and Native American Civilizations*. 3rd ed. Halifax: Fernwood Publishing, 2006.

Paxton, Katrina A. "Learning Gender: Female Students at the Sherman Institute, 1907–1925." In *Boarding School Blues: Revisiting American Indian Educational Experiences*, edited by Clifford E. Trafzer, Jean A. Keller, and Lorene Sisquoc, 174–86. Lincoln: University of Nebraska Press, 2006.

Petoukhov, Konstantin. "An Evaluation of Canada's Truth and Reconciliation Commission through the Lens of Restorative Justice and the Theory of Recognition." MA thesis, University of Manitoba, 2011.

Philp, Kenneth R. *John Collier's Crusade for Indian Reform, 1920–1954*. Tucson: University of Arizona Press, 1977.

Piatote, Beth. *Domestic Subjects: Gender, Citizenship, and Law in Native American Literature*. New Haven, CT: Yale University Press, 2013.

Pile, Scott. "Introduction: Opposition, Political Identities, and Spaces of Resistance." In *Geographies of Resistance*, edited by S. Pile and M. Keith, 1–32. London: Routledge, 1997.

Ponting, J. Rick, and Roger Gibbons. *Out of Irrelevance: A Sociopolitical Introduction to Indian Affairs in Canada*. Toronto: Butterworth and Company, 1980.

Powell, Christopher. *Barbaric Civilization: A Critical Sociology of Genocide*. Montreal: McGill-Queen's University Press, 2011.

———. "What Do Genocides Kill? A Relational Conception of Genocide." *Journal of Genocide Research* 9, 4 (2007): 527–47.

Powell, Christopher, and Julia Peristerakis. "Genocide in Canada: A Relational View." In *Colonial Genocide and Indigenous North America*, edited by Andrew Woolford, Jeff Benvenuto, and Alexander Laban Hinton, 70–92. Durham, NC: Duke University Press, 2014.

Power, Samantha. *A Problem from Hell: America and the Age of Genocide*. New York: Harper, 2003.

Prucha, Francis Paul. *The Churches and the Indian Schools, 1888–1912*. Lincoln: University of Nebraska Press, 1979.

———. *The Great Father: The United States Government and the American Indians, Volumes I and II*. Lincoln: University of Nebraska Press, 1984.

Raibman, Roberta. "'In Loco Parentis': G. H. Raley and a Residential School Philosophy." *Journal of the Canadian Church Historical Society* 38 (1996): 29–52.

Raibmon, Paige. "'A New Understanding of Things Indian': George Raley's Negotiation of the Residential School Experience." *BC Studies* 110 (1996): 69–96.

Ratner, R. S., and Andrew Woolford. "Mesomobilization and Fragile Coalition: Aboriginal Politics and Treaty-Making in British Columbia." *Research in Social Movements, Conflicts, and Change* 28 (2008): 113–36.

Ratner, R. S., Andrew Woolford, and Andrew Patterson. "Obstacles on the Path to Post-Genocide Repair: A Comparative Analysis, 1945–2010." *International Journal of Comparative Sociology* 55, 4 (2014): 229–59

Reading, Charlotte Loppie, and Fred Wien. *Health Inequalities and Social Determinants of Aboriginal Peoples' Health*. Prince George: National Collaborating Centre for Aboriginal Health, 2009.

Regan, Paulette. *Unsettling the Settler Within: Indian Residential Schools, Truth Telling, and Reconciliation in Canada*. Vancouver: UBC Press, 2011.

Reyhner, Jon, and Jeanne Eder. *American Indian Education: A History*. Norman: University of Oklahoma Press, 2004.

Riney, Scott. *The Rapid City Indian School 1898–1933*. Norman: University of Oklahoma Press, 1999.

———. "Review: *Education by Hardship: Native American Boarding Schools in the U.S. and Canada*." *Oral History Review* 24, 2 (1997): 117–23.

Roessel, Ruth, and Broderick H. Johnson, eds. *Navajo Livestock Reduction: A National Disgrace*. Chinle, AZ: Navajo Community College Press, 1974.

Rosenberg, Sheri P. "Genocide Is a Process, Not an Event." *Genocide Studies and Prevention* 7, 1 (2012): 16–23.

Rothman, David. *The Discovery of the Asylum: Social Order and Disorder in the New Republic.* Boston: Little, Brown, 1971.

Rusco, E. R. "John Collier, Architect of Sovereignty or Assimilation?" *American Indian Quarterly* 15, 1 (1991): 49–55.

Ryerson University's Aboriginal Education Council. "Egerton Ryerson, the Residential School System, and Truth and Reconciliation." Toronto: Ryerson, 2010. http://www .ryerson.ca/content/dam/aec/pdfs/egerton%20ryerson_fullstatement.pdf.

Sando, Joe S. *The Pueblo Indians.* San Francisco: Indian Historian Press, 1976.

———. *Pueblo Nations: Eight Centuries of Pueblo Indian History.* Santa Fe: Clear Light Publishers, 1992.

Sarche, Michelle, and Paul Spicer. "Poverty and Health Disparities for American Indian and Alaska Native Children: Current Knowledge and Future Prospects." *Annals of the New York Academy of Sciences* 1136 (2008): 126–36.

Satzewich, Vic, and Linda Mahood. "Indian Agents and the Residential School System in Canada, 1946–1970." *Historical Studies in Education* 7, 1 (1995): 45–69.

Saunders, Francis. *The Indians of the Terraced Houses.* New York: G. P. Putnam and Sons, 1912.

Schabas, W. A. "Genocide and the International Court of Justice: Finally, a Duty to Prevent the Crime of Crimes." *Genocide Studies and Prevention* 2, 2 (2007): 101–22.

Schaller, Dominik J. "From Lemkin to Clooney: The Development and State of Genocide Studies." *Genocide Studies and Prevention* 6, 3 (2011): 245–56.

Schaller, Dominik J., and Jurgen Zimmerer. "Settlers, Imperialism, Genocide: Seeing the Global without Ignoring the Local—Introduction." *Journal of Genocide Research* 10, 2 (2008): 191–99.

Schissel, Bernard, and Terry Wotherspoon. *The Legacy of School for Aboriginal People: Education, Oppression, and Emancipation.* Don Mills, ON: Oxford University Press, 2003.

Schwartz, E. A. "Red Atlantis Revisited: Community and Culture in the Writings of John Collier." *American Indian Quarterly* 18, 4 (1994): 507–31.

Scott, James C. *Domination and the Arts of Resistance: Hidden Transcripts.* New Haven, CT: Yale University Press, 1990.

———. *Thinking like a State: How Certain Schemes to Improve the Human Condition Have Failed.* New Haven, CT: Yale University Press, 1998.

Sealey, D. B. *The Education of Native Peoples in Manitoba. Monographs in Education Series.* Winnipeg: University of Manitoba, 1980.

Shaw, Martin. *What Is Genocide?* London: Polity, 2007.

Short, Damien. "Australia: A Continuing Genocide?" *Journal of Genocide Research* 12, 1 (2010): 45–68.

———. "Cultural Genocide and Indigenous Peoples: A Sociological Approach." *International Journal of Human Rights* 14, 6 (2010): 833–48.

Sibley, David. *Geographies of Exclusion*. London: Routledge, 1995.

Silko, Leslie Marmon. *Ceremony*. New York: Penguin, 1977.

Simpson, Leanne. *Dancing on Our Turtle's Back: Stories of Nishnaabeg Re-Creation, Resurgence, and a New Emergence*. Winnipeg: Arbeiter Ring, 2011.

Sinclair, Raven. "Identity Lost and Found: Lessons from the Sixties Scoop." *First Peoples Child and Family Review* 3, 1 (2007): 65–82.

Smith, Andrea. "Boarding School Abuses, Human Rights, and Reparations." *Social Justice* 31, 4 (2004): 89–102.

———. "Boarding School Abuses, Human Rights, and Reparations." *Journal of Religion and Abuse* 8, 2 (2006): 5–21.

———. *Indigenous Peoples and Boarding Schools: A Comparative Study*. Permanent Forum on Indigenous Issues, Eighth Session, New York, May 18–29, 2009.

Smith, Derek. "The 'Policy of Aggressive Civilization' and Projects of Governance in Roman Catholic Industrial Schools for Native Peoples in Canada, 1870–95." *Anthropologica* 43, 2 (2001): 253–71.

Smith, Donald A. "John A. Macdonald and Aboriginal Canada." *Historic Kingston* 50 (2002): 9–30.

Smith, Linda Tuhiwai. *Decolonizing Methodologies: Research and Indigenous Peoples*. 2nd ed. London: Zed Books, 2012.

Smith, Maureen. 2001. "Forever Changed: Boarding School Narratives of American Indian Identity in the U.S. and Canada." *Indigenous Nations Studies Journal* 2, 2 (2001): 57–82.

Smith, Sherry L. "Reconciliation and Restitution in the American West." *Western Historical Quarterly* 41 (2010): 5–25.

Snow, David A., and Robert D. Benford. "Ideology, Frame Resonance, and Participant Mobilization." *International Social Movement Research* 1 (1988): 197–217.

———. "Master Frames and Cycles of Protest." In *Frontiers in Social Movement Theory*, edited by A. D. Morris and C. McClurg Mueller, 133–55. New Haven, CT: Yale University Press, 1992.

Sofsky, Wolfgang. *The Order of Terror: The Concentration Camp*. Translated by William Templar. Princeton, NJ: Princeton University Press, 1993.

Sousa, Ashley Riley. "'They Will Be Hunted Down like Wild Beasts and Destroyed': A Comparative Study of Genocide in California and Tasmania." *Journal of Genocide Research* 6, 2 (2004): 193–209.

Sowby, Joyce Katherine. "Macdonald the Administrator: Department of the Interior and Indian Affairs, 1878–1887." PhD diss., Queen's University, 1984.

Sproule-Jones, Megan. "Crusading for the Forgotten: Dr. Peter Bryce, Public Health, and Prairie Native Residential Schools." *Canadian Bulletin of Medical History* 12 (1996): 199–224.

Stannard, David E. *American Holocaust: Columbus and the Conquest of the New World.* New York: Oxford University Press, 1992.

Stanton, Kim. "Canada's Truth and Reconciliation Commission: Settling the Past?" *International Indigenous Policy Journal* 2, 3 (2011): n. pag. http://ir.lib.uwo.ca /iipj/vol2/iss3/2.

Stedman-Jones, David. *Masters of the Universe: Hayek, Friedman, and the Birth of Neoliberal Politics.* Princeton, NJ: Princeton University Press, 2012.

Stoler, Laura Ann. *Carnal Knowledge and Imperial Power: Race and the Intimate in Colonial Rule.* Berkeley: University of California Press, 2002.

Stonechild, A. Blair. "The Indian View of the 1885 Uprising." In *Sweet Promises: A Reader on Indian-White Relations in Canada,* edited by J. R. Miller, 259–76. Toronto: University of Toronto Press, 1991.

Straus, Scott. "Contested Meanings and Conflicting Imperatives: A Conceptual Analysis of Genocide." *Journal of Genocide Research* 3, 3 (2001): 349–75.

Szasz, Margaret Connell. *Education and the American Indian: The Road to Self-Determination since 1928.* Albuquerque: University of New Mexico Press, 1999.

———. "'I Knew How to Be Moderate. And I Knew How to Obey': The Commonality of American Indian Boarding School Experiences, 1750s–1920s." *American Indian Culture and Research Journal* 29, 4 (2005): 75–94.

———. *Indian Education in the American Colonies, 1607–1783.* Albuquerque: University of New Mexico Press, 1988.

Tate, Michael L. "From Scout to Doughboy: The National Debate over Integration of American Indians into the Military, 1891–1918." *Western Historical Quarterly* 17 (1986): 416–37.

Tatz, Colin. "Confronting Australian Genocide." *Aboriginal History* 25 (2001): 16–25.

———. "Genocide Studies: An Australian Perspective." *Genocide Studies and Prevention* 6, 3 (2011): 231–44.

Tavuchis, Nicholas. *Mea Culpa: A Sociology of Apology and Reconciliation.* Stanford, CA: Stanford University Press, 1991.

Taylor, Jonathan B. *Determinants of Development Success in the Native Nations of the United States.* Tucson: Native Nations Institute for Leadership, Management, and Policy; Cambridge, MA: Harvard Project on American Indian Economic Development, 2008.

Tennant, Paul. *Aboriginal Peoples and Politics.* Vancouver: UBC Press, 1990.

Terry, M. J. "Kelengakutelleghpat: An Arctic Community-Based Approach to Trauma." In *Secondary Traumatic Stress: Self-Care Issues for Clinicians, Researchers, and Educators*, edited by B. H. Stamm, 149–78. Baltimore, MD: Sidron Press, 1995.

Theriault, Henry. "Against the Grain: Critical Reflections on the State and Future of Genocide Scholarship." *Genocide Studies and Prevention* 7, 1 (2012): 123–44.

Thompson, Hildegard. *The Navajos' Long Walk for Education: A History of Navajo Education*. Tsaile, Navajo Nation, AZ: Navajo Community College Press, 1975.

Thornton, Russell. *American Indian Holocaust and Survival: A Population History since 1492*. Norman: University of Oklahoma Press, 1987.

———. "Native American Demographic and Tribal Survival into the Twenty-First Century." *American Studies* 46, 3–4 (2005): 23–38.

Tickell, Adam, and Jamie A. Peck. "Social Regulation after Fordism: Regulation Theory, Neoliberalism, and the Global-Local Nexus." *Economy and Society* 24, 3 (1995): 357–86.

Tinker, George. *Missionary Conquest: The Gospel and Native American Cultural Genocide*. Minneapolis: Fortress Press, 1993.

Titley, E. Brian. *A Narrow Vision: Duncan Campbell Scott and the Administration of Indian Affairs in Canada*. Vancouver: UBC Press, 1986.

Tobias, John L. "Protection, Civilization, Assimilation: An Outline History of Canada's Indian Policy." In *Sweet Promises: A Reader on Indian-White Relations in Canada*, edited by J.R. Miller, 127–44. Toronto: University of Toronto Press, 1991.

Torpey, John. *Making Whole What Has Been Smashed: On Reparations Politics*. Cambridge, MA: Harvard University Press, 2006.

Torpey, John, ed. *Politics and the Past: On Repairing Historical Injustices*. Lanham, MD: Rowman and Littlefield, 2003.

Trafzer, Clifford E., Jean A. Keller, and Lorene Sisquoc. "Introduction: Origin and Development of the American Indian Boarding School System." In *Boarding School Blues: Revisiting American Indian Educational Experiences*, edited by Clifford E. Trafzer, Jean A. Keller, and Lorene Sisquoc, 1–34. Lincoln: University of Nebraska Press, 2006.

Trafzer, Clifford E., Jean A. Keller, and Lorene Sisquoc, eds. *Boarding School Blues: Revisiting American Indian Educational Experiences*. Lincoln: University of Nebraska Press, 2006.

Travis, Hannibal. "On the Original Understanding of the Crime of Genocide." *Genocide Studies and Prevention* 7, 1 (2012): 30–55.

Trennert, Robert A. *The Phoenix Indian School: Forced Assimilation in Arizona, 1891–1935*. Norman: University of Oklahoma Press, 1988.

Trevithick, Scott. "Native Residential Schooling in Canada: A Review of Literature." *Canadian Journal of Native Studies* 18, 1 (1998): 49–86.

Truth and Reconciliation Commission of Canada. *They Came for the Children: Canada, Aboriginal Peoples, and Residential Schools.* Winnipeg: Truth and Reconciliation Commission of Canada, 2012.

Upton, L. F. S. "The Extermination of the Beothucks of Newfoundland." In *Sweet Promises: A Reader on Indian-White Relations in Canada*, edited by J. R. Miller, 68–92. Toronto: University of Toronto Press, 1991.

van Krieken, Robert. "The Barbarism of Civilization: Cultural Genocide and the 'Stolen Generations.'" *British Journal of Sociology* 50, 2 (1999): 297–315.

———. "Rethinking Cultural Genocide: Aboriginal Child Removal and Settler-Colonial State Formation." *Oceania* 75 (2004): 125–51.

Vansina, Jan. *Oral Tradition as History. Madison: University of Wisconsin Press, 1985.*

Veracini, Lorenzo. *Settler Colonialism: A Theoretical Overview.* London: Palgrave Macmillan, 2010.

Verdeja, Ernesto. "On Situating the Study of Genocide within Political Violence." *Genocide Studies and Prevention* 7, 1 (2012): 81–88.

Vizenor, Gerald. *Survivance: Narratives of Native Presence.* Lincoln: University of Nebraska Press, 2008.

Wacquant, Loïc. *Punishing the Poor: The Neoliberal Government of Social Insecurity.* Durham, NC: Duke University Press, 2009.

Wegner, Tisa. *We Have a Religion: The 1920s Pueblo Indian Dance Controversy and American Religious Freedom.* Chapel Hill: University of North Carolina Press, 2009.

Weisiger, Marsha. *Dreaming of Sheep in Navajo Country.* Seattle: University of Washington Press, 2009.

Wesley-Esquimaux, Cynthia C., and Magdelena Smolewski. *Historic Trauma and Aboriginal Healing.* Ottawa: Aboriginal Healing Foundation, 2004.

Whalen, Kevin. "Finding the Balance: Student Voices and Cultural Loss at Sherman Institute." *American Behavioral Scientist* 58, 1 (2014): 124–44.

Whitbeck, Les B., Gary W. Adams, Dan R. Hoyt, and Xiaojin Chen. "Conceptualizing and Measuring Historical Trauma among American Indian People." *American Journal of Community Psychology* 33, 3–4 (2004): 119–30.

White, Richard. *The Roots of Dependency: Subsistence, Environment, and Social Change among the Choctaws, Pawnees, and Navajos.* Lincoln: University of Nebraska Press, 1988.

Wilner, Isaiah Lorado. "A Global Potlatch: Identifying the Indigenous Influence on Western Thought." *American Indian Culture and Research Journal* 37, 2 (2013): 87–114.

Wilson, Daniel, and David Macdonald. *The Income Gap between Aboriginal Peoples and the Rest of Canada.* Ottawa: Canadian Centre for Policy Alternatives, 2010.

Wilson, Richard A. *The Politics of Truth and Reconciliation in South Africa: Legitimizing the Post-Apartheid State.* Cambridge, UK: Cambridge University Press, 2001.

Wilson, Wasiyatawin Angela. *Remember This! Dakota Decolonization and the Eli Taylor Narratives.* Lincoln: University of Nebraska Press, 2005.

Witherspoon, Gary. *Language and Art in the Navajo Universe.* Ann Arbor: University of Michigan Press, 1977.

Wolfe, Patrick. "Settler Colonialism and the Elimination of the Native." *Journal of Genocide Research* 8, 4 (2006): 387–409.

———. *Settler Colonialism and the Transformation of Anthropology: The Politics and Poetics of an Ethnographic Event.* London: Cassell, 1999.

———. "The Settler Complex: An Introduction." *American Indian Culture and Research Journal* 37, 2 (2013): 1–22.

Woolford, Andrew. *Between Justice and Certainty: Treaty-Making in British Columbia.* Vancouver: UBC Press, 2005.

———. "Discipline, Territory, and the Colonial Mesh: Boarding/Residential Schools in the U.S. and Canada." In *Colonial Genocide in Indigenous North America*, edited by Andrew Woolford, Jeff Benvenuto, and Alexander Laban Hinton, 29–48. Durham, NC: Duke University Press.

———. "Genocide, Affirmative Repair, and the British Columbia Treaty Process." In *Transitional Justice: Global Mechanisms and Local Realities after Genocide and Mass Atrocity*, edited by A. L. Hinton, 137–56. Newark, NJ: Rutgers University Press, 2011.

———. "Governing through Repair: Transitional Justice and Indigenous Peoples in Canada." In *Facing the Past: Finding Remedies for Grave Historical Injustice*, edited by Peter Malcontent. Antwerp: Intersentia Publishers, forthcoming.

———. "Nodal Repair and Networks of Destruction: Residential Schools, Colonial Genocide, and Redress in Canada." *Settler Colonial Studies* 3, 1 (2013): 61–77.

———. "Ontological Destruction: Genocide and Aboriginal Peoples in Canada." *Genocide Studies and Prevention: An International Journal* 4, 1 (2009): 81–97.

———. "Transition and Transposition: Genocide, Land, and the British Columbia Treaty Process." *New Proposals: Journal of Marxism and Interdisciplinary Inquiry* 4, 2 (2011): n. pag. http://ojs.library.ubc.ca/index.php/newproposals/article/view/2010.

Woolford, Andrew, and Amelia Curran. "Community Positions, Neoliberal Dispositions: Neoliberalism, Welfare, and Reflexivity within the Social Service Field." *Critical Sociology* 39, 1 (2013): 45–63.

———. "Limited Autonomy, Neoliberal Domination, and Ethical Distancing in the Social Services." *Critical Social Policy* 31, 4 (2011): 583–606.

Woolford, Andrew, and Amanda Nelund. "The Responsibilities of the Poor: Performing Neoliberal Citizenship within the Social Service Field." *Social Service Review* 87, 2 (2013): 292–318.

Woolford, Andrew, and R. S. Ratner. *Informal Reckonings: Conflict Resolution in Mediation, Restorative Justice, and Reparations.* London: Routledge-Cavendish, 2008.

Woolford, Andrew, and Jasmine Thomas. "Genocide and Aboriginal Peoples in Canada: A Dialogue in Waiting." In *The Ethnocide and Genocide of Indigenous Peoples*, edited by S. Totten and R. Hitchcock, 61–86. Edison, NJ: Transaction Publishers, 2010.

Woolford, Andrew, and Stefan Wolejszo. "Collecting on Moral Debts: Reparations, the Holocaust, and the Porrajmos." *Law and Society Review* 40, 4 (2006): 871–902.

Wotherspoon, Terry, and Vic Satzewich. *First Nations: Race, Class, and Gender Relations.* 2nd ed. Regina, SK: Canadian Plains Research Center, 2000.

Zimmerer, Jürgen. "Colonialism and the Holocaust—Toward an Archeology of Genocide." *Development Dialogue—Revisiting the Heart of Darkness* 50 (2008): 95–123.

INDEX

agricultural production (*cont.*)
350n37, 352n62; equipment for, 180;
gender roles in, 167; and Indian
Problem, 61; for Indigenous food,
250; of Pueblos, 130, 223, 230; at
schools, 75, 78, 103, 127–28, 156–
58, 216, 230, 250; self-sufficiency
through, 247–48; U.S. legislation
on Indigenous, 91. *See also* employment; livestock

Aguilar, Santana, 237

AIS. *See* Albuquerque Indian School
(AIS)

Alaskan Native peoples, 261–62

Alberni Indian Residential School, 271

Alberta, 68

Albuquerque Indian School (AIS), *100*,
121, *131*; after effects of, 263; army
enlistees at, 147; arts education at,
157; citizenship training at, 207–
9; comparison to other schools,
99–103, 231; competition and
cooperation of, 114–16; compulsory
attendance at, 73; deaths at, 235,
358n18; Diné at, 222, 223, 225;
discipline at, 144–48, *149*, 151, 152,
154, 158; domestic arts at, 159, *160*;
girls at, *170*, *172*, *173*; languages at,
192; lawsuits against, 148, 338n42;
location of, 228–29; Mexican students at, 253; overview of, 99–103;
parental role at, 129, 218–19; Pueblo
students at, 119, 120, 218–19, 230;
records at, 180; research on, 13, 17;
resistance at, 132, 136, 137, 217–20;
school song of, 207–9; social events
at, 163–64; sports at, *165*; staff of,
124, *205*; student experiences at,
79, 104–5, *196*, *198*, 232; student

government at, 205–6; uniforms at,
146; willing student at, 162

Albuquerque NM, 133, 162–63

alcohol consumption, 26, 126, 187, 192,
260–62

Alderville, 302n6

Alexander, Jeffrey, 15

Alexander Boarding School. *See* Fort
Alexander Indian Residential School
(FAIRS)

Algiers, 65

Alien Tort Claims Act, 274

allotment, 64, 82–84, 206, 318n71. *See
also* Dawes Act; land dispossession

All Pueblos Council, 130

alternative dispute resolution (ADR),
272–73, 361n63

American Board of Commissioners for
Foreign Missions, 53

American Indian Defense Association,
83

American Indian Education (Reyhner
and Eder), 5–6

American Indian/First Nations Schooling
(Glenn), 7

American Indian Law Alliance, 276

American Indian Wars, 48, 58–60, 63,
265, 317n58

American-Mexican War, 101

American Southwest, 14, 127, 153–54,
179, 232, 266, 319n75, 331n88

American West, 316n44

Amherst University, 159

Anglican Church, 68, 76–78, 112, 129,
200–201, *202*, 272

Anishinaabe. *See* Ojibway Indians

Annett, Kevin, 31

Apache Indians, 17, 102–5, 113, 230, 231.
See also Jicarilla Apache Indians

apologies. *See* reconciliation

Arapaho Indians, 66

Archulet, Rosalie, 158–59

Arendt, Hannah, 42

Arizona, 91, 101, 114, 220, 248, 326n7

Armenia, 22, 214

Armijo, Lupe, 237

Armijo, Petra, 237

Armstrong, Samuel Chapman, 67, 143, 145, 153, 178, 255–56, 291, 319n82

arts, Indigenous, 105, 120, 157, 159, 164. *See also* culture; weaving

arts education, 157. *See also* curriculum

Assembly of First Nations, 15, 93, 269, 271–73, 280, 360n42, 362n93

Assembly of Manitoba Chiefs, 15, 184, 271

assimilation: alternatives to, 63, 317n65; by biological absorption, 255, 308n18; as cultural genocide, 24, 31, 36–37, 83, 264–65, 309n32; of Diné, 220–21; and gender roles, 173; and health, 238–41, 243; and Indian Problem, 57–62, 64, 69, 316n44, 316n49, 318n71, 320n93; by land ownership, 230–31; in modern Indigenous education, 298, 299; post–World War II, 92; and redress, 283, 293, 294, 296; scholarship on, xii, 291; by Treaty of 1868, 222; of Utes, 129. *See also* civilization; cultural genocide

assimilative education: blood quantum in, 255–56; at boarding schools, 2–8, 10, 17, 19, 27, 31, 36, 38, 44–45, 87–88, 104, 105, 108, 111, 115, 119, 120, 122, 218, 292, 327n27, 330n75; challenges in U.S., 86–87; comparison of policy on, 264; compulsory

participation in, 71–74; concept of hell in, 244–45; at day schools, 115; demise of, 88–95; for Diné, 223; history of, 51–56; implementation of, 74–80; and Indian Problem, 47–48, 56–57, 62–70, 81–86, 319n82; institutionalization of, 66–71; and land dispossession, 229–30; responses to, 97, 99, 126–27, 133, 137–38, 174–76, 196–97; school staff resistance to, 124–25, 333n116; techniques of, 139–43, 151–53, 158–67, 175–78, 180–83, 191, 196, 197, 203–4, 207–10, 213–14, 233, 244–49, 252–53, 257, 335n1, 356n132. *See also* education; Indigenous education; schools

Assiniboine, Annie, 137, 344n32

Athens, 22

Atkins, John, 54

Augustine, Katherine, 157

Auschwitz, 360n57

Australia, 7, 43–44, 277, 304n28, 308n18, 312n77

axes, 251

Baca, Mr. (Laguna Pueblo), 193

"bad man" clause, 275, 358n26

Bagot Commission, 61, 62

banishment, 317n65

barbarity, 22–23

Barrows, William, 318n74

Barta, Tony, 27

Battleford Industrial School, 68

Bauman, Zygmunt, 317n65

Baxter class action lawsuit, 273, 361n66

Bays, Eric, 38

BC Treaty Process, 360n55

Beardsley, Monroe, 30

Beatty, Willard Walcott, 85, 86, 118, 163, 183

Beccaria, Cesare, 186

Becenti, Rex, Jr., 229

Begay, Austin, 246

Begay et al. v. The United States, 265, 358n26

Behind Closed Doors (Fortier), 347n85

Benally, Andrea (Diné), 201

benevolence: as assimilative technique, 203; at boarding schools, 38, 39, 118, 125, 193–97, 204–5, 265, 333n108; and genocidal intent, 35, 36, 43–44, 312n75; and Indian Problem, 291; of Indigenous education, 38, 72, 90, 101–2, 156, 299. *See also* social welfare

Benvenuto, Jeff, 309n45

Beothuks, 310n52

Berens River community, 110, 112

BIA. *See* Bureau of Indian Affairs (BIA)

Bill C-31, 254–55, 316n48

Bill of Indian Rights, 83–84

Bineziikwe, Ozaawi, 204–5, 245

biological absorption, 65, 241, 253–55, 258, 308n18

bison, 35, 55, 69

Bissett, Dr., 242

Black Freedom Movement, 264. *See also* African Americans

Blake, S. H., 77–78

blood, 58–59, 178, 253–58, 268, 292. *See also* half-bloods; race

Bloodvein community, 112

Boarding School Healing Project (BSHP), 276

boarding schools: archives of, 16–17, 99, 103, 123–24, 137, 165, 178–80; as benevolent experiment, 3, 14, 66, 138, 302n6, 302n8; closure of, 88–95, 115, 259; comparison of, 2–9, 48, 97–99, 291–93; competition and cooperation among, 110–18; compulsory attendance at, 48, 73, 94, 122, 126–30, 217–18; cultural genocide at, 10–12, 27, 30, 247, 290; deaths in, 30, 76, 104, 107, 235–38, 240, 310n53; definition of, 301n4, 322n115; early experiments with, 52, 54; funding of, 7, 54, 68, 74–78, 80–81, 84–90, 102, 103, 112, 113, 117, 181, 216, 217, 242, 253, 292, 320n85, 353n75; health at, 234–35, 237–42, 353n75, 354n87; implementation of, 66, 74–80; and Indian Problem, 57, 61–63, 67–71, 291, 295; intent of Canadian, 35–36, 55–56, 68, 320n85, 331n83; living conditions at, 247–49; negative outcomes of, 19–20, 90, 225, 266–67, 304n29; policy for U.S., 80–88, 94, 121, 222–24; positive outcomes of, 8, 14, 16, 44–45, 124–25, 160–62, 165, 166, 183, 196, 248, 304n25; research on, 12–17, 354n92; students' impressions of, 233; technologies of self in, 139, 335n2. *See also* education; Indian Residential School system; schools; *specific schools*

boarding school staff: assimilative techniques of, 139, 147, 149, 161, 163, 171–75, 186–97, 204–5, 233, 252, 257, 354n92; benevolence of, 38, 193, 195–97, 204–5; civilians as, 88; and colonialism, 4, 12; competition and cooperation among, 115, 129, 330n75; at FAIRS, 109, 205, 329n54; and health, 240; management of,

Cameron, Sam, 116

"camp," 354n92

Canada: agricultural production in, 352n62; assimilative education in, 2–3, 51–56, 175, 229, 244–45, 336n2; boarding schools in, 5–9, 35–38, 54–55, 68, 74–78, 87–95, 111–18, 184; boarding school staff in, 122–26, 203, 333n108, 333n116; colonial genocide in, 304n27; compulsory attendance in, 73–74; cultural genocide in, 25, 31, 35, 308n18; deaths in, 30, 76, 243, 310n53; definition of Aboriginal peoples in, 301n4; disciplinary model in, 141–44, 149–58, 337n19; health in, 234–35, 237–42, 249–50, 353n71, 353n75; Indian Problem in, 47–48, 58–62, 65, 69–71, 74–75, 291–92, 295, 297, 316n48, 320n93; Indian status in, 58, 254–56, 316nn48–49, 357n137; Indigenous-controlled schools in, 93; land dispossession in, xi–xii, 328n37; and National Resolution Framework, 271–72; oral histories in, 16, 225; policy enforcement in, 215, 225–26; record keeping in, 180–84; redress in, 259–65, 267–77, 278–87, 292–96, 359n40, 360n55, 361n66; research on schools in, 13, 16–18; resocialization in, 200–201, 204–5, 347n85; social welfare model in, 82; student resistance in, 132–33, 137; time management in, 231; types of schools in, 322n115; violence in, 185, 189–91. See also governments; Indian Residential School system; North America; specific provinces

Canadian Bar Association, 273

Canadian Department of Indian Affairs: on abuse reports, 126; complaints to, 128; on curriculum, 144; on discipline, 123, 149–50; on health, 237, 242; and Indian Problem, 61, 69–70, 77–78; leadership of, 80, 320n94; policy enforcement of, 215; on runaways, 137; staff of, 292; in United States, 71. See also agents, Indian; governments

Canadian Department of Indian Affairs and Northern Development, 106, 107

Canadian Department of the Interior, 237–38, 320n94

Canadian House of Commons, 272–74

Canadian Indian Research and Aid Society, 64

Canadian Indian School Service, 203

Canadian Pacific Railway, 47–48

Canyon de Chelley, 220–21

capitalism: assimilative education for, 160; comparison to colonialism, 42; and land ownership, 230, 231; and livestock reduction, 224, 350n37; and redress, 270, 360n55; and settler colonial mesh, 302n9. See also economy

carceral institutions: assimilation through, 88; Diné in, 221; discipline in, 141, 336n11; experiments in, 38, 66–67, 145; and Indigenous education, 297, 299; for Indigenous "problems," 261; and redress, 287; students in, 188. See also Fort Marion prison; guardhouses; workhouses

Carlisle Indian School: benevolence at, 203; competition of, 114; deaths at,

219; experiments at, 67, 291; living conditions at, 249; military-style marching at, 145; operations at, 71; oversight of, 7; Pueblo students at, 100

Carson, Kit, 220–21

Cart, S. M., 103–4, 113–14, 120, 145–46, 185, 222

Carthage, 22

casinos, 268

Catholic Church: in Canada, 55–56, 76, 109–12, 126, 129, 143–44, 150, 151, 173–74, 200–201, 202, 225, 241–42, 244; and compulsory attendance, 73; Indigenous adaptation of, 246; school staff from, 123; in United States, 70, 113, 146–47

Catholic Hierarchy of Canada, 143, 173–74

cemeteries, 216. *See also* deaths

Center for Southwest Research, 14–15

Ceremony (Silko), 358n18

Chalk, Frank, 28, 29

Chapman, H. H., 256

Charlie, John, 130

Chaske, John, 107, 328n47

Chemawa Indian School, 277

Chemawa OR, 157

Cherokee Indians, 105, 277, 319n78, 320n86

Cherokee National Council, 319n78

Cheyenne Indians, 66, 105

Chickasaw Indians, 320n86

Child, Brenda, 133, 203, 226, 248

children: abuse of, 55; adoption of, 90, 92, 205, 254, 260; assimilation of, 63–64; care for, 172, 175; genocide against, 25, 26, 35, 36; Indian status of, 254–55; proprietorship of

Indigenous, 226, 351n42; use in fur trade, 52; welfare services for, 88–92. *See also* boys; girls; students

Children of the Earth high school, 297–98

Chilocco Indian Residential School, 171, 267

Chin, Mr. (adjudicator), 273

Chippewa Indians, 102

Choctaw Indians, 277, 320n86

Christianity: and boarding school differences, 7; in Canadian boarding schools, 18, 62, 70, 74, 88, 111–13, 149–53, 183–84, 291; in early education efforts, 51, 52, 54; and gender roles, 171; imposition of, 73, 101, 209; and Indian Problem, 63–64, 84; as nonhuman actor, 246–47, 257–58; in U.S. boarding schools, 146–47, 263. *See also* missionary societies; religion

Churchill, Ward, 6, 265–66

Church of England, 112

citizenship: in Canada, 68, 89; by education, 49, 68, 81–82, 86, 89, 91, 104, 105, 111, 154, 158, 175, 178–79, 206–9, 249; and gender roles, 167; and genocide, 172; legislation on, 64–65, 206–7; of Pueblos, 101; by staff-student relationships, 203; Treaty of 1868 on, 222

civilization: in Canada, 55; definition of, 30n5; desire for, 160; of Diné, 221; by discipline, 140, 152–55, 158–59, 177; by education, 53, 63–72, 120, 125, 126, 156, 166, 204, 318n71, 333n116; by gender roles, 170–72; and genocide, 33, 36–37, 312n77; and health, 238–41, 354n87; and Indian

culture (*cont.*)
85, 86, 91–94, 151, 154, 157, 182, 183, 192–93; school desertion for, 136–37. *See also* arts, Indigenous; dancing; language
culture, Western, 160, 175, 196–97, 240–41
Cumming, Margaret, 106
Curcio, Andrea, 275–78
curriculum: in Canada, 75, 108, 144, 154, 167, 182, 210; in United States, 85–87, 105, 154–57, 183. *See also* academic instruction; agricultural instruction; arts education; domestic arts; industrial schools; textbooks; trades; vocational education
Curtis Act (1924), 207

Dadrian, Vahakn, 305n42
Daggit, E., 174
Dakota Sioux Indians, 17, 106–8, 250, 328n37, 328n47
Dakota War of 1862, 328n37
dancing, 120, 122, 151, 153, 163–64, 188, 192–93, 247. *See also* culture
Danziger, Edmund, Jr., 8
Dartmouth College, 53
Davin, Nicholas Flood, 68, 71, 118, 320n85
Dawes Act, 58, 64–65, 83–84, 206, 229–30, 318n74. *See also* allotment; land; land dispossession
day schools: in Canada, 54–55, 68, 69, 75, 78, 106, 109, 110, 116–17, 122, 281, 282, 328n37, 331n83; comparison of, 98, 153; compulsory attendance at, 73, 126; cultural violence at, 191; operations at, 292; protest against, 128; research on, 13,

18–19, 214; in United States, 78–80, 85–87, 104, 114–16, 222–24, 248, 331n79. *See also* schools
deaths: at boarding schools, 30, 76, 104, 107, 219, 235, 236, 238, 240, 243, 279, 310n53; of Diné, 220; from resistance, 136, 335n146; of U.S. Indigenous, 262, 358n18. *See also* cemeteries; killing; suicide
decolonization, xiii, 287, 293–98, 306n3, 364n5
Decoration Day, 207
DeHuff, Elizabeth, 120
DeHuff, John: discipline by, 151, 158, 173, 187; on health, 236–37; on Indigenous culture, 192–93; leadership of, 111, 120–22; on pregnant students, 174; records of, 179
dehumanization, 32, 33, 37
Denetdale, Jennifer, 350n34
Dennis, John Stoughton, 320n85
Department of Mines and Resources (Canadian), 118
desire, 140, 141, 159–67, 175, 182, 196, 210, 252–53, 264–65, 340n82. *See also* inducements
destruction: by colonization, 3–12, 19, 298–99; of Diné, 220–22; by disease, 234, 243; by education, 36, 49, 72, 74, 87–88, 93–95, 133, 266–67, 295; by genocide, 22–41, 45, 289, 290, 294, 306n3, 307n5, 309n45, 311n65, 311n67; of group identity, 31–37, 54, 62, 83, 183, 194–95, 265, 286, 348n1; of Indigenous gender roles, 175; of Indigenous gods, 245–46; by nonhuman actors, 213, 214, 216, 233, 348n4; resistance to, 209–11. *See also* cultural genocide; genocide; violence

Eliot, John, 51
Ellinghaus, Katherine, 308n18
Ellis, Clyde, 44, 133
employment: with boarding schools, 88, 203–4; discipline for, 141, 152, 153, 155, 175; education for, 67, 79–80, 104, 108, 116, 126, 172; opportunities for Indigenous, 84, 85, 92, 171, 248, 261, 262; records on Indigenous, 151, 180. *See also* agricultural production; boarding school staff; civil service; labor; vocational education
England, 55. *See also* British Empire
English language, 51, 54, 108, 127, 157, 191, 221, 233, 244. *See also* language
ethnic groups, 28, 33, 37
ethnocentrism, 49, 50
ethnocide, 10, 25, 27, 30
etiquette, 153–55, 164, 167, 191
European image: by discipline, 143, 144, 153–58; of five civilized tribes, 320n86; and gender roles, 171, 173, 175; of God, 245; and group destruction, 54, 191, 253–54; and health, 235, 238–39; imposition of, 33, 34, 37, 43–44, 56, 60, 63, 67–68, 71, 74, 94, 120, 198, 203, 209, 215, 228, 231, 266; individualism in, 197–98; by knowledge, 182; nature and culture in, 234; by self-sufficiency, 248; of women, 204
European schooling: discipline in, 141; history of, 51; at Indigenous boarding schools, 7, 50, 79, 121, 297; records about, 178; resistance to, 52, 223–24, 229; strategic use of, 127; time of exposure to, 232
Evans, James, 55

Evans, Raymond, 27
exceptionalism, 33

FAIRS. *See* Fort Alexander Indian Residential School (FAIRS)
family: and cultural genocide, 36, 290; effects of colonialism on, 260, 261; form of life in, 360n57; gender roles in, 167, 168, 170–72; and health, 237; knowledge about Indigenous, 178, 183; role in education process, 122, 133, 135–37, 218, 223–24, 232–33, 248–53; school community as, 197–99, 203–6, 209, 333n108; separation from, 19, 48, 52, 67, 81, 148, 198–201, 210, 222, 226–28, 232, 267, 338n42; violence toward, 184, 272–73. *See also* communities; parents
Faris, Chester E., 105, 111
fear, 40, 244–45
Fear-Segal, Jacqueline, 9–10, 161
federal mothers, 203, 204. *See also* boarding school staff; women
Federal Torts Claim Act, 275
Feierstein, Daniel, 29
Fein, Helen, 28, 29
feminism, 171, 172, 204. *See also* women
Fergusson, Erna, 129
Ferrier, Russell T., 181
Field Manual for Agency Superintendents, 125
field matrons, 170–71, 186–87. *See also* boarding school staff; women
fiestas. *See* culture; dancing; social life
File Hills reserve, 238
Filles de la Croix. *See* Sisters of the Cross

gender roles, 141, 167–75, 207, 248–49.
    See also boys; girls; women
General Allotment Act. *See* Dawes Act
genocide: at Acoma, 310n52; by assimi-
    lation, 7, 19, 54, 94–95, 137–38,
    166–67, 309n32; and blood, 253–54;
    by colonization, 5, 6, 40–45, 63,
    265–66, 304nn27-28, 317n65; defi-
    nitions of, 21–41, 45, 303n15, 307n5,
    311n58, 311n65, 311n67; discourse
    of, 57, 316n44; by disease, 238, 243;
    livestock reduction as, 224, 351n38;
    as process, 24, 26, 40–45, 88,
    98, 133, 234, 313n87, 314n101; and
    redress, 263, 265, 269, 277, 293–99;
    resistance to, 209–10, 214; scholar-
    ship on, xi–xiii, 4, 6, 8–13, 18, 22–45,
    213, 214, 234, 289, 296, 303n14,
    304nn27-29, 305n31, 305n36,
    305n42, 306n3, 308n18, 313n87,
    313n101; and symbolic violence, 210;
    targets of, 22, 31–33, 44, 45, 133–36,
    214, 254, 306n3, 311n58, 313n101;
    at U.S. and Canadian schools, 99.
    See also colonial genocide; cultural
    genocide; destruction; Holocaust;
    violence
geography of resistance, 217–18,
    349n18. *See also* resistance
Germany, 42, 65, 360n57
girls: bodies of, 173, 174, 256; com-
    plaints about staff, 123; curriculum
    for, 108, 110, 153, 157, 160; in Decora-
    tion Day parade, 207; discipline of,
    186, 188; lawsuits of, 265; morality
    of, 173–74; resocialization of, 203; at
    schools, 69, 170, 320n85; at social
    events, 163–64; weaving of, 159;
    work for whites, 158, 173, 342n125.

See also children; gender roles;
    students; women
"giving face," 14, 305n44
Glenn, Charles, 7, 264
Goffman, Erving, 140–41
Gorman, C. (Diné), 240–41
Gover, Kevin, 277
governments: on assimilative educa-
    tion, 2–3, 7, 13, 17, 18, 49, 52, 53,
    56, 67–80, 87–95, 99–102, 110–13,
    291–92; assimilative techniques
    of, 139, 143–44, 147, 171, 177; and
    biological absorption, 308n18;
    colonialism by, 4, 11–12; of Diné,
    224; and disease, 353n71; fund-
    ing of boarding schools, 103, 104,
    106, 109, 116–17, 181, 217, 253; on
    gender relations, 172–74; genocide
    by, 35, 36, 307n5; humanitarian-
    ism of, 291; on Indian Problem,
    47, 48, 56–69, 81, 108, 118–19,
    197, 233, 250, 317n58, 318n66,
    323n129; on Indigenous inferior-
    ity, 255; Indigenous obligation
    to, 127; of multiple groups, 32;
    Pueblos' experience with, 101, 130,
    131; on punishments and violence,
    121, 123, 129; redress by, 263–66,
    270–75, 281, 284–87, 292–93, 299,
    359n29, 360n55; withholding of
    resources, 250–51. *See also* Bureau
    of Indian Affairs (BIA); Canada;
    Canadian Department of Indian
    Affairs; colonialism; macrolevel;
    politics; treaties; United States
Gradual Civilization Act (1857), 62
Gradual Enfranchisement Act (1869),
    58, 320n93
Graham, Commissioner, 226

Indian Self-Determination Act (1975), 106, 267–68

The Indians of the Terraced Houses (Saunders), 121

indigenocide, 27–28

Indigenous education: assimilative techniques in, 139–40; Canadian policy on, 215, 251; comparisons of Canada and U.S., 98; desire for, 103, 126–32, 196, 223, 229, 233; funding of, 53, 54, 71, 292; inadequacy of, 261, 262; and Indian Problem, 2–3, 47, 51–56, 62, 70–71, 77–78, 318n71; information sharing about, 117–18; and knowledge of Indians, 182–83; nature of, 223–24, 247, 297–99; normalization of, 232–33; overview, 49–56; at PLPIRS, 108; precontact, 50; responsibility for, 90, 266, 267, 359n32; Richard Pratt's experiment in, 66–68; U.S. policy on, 80–88, 91–92, 94, 111, 114–17, 121, 221–23. *See also* assimilative education; education

Indigenous peoples: agency of, 44, 56, 62–66, 94, 100, 112–13, 127, 129, 132–33, 139–40, 195, 205, 213–14, 266–69, 313n101, 315n39, 345n50; apologies to, 16, 272, 274, 277–80, 287; ascribed faith of, 110, 112, 113; biological absorption of, 24, 308n18; biological warfare against, 352n71; blood quantum of, 58–59, 254–56; bodies of, 153, 173, 174, 235–37; debasement of, 33, 60, 72, 113–14, 142, 159–61, 165, 192, 193, 198, 209, 238–39, 243–45, 248–50, 255–56, 354n87, 354n92; definition of American, 301n4; economic value

of, 56; gender roles of, 167–68; genocide against, 25–27, 35–37, 43; gods of, 245–46; healing practices of, 240–41; homogenization of, 57–59, 82, 101, 180; identification with land, 34, 64–65, 140, 210–11, 229–30, 318n66; knowledge about, 177–84, 240, 241; legal status of, 58, 254–56, 268, 316nn48-49; lifestyles of, 130, 210–11, 263, 271, 360n57; living conditions of, 170; paid for school enrollment, 104; populations of, 56, 99, 241, 261–62; protection of, 28, 53–54, 57, 62, 91–92; scholarship on, xi–xiii, 17, 182–83, 301n4; as school staff, 91–93, 125, 203–4, 205, 333n116; school staff attitudes toward, 119, 331n88; self-image of, 161–62; U.S. policy on, 91, 141, 336n15; utility of, 142, 159, 337n19; values of, 16, 210–11, 306n49, 309n50; as wards of state, 101, 130–31, 209. *See also* specific groups

Indigenous rights: and boarding school experiences, 8, 195; in Canada, 48, 58, 268–69; and Indian Problem, 59–60, 63, 64, 89; John Collier on, 82–84; and nonhuman actors, 214, 219; and redress, 263–64, 267–69; of students, 206–7. *See also* reformers

Indigenous Women's Network, 276

individualism: detrimental effects of, 260; and gender roles, 171; and overcrowding, 217; and poverty, 247, 251; and redress, 276, 282–83; by resocialization, 197–98, 203, 206, 209, 347n76; of students, 181. *See also* collective identity; group life

laws (*cont.*)

    status, 58, 254–56, 316nn48-49; on Indigenous rights, 83–84; on names, 191–92; as nonhuman actors, 214; for redress, 267–77, 286, 361n63; resistance to, 174

lawsuits: against boarding schools, 15, 148, 184–85, 263, 271–74, 280–83, 338n42, 361n66, 363nn100-101; in United States, 264, 265, 275–76

leg irons, 187. *See also* punishment

Lemkin, Raphael: on collective identities, 33; on genocide, 10, 11, 21–27, 29, 31, 34, 45, 54, 289, 304n29, 305n31, 308n14; on group diversity, 83

Letgers, Lytman, 311n67

Leung, Francis, 157

Leupp, Francis, 80, 87, 115, 204, 222, 239

Lévi-Strauss, Claude, 317n65

Liberal Party (Canada), 75, 268–69. *See also* politics

livestock, 84, 168, 201, 220, 223, 224, 351n38, 352n62. *See also* agricultural production

Logan, Indian Agent, 122

logic of elimination, 45, 298

Lomawaima, K. Tsianna, 44, 133, 171, 173, 304n25

Lonergan, P. T., 128

Long Plain First Nation, 109, 352n62

Long Plain Reserve, 99, 106, 108, 122, 273

Long Walk, 220–22. *See also* removal

Lorne, Lord, 47

love, 199–201, 203–5, 216

Lucero, Tony, 198

Lukes, Stephan, 161

Lummis, Charles, 148, 219, 338n42

Macdonald, John A., 68, 69, 319n85, 320n94, 353n71

Mackenzie River, 56

Macrae, J. A., 69

macrolevel: boarding schools at, 5, 98, 110; genocide at, 41; Indian Problem at, 47; research on, 13, 18; of settler colonial mesh, 3, 4, 45, 291. *See also* governments; settler colonial mesh

Madrid, 22

Malinowski, Bronislaw, 26

managerialism, 147–48, 158, 177–78, 181

manifest destiny, 10, 33. *See also* land dispossession

Manitoba: blood quantum in, 256; boarding schools in, 106, 108, 109; citizens' rights in, 68; comparison of schools in, 99; compulsory attendance in, 251; concept of hell in, 244, 245, 247; cultural genocide in, 41; Dakota Sioux Indians in, 106–7, 328n37; desire in, 165, 166; disciplinary model in, 149, 158; food in, 249–52; gender roles in, 167, 173–74; health in, 239–43; overcrowding in, 217; oversight of schools in, 215; prisoners in, 261; record keeping in, 181–84; research in, 12; resocialization in, 200–209; settlement of, 55; student placement in, 117, 331n83; students in, 111–12, 292; time in, 231–33; violence in, 123, 184–85, 189, 191, 197. *See also* Canada

Mann, Cornelius, 112

Mann, James, 112

Mann, Michael, 309n32

Mann, William, 128
manners. *See* etiquette
Manuelito, 221
Manuelito area, 133
marching, 145, 148, 160, 186, 207
Margolis, Eric, 347n76
Marmon, Mrs. Walter K. (Suzy), 162–63, 249
marriage, 174, 200, 254, 255, 284, 308n18, 316n48
maternalism, 171. *See also* women
Mayhew, Thomas, Jr., 51
McBeth, Sally, 133
McGill, Harold, 241–42
McKinney, Lillie G., 218
McLean, J. D., 128–29
McNeill, John A., 116–17
measles, 239. *See also* health
media, 15, 218–19, 277, 281
Meeker, Nathan C., 129
Melos, 22
memoirs, 8, 38, 125, 184, 226–27, 344n19, 347n85. *See also* students, school experiences of
Memorial Day. *See* Decoration Day
memory, 226–29, 246, 253, 282–85
Menaul School, 162–63
mental health, 261, 262, 274, 282–85. *See also* health
mentors, 155. *See also* boarding school staff
Meriam Report, 80–88, 92, 108, 117, 266
Merrick, Flora, 272–73
mesolevel: assimilative techniques at, 139, 147, 183, 209; boarding schools at, 98, 110–11, 120, 137, 138, 291, 292; genocide at, 41; Indian Problem at, 47, 65, 66, 74; nonhuman

actors at, 214, 215; research on, 13, 18; of settler colonial mesh, 3–5, 45, 291. *See also* settler colonial mesh
Methodists, 76, 78, 106
Métis, 55, 68–69, 256, 319n85
Mexicans, 214, 223, 253, 356n132
Mexico, 101, 130, 218, 232
microlevel: assimilative techniques at, 139, 183, 197, 209, 213–15, 245, 247, 257; boarding schools at, 87, 98, 111, 137, 138, 292; genocide at, 41, 243; Indian Problem at, 66; redress at, 259, 262, 299; research on, 12–19; of settler colonial mesh, 3–5, 45, 291. *See also* settler colonial mesh
Midewiwin, 50
Mi'kmaq, 32
military: and compulsory attendance, 120; and cultural genocide, 11–12; of Diné, 179; disciplinary model of, 141–53, 149, 158–61, 167, 175, 181, 186, 200, 336n15, 337n31; elements in schools, 67, 104, 105, 164, 209; and Indian Problem, 47–48, 56, 59, 62, 94, 291; and Indigenous children, 52; Indigenous peoples in, 116, 179; of Métis, 69; Pueblos' cooperation with, 101. *See also* United States Army
Miller, J. R., 8, 9, 52, 112–13, 123, 132–33, 150, 156
Miller family, 132
Milloy, John, 77, 154, 237
mining industry, 59, 84, 224
Minnesota, 68
Missionary Monthly, 108
missionary societies, 35, 39, 47, 84, 291, 316n44. *See also* Christianity; religion

mission schools: assimilative education at, 2, 53, 66, 74–78, 84–85; in Canada, 55–56, 68, 109; comparison of, 99; funding of, 54, 74–76, 78, 111, 114; health at, 238, 354n87; operations at, 292; oversight of, 215; purposes of, 51, 56; research on, 13; resistance to, 122; student experiences at, 198, 223, 275; teachers at, 123; in United States, 100, 113–14, 119, 218, 232. *See also* religion; schools

Mission Society of the Church in Canada, 77–78

Mohawk Institute, 56, 71, 273, 361n66

Mohonk Conferences, 64, 65, 70, 159–60

Mojave Indians, 102

Montenegro, 311n71

Montoya, Virginia, 158–59

Montreal, 55–56

Moore, P. E., 242–43

Moore, Thomas, 153

morality: and discipline, 141, 151, 154, 175; in gender roles, 171–74; and genocide, 10–11, 24, 34, 305n31, 305n36; of group identity, 311n57; and Indian Problem, 57; legislation regarding, 53; and school attendance, 72, 126; violations of, 128. *See also* sexual mores

Morgan, Thomas J., 78, 115, 219

Morrisseau, Leo, 150

Mosby, Ian, 249–50

Moses, A. Dirk, 26, 43–44, 314n101

Mount Elgin, 302n6

Mount Pleasant School District, 108

Mount Taylor, 133

movies, 165–67

Muckle, A. A., 231

Muncey school, 71

murder. *See* killing

Musa Dagh, 214

Muscogee Indians. *See* Creek Indians

music. *See* arts education; songs, school

Muslims, 311n71

nádleeh, 168

Nambe Pueblo, 153–54

names, 191–92, 198, 222, 249

National Resolution Framework, 271–72

nations: building of, 35, 57, 59, 60, 68, 155, 281; destruction through genocide, 25, 28, 33, 37; loyalty to, 207, 208–9; redress efforts by, 264, 270–71

Native American Apology Resolution, 277

Navajo. *See* Diné

Navajo Community College, 92, 266

Navajo Educational Emergency Program, 223

Navajo-Hopi Rehabilitation Act, 223

Navajo Museum and Cultural Center, 220

Navajo Treaty (1876), 359n26

Navajo Tribal Council, 168, 222–23

Nazis, 22–24, 38, 42, 306n3, 310n57

Neary, Bernard, 344n32

neoliberalism, 20, 89, 262, 269–71, 286, 287. *See also* economy; politics

net of incorporation, 302n9

New Brunswick, 56

New Deal, 84, 182

New England Company, 56

Newfoundland, 310n52

New France, 52

New Guinea, 65

New Hampshire, 53

New Mexico: blood quantum in, 256; compulsory attendance in, 72–73, 120, 232; cultural genocide in, 41; Diné in, 221; disciplinary model in, 146–51, 154, 158, 188–89; food in, 249, 252–53; gender roles in, 167, 172–74; geography of, 214; health in, 239–40; inducements in, 162–66; land ownership in, 319n75; mission schools in, 51; overcrowding in, 217; religion in, 245–47; research in, 12; resocialization in, 201–9; schools in, 99, 101, 114; statehood of, 101; students in, 219, 232–33, 263, 292; taxation in, 130; Ute Indians in, 129; violence in, 185, 189–91, 197. *See also* Albuquerque Indian School (AIS); Santa Fe Indian School (SFIS); United States

New York Times editorial, 318n66

New Zealand, 7

Nichols, Roger L., 77

Niezen, Ronald, 265

Niza, Fray Marcos de, 232

nomadism, 140, 143, 230–31, 350n34, 354n87

nonhuman actors: Anishinaabe on, 296, 364n6; assimilation through, 213–14, 257, 335n1; and colonialism, 4–5, 12, 303n14, 305n41; research on, 19; responses to boarding schools, 97; sheep as, 224, 351n38. *See also* Actor Network Theory (ANT)

nonreservation schools: in Canada, 228; comparison of, 98, 99; Diné at, 223, 225; health at, 236; Henry Pratt's vision of, 67; operations at, 292; records of, 178; in United States, 78–79, 104, 114–15, 230. *See also* schools

Nordstrom, C. E., 330n72

North America: British dominance of, 56–58; comparison of boarding schools in, 7, 97–99; demise of boarding schools in, 88–95; disease in, 234; education in precontact, 50; genocide scholarship in, xii–xiii, 26; Indigenous-settler relations in, 32, 36–37, 45, 298; redress efforts in, 259–60, 269–70. *See also* Canada; United States

Northern Pueblos Agency, 111, 115

Northwest Rebellion of 1885, 68

North-West Territories, 55, 75

Norway House, 110

nuns: in Canada, 1, 55–56, 109, 168, 175, 329n54; on damnation, 245; as surrogate parents, 198, 199, 205; violence of, 189, 193–94, 201, 252. *See also* religion

Nuremberg indictment, 24

nutrition, 75, 80, 81, 235, 241, 249–50. *See also* food

Obama, Barack, 277

obedience. *See* discipline

Oblate Catholic Indian Missions, 242

Oblates of Mary Immaculate, 55–56, 68, 109, 112, 150, 272, 329n54

O'Connor, Bishop Hubert, 271

Office of the Commissioner of Indian Affairs, 185, 247

Ojibway Indians: agricultural production of, 352n62; cosmology of, 296, 364n6; diet of, 250; education of, 50, 108, 109; identity of, 211; language of, 244; reservation of, 106, 109–10; study of, 17

policing: as assimilative technique, 209; and colonialism, 4; and cultural genocide, 12; and education, 47–48, 94; and redress, 287; of truants, 73, 129–30, 135–36, 179; in U.S. school system, 81–82, 120

politics: and assimilative education, 52, 56, 75, 77, 84, 88–90; and genocide, 12, 23, 28, 305n31; and Indian Problem, 291; Indigenous involvement in, 205; and redress, 20, 262, 267–71, 286, 293–94, 359n40; and will to assimilate, 64. *See also* governments; Liberal Party (Canada); neoliberalism

Portage la Prairie Indian Residential School (PLPIRS), *107*; agricultural production near, 352n62; appearance of, 165–66; comparison to other schools, 99; discipline at, 149, 189; domestic arts at, *169*; economic assimilation at, 231; gender roles at, *173*; labor at, 156; location of, 226, 228; names of, 106; overcrowding at, 217; overview of, 106–9; research on, 13; resistance at, 132, 137; resocialization at, 200; spiritual practices at, 246; staff of, 122–24; student experiences at, 116, 272–73, 278, 285; violence at, 190, 193–94

Posha, John, 107, 328n47

poststructuralism, 42

potlatch, 48

poverty: and colonialism, 19, 261; desire to escape, 162; as nonhuman actor, 97, 247–53; at Sagkeeng, 109; on U.S. reservations, 261–62. *See also* economy

Powell, Christopher, 29

power, technology of, 139, 191, 195, 335n2, 348n1

practical jokes, 132

Pratt, Richard H.: disciplinary model of, 145, 148, 157–58, 336n15; educational experiment of, 66–68, 71, 153, 291, 319n82; on Indian Problem, 94, 95, 197–98; on miscegenation, 254; paternalism of, 203; on school locations, 218, 228

praying towns, 51. *See also* religion

Presbyterian Church, 53, 76, 78, 100, 106, 107, 150, 272

president of United States, 316n44

preventorium, 241–43

priests, 198–201, 205, 245. *See also* Franciscans; Jesuits; religion

principals: autonomy of, 118–19; in Canada, 122, 123, 137, 227; cooperation with agents, 125; and discipline, 147, 188, 189; on Indigenous inferiority, 255; record keeping by, 181; at SFIS, 216; violence toward, 132. *See also* boarding school staff

prisons. *See* carceral institutions; Fort Marion prison

private schools, 73, 93. *See also* schools

The Problem of Indian Administration. See Meriam Report

production, technologies of, 139, 335n2

Protestants, 51, 56, 70, 73, 84, 111, 113, 126, 146, 291

Protestant work ethic, 318n71

Provencher, Joseph, 55

Prucha, Francis Paul, 316n44

public schools, 18–19, 72–73, 89–93, 223, 248, 292, 325n176. *See also* schools

Reel, Estelle, 72, 79, 156–59, 178–81, 204, 255–56

reform: of appearance, 194; and assimilation, 64–65, 139, 175–76, 209, 336n2; by colonization, 5, 6, 42; of Diné, 221; by discipline, 141, 150, 155; by education, 16, 19, 51, 54, 60–63, 66, 74, 78, 81–84, 111, 133, 238, 295, 354n92; of gender roles, 170–72; and genocidal intent, 37–38; and health, 239–40, 249, 354n87; inducements for, 162; and knowledge, 180–83; and nonhuman actors, 215, 245; for redress, 267–68; by resocialization, 197–211; and symbolic violence, 195

reformers: and genocide, 12; on Indian Problem, 64, 291, 316n44, 318n71; on Indigenous education, 70; and land dispossession, 229–30; and nonhuman actors, 214; observations of, 188, 264; and power of desire, 161; for religious conversion, 150. *See also* Indigenous rights; "self-help" associations

Regan, Paulette, xii, 294, 295

Regina Indian Industrial School, 153

religion: as assimilative technique, 161, 209, 243–47, 257–58; benevolence of, 39; in Canadian boarding schools, 6, 7, 48, 55–56, 62, 71, 74–78, 87, 88, 90, 91, 94, 111–12, 122, 129, 141–44, 149–53, 158–59, 165–67, 173–74, 181–84, 200–201, 215, 244–47, 291, 320n85, 337n19, 351n42; discipline through, 186; and ethnocide, 30; and genocide, 24–28, 33–37; and Indian Problem, 63, 94, 291–92; Indigenous rights

to, 83, 88; Pueblo education in, 232; records on students', 180; in U.S. boarding schools, 146–47, 152. *See also* Christianity; missionary societies; mission schools; nuns; praying towns; priests

removal: and assimilative education, 48, 52, 61, 67, 69, 75, 78–81, 88, 90, 115, 188, 203, 215, 224, 254; of Cherokee, 319n78; of Diné, 129, 220–22, 224; and Indian Problem, 59; of non-Indigenous students, 253; of sick students, 240; in United States, 58, 218, 267, 277, 323n129. *See also* Long Walk; sixties scoop

reparations, 264, 266, 269–71, 274, 276, 286, 295. *See also* compensation programs; redress

reservations: in Canada, 47–48, 55, 58, 75–76, 89, 93, 106–10, 241, 322n129; comparison with schools, 196, 198; desire to escape, 162, 284; Diné at, 221; and Indian Problem, 59–64, 68; living conditions on, 247–50, 261–62; "self-help" associations on, 152; students' return to, 71, 78, 79, 82, 104, 119–22, 133–37, 158, 178–79, 192–99, 203–4, 218, 225–29, 232, 236–37, 240, 263. *See also* communities

reservation schools, 67, 75, 78, 79, 98, 114–15, 251, 292, 322n115. *See also* schools

residential schools. *See* boarding schools

resistance: and assimilative techniques, 139–40, 166–67, 171–75, 183, 190, 191, 195, 209–13; to Canadian educational policies, 93, 225–28; of

230; records at, 179, 180; research on, 13; staff of, 119–22, 124–25; student experiences at, 248; truancy at, 133–36; violence at, 185, 187, 188. *See also* Institute of American Indian Arts

school buildings: in Canada, 76, 106, 109, 110, 165–66, 217, 226, 237–38, 242; complaints about, 129, 131, 247; as nonhuman actors, 215–17; in United States, 105, 221, 223, 267. *See also* dormitories; space
schools: comparison of, 97–99, 137–38; competition and cooperation among, 110–18, 218, 226, 330n75, 330nn72-73, 351n42; compulsory attendance at, 48, 60, 66, 71–74, 81–82, 117, 122, 125, 180, 221–22, 250–53, 257, 319n78; criticism of, 104, 128–31; cultural genocide in, 41; debasement at, 33; enrollment in Canadian, 55, 56, 90, 98, 106–10, 122–23, 181, 217, 226, 231–32; enrollment in U.S., 73, 91–92, 98, 100, 102–5, 113–15, 119–20, 172, 179–80, 222–25, 232, 235, 325n176; funding of, 68, 80, 93, 98, 103–6, 111, 115, 116; Indigenous control of, 91–93, 106, 259, 266, 267; inspection of Canadian, 215, 217, 225; locations

of, 75–77, 129–30, 214–19, 225–29, 263; loyalty to, 207–9; nature of, 297; normalization of, 232–33; types of, 54, 78–79, 292, 322n115. *See also* assimilative education; boarding schools; day schools; education; industrial schools; mission schools; nonreservation schools; private schools; public schools; reservation schools; seminaries

Schurz, Carl, 60–61, 68
scorched earth campaign, 220–21
Scott, Duncan Campbell, 76, 77, 80, 94, 95, 227, 237, 308n18
Scott, James C., 56–57, 349n18
self, technologies of, 139, 197, 335n2
self-destruction, 26
self-determination: boarding school staff on, 193; denial of, 34, 298; discipline through, 142, 147–49; and genocide, 307n3, 311n58; of groups, 32; in Indigenous education, 92, 93, 108, 205–6, 223; Indigenous rights to, 83–84, 88, 182, 266–70, 359n32; of Pueblos, 130. *See also* group life
"self-help" associations, 152–53. *See also* reformers
self-improvement, 60, 72, 120, 155, 218, 230
Selkirk, 225
Sells, Cato, 157, 239
seminaries, 51, 52, 141, 244. *See also* schools
Seminole Indians, 320n86
semiotics, 335n1
Seneca Indians, 102
Seowtewa, Alex, 246
Serbia, 311n71
settlement agreement, 273–74, 281, 286

students (*cont.*)
215–16, 225–27, 231–33, 244–45, 248–55, 272–75, 278, 297, 347n85; segregation of male and female, 170; separation from siblings, 201, 216. *See also* boys; children; girls; runaway students; truancy
subversion: of assimilative techniques, 139–40, 166, 215, 216; in boarding schools, 97, 99, 132, 133, 138; of gender roles, 168, 172; of settler colonialism, 4, 9, 13, 295; through memory, 226–27. *See also* resistance
Sudan, 293
suicide, 260–62. *See also* deaths
summer vacations, 128, 158, 174, 201, 232, 263. *See also* reservations, students' return to
sun dance, 247. *See also* dancing
Sunday Post, 218–19
superintendents: authority of, 111, 119–22; benevolence of, 196; competition and cooperation of, 113–15, 125, 330n75; discipline by, 128, 185–88, 344n32; on home visits, 229; on Mexican students, 253; records of, 178–80; on school environments, 219–20; at SFIS, 119–20, 157, 219, 253; and social activities, 163–64. *See also* boarding school staff
A Survey of the Contemporary Indians of Canada. See Hawthorn Report
survival: and assimilative techniques, 139–40, 166; of boarding schools, 15, 16, 233; of colonization, 5; of cultural genocide, 9, 29, 33–34, 295, 309n45; by Diné, 224, 246; by memory, 226–27; and modern Indigenous education, 298, 299

survivance, 139–40, 246
Swan Lake community, 108, 116
Swinford, Inspector, 122
symbolic violence, 127, 139, 177, 184–97, 209, 210, 263–65, 299, 335n2, 346n51. *See also* violence
Syria, 293
Szasz, Margaret Connell, 48, 85, 359n32

Tafoya, Richard, 128
Talehaftewa, Herbert, 127
Taos Pueblo, 83, 113, 188
taxation, 130
teachers: and assimilative techniques, 166, 171, 172, 175, 178, 180, 188, 193; complaints about, 127–28; hiring and firing of, 53, 112, 126; on Indigenous inferiority, 255; Indigenous peoples as, 319n78; in integrated schools, 92; quality of, 123–25, 217, 221, 333n108, 333n116; salaries of Canadian, 106; as surrogate parents, 199; training of, 80, 87; and U.S. policy, 86–87. *See also* boarding school staff
technology, 139, 224–25, 335nn1-2
Teec Nos Pos Boarding School, 265
Tenorio, Frank, 115
terror, 29
Tesuque Pueblo, 114
textbooks, 87, 93, 183. *See also* curriculum
Thatcher, Margaret, 270
theft, 125, 132, 187
Theriault, Henry, 32–33, 294
Third Punic War, 22
Thompson, Hildegard, 86, 163
Thornton, Russell, 352n71

United States (*cont.*)
schools in, 5–9, 67–68, 78–80, 90–95, 108, 111–18, 184, 319n85, 320n85; cultural genocide in, 10, 25, 35, 308n18; Dakota Sioux Indians in, 328n37; deaths in, 30, 243; disciplinary model in, 141–44, 147, 150, 152–58, 336n15; health in, 234–35, 239, 241; Indian Problem in, 58–64, 70–71, 291, 295, 316n44, 317n58, 318n66; knowledge of Indians in, 178–82; locations of schools in, 228–29; New Mexico as part of, 101; policy in, 58, 64, 80–88, 90–95, 111, 114–17, 121, 141, 182–83, 188, 191–92, 204–7, 221–25, 229–30, 247, 250–51, 255, 262–68, 285–86, 316n44, 316n48, 318n66, 318n71, 336n15, 358n25; Pueblo peoples in, 130, 218, 232; Raphael Lemkin to, 22; redress in, 259–69, 275–78, 285–86, 294–96; research on schools in, 13–18; school attendance in, 66, 72–74, 81–82, 319n78, 325n176; student resistance in, 132–37; teachers in, 124; time management in, 231; types of schools in, 322n115; violence in, 185–91. *See also* American Southwest; governments; North America; specific states
United States Army, 129, 145–47, 179, 220–21. *See also* military
United States Congress, 53, 64, 130, 222, 223. *See also* Continental Congress
United States Department of the Interior, 118, 152, 170–71, 174, 320n85, 336n15
United States Industrial School at Santa Fe. *See* Santa Fe Indian School (SFIS)

United States War Department, 336n15
universalism, liberal, 63
University of New Mexico, 14, 103
Ute Indians, 105, 129, 235

Valencia, Jose Domingo, 128
Valentine, Commissioner, 356n132
vandalism, 22–23
Vankoughnet, Lawrence, 320n94
van Krieken, Robert, 35, 312n77
Veracini, Lorenzo, 287, 317n65
Verdeja, Ernesto, 41, 214
victimization, 12, 21, 28, 44, 265, 274, 305n42, 313n101
Viets, Andrew H., 103, 130–31
Vigil, Clemente, 153–54
violence: at boarding schools, 2, 6, 15, 16, 19, 49, 126, 137, 138, 206, 210, 297; by colonists, 59, 69, 262, 287; control through, 177, 184–97, 252, 255, 256; and discipline, 141, 201, 244–45, 336n14; as form of resistance, 131–32, 174–75; and genocide, xii, 30, 32, 41, 310n52; government threats of, 129; legacy of, 260, 263, 279, 284, 358n18; redress for, 271–74, 277, 278, 281–84, 361n66; survival stories of, 184, 265, 267, 271, 275, 344n19, 358n26. *See also* destruction; genocide; killing; punishment; sexual violence; symbolic violence; war
Vizenor, Gerald, 139–40
vocational education: at Canadian boarding schools, 106, 144; goals of, 156–57; at U.S. boarding schools, 79–80, 85, 105, 116, 172, 223, 331n79. *See also* curriculum; domestic arts; employment; industrial schools; trades

Wacquant, Loïc, 302n9
Waite, J., 116
Walker, Francis Amasa, 59–60
war: cost of, 59–63, 317n58; and disease, 352n71; in Indigenous culture, 192; and military discipline, 161; and Treaty of Guadalupe-Hidalgo, 101; in United States, 323n129; violence in, 177. *See also* American Indian Wars; violence
Warkentin, B., 150–51, 182
Warner, Mr. (Diné), 162
War of 1812, 62, 315n39
Washington, D.C., 68, 320n85
Washington, George, 317n58
weaving, 159. *See also* arts, Indigenous
Wesleyan missionaries, 55
Whalen, Kevin, 304n29
Wheelock, Eleazor, 51
White, Richard, 350n37
White Earth, 248
white people: and allotment, 64; as boarding school staff, 103, 204, 205; gender roles of, 171; genocidal intent of, 35, 54; health of, 239–43; Indian laborers with, 158; Indigenous integration with, 67, 90–92, 195, 228, 229, 246, 253, 254, 280, 316n49, 345n50; Indigenous segregation from, 52, 59, 60, 84; individualism of, 197–98; land acquisition of, 319n75; and nonhuman actors, 214, 216; student attitudes toward, 15–16, 164; treaties with, 275. *See also* race
White River CO, 129
William, Victor Christian, 112
Williams Lake Indian Residential School, 271

Wilner, Isaiah Lorado, 309n50
Wilson, Marie, 280
Window Rock AZ, 220
Winnipeg, 109, 297–98, 320n85
Winnipeg River, 109, 110
Winnipeg Truth and Reconciliation Commission, 244–45
Wolfe, Patrick, 43, 45, 229, 296, 302n7, 316n49
women, 124, 168, 171, 203, 224, 254–55, 310n52, 316n48, 331n88. *See also* federal mothers; feminism; field matrons; gender roles; girls; maternalism
Women of Color Against Violence, 276
Women's Missionary Society of the Presbyterian Church, 106
workhouses, 51, 79, 141. *See also* carceral institutions
Working Group on Truth and Reconciliation and the Exploratory Dialogues, 273
world systems theory, 42, 302n9
World War I, 147, 206
World War II, 85–86, 89, 92, 105, 147, 154, 222–23, 264, 273
Wounded Knee uprising, 267
Wright, A. O., 186, 253

Yankton Sioux, 275
Yazzie, Ray, 164

Zephier, Sherwyn, 275
Zia (village), 134
Zimbardo, Philip, 38
Zimmerer, Jurgen, 42
Zuni Church of Our Lady of Guadalupe, 246
Zuni Indians, 102, 105, 219, 232, 246

To order or obtain more information on these or other
University of Nebraska Press titles, visit nebraskapress.unl.edu.

CPSIA information can be obtained at www.ICGtesting.com
Printed in the USA
LVOW10*1950310815

452238LV00004B/19/P